MARGARET THATCHER
In Her Own Words

Other books by Iain Dale

As I Said to Denis: The Margaret Thatcher Book of Quotations
(Robson Books, 1997)

Memories of Maggie (Politico's, 2000)

Margaret Thatcher: A Tribute in Words & Pictures
(Weidenfeld & Nicolson, 2005)

MARGARET THATCHER

In Her Own Words

Edited by
IAIN DALE

First published in Great Britain in 2010 by

Biteback Publishing Ltd
Westminster Tower
3 Albert Embankment
London
SE1 7SP

ISBN 978-1-84954-055-1

10 9 8 7 6 5 4 3 2 1

A CIP catalogue record for this book is available from the British Library.

Set in Adobe Garamond by Soapbox

Printed and bound in Great Britain by
TJ International, Padstow, Cornwall

I dedicate this book to the memory of my grandmother, Constance Dale, who died in 1979. She cried with joy on the day she heard a woman had been elected leader of the Conservative Party.

CONTENTS

ACKNOWLEDGEMENTS

I am grateful to Chris Collins of the Margaret Thatcher Foundation for his help and co-operation in the compilation of this book, and the accompanying CD box set of Margaret Thatcher's speeches. His work for the Margaret Thatcher Foundation is beyond compare and the MargaretThatcher.org website is a treasure trove of Thatcher words. I highly recommend it.

I would also like to thank Grant Tucker, my executive assistant, for his assistance and enthusiasm in tracking down some elusive quotes. Grant is a mere 18-years-old and was born two years after Margaret Thatcher fell from power, yet he seems to know more about her life and achievements than I do. Grant is living proof that Margaret Thatcher's legacy will be handed down through the generations.

Iain Dale
Tunbridge Wells
October 2010

FOREWORD

I became a Thatcherite at the age of sixteen. Thirty-two years later I still hold to the beliefs and values that defined Margaret Thatcher's time in office. Twenty years after her fall from power, Margaret Thatcher and her legacy still have an important and telling influence on British political life, in the same way that Gladstone and Disraeli did a century earlier. Even though she hasn't made a full speech for ten years, she retains the ability to make news and influence current day politicians in a way which no other politician can. But with her legacy come a lot of myths, myths which I hope this book can help dispel.

She is loved and hated in equal measures. The bile and venom on the internet whenever her name is mentioned has to be seen to be believed. She is often held to be responsible for all the ills of today's economy and society, even though it is two decades since she left Downing Street. She was inexplicably blamed for the recent banking crisis, her critics conveniently ignoring that it was the Labour government who introduced a new system of banking regulation in the late 1990s.

But those of us who remain firm adherents and defenders of the Thatcherite legacy must also recognise that times move on and that what was right for the country in the 1980s might not be the medicine that the country needs now. I think the secret is to understand how Thatcherite principles can be applied to today's politics, rather than get hung up on individual policies.

Perhaps, though, the main lesson which today's politicians must learn from Margaret Thatcher is to look at her policy of 'sound money'. We seem to conveniently forget how much of a basket case the British economy was in 1979, when the Conservatives won the election. Only three years earlier the Labour Chancellor, Denis Healey, had humiliatingly been forced to go to the IMF. Nationalised industries were overmanned and inefficient and British industry was clinging onto the glories of an industrial past, without realising that other countries were overtaking us in an increasingly competitive international market. It wasn't the Thatcher government which decimated British manufacturing in the 1980s. It was weak management and rampant trade unions which combined to prevent the modernisation of working practices that were proving so disastrous to the British car, steel and coal industries among many others. Margaret Thatcher forced industrial leaders to wake up to the fact that without standing up to the trade unions they might as well give up.

She also woke up a nation which had got used to its decline in world influence, and had never really recovered from Suez. It wasn't just the Falklands War that put the Great back into Great Britain, it was the strong diplomacy deployed in her dealings with the European Community and the Soviet bloc that restored a pride and self respect to Britain, which had been missing for decades. And it brought a new respect from other countries and world leaders. We were no longer regarded as a soft touch in international negotiations. All this came as a deep shock to the Foreign Office mandarins, who were in the business of 'managing decline'.

Margaret Thatcher is the reason I became actively involved in politics. She inspired me, as a 16-year-old, to join the Conservative Party and do my bit to help revive Britain. One of the tasks of today's political leaders is to provide a lead, to inspire, to motivate. Margaret Thatcher was able to do that in a way few politicians in this country have been able to emulate. My first tentative footstep into the political arena was to set up a Conservative organisation in 1982 at the very left wing University of East Anglia. Only a few months later followed my first encounter with Margaret Thatcher when she invited the chairmen of the various University Conservative Associations to a reception at No. 10.

For a country boy like me, it was unbelievable to have been invited and it was something I had been looking forward to for months. Just to climb those stairs with the portraits of all past Prime Ministers on the wall, was worth the trip on its own. And there at the top of the stairs was the Prime Minister. She had obviously perfected the art of welcoming people to receptions and as she shook you by the hand and wished you had a good evening, she moved you on into the room without you even knowing she was doing it. Most of the Cabinet were there – I remember discussing with Cecil Parkinson the number of free running shoes he had been sent after a recent profile had announced to the world that he was a keen runner. He offered me a pair but it turned out his feet were much smaller than mine! We were constantly plied with wine and I made a mental note to stop at two glasses. But after the second glass was emptied I felt rather self-conscious without a glass in my hand so grabbed another. Just as the Prime Minster walked by I took a sip. All I remember is my stomach heaving and me thinking that I was about to throw up at the Prime Minister's feet, thus ending a glorious political career which had hardly got off the ground. Luckily I managed to control my stomach and all was well. It turned out that it was whisky in my glass, rather than white wine.

Later in the evening, as I was talking to my local MP, Alan Haselhurst, the division bell sounded. Although there were at least forty MPs there, none made a move to leave to go and vote over the road in the House of Commons. Mrs Thatcher started to look rather irritated and was obviously none too impressed. In the end she walked to the middle of the room, took off one of her shoes and banged it on the floor. There was instant silence. The Prime Minister then spoke. 'Would all Conservative MPs kindly leave the building immediately,' she instructed. 'And the rest of us will stay and enjoy ourselves!' Naturally we all laughed uproariously, enjoying the sight of the MPs trooping out of the room in a somewhat sheepish manner.

After I graduated I went to work at the House of Commons as a researcher for a Norfolk Member of Parliament. He was not a particularly well-known MP and never courted publicity. He had a marginal seat and devoted himself to his constituency rather than join the rent-a-quote mob. It served him well as he held his seat for the next two elections. If ever there was an MP less likely to be involved in sleaze it was him. But one day, a careless error by me left him open to charges of dirty dealing. We ran a businessman's club in the constituency, called The Westminster Circle. It served two purposes – one to keep the MP in touch with local businesses and secondly to raise a little more money for the very poor constituency association. For £100 a year business people joined and were given a dinner in the House of Commons, usually addressed by a Cabinet minister, and another dinner in the constituency, addressed by a more junior minister. These clubs were common in all parties up and down the country. But in a publicity leaflet designed to attract new members I used the phrase 'with direct access to government minister'. By this I had meant they would be able to meet and speak to a government minister at the dinner. In those pre 'cash for questions' days we were all rather innocent. But it proved to be my undoing – and very nearly my employer's.

Early one Tuesday afternoon he found out that at that day's Prime Minister's Question Time, the Liberal leader, David Steel, would raise this subject with the Prime Minister. He immediately went to see her in her office behind the Speaker's Chair. He must have been quaking in his boots but he later told me she had been brilliant. She sat him down, offered him a coffee and heard him out. She did not disguise her dislike for Steel and thought it was typical of him to operate in this manner. She told him she would let Steel have both barrels, and of course she did! He returned to the Office after PM's Question Time and related the events of the day to me. I had been completely oblivious, which was just as well as I would no doubt have been having a premonition of what a P45 looked like.

A few months later I was having lunch with a couple of Tory MPs in the Members' Cafeteria. We had just finished our lunch when in walked Mrs T and her entourage. She grabbed a tray and chose a light lunch of Welsh rarebit. Unfortunately, as we had finished, I did not have cause to hang around too much longer so left the room, cursing that we had decided to have an early lunch. A few minutes later I realised I had left some papers and magazines on the table in the cafeteria and returned to retrieve them. As luck would have it, the Thatcher group had sat themselves at the table we had been sitting at and Mrs T had her elbow plonked on my papers. I decided to summon up the courage and interrupt them to ask for my papers. Just as I had started I looked down at the pile of papers and to my horror saw that my copy of the new issue of *Private Eye* was on the top of them and with a front cover of a particularly nasty photo of Denis Thatcher. Mrs Thatcher cottoned on to what I wanted, removed her elbow, and gazed down at the offending magazine. My heart stopped. 'Oh, *Private Eye*, Denis loves it,' she gushed. To my external shame, I just picked it up, along with the rest of my papers, made my excuses and left. What a wimp.

In 1995 I took an American friend, Daniel Forrester, to the T. E. Utley Young Journalist of the Year awards at the Reform Club. Lady Thatcher had been invited to present the awards. She treated us to a half hour impromptu speech on political issues of the moment, which seemed to go by in about five minutes – quite an achievement as her entire audience had to remain standing throughout. After she had finished Daniel whispered to me: 'I have to meet her, what should I do?' Knowing her penchant for strapping, six feet tall, dark-haired American men I encouraged him to go and introduce himself. He suddenly got cold feet so eventually I dragged him over to where she was talking to several of the award winners. In typically American style he launched into a sycophantic introduction which immediately attracted her attention. 'Mrs Thatcher,' he began. I kicked him. 'Er, Lady Thatcher,' he hurriedly corrected himself, 'May I say how much our country misses your leadership. . . ' and he continued in that vein for a few seconds. While he was speaking, the diminutive figure of the Iron Lady (for she is much smaller in height than most people imagine) stared up at him, her eyes never leaving his. When he had finally finished having his say, Lady Thatcher hardly paused or breathed. 'Your President, President Clinton.' She paused, heightening the drama for my American friend. 'He is a great communicator.' Up came the forefinger, almost prodding

Daniel's chest. Then in a particularly contemptuous tone, came the pièce de résistance: 'The trouble is, he has absolutely nothing to communicate.' With that she was away. It was almost a flounce. Daniel eventually came down from whichever cloud he had been on – probably nine – and said, 'I'll remember that for the rest of my life' – and as a well-known critic of Bill Clinton, has been dining out on it ever since.

Another encounter came at a retirement party for ITN's much missed political editor Michael Brunson. My friend Alan Duncan, the Tory MP for Rutland, started a conversation with her and she suddenly asked where Denis had disappeared off to as they had to leave for dinner. Being of diminutive stature, and me being over six feet tall, she asked me to scan the room. Both of them looked at me expectantly. To my horror I spied Denis on the other side of the room talking to Michael Heseltine. I summoned up all the courage at my disposal and explained where he was. Lady Thatcher's eyes became even bluer than normal and she exclaimed: 'Denis and I are having dinner with Cap Weinberger tonight. I think he's rather more important than THAT man, don't you?! If Denis isn't over here within one minute I shall go over and stare at them.' Luckily for Michael Heseltine, she didn't have to.

Early in 2005 I invited Lady Thatcher to come to a fundraising party to raise money for my campaign as Conservative candidate for North Norfolk. To my delight she accepted and on a cold March evening turned up on time to work a room of fifty friends and political acquaintances. And boy did she work! She was particularly pleased to meet the teenagers present, including one with a particularly eye-catching piece of metal face jewellery. My task for the evening was to guide Lady T around the room so she could meet everyone. It was a thankless task. The Iron Lady decided where she was going and no amount of me tugging at her elbow was going to persuade her otherwise!

And then, in November 2005 I launched my book, *Margaret Thatcher: A Tribute in Words & Pictures*, at a function in the City of London, kindly hosted by the Corporation of London. Lady

Thatcher agreed to attend and made a point of speaking to everyone in the room while she was there. Especially poignant for me, was the sight of her having a protracted chat with my two nieces, Isabella and Ophelia Hunter, who were then aged ten and six. It was a very touching moment as they posed for pictures. It brought back a memory from 1988, when my cousin Nicola's daughter Emma – then an infant – asked her mother: 'Mummy, can a man be Prime Minister?' She soon found out that the answer was no. . . .

The last time I spoke to Lady Thatcher was in January 2009 when I went to the Carlton Club for a drinks party hosted by Liam Fox. I was delighted to see Lady Thatcher arrive and looking absolutely fantastic. For a woman of eighty-three and supposedly in frail health, she looked absolutely stunning.

I had a couple of minutes talking to her and told her it was twenty-six years to the day that I first met her at a reception for Conservative students at 10 Downing Street. 'I think I remember that,' she said. 'It was so nice to see so many young people in the building. That didn't happen very often.' We talked a little about newspapers and she said: 'I never read them. I had Bernard to do it for me.' Everyone needs a Bernard...

As I left the Carlton Club, a thought struck me. If Lady T were in her heyday and had to take over as Prime Minister now, what would she do? If I had asked her, I know exactly what her reply would have been. 'Restore sound money, dear,' she would have said. And you know what? She'd have been dead right.

Margaret Thatcher was never a natural orator. Public speaking was a skill which had to be learnt. She knew it was a weakness and had the self-knowledge to recognise that she needed to do something about it. Enter stage left Ronald Millar and stage right Gordon Reece. It was Millar who fed her the lines and Reece who told her how to deliver them. Reece persuaded her to have voice coaching and to lower her rather shrill voice. And between them, they helped Margaret Thatcher become a professional and at times inspirational platform speaker. Her conference speeches, initially delivered from a text, but later from an autocue (a trick she learned from another Ronald, President Reagan) became real landmarks in the political year. Indeed, in later years she became much more confident and delivered some very good jokes. It is a moot point as to how funny she found them herself, it has to be said. See Appendix 1 for John Whittingdale's hilarious tale of how Margaret Thatcher came to perform the *Monty Python* 'Dead Parrot' sketch, ridiculing the newly formed Liberal Democrats, in her 1990 party conference speech.

This is not a book to be read from cover to cover. It is a book to be dipped in and out of. But I hope it provides entertainment, information and inspiration.

Iain Dale
Tunbridge Wells
October 2010

PART ONE

The Path to Power

1925–70

I wasn't lucky – I deserved it.

Receiving a prize for poetry, aged 9

Every Conservative desires peace. The threat to peace comes from Communism, which has powerful forces ready to attack anywhere. Communism waits for weakness, it leaves strength alone. Britain therefore must be strong, strong in arms, and strong in faith in her own way of life.

Margaret Roberts' election leaflet, 1950

MAIDEN SPEECH IN THE HOUSE OF COMMONS

February 1960

Public Bodies (Admission of the press to Meetings) Bill
Order for Second Reading read

Mrs Margaret Thatcher (Finchley): I beg to move, that the Bill be now read a Second time.

This is a maiden speech, but I know that the constituency of Finchley which I have the honour to represent would not wish me to do other than come straight to the point and address myself to the matter before the House.

I cannot do better than begin by stating the objects of the Bill in the words used by Mr Arthur Henderson when he introduced the Bill which became the Local Authorities (Admission of the Press to Meetings) Act, 1908, which was also a Private Member's Measure. He specified the object and purpose as that of guarding the rights of members of the public by enabling the fullest information to be obtained for them in regard to the actions of their representatives upon local authorities.

It is appropriate at this stage to mention that the public does not have a right of admission, either at common law or by statute, to the meetings of local authorities. Members of the public are compelled, therefore, to rely upon the local Press for information on what their elected representatives are doing. The original Measure was brought as a result of a case in which the representatives of a particular paper were excluded from a particular meeting.

The public has the right, in the first instance, to know what its elected representatives are doing. That right extends in a number of directions. I do not know whether hon. Members generally appreciate the total amount of money spent by local authorities. In England and Wales, local authorities spend £1,400 million a year and, in Scotland, just over £200 million a year. Those sums are not insignificant, even in terms of national budgets. Less than half is raised by ratepayers' money and the rest by taxpayers' money, and the first purpose in admitting the Press is that we may know how those moneys are being spent.

In the second place, I quote from the Report of the Franks Committee: "Publicity is the greatest and most effective check against any arbitrary action."

That is one of the fundamental rights of the subject. Further, publicity stimulates the interest of local persons in local government. That is also very important. But if there is a case for publicity, there is also a case for a certain amount of private conference when personal matters are being discussed and when questions are in a preliminary stage. It is in trying to find a point of balance between these two aspects—the public right of knowledge and the necessity on occasion for private conference—that the difficulty arises.

An attempt was made by the 1908 Act to meet this difficulty, and I now turn to the history of the Measure which I am about to present. Provision was made by the 1908 Act for Press representatives to attend meetings of local councils and meetings of education committees in so far as they had delegated powers, and, also a number of other bodies which have now ceased to exist because successive Parliaments have substituted new bodies to carry out the powers which the 1908 Act formerly permitted the Press to publicise.

Long before the events of the past summer, there was a very good case for amending the 1908 Act. The first good case arose when the Local Government Act, 1929, abolished boards of guardians, to whose meetings the Act admitted the Press. Boards of Guardians were responsible for the administration of hospitals and many other matters. The first attempt to bring the law of 1908 up-to-date came in 1930, when the right hon. Member for South Shields (Mr Ede) introduced a Private Members' Measure, which I am happy and relieved to learn received a Second Reading. It did not get any further because of a rather precipitate change of

Government, which I do not think even the most optimistic hon. Member opposite would believe was imminent at the moment. The case for the Bill then was that boards of guardians no longer existed and the Act needed amending, firstly, by reference to its past performance, and secondly, by reference to the new legislation of 1929.

Then came another major local government Measure, the Local Government Act, 1933. That Act has very considerable significance, because in Section 85 local authorities were empowered to appoint any committees they chose. As a result, many authorities began to go into committee of the full council, not merely for the purpose which is in the spirit of the 1908 Act—that is to say, in order to discuss something which was truly of a confidential nature—but in order merely to exclude the Press, without addressing their minds to whether such exclusion was justified by reference to the matter to be discussed. That began to provide the first major legal loophole in the Act. Where previously local authorities had to deliberate in open council, with the exception of circumstances arising from the business which justified the exclusion of the Press after that Act they were enabled to resolve themselves into committee merely as a matter of administrative convenience.

Two more Private Members' Measures attempted to bring the 1908 Act up-to-date—one introduced in 1949 by the hon. Member for Westbury (Sir R. Grimston), and the other introduced in 1950 by the hon. Member for Solihull (Mr M. Lindsay). In the meantime, the need was becoming even greater, because in 1944 came the Education Act, which removed from the sharp light of publicity education committees which had been within purview of the 1908 Act. So we find that the purpose of this Act which governs the position now is no longer effective, because its provisions have become greatly out-dated. This is one of the major grounds for attempting now to bring the 1908 Act up-to-date and make its purpose effective by means of a new Act.

I now turn to the Bill before the House and will try to deduce its general principle from the Clauses there set down. There are six points I should like to make. The first point is, on what occasions in local authority work will this Bill entitle the Press to be present? I use the word "entitled" because there are many authorities which already practise the admission of the Press to a far greater extent than the Bill would necessitate their doing if it became law. This is meant to establish a minimum legislative code of practice for the local authorities. Therefore, the first question is to which meetings of local authorities would the Press be entitled to be admitted by virtue of the Bill. I would refer hon. Members to Clause 2 (2), which contains the major point with reference to committees, and I will try to put the point in fairly simple language—rather simpler than the complicated drafting we find here.

May I point out that committees of local authorities whose only power is to recommend a course of action to the council—a course of action which must be taken by the council and which cannot be taken by the committee without reference back—are not included at all in the Bill? Therefore, any committee of a local authority whose only task is to recommend a course of action to the council is not within the purview of the Bill.

I am well aware that a number of committees of local authorities have two different kinds of power—power to recommend and power to discharge the function of the local authority itself because that local authority has specifically delegated that task to the committee. Where the committee has both of these functions, it comes within the realm of the Bill if, and only if, a substantial part of its functions consists in discharging delegated powers. Where a committee only has the odd delegated power referred to it, it will not come within the Bill. Where local authorities have made a practice, as some have, of delegating their own functions to committees, these committees have substantial delegated powers, and therefore come within this Clause.

The Press will be admitted to the main council meetings of local authorities and to those meetings which effectively discharge the functions of the council; that is, the committees with substantial delegated powers, but others are not included. I know that some authorities include them, and I would like to see more authorities include them, because I think it would be in the interests of local government, but they are not entitled to be included under this Bill.

Having got the Press in to these meetings, or having entitled them to be in, there must inevitably be occasions, such as personal circumstances coming under discussion, matters preliminary to legal proceedings, matters with regard to the acquisition of land, or such matters which would inevitably come up, when the Press were entitled to be present, unless some effective provision was made to exclude the Press on these occasions.

My second point, therefore, is: having got the Press in, upon what grounds is a local authority entitled to exclude it? There must inevitably be some occasions. We have had great difficulty in drafting the Clause to fit all cases. I had hoped to draw up a schedule of circumstances in which local authorities would be entitled to exclude the Press. That was not possible, and we have had to go back to a kind of omnibus Clause. I refer hon. Members to Clause 1 (2), which is the operative Clause for this purpose. I suggest most earnestly that when the Press is excluded it must be because of some particular reason arising from the proceedings of the local authority at the time, and there must be very good reason for the exclusion. The real reason for excluding the Press is that publicity of the matter to be discussed would be prejudicial to the public interest.

> If you want anything said, ask a man. If you want anything done, ask a woman.
>
> *20 May 1964*

There are two prongs to this Clause. Publicity would be prejudicial for two main groups of reasons. The first group is where the matters under discussion are of a confidential nature. They may relate to personal circumstances of individual electors. They may relate to a confidential communication from a Government Department asking local authorities for their opinion on a subject which the Minister would not like to be discussed in open session until he is a good deal further on and has received the views of local authorities.

There is another group of subjects which perhaps could not be strictly termed confidential but where it would be clearly prejudicial to the public interest to discuss them in open session. They may relate to staff matters, to legal proceedings, to contracts, the discussion of which tender to accept and other such matters. On this prong the Press has to be excluded for a special reason which would need to be stated in the resolution for exclusion. Where the matter is confidential it would not need to be specified further in the resolution for exclusion. Where it was for a special reason, that reason would need to be specified in broad general terms in the resolution for exclusion. This subsection is effective and wide enough in its drafting to cover all occasions upon which a local authority could possibly have good grounds for going into private session. Those are the two main operative Clauses of the Bill.

My third point relates to documents. I understand that there is a very wide variation in practice between the number of documents which different local authorities give to the Press. I do not know how many hon. Members have tried to obtain information about a local authority of which they are not a member but happen to be a ratepayer. One sometimes goes to a council meeting without any idea of what is to be discussed. One sits there for about 15 minutes and all one hears is numbers being counted up to about twenty and starting all over again. Unless the Press, which is to report to the public, has some idea from the documents before it what is to be discussed, the business of allowing the Press in becomes wholly abortive. Therefore, Clause 1 (3, *b*) makes provision for a limited number of documents to be supplied to the Press at its request in advance of the meeting. It specifies that the agenda must be supplied to the Press if it so requests and is prepared to pay for it.

Agendas vary very much. Some are couched in terms which do not betray for one moment the subject which is to be discussed.

One sees such items as "To discuss the proposal of Mr Smith" and, "To receive the recommendation of Mr Jones". As distinct from the supporting accompanying documents, the agenda itself is usually a comparatively brief document. I have, therefore, thought fit to put into the subsection a provision that the agenda shall be supplied to the Press together with such further statement or particulars as are necessary to convey to an outside person the nature of the subject to be discussed. Therefore, the Press must have some idea from the documents what is the true subject to be discussed at meetings to which its representatives are entitled to be admitted.

You know how it is, if your hair looks awful, you feel awful.

Daily Mail, July 1965

If the whole agenda was supplied, it might include some things which would be likely to be taken when the Press was excluded. I understand that the practice in many councils is to have Part I and Part II, to take subjects in public session first, and then have a resolution and go into camera for the next group of subjects which come up in private. The corporation, acting through its proper officer, to whom it would have to give instructions, is entitled to exclude from the agenda matters which are likely to be taken in camera so that no confidential matters will leak out by that process. Another provision in the Clause is that the corporation may, if it thinks fit—not must—include supporting committee reports or documents, but it would have to exercise its mind to include them. The Press would not be able to demand such documents as of right.

Fourthly, I have been approached and asked about the question of qualified privilege for local councillors and people who serve on local authorities. I have been approached by people who suggest that the privilege should be made absolute. I could not possibly accede to that, as I think that absolute privilege should be given very rarely indeed. However, there is a consequential provision in the Bill which means that where qualified privilege at present exists for statement made by people serving on local authorities that qualified privilege shall not cease to exist merely because the Press is present. That retains the present position and removes one of the reasons why people can object to the Press being present, because unless there were a consequential provision it might serve to remove the qualified privilege.

Fifthly, I understand from various sources that my proposals are under some criticism because they contain no sanctions or penalties upon local authorities. I should therefore like to state briefly what I am advised the position is when any statute is breached. There are general sanctions available at law for this purpose. Where a public right is infringed, as it would be in the event of the Bill becoming law and local authorities wrongfully excluding the Press, any person can apply to either the Attorney-General or the Solicitor-General for what is known as a relator action. He must state on the application the grounds and enclose counsels opinion that there is a good cause of action, that is to say, that it is probable that the council wrongfully excluded under particular circumstances. The person must supply also—I have no doubt that this is very important—a solicitor's certificate to the effect that the person to take action and to go to the courts is a person who is likely to be able to meet the costs, because the Attorney-General will not foot the bill. He only lends his name to the action.

A very good talker, but he is not a doer.

On Harold Wilson, February 1966

When that is done, the courts can adjudicate on whether that exclusion was legal or illegal. In the event of the litigant getting a declaration that the exclusion was illegal, he would get costs, and the district auditor already has power to surcharge those costs upon the members of the local authority whose misconduct was responsible for the illegal action occurring. I submit that those sanctions that are available by the ordinary law are sufficient to enable this Measure to be enforced.

My sixth point relates to the Schedule. I shall not go through the Schedule in any great detail, except to point out that a considerable number of the bodies referred to in it are the successors in title to those mentioned in the 1908 Act—the divisional executives established under the Education Act, the regional hospital boards and so on. Hon. Members will note that some committees of authorities are specifically excluded—those whose functions consist solely of determining matters of a confidential nature.

For example, committees of regional hospitals boards are specifically excluded. Committees of executive councils are specifically excluded, which means that any disciplinary matter relating to doctors, nurses, and so on, would not come before the public eye because the committee discharging the function does not come within this Measure.

I hope it is evident from what I have said that we are trying very hard to put into the form of legislation a code of practice that will safeguard the rights of the public. There was, last summer, one instance of the letter of the 1908 Act being contravened, and in a number of instances certainly the spirit of that Act was contravened. It is not, therefore, only a matter of bringing the 1908 Act up to date; because of the abuse of the law, there is a case for safeguarding the rights of the citizen. I hope that hon. Members will think fit to give this Bill a Second Reading, and to consider that the paramount function of this distinguished House is to safeguard civil liberties rather than to think that administrative convenience should take first place in law.

Finally, Mr Speaker, I should like to acknowledge the help given to me by [Henry Brooke] my right hon. Friend and his Department which, I understand, has been as great as any Government Department could give to a private Member. I want also to acknowledge the help of those who have been good enough to subscribe their names to the Bill, and I should like to thank the House for its very kind indulgence to a new Member.

FIRST BROADCAST INTERVIEW AS A MEMBER OF PARLIAMENT

ITN, transmitted 11 February 1960

David Rose: After an exceptional maiden speech, one daring reporter even asked if she thought she would ever reach the front benches.

Margaret Thatcher: Well, I think we'll just try to be a very good back-bencher first—certainly until these two are a little older, I couldn't take on any more political responsibilities—these responsibilities are quite enough.

DR: Have you been able to combine your political life with looking after a family, running a home?

MT: Well, I mainly do the catering here—I love cooking and I do the shopping, and always a big batch of cooking at the weekend, and of course there are the parliamentary recesses, which coincide with the school holidays, so I can see quite a good bit of the children and take them out, and at half term they come up to the House of Commons and have lunch with me.

INTERVIEW ON FIRST DAY AS MINISTER FOR PENSIONS

ITN, 12 October, 1961

Interviewer: Today was the first day at her new job for Mrs Margaret Thatcher, MP for Finchley. She was appointed Joint Parliamentary Secretary to the Ministry of Pensions in the Government changes this week. I went to the Ministry this afternoon and asked Mrs Thatcher—the mother of six year old twins—how she'd be able to cope with the extra work?

Interviewer: Will you be able to cope with the extra work? [Broadcast interview begins here]

MT: Well, I'm quite happy about it, because it means that one has a definite job to get down to rather than having a roving brief throughout the whole of the political scene.

Interviewer: What's it going to mean in your home life—obviously you are going to have to make some adjustments?

MT: I think it is going to be even more organisation and method: I'm a great believer in those two things, but in any case I could never do it if not for the fact that my home is within thirty five minutes of Westminster. I have an excellent nanny-housekeeper who helps immensely, I see the children every morning and they are at school all day and of course I make a point of seeing and being with them at weekends.

Interviewer: Your husband's abroad a good deal, I think. Will you have two different timetables, one for when he is away, and one for when he is at home?

MT: Well, not quite that. We do most of the domestic things while [Denis Thatcher] he is away, you know in redecoration, and so on, so that the household isn't put out when he is at home, but he does travel on export duties quite a bit.

Interviewer: What do you feel about this particular appointment, is it one that you looked forward to when you were indulging your pipe dreams?

MT: Well, I haven't thought of having any appointment, really, certainly not so soon, but I am very happy about it, because I think it offers scope both for the human side, which is helping people who are in need of help and also on the financial side and seeing that the scheme is sound.

Interviewer: Tell me what happens on your, so to speak, your first day when the new girl comes in, what happens?

MT: Well, I was as curious about that as you. I've had a very pleasant morning, I was received by the [John Boyd-Carpenter] Minister as soon as I came in and introduced to the various heads of departments and my sphere of duty was well-defined and I shall be given an enormous amount of homework to take away for the weekend.

SPEECH TO THE 1966 CONSERVATIVE PARTY CONFERENCE

Winter Gardens, Blackpool. 12th October 1966

First I should like to thank and congratulate Mr Don Williams on the excellent and reasoned way in which he proposed this important motion. He, and every one of the speakers who spoke to the motion, has already shown that this nation is absolutely fed up with the Socialist path of higher and higher taxation. Last year the total tax burden on this country had risen to 34.6% of the gross national product, a higher proportion than for 13 years past. It is a Socialist proportion, it is travelling upwards and in the wrong direction. Perhaps it would be easier if I put it another way: when we left office in 1964 the total burden of tax per head of the population was £180. High enough in all honesty. Two years later that total burden per head has risen by nearly £50 to £229 per head. Small wonder that we have a tremendous number of motions on the subject of taxation and you are asking us to reduce the burden of direct taxation on the people of this country.

I accept the need for incentives, the need for an incentive to individuals on the shop floor. There have been some very interesting statistics published recently. They show that during the period of increased personal taxation over the last two years there has been a reduction in the average working week of nearly one and a half hours. This shows what the proposer and speakers have already pointed out, that people have come to a point when, rather than work longer, they would take more leisure because tax means the extra work is not worth the effort. That extra one and a half hours a week from all persons in manufacturing industry would have sent our production soaring upwards instead of remaining static where it has been for virtually two years. There must, of course, also be incentives at the top. Now it is very interesting to see a person's reaction if you say to him, "Look, you are in the top 2% of incomes." In America or in Germany if one said that to a person he would take it as a tremendous compliment and it would be an enormous source of pride. Here there tends to be a slight guilt complex about it. Now this is absolute nonsense. We want the people with high earning capacity to stay in this country, to develop our industries and to bring a higher standard of living here.

[The Selective Employment Tax] is sheer cockeyed lunacy. The Chancellor needs a woman at the Treasury.

March 1966

A short time ago Gallup Poll did a survey which was published in the *Sunday Telegraph* on 24th July. These were its findings: "The majority of Britain's leading industrialists would emigrate if they were younger men at the start of their careers. ... The Government, it is felt, has not done what it should have done to provide incentives to increase production." What an indictment of a Socialist Government. The people we can do without are Harold Wilson, and George Brown, Mr Callaghan and Douglas Jay! Their policy results in the next generation's top people going abroad. They will take with them all hope for a higher standard of living for all of our people. So I fully accept the need for a taxation system that provides for incentives right throughout the whole system.

Naturally you will ask, "Can it be done?" Not under the present lot! It cannot because they do not want to and they would not. Mr Macleod could certainly do it and Rab Butler certainly did. Let us draw quickly one parallel: we have been talking here of 1951, let us see how Rab Butler tackled it. He became Chancellor when there was a deficit running at the rate of £800 million a year, a familiar figure. But it did not dismay him at all. He became Chancellor at a time when the reserves of this country had just lost some £547 million within the previous six months. But he did not go about shouting about the position, he took firm steps in which the world had confidence. May I point out that he did not, at that time, as Callaghan has, have an enormous build-up of stocks, nor £11,000 million of overseas investments, because of course he came into power after six years of Socialism and not after 13 years of Conservatism. He dealt with the economic crisis, and within 18 months of taking office produced an incentive budget of the type you are asking us to introduce now. He reduced the direct rates of income tax. He gave increased personal relief and he restored capital allowances, incentives for companies, incentives for individuals.

> I don't want to give my life over to politics. I don't think I'd have the ability and I'd never be given the chance.
>
> *On the possibility of becoming Prime Minister, Sunday Times, March 1967*

That is the Budget we could have had last April if we had had a Tory Government returned in 1964.

A number of speakers have referred to the other side of the coin of lower direct taxation. It is, of course, Government expenditure. I accept that we must take a much more discriminating line towards Government expenditure. We cannot afford unlimited increases. The other day I looked at the figures of increased Government expenditure under this Government. They were given in the House of Commons in May. I think when they were written down in a column they shook us all. Remembering that the Government, when it was returned in 1964, shouted that it had an economic crisis you would have thought that it would have reduced total Government expenditure. Not a bit of it; in that first year it increased it by £1,100 million. In the second year it increased it again, and this year the present Government is spending more than £2,000 million than the last Conservative Government, an average of increased Socialist Government expenditure of over £1,000 million a year. Small wonder we have a balance of payments crisis still, small wonder that we have stagnant production. This is also one of the causes of the tremendous increase in taxation that we have seen. If you run all the Budgets in a race called the high taxation stakes, I am glad to say that Conservative Budgets would not come in any of the first four places. The topmost prize for increased taxation would go to Hugh Gaitskell in 1951. The second prize for increased taxation would go to Callaghan in 1966. The third prize to Callaghan in 1965. The fourth prize to Callaghan in 1964. This chap Callaghan must go!

There have been some hard words said about the Selective Employment Tax. Quite right. I said some hard words about it myself in the House of Commons—and what I said was but a shadow of what Iain Macleod and I thought. It is an absolutely ridiculous tax, and I agree that it must go. How any intelligent person who wanted to collect £240 million in revenue could think up a system of taking in £1,130 million and paying back, through seven Government Departments, £890 million, I do not know. If the Greeks had invented such a system, they would have had a word for it. As they have not, I suggest we fall back on one frequently used by Quintin Hogg.

It is a recipe for rising prices; and it falls heavily on the weakest—quite different from what Callaghan promised during the election, when he said, "We shall set the burdens on the shoulders of those who are able to carry them, on the strongest and not the weakest." Within weeks of that promise, he was attempting to put a tax on charities and on the disabled. It was absolutely monstrous, and it was stopped because of the Conservative Opposition.

I turn now to a completely different subject but one which I believe to be absolutely vital. It is illustrated already by some of the changes in the tax system. This Government are undermining legal rights and respect for the law. Our legal system and the rule of law are far more responsible for our traditional liberties than any system of "one man one vote". Any country or Government which wants to proceed towards tyranny starts to undermine legal rights and to undermine the law.

> No woman in my time will be Prime Minister or Foreign Secretary – not the top jobs. Anyway I wouldn't want to be Prime Minister. You have to give yourself 100% to the job.
>
> *1969*

This process started with the Finance Bill of 1965, with which you will be familiar. It set out to introduce a system which was modern, simple and purposive. It is not modern: it is the old continental system which this Government was adopting at the very moment the Continent was abandoning it in favour of ours. Nor is it simple. They started with a system which, I admit, was difficult for the taxpayer to understand, and they finished up with one which was impossible even for the lawyers to understand. Now, therefore, we have reached a position where one has to ask the Revenue what they think the law is. This is legislation within legislation, and it is quite wrong. You cannot now look at the law to see what your rights are. This Act too must be drastically revised, so drastically that if will be unrecognisable by the time we have finished the revision.

Of course, it was a purposive Act, because it was intended, I believe, to take away people's rights. It has been followed by other legislation which does the same, by legislation which destroys the sanctity of contract, which compels an employer to break his honourable commitment with his employee. It is the same point—destroying respect for the law. It was followed by the investment grants legislation—no longer a legal right, but you have to go and ask the Government. It was followed by the S.E.T. legislation, when the Minister of Labour is given colossal arbitrary powers to decide whether persons shall have a premium or rebate or have to pay a penalty. All this is fundamentally wrong for Britain. It is a step not merely towards Socialism but towards Communism.

It is the fundamental strategy that is wrong, and the fundamental strategy that we must reverse. If Harold Wilson had gone to the electorate in 1964 and said, "In the next two years I am going to increase taxation by £1,200 million, I am going to introduce a taxation system that no one will be able to understand, and I am going to fine an employer if he dares to pay an employee more without my permission and on top of that I am going to pay myself 50 per cent more than any other Prime Minister for doing it," he would have been totally and utterly rejected, as he should have been. He is, as one of our speakers pointed out, an apostle of change, a change to more power for politicians over people and their pockets. I reject that kind of change; we are more interested in progress than in change, progress through increased personal responsibility and increased personal endeavour. That is the policy enshrined in this motion, and I gladly accept it.

CONSERVATIVE POLITICAL CENTRE LECTURE, 'WHAT'S WRONG WITH POLITICS?'

Conservative Party Conference, Blackpool, 11 October 1968

Criticism of politics is no new thing. Literature abounds with it.

In Shakespeare we find the comment of King Lear:

> *'Get thee glass eyes;*
> *'And, like a scurvy politician, seem*
> *'To see the things thou dost not.'*

Richard Sheridan, reputed to have made one of the greatest speeches the House of Commons has ever heard (it lasted 5 hours and 40 minutes), commented that 'conscience has no more to do with gallantry than it has with politics'. Anatole France was perhaps the most scathing: 'I am not so devoid of all talents as to occupy myself with politics.'

Nor have political leaders escaped criticism:

> *'Disraeli unites the maximum of Parliamentary cleverness with the minimum of statesmanlike capacity. No one ever dreams to have him lead. He belongs not to the bees but to the wasps and the butterflies of public life. He can sting and sparkle but he cannot work. His place in the arena is marked and ticketed for ever.'*

This from the Controller of the Stationery Office, in 1853, quoted in *The Statesman* by Henry Taylor. There is no need to remind you how utterly wrong that judgment was.

There are even some things that have improved over the years. Bribery and corruption, which have now gone, used to be rampant. The votes of electors were purchased at a high price. The famous Lord Shaftesbury when he was Lord Ashley, spent £15,600 on successfully winning Dorset in 1831. It is interesting to note that £12,000 of this went to public houses and inns for the refreshment of the people. And this when gin was a penny a glass! Some forty years before, Lord Penrhyn spent £50,000 on his campaign—and then lost!

But we can't dismiss the present criticisms as easily as that. The dissatisfaction with politics runs too deep both here and abroad. People have come to doubt the future of the democratic system and its institutions. They distrust the politicians and have little faith in the future.

Let us try to assess how and why we have reached this pass. What is the explanation? Broadly speaking I think we have not yet assimilated many of the changes that have come about in the past thirty to forty years.

First, I don't think we realise sufficiently how new our present democratic system is. We still have comparatively little experience of the effect of the universal franchise which didn't come until 1928. And the first election in this country which was fought on the principle of one person one vote was in 1950. So we are still in the early stages of dealing with the problems and opportunities presented by everyone having a vote.

Secondly, this and other factors have led to a different party political structure. There is now little room for independent members and the controversies which formerly took place outside the parties on a large number of measures now have to take place inside. There is, and has to be room for a variety of opinions on certain topics within the broad general principles on which each party is based.

Thirdly, from the party political structure has risen the detailed programme which is placed before the electorate. Return to power on such a programme has led to a new doctrine that the party in power has a mandate to carry out everything in its manifesto. I myself doubt whether the voters really are endorsing each and every particular when they return a government to power.

I'm not hard, I'm frightfully soft – but I will not be hounded.

Daily Mail, 1972

This modern practice of an election programme has, I believe, influenced the attitudes of some electors; all too often one is now asked 'what are you going to do for me?' implying that the programme is a series of promises in return for votes. All this has led to a curious relationship between elector and elected. If the elector suspects the politician of making promises simply to get his vote, he despises him, but if the promises are not forthcoming he may reject him. *I believe that parties and elections are about more than rival lists of miscellaneous promises—indeed, if they were not, democracy would scarcely be worth preserving.*

Fourthly, the extensive and all-pervading development of the welfare state is also comparatively new, not only here but in other countries as well. You will recollect that one of the four great freedoms in President Roosevelt's wartime declaration was 'freedom from want.' Since then in the Western world there has been a series of measures designed to give greater security. I think it would be true to say that there is no longer a struggle to achieve a basic security. Further, we have a complete new generation whose whole life has been lived against the background of the welfare state. These developments must have had a great effect on the outlook and approach of our people even if we cannot yet assess it properly.

> Please don't use the word tough. People might get the impression that I don't care. And I do care very deeply. Resilient, I think.
>
> *August 1973*

Fifthly, one of the effects of the rapid spread of higher education has been to equip people to criticise and question almost everything. Some of them seem to have stopped there instead of going on to the next stage which is to arrive at new beliefs or to reaffirm old ones. You will perhaps remember seeing in the press the report that the student leader Daniel Cohn-Bendit has been awarded a degree on the result of his past work. His examiners said that he had posed a series of most intelligent questions. Significant? I would have been happier had he also found a series of intelligent answers.

Sixthly, we have far more information about events than ever before and since the advent of television, news is presented much more vividly. It is much more difficult to ignore situations which you have seen on film with your own eyes than if you had merely read about them, perhaps skimming the page rather hurriedly. Television is not merely one extra means of communication, it is a medium which because of the way it presents things is radically influencing the judgments we have to make about events and about people, including politicians.

Seventhly, our innate international idealism has received many nasty shocks. Many of our people long to believe that if representatives of all nations get together dispassionately to discuss burning international problems, providence and goodwill will guide them to wise and just conclusions, and peace and international law and order will thereby be secured. But in practice a number of nations vote not according to right or wrong even when it is a clear case to us, but according to their national expediencies. And some of the speeches and propaganda to explain blatant actions would make the angels weep as well as the electorate.

All of these things are a partial explanation of the disillusion and disbelief we encounter today. The changes have been tremendous and I am not surprised that the whole system is under cross-examination. I welcome healthy scepticism and questioning. *It is our job continually to retest old assumptions and to seek new ideas. But we must not try to find one unalterable answer that will solve all our problems for none can exist.*

You may know the story of the soldier of fortune who once asked the Sphinx to reveal the divine wisdom of the ages in one sentence, and the Sphinx said 'Don't expect too much.'

In that spirit and against the background I have sketched, let us try to analyse what has gone wrong.

I believe that the great mistake of the last few years has been for the government to provide or to legislate for almost everything. Part of this policy has its roots in the plans for reconstruction in the postwar period when governments assumed all kinds of new obligations. The policies may have been warranted at the time but they have gone far further than was intended or is advisable. During our own early and middle period of government we were concerned to set the framework in which people could achieve their own standards for themselves, subject always to a basic standard. But it has often seemed to me that from the early 1960s the emphasis in politics shifted. At about that time 'growth' became the key political word. If resources grew by X per cent per annum this would provide the extra money needed for the government to make further provision. The doctrine found favour at the time and we had a bit of a contest between the parties about the highest possible growth rate. Four per cent or more. *But the result was that for the time being the emphasis in political debate ceased to be about people and became about economics.* Plans were made to achieve a 4 per cent growth rate. Then came the present government with a bigger plan and socialist ideas about its implementation, that is to say if people didn't conform to the plan, they had to be compelled to. Hence compulsion on Prices and Incomes policy and with it the totally unacceptable notion that the government shall have the power to fix which wages and salaries should increase.

We started off with a wish on the part of the people for more government intervention in certain spheres. This was met. But there came a time when the amount of intervention got so great that it could no longer be exercised in practice by government but only by more and more officials or bureaucrats. Now it is difficult if not impossible for people to get at the official making the decision and so paradoxically although the degree of intervention is greater, the government has become more and more *remote* from the people. The present result of the democratic process has therefore been an increasing authoritarianism.

> It costs as much to train a bad teacher as it does to train a good teacher.
>
> *August 1973*

During July the *Daily Telegraph* published a rather interesting poll which showed how people were reacting against this rule of impersonal authority. The question was 'In your opinion or not do people like yourselves have enough say or not in the way the government runs the country (68 per cent not enough), the services provided by the nationalised industries (67 per cent not enough), the way local authorities handle things (64 per cent not enough—note this rather high figure; people don't like remote local authorities any more than they like remote governments).'

Recently more and more feature articles have been written and speeches made about involving people more closely with decisions of the government and enabling them to participate in some of those decisions.

But the way to get personal involvement and participation is not for people to take part in more and more government decisions but to make the government reduce the area of decision over which it presides and consequently leave the private citizen to 'participate', if that be the fashionable word, by making more of his own decisions. What we need now is a far greater degree of personal responsibility and decision, far more independence from the government, and a comparative reduction in the role of government.

These beliefs have important implications for policy.

First Prices and Incomes policy. The most effective prices policy has not come by controlling prices by the government, through the Prices and Incomes Board, but through the Conservative way of seeing that competition flourishes. There have been far more price cuts in the supermarkets than in the nationalised industries. This shows the difference between the government doing the job itself and the government creating the conditions under which prices will be kept down through effective competition.

On the Incomes side, there seemed to be some confusion in the minds of the electorate about where the parties stood. This was not surprising in the early days because a number of speeches and documents from both sides of the House showed a certain similarity. For example, here are four separate quotations—two from the Labour Government and two from our period of office. They are almost indistinguishable.

1. 'Increases in the general level of wage rates must be related to increased productivity due to increased efficiency and effort.' (White Paper on Employment Policy, 1944)
2. 'It is essential therefore that there should be no further general increase in the level of personal incomes without at least a corresponding increase in the volume of production.' (Sir Stafford Cripps, 1948)
3. 'The Government's policy is to promote a faster rate of economic growth ... But the policy will be put in jeopardy if money incomes rise faster than the volume of national production.' (Para. 1 of Incomes Policy, *The Next Step*, Cmnd 1626, February 1962)
4. '...the major objectives of national policy must be...to raise

productivity and efficiency so that real national output can increase and so keep increases in wages, salaries and other forms of income in line with this increase.' (Schedule 2, Prices and Incomes Act, 1966) All of these quotes express general economic propositions, but the policies which flowed from those propositions were very different. We rejected from the outset the use of compulsion. This was absolutely right. The role of the government is not to control each and every salary that is paid. It has no means of measuring the correct amount. Moreover, having to secure the state's approval before one increases the pay of an employee is repugnant to most of us.

We should back the workers, not the shirkers.

February 1974

There is another aspect of the way in which Incomes policy is now operated to which I must draw attention. We now put so much emphasis on the control of incomes that we have too little regard for the essential role of government which is the control of money supply and management of demand. Greater attention to this role and less to the outward detailed control would have achieved more for the economy. It would mean, of course, that the government had to exercise itself some of the disciplines on expenditure it is so anxious to impose on others. It would mean that expenditure in the vast public sector would not have to be greater than the amount which could be financed out of taxation plus genuine saving. For a number of years some expenditure has been financed by what amounts to printing the money. There is nothing *laissez-faire* or old-fashioned about the views I have expressed. It is a modern view of the role the government should play now, arising from the mistakes of the past, the results of which we are experiencing today.

The second policy implication concerns taxation and the social services. It is no accident that the Conservative Party has been one which has reduced the rates of taxation. The decisions have not been a haphazard set of expediencies, or merely economic decisions to meet the needs of the moment. They have stemmed from the real belief that government intervention and control tends to reduce the role of the individual, his importance and the desirability that he should be primarily responsible for his own future. When it comes to the development of the social services, the policy must mean that people should be encouraged if necessary by taxation incentives to make increasing provision for themselves out of their own resources. The basic standards through the state would remain as a foundation for extra private provision. Such a policy would have the advantage that the government could concentrate on providing things which the citizen can't. Hospitals are one specific example.

The other day I came across a quotation which you will find difficult to place.

> *'Such a plan as this was bound to be drastic and to express nothing less than a new pattern ... (for the hospitals of this country) ... Now that we have it, we must see that it lives. As I have said before it is a plan which has hands and feet. It walks and it works. It is not a static conception stated once and for all but something which is intended to live and to be dynamic ... My Ministry will constantly be carrying this review forward so that there will always be ten years work definitely projected ahead.' (Hansard, 4th June 1962, Col. 153.)*

No, it doesn't come from Harold Wilson. It is not about our enormous overall plan, but a very limited plan in a small area in which the government could make a distinctive contribution. It was Enoch Powell introducing his ten-year hospital plan in the House of Commons on 4th June 1962.

To return to the personal theme, if we accept the need for increasing responsibility for self and family it means that we must stop approaching things in an atmosphere of restriction. There is nothing wrong in people wanting larger incomes. It would seem a worthy objective for men and women to wish to raise the standard of living for their families and to give them greater opportunities than they themselves had. I wish more people would do it. We should then have fewer saying 'the state must do it.' What *is wrong* is that people should want more without giving anything in return. The condition precedent to high wages and high salaries is hard work. This is a quite different and much more stimulating approach than one of keeping down incomes.

Doubtless there will be accusers that we are only interested in more money. This just is not so. Money is not an end in itself. It enables one to live the kind of life of one's own choosing. Some will prefer to put a large amount to raising material standards, others will pursue music, the arts, the cultures, others will use their money to help those here and overseas about whose needs they feel strongly and do not let us underestimate the amount of hard earned cash that this nation gives voluntarily to worthy causes. The point is that even the Good Samaritan had to have the money to help, otherwise he too would have had to pass on the other side. In choice of way of life J. S. Mill's views are as relevant as ever.

> *'The only freedom which deserves the name is that of pursuing our own good in our own way so long as we do not deprive others of theirs, or impede their efforts to obtain it ... Mankind are greater gainers by suffering each other to live as seems good to themselves than by compelling each to live as seems good to the rest.'*

These policies have one further important implication. Together they succeed at the same time in giving people a measure of *independence from the state*—and who wants a people dependent on the state and turning to the state for their every need—also they succeed in drawing power away from governments and diffusing it more widely among people and non-governmented institutions.

The second mistake politics have made at present is in some ways related to the first one. We have become bewitched with the idea of size.

As a result people no longer feel important in the scheme of things. They have the impression that everything has become so big, so organised, so standardised and governmentalised that there is no room for the individual, his talents, his requirements or his wishes. He no longer counts.

It is not difficult to see how this feeling has come about. In industry the merits of size have been extolled for some years now and too little attention given to its demerits. Size brings great problems. One of the most important is the problem of making and communicating decisions. The task of decision tends to be concentrated at the top, and fewer people get used to weighing up a problem, taking a decision, sticking to it and carrying the consequences. The buck is passed. But even *after* a decision has been made, there is the problem of communicating it to those who have to carry it out in such a way that it is understood, and they are made to feel a part of the team. In a large-scale organisation, whether government, local government or industry, failure to do this can lead to large-scale mistakes, large-scale confusion and large-scale resentment. These problems, can, and must be, overcome, but all too often they are not.

> It will be years, and not in my time, before a woman will lead the Party or become Prime Minister.
>
> *1974*

The third mistake is that people feel they don't count when they try to get something done through government agencies.

Consider our relations with government departments. We start as a birth certificate; attract a maternity grant; give rise to a tax allowance and possibly a family allowance; receive a national health number when registered with a doctor; go to one or more schools where educational records are kept; apply for an educational grant; get a job; start paying national insurance and tax; take out a television and a driving licence; buy a house with a mortgage; pay rates; buy a few premium bonds; take out life assurance; purchase some shares; get married; start the whole thing over again; receive a pension and become a death certificate and death grant, and the subject of a file in the Estate Duty Office! Every one of these incidents will require a form or give rise to some questions, or be recorded in some local or national government office. *The amount of information collected in the various departments must be fabulous. Small wonder that life really does seem like 'one damned form after another'.*

A good deal of this form-filling will have to continue but I think it time to reassert a right to privacy. Ministers will have to look at this aspect in deciding how to administer their policies. There is a tendency on the part of some politicians to suggest that with the advent of computers all this information should be centralised and stored on magnetic tape. They argue that this would be time-saving and more efficient. Possibly it would; but other and more important things would be at stake. There would be produced for the first time a personal dossier about each person, on which everything would be recorded. In my view this would place far too much power in the hands of the state over the individual. In the USA there is a Congressional enquiry sitting on this very point because politicians there have recognised the far-reaching dangers of such a record.

Fourthly, I believe that there is too great a reliance on statistical forecasts; too little on judgment.

We all know the old one about lies, damned lies and statistics, and I do not wish to condemn statistics out of hand. Those who prepare them are well aware of their limitations. Those who use them are not so scrupulous.

Recently the economic forecasts have been far more optimistic than the events which happened. The balance of payments predictions have been wrong again and again.

For example, in February this year the National Institute of Economic and Social Research forecast predicted a *surplus* of £100m in the second half of this year. In August they predicted a *deficit* of £600m for the whole of this year, but a surplus of £250m *next* year.

They commented, 'The balance of payments forecast taken year by year look a lot worse than previously estimated, but the difference is largely one of timing—with the movement into surplus coming later, and with a still large rate of improvement.'

The truth is that statistical results do not displace the need for judgment, they increase it. The figures can be no better than the assumptions on which they are based and these could vary greatly. In addition, the unknown factor which, by its very nature is incapable of evaluation, may well be the determining one.

Fifthly, we have not yet appreciated or used fully the virtues of our party political system. The essential characteristic of the British Constitutional system is not that there is an alternative personality but that there is an alternative policy and a whole alternative government ready to take office. As a result we have always had an Opposition to act as a focus of criticism against the government. We have therefore not suffered the fate of countries which have had a 'consensus' or central government, without an official opposition. This was one of the causes of trouble in Germany. Nor do we have the American system, which as far as Presidential campaigns go, appears to have become almost completely one of personalities.

Look Keith, if you're not going to stand, I will.

To Sir Keith Joseph after he decided not to stand against Edward Heath for the Party Leadership

There are dangers in consensus; it could be an attempt to satisfy people holding no particular views about anything. It seems more important to have a philosophy and policy which because they are good appeal to sufficient people to secure a majority.

A short time ago when speaking to a university audience and stressing the theme of second responsibility and independence a young undergraduate came to me and said 'I had no idea there was such a clear alternative.' He found the idea challenging and infinitely more effective than one in which everyone virtually expects their MP or the government to solve their problems. The Conservative creed has never offered a life of ease without effort. Democracy is not for such people. Self-government is for those men and women who have learned to govern themselves.

No great party can survive except on the basis of firm beliefs about what it wants to do. It is not enough to have reluctant support. We want people's enthusiasm as well.

INTERVIEW ON 'VAL MEETS THE VIPS' WITH VALERIE SINGLETON

BBC Children's TV, 5 March 1973

Roger: [Question paraphrased] Good to see a woman Prime Minister?

Mrs Thatcher: I think it depends on who the person is. I don't think there will be a woman Prime Minister in my lifetime. And I don't think it depends so much on whether it's a man Prime Minister or a woman Prime Minister as whether that person is the right person for the job at that time. And it's very difficult to foresee what may happen many, many years ahead.

Val Singleton: [Question paraphrased] Prejudice or...

MT: Not wholly...

VS: [Question paraphrased]...or because women don't desire to become Prime Minister?

MT: ... let's be. It's not wholly prejudice, let's be fair. I don't think we have enough women with the same range of experience in politics as men have had. And it is important, whoever becomes Prime Minister, that they've had quite a wide range of experience in top political jobs. And we haven't yet worked up sufficient women...

VS: [Question paraphrased] Graham Hill said last week women not aggressive enough to be grand prix drivers. Not the reason on lack of aggression in women?

MT: I wouldn't say that I was guilty of lack of aggression sometimes.

VS: [Question paraphrased] Roger, would you like a woman Prime Minister?

> I've got my teeth into him, and I'm not going to let go.
>
> *On Edward Heath during the leadership contest, February 1975*

Roger: [Question paraphrased] Don't know. Would be new thing. Might change some ideas. Depends on whose side and experience.

VS: You wouldn't mind voting for a woman when you are old enough?

Roger: [Question paraphrased] If suitable for the job.

MT: But Roger, there are one or two women Prime Ministers in other countries of course, in India, in Israel, and in Ceylon. They've got women Prime Ministers, and seem to have done quite well with women Prime Ministers, so I don't think we've failed as a sex.

Eileen Conroy: If given chance to be PM, do you have enough [experience]?

MT: (Laughs) My goodness me, it's a pretty penetrating question, isn't it? I would not wish to be Prime Minister, dear. I have not enough experience for that job. The only full ministerial position I've held is Minister of Education and Science. Before you could even think of being Prime Minister, you'd need to have done a good deal more jobs than that.

VS: Mrs Thatcher, thank you very much indeed for being our guest today.

PART TWO

Opposition

1975–79

I'll always be fond of dear Ted, but there's no sympathy in politics.

On former Prime Minister Edward Heath, 1975

To yesterday's men, tomorrow's woman says 'hello'.

11 February 1975

REMARKS AT A PRESS CONFERENCE SHORTLY AFTER BEING ELECTED LEADER OF THE CONSERVATIVE PARTY

Grand Committee Room, House of Commons, 11 February 1975

Margaret Thatcher: *[Reading written statement]* To me it's like a dream that the next name in the line Harold Macmillan, Alec Douglas-Home and Edward Heath is Margaret Thatcher. Each has brought his own style of leadership and stamp of greatness to the task. I shall take on the work with humility and dedication. I'd like to say "Thank you" for the trust and confidence my supporters have placed in me, and a special thank you to Airey Neave and Bill Shelton and our splendid helpers for their all-out effort on my behalf.

It is important to me that this prize has been won in open electoral contest with four other potential leaders. I know that they'll be disappointed, but I hope that we shall soon be back working together as colleagues for the things in which we believe.

There is much to do and I hope you will allow me time to do it thoughtfully and well.

Finally, I would like to pay tribute to the Chief Whip and his staff, and to Robert Carr for carrying on so magnificently during this period of uncertainty.

English Male Questioner: Mrs Thatcher, do you envisage any substantial changes in your Shadow Cabinet?

MT: No, there will be some changes I expect, but it will be a blend of continuity and change.

American Male Questioner: Mrs Thatcher what would you like to say to people who are still sceptical about the idea of a lady leader?

MT: Give me a chance! *[Laughter]*

English Male Questioner: Are you surprised, Mrs Thatcher, that the male-dominated Parliamentary Party have elected you?

MT: No, they seem to like ladies. *[Laughter]*

Female Questioner: Mrs Thatcher, have you spoken to your husband?

MT: Yes, you always ask me that! *[Laughter]* You always ask me the personal questions.

Same Questioner: What did you tell him and what did he say?

I sometimes think the Labour Party is like a pub where the mild is running out. If someone does not do something soon, all that is left will be bitter and all that is bitter will be left.

1975

MT: As I told the chaps in the Grand Committee Room, the tape seems to get there faster than the British Post Office telephone calls. He knew already, he was absolutely thrilled. He'll be up shortly.

Same Questioner: He'll be home shortly?

MT: Yes.

Same Questioner: And what do you plan for … tonight?

MT: Well, I just have to carry on working.

Same Questioner: What about him?

MT: Well, he'll have work to do too.

American Male Questioner: How do you feel Mrs Thatcher about facing Harold Wilson?

MT: Ah, about the same as he will facing me. *[Much laughter]* Next one, come on.

American Male Questioner: Mrs Thatcher you said that sex was not the issue and so did the other candidates. What was the issue you think that put you over the top of a Tory …?

MT: I would like to think it was merit?

Same Questioner: Could you expand on that?

MT: No, it doesn't need expansion. You chaps don't like short answers. Or direct answers. Men like long rambly, waffly answers.

Far Eastern Male Questioner: Mrs Thatcher, do you intend to put any other women in your Shadow Cabinet?

MT: Er, I have not yet made any decisions about the Shadow Cabinet yet, with two exceptions. I am pledged to offer Mr Heath a place if he wishes to have it, and also I hope that former, that …er, the people who contested in the second round who are members of Shadow Cabinet will continue to be members of Shadow Cabinet.

Foreign Male Questioner: Mrs Thatcher do you view your victory today as a victory for Margaret Thatcher alone or do you view it as well as a victory for women in Britain?

MT: Neither. No one can win alone. Ever. You can only win by having a lot of people thinking and working the way you do. It's not a victory for Margaret Thatcher, it's not a victory for women. It is a victory for someone in politics.

American Female Questioner: Mrs Thatcher, how would you unite your party with …? *[Final words of question inaudible]*

MT: Well, one has a wonderful opportunity. After all the vote for me was greater than the votes for all other candidates put together, and the consultations with the constituency last weekend were very favourable. That's a marvellous basis on which to go forward. Next question.

I am not a consensus politician–I'm a conviction politician.

1975

Female American Questioner: Mrs Thatcher have you had any message from the Queen?

MT: Oh indeed no, no, one would not...*[laughter]*...expect that. One would not expect that, one doesn't. This is a party, this is a party political thing.

Male Questioner: Mrs Thatcher...*[words inaudible]*...that you would be going to the Palace?

MT: No, no, one is, er, not until one's prime minister. I hope that will happen one day.

American Male Questioner: Mrs Thatcher *[words inaudible]* real changes of direction in Tory economic policy under your leadership?

MT: Uh, well, one will obviously consult with those in the Shadow Cabinet who will be responsible for economic policy. And if you're going to ask me who those will be—I don't know. *[Sighs]*

Male Questioner: ...one said your election would ensure that the Conservatives are in Opposition for another ten years.

MT: I think they are wrong. *[Shouts of"Hear, Hear"]* It seems to me that Mrs Gandhi 's election in India ensured the election of her party for a very long period in office.

American Male Questioner: Mrs Thatcher do you regard yourself as a, as a Mrs Gandhi…

MT: No. I regard myself as Margaret Thatcher

Male Questioner ***[Michael Cockerell, BBC]*****:** Mrs Thatcher, what is your opinion of Mr Whitelaw?

MT: A very good chap. *[Pauses]* I've had a very nice message of support from him since the ballot.

English Male Questioner: What quality would you most like the Tory Party displaying under your leadership?

MT: Win … the winning quality.

Same Questioner: What sort of philosophical quality?

MT: A Conservative philosophical quality. A distinctive Conservative philosophy. Oh, you don't win by just being against things, you only win by being *for* things and making your message perfectly clear.

Same Questioner: For what?

MT: For a free society with power well distributed amongst the citizens and *not* concentrated in the hands of the state. And the power supported by a wide distribution of private property amongst citizens and subjects and not in the hands of the state.

Same Questioner: How long do you think it will be before you fight an election on this…?

MT: I have no idea. That—the calling of an election—is a matter for the Prime Minister of the day and not for the Leader of the Opposition and he'll call it naturally at a time most suitable to him.

Questioner: ...The Government's majority is very small...

MT: No, it's very large really, over...over, um, it's very large over the Conservative Party.

Same Questioner: *[words inaudible]* May I ask you...*[words inaudible]* Would you seek a coalition, or would you seek an election or would you seek...*[words inaudible]*

MT: I believe there's a classic answer to that, er—we'll just wait and see. I think that's shorter than saying "that's a hypothetical question".

American Female Questioner: Mrs Thatcher do you *[words inaudible]* ... if you will be able to attract finance to the Conservative Party, which I understand is short of money?

MT: We're always short of money. We need a lot more. Do you think we should take a collection at the door? Do you think we should take a collection at the door? *[laughter]*

Male Questioner: *[words inaudible]*

MT: We need more women to come forward to stand for election. I hope they will. I think it is somewhat of a disappointment that after years and years of higher education for women we haven't got more coming forward for Parliamentary candidature. A lot of them, of course, are candidates and local councillors.

American Male Questioner: Mrs Thatcher do you have anything in particular to working class Tory...*[words inaudible]*

MT: Yes. Vote Conservative next time.

English Male Questioner: You said that the Labour Government has a very large majority in practice. Does this mean that you don't expect to be able to get a decisive Parliamentary defeat on the Labour Party?

MT: No, no no. It's just a question of *fact*, it's not a question of opinion. They have a considerable majority over the Conservative Party. It is only if *all* the Opposition parties combine that they have a very *narrow* majority, but for most purposes they have quite a good majority.

> We must have an ideology. The other side have an ideology they can test their policies against. We have one as well.
>
> *1975*

Same Questioner: And you don't think the chances of…*[words inaudible]*…the total anti-government to come into the lobbies…*[words inaudible]*…is particularly great in the forseeable future?

MT: Well, it just depends what the occasion is and what the issue is. We had run reasonably close, I think we ran … the closest we ran was about eleven. I think we did that on the Finance Bill. Er, I'm sorry, of course we won over the earning rule. Yes, that can happen. It is an issue that goes across political boundaries, and some people are prepared to cross-vote.

American Female Questioner: Is it your view that…*[words inaudible]*…Mr Powell…*[words inaudible]*…might be good for the Conservative Party?

MT: I have already said that Mr Powell would not be included in my team.

Questioner: Given the dreadful state of the British economy, do you have any…*[words inaudible]*

MT: No. At the moment we are not responsible for the state of the British economy. That is a matter for the Chancellor of the Exchequer. My views are made very clear in budget statements and on second reading of Finance Bill and *in extenso* on the several clauses in the Finance Bill and I think it is better to read those than try to summarise them.

Questioner: *[words inaudible]*

MT: That was set out in the debate last week, a two-day debate that we had last week. Right, thank you. Thank you very much. I think there are one or two interviews to be done…

PARTY POLITICAL BROADCAST

5 March 1975

I see the Socialists have been celebrating twelve months in office. I wonder why?

What exactly is it this Government feels so proud of?

A year that has seen the greatest acceleration of wage and price inflation in modern British history hardly seems a good excuse for dancing in the streets.

Can the cause of their rejoicing be the bigotry of Mr Benn?

The foolishness of Mr Foot?—presided over by the wiliness of Mr Wilson, putting party before country in the name of Labour unity.

Labour united? I hardly think so.

Only last Saturday we were treated to the spectacle of one of the most senior Members of the Government publicly accusing another senior Member of "economic illiteracy".

And in the same speech Michael Foot informed the nation, "I want to move towards a socialist society as fast as I can."

Well, Mr Foot, I don't.

What I want to do is to lead the people of this country away from the quicksands of Socialism. I don't think they want a Socialist society as fast as they can—or even as slow as they can. I don't think they want a Socialist society at all. Certainly a majority has never voted for it—least of all for the particular brand of Marxist socialism peddled so assiduously by Mr Foot and Mr Benn and their friends.

To stop the drift towards their kind of Britain and all that it implies will not be easy. It will call for hard, dedicated and united work by all those who do not want this country taken over root and branch by a carefully organised and highly articulate minority of the Socialist Party, itself of course a minority. But if the danger is recognised in time it can be stopeed in its tracks—tracks that are daily becoming more clearly defined. Indeed it must be stopped, if we are going to restore the standards on which this nation was greatly built, on which it greatly thrived and from which in recent years it has greatly fallen away.

> We must build a society in which each citizen can develop his full potential, both for his benefit and for the community as a whole.
>
> *1975*

So I say now to all our people, and particularly those in the Midlands and the North—and to my friends in Scotland who welcomed me so unforgettably the other day—but who may have felt in the past that there was not all that difference between the Parties, that it didn't really matter who was in office, I say to you: come back into the fight. There's all the difference in the world. Join hands with us in the Conservative Party and help us rid the nation of this Socialist albatross.

But wishing won't make it so. It has to be worked for—and that, as the new Leader of the Conservative Party, I pledge myself to do with all my heart and strength.

To those who have been tempted to turn left, let me say this—in words attributed to Abraham Lincoln: You cannot strengthen the weak by weakening the strong. You cannot bring about prosperity by discouraging thrift. You cannot help the wage earner by pulling down the wage payer. You cannot further the brotherhood of man by encouraging class hatred. You cannot help the poor by destroying the rich. You cannot keep out of trouble by spending more than you earn. You cannot build character and courage by taking away man's initiative and independence. You cannot help men permanently by doing for them what they could and should do for themselves.

It's been said that all that politicians are doing now is re-arranging the deck chairs on the Titanic.

Well, here is one who isn't. Help me to help you.

Good night.

SPEECH TO THE CONSERVATIVE PARTY CONFERENCE

Winter Gardens, Blackpool, 10 October 1975

The first Conservative Party Conference I attended was in 1946. I came to it as an undergraduate representing Oxford University Conservative Association (I know our Cambridge supporters will not mind). That Conference was held in this very hall and the platform then seemed a long way away, and I had no thought of joining the lofty and distinguished people sitting up there. But our Party is the Party of equality of opportunity—as you can see.

You will understand, I know, the humility I feel at following in the footsteps of great men like our Leader that year, Winston Churchill a man called by destiny who raised the name of Britain to supreme heights in the history of the free world. In the footsteps of Anthony Eden, who set us the goal of a property-owning democracy—a goal we still pursue today. Of Harold Macmillan whose leadership brought so many ambitions within the grasp of every citizen. Of Alec Douglas-Home whose career of selfless public service earned the affection and admiration of us all. And of Edward Heath who successfully led the Party to victory in 1970 and brilliantly led the nation into Europe in 1973.

During my lifetime, all the leaders of the Conservative Party have served as Prime Minister. I hope the habit will continue. Our leaders have been different men with different qualities and different styles. But they have one thing in common. Each met the challenge-of-his-time. What is the challenge of our time? I believe there are two—to overcome the country's economic and financial problems, and to regain our confidence in Britain and ourselves.

> Freedom under the law must never be taken for granted.
>
> *1975*

The economic challenge has been debated at length in this hall. Last week it gave rise to the usual scenes of cordial brotherly strife. Day after day the comrades called one another far from comradely names, and occasionally, when they remembered, they called us names too. Some of them, for example, suggested that I criticised Britain when I was overseas. They are wrong. It wasn't Britain I was criticising. It was Socialism. And I will go on criticising Socialism, and opposing Socialism because it is bad for Britain—and Britain and Socialism are not the same thing. As long as I have health and strength, they never will be. But whatever could I say about Britain that is half as damaging as what this Labour Government have done to our country?

Let's look at the record. It is the Labour Government that have caused prices to rise at a record rate of 26 per cent a year. They told us that the Social Contract would solve everything. But now everyone can see that the so-called contract was a fraud—a fraud for which the people of this country have had to pay a very high price. It is the Labour Government whose policies are forcing unemployment higher than it need have been—thousands more men and women lose their jobs every day. There are going to be men and women many of them youngsters straight out of school—who will be without a job this winter because Socialist Ministers spent last year attacking us, instead of attacking inflation.

And it's the Labour Government that have brought the level of production below that of the 3-day week in 1974. We've really got a 3-day week now,—only it takes five days to do it. It's the Labour Government that have brought us record peace-time taxation. They've got the usual Socialist disease—they've run out of other people's money. And it's the Labour Government that have pushed public spending to record levels. And how've they done it? By borrowing, and borrowing and borrowing. Never in the field of human credit has so much been owed. But serious as the economic challenge is, the political and moral challenge is just as grave, perhaps more so.

> Never in the history of human credit has so much been owed.
>
> *1975*

Economic problems never start with economics. They have deeper roots—in human nature and in politics. They don't finish at economics either. Labour's failure to cope, to look at the nation's problems from the point of view of the whole nation, not just one section of it, has led to loss of confidence and a sense of helplessness. With it goes a feeling that Parliament, which ought to be in charge, is not in charge—that the actions and the decisions are taken elsewhere. And it goes deeper than that. There are voices that seem anxious not to overcome our economic difficulties, but to exploit them, to destroy the free enterprise society and put a Marxist system in its place.

Today those voices form a sizeable chorus in the Parliamentary Labour Party. A chorus which, aided and abetted by many Constituency Labour Parties, seems to be growing in numbers. Anyone who says this openly is promptly accused of seeing Reds Under the Bed. But look who's seeing them now! On his own admission, Mr Wilson has at last discovered that his own Party is infiltrated by extreme left-wingers—or to use his own words it is infested with them. When even Mr Wilson gets scared about their success in capturing key positions in the Labour Party, shouldn't the rest of us be? And shouldn't the rest of us ask him "Where have you been while all this has been going on, and what are you doing about it?" The answer is nothing.

I sometimes think the Labour Party is like a pub where the mild is running out. If someone doesn't do something soon, all that's left will be bitter. And all that's bitter will be Left.

Whenever I visit Communist countries, their politicians never hesitate to boast about their achievements. They know them all by heart and reel off the facts and figures, claiming that this is the rich harvest of the Communist system. Yet they are not prosperous as we in the West are prosperous, and they are not free as we in the West are free. Our capitalist system produces a far higher standard of prosperity and happiness because it believes in incentive and opportunity, and because it is founded on human dignity and freedom. Even the Russians have to go to a capitalist country, America to buy enough wheat to feed their people. And that after more than 50 years of a State controlled economy. Yet they boast incessantly while we, who have so much more to boast about, forever criticise and decry. Isn't it time we spoke up for our way of life? After all, no Western nation has to build a wall round itself to keep its people in.

So let us have no truck with those who say the free enterprise system has failed. What we face today is not a crisis of capital ism, but of Socialism. No country can flourish if its economic and social life is dominated by nationalisation and state control. The cause of our shortcomings does not therefore lie in private enterprise. Our problem is not that we have too little socialism. It is that we have too much. If only the Labour Party in this country would act like Social Democrats in West Germany. If only they would stop trying to prove their Socialist virility by relentlessly nationalising one industry after another.

Of course, a halt to further State control will not on its own restore our belief in ourselves, because something else is happening to this country. We are witnessing a deliberate attack on our values, a deliberate attack on those who wish to promote merit and excellence, a deliberate attack on our heritage and great past. And there are those who gnaw away at our national self-respect, rewriting British history as centuries of unrelieved gloom, oppression and failure. As days of hopelessness—not Days of Hope.

And others, under the shelter of our education system, are ruthlessly attacking the minds of the young. Everyone who believes in freedom must be appalled at the tactics employed by the far Left in the systematic destruction of the North London Polytechnic. Blatant tactics of intimidation, designed to undermine the fundamental beliefs and values of every student. Tactics pursued by people who are the first to insist on their own civil rights while seeking to deny them to the rest of us. We must not be bullied and brainwashed out of our beliefs. No wonder so many of our people—some of the best and brightest—are depressed and talk of emigrating.

> When you take into public ownership a profitable industry the profits soon disappear. The goose that laid the golden eggs goes broody. State geese are not great layers.
>
> *1976*

Even so, I think they are wrong at giving up too soon. Many of the things we hold dear are threatened as never before, but none has yet been lost. So stay here. Stay and help us defeat Socialism, so that the Britain you have known may be the Britain your children will know. Those are the two great challenges of our time. The moral and political challenge, and the economic challenge. They have to be faced together—and we have to master them both.

What are our chances of success? It depends what kind of people we are. Well, what kind of people are we? We are the people that in the past made Great Britain the Workshop of the World. The people who persuaded others to buy British not by begging them to do so, but because it was best. We are a people who have received more Nobel prizes than any other nation except America, and head for head we have done better than America. Twice as well, in fact. We are the people who, among other things, invented the computer, refrigerator, electric motor, stethoscope, rayon, steam turbine, stainless steel, the tank, television, penicillin, radar, jet engine, hovercraft, float glass and carbon fibres. Oh, and the best half of Concorde. We export more of what we produce than either West Germany, France, Japan or the United States. And well over 90% of these exports come from private enterprise. It's a triumph for the private sector and all who work in it. Let us say so, loud and clear.

With achievements like that who can doubt that Britain can have a great future? What our friends abroad want to know is whether that future is going to happen. Well, how can we Conservatives make it happen? Many of the details have already been dealt with in the various debates. But policies and programmes should not be just a list of unrelated items. They are part of a total vision of the kind of life we want for our country and our children. Let me give you my vision.

A man's right to work as he will to spend what he earns to own property to have the State as servant and not as master these are the British inheritance. They are the essence of a free economy. And on that freedom all our other freedoms depend. But we want a free economy, not only because it guarantees our liberties, but also because it is the best way of creating wealth and prosperity for the whole country. It is this prosperity alone which can give us the resources for better services for the community, better services for those in need. By their attack on private enterprise, this Labour Government have made certain that there will be next to nothing available for improvements in our social services over the next few years. We must get private enterprise back on the road to recovery, not merely to give people more of their own money to spend as they choose, but to have more money to help the old and the sick and the handicapped. The way to recovery is through profits. Good profits today, leading to high investment, well-paid jobs and a better standard of living tomorrow.

No profits mean no investment, and a dying industry geared to yesterday's world. Other nations have recognised that for years now. They are going ahead faster than we are; and the gap between us will continue to increase unless we change our ways. The trouble here is that for years the Labour Party have made people feel that profits are guilty-unless proved innocent. But when I visit factories and businesses I do not find that those who actually work in them are against profits. On the contrary, they want to work for a prosperous concern. With a future—their future. Governments must learn to leave these companies with enough of their own profits to produce the goods and jobs for tomorrow. If the Socialists won't or can't there will be no profit making industry left to support the losses caused by fresh bouts of nationalisation.

I have changed everything.

1976

And if anyone says I am preaching laissez-faire, let me say this. I am not arguing, and never have argued, that all we have to do is to let the economy run by itself. I believe that, just as each of us has an obligation to make the best of his talents so governments have an obligation to create the framework within which we can do so. Not only individual people, but individual firms and particularly small firms. Some of these will stay small but others will expand and become the great companies of the future. The Labour Government have pursued a disastrous vendetta against small businesses and the self-employed. We will reverse their damaging policies.

Nowhere is this more important than in Agriculture—one of our most successful industries made up entirely of small businesses. We live in a world in which food is no longer cheap or plentiful. Everything we cannot produce here must be imported at a high price. Yet the Government could not have destroyed the confidence of the industry more effectively if they had tried deliberately to do so, with their formula of empty promises and penal taxation. So today what is the picture? Depressed profits, low investment, no incentive, and overshadowing everything government spending, spending far beyond the taxpayers means.

To recover, to get from where we are to where we want to be, will take time. "Economic policy" wrote Maynard Keynes "should not be a matter of tearing up by the roots but of slowly training a plant to grow in a different direction" It will take time to reduce public spending, rebuild profits and incentives, to benefit from the investments which must be made. The sooner that time starts, the better for Britain's unemployed. One of the reasons why this Labour Government has incurred more unemployment than any Conservative Government since the War is because they have concentrated too much on distributing what we have, and too little on seeing that we have more.

We Conservatives hate unemployment. We hate the idea of men and women not being able to use their abilities. We deplore the waste of national resources, and the deep affront to peoples' dignity from being out of work through no fault of their own. It is ironic that we should be accused of wanting unemployment to solve our economic problems by the very Government which has produced a record post-War unemployment, and is expecting more. The record of Mr Wilson and his colleagues on this is unparalleled in the history of political hypocrisy. We are now seeing the full consequences of nearly twenty months of Labour Government. They have done the wrong things at the wrong time in the wrong way. They have been a disaster for this country.

Now let me turn to something I spoke about in America. Some Socialists seem to believe that people should be numbers in a State computer. We believe they should be individuals. We are all unequal. No one, thank heavens, is like anyone else, however much the Socialists may pretend otherwise. We believe that everyone has the right to be unequal but to us every human being is equally important. Engineers, miners, manual workers, shop assistants, farm workers, postmen, housewives—these are the essential foundations of our society. Without them there would be no nation. But there are others with special gifts who should also have their chance, because if the adventurers who strike out in new directions in science, technology, medicine, commerce and industry the arts are hobbled, there can be no advance. The spirit of envy can destroy. It can never build. Everyone must be allowed to develop the abilities he knows he has within him, and she knows she has within her, in the way they choose.

Freedom to choose is something we take for granted—until

it is in danger of being taken away. Socialist governments set out perpetually to restrict the area of choice, Conservative governments to increase it. We believe that you become a responsible citizen by making decisions yourself, not by having them made for you. But they are made for you under Labour all right. Take education. Our education system used to serve us well. A child from an ordinary family, as I was, could use it as a ladder as an advancement. But the Socialists are better at demolition than reconstruction, are destroying many good grammar schools. Now this is nothing to do with private education. It's opportunity and excellence in our State schools that are being diminished under Socialism. And naturally enough, parents don't like this. But in a Socialist society parents should be seen and not heard.

And another denial of choice is being applied to health. The private sector helps to keep some of our best doctors here, and so are available part time to the National Health Service. It also helps to bring in more money for the general health of the nation. But under Labour, private medicine is being squeezed out, and the result will be to add to the burden on the National Health Service without adding one penny to its income. Let me make this absolutely clear. When we return to power we shall reverse Mrs Castle's stupid and spiteful attack on hospital pay beds. We Conservatives do not accept that because some people have no choice, no one should have it. Every family should have the right to spend their money, after tax, as they wish, not as the Government dictates. Let us extend choice, the will to choose and the chance to choose.

I want to come now to the argument which Mr Wilson is trying to put across the country: namely that the Labour Party is the natural party of Government because it is the only one that the Trade Unions will accept. From what I saw on television last week, the Labour Party did not look like a party of Government at all, let alone a natural one. But let's examine the argument. If we are to be told that a Conservative Government could not govern because certain extreme leaders would not let it, then General Elections are a mockery we've arrived at the one party state, and parliamentary democracy in this country will have perished. The democracy for which our fathers fought and died is not to be laid to rest as lightly as that.

When the next Conservative Government comes to power many Trade Unionists will have put it there. Millions of them vote for us at every Election. I want to say this to them, and to every one of our supporters in industry. Go out and join in the work of your Union. Go to its meetings—and stay to the end. Learn the Union rules as well as the Far Left know them, and remember this. If Parliamentary democracy dies, free Trade Unions die with it.

> I've got no hang-ups about my background, like you intellectual commentators in the south east. When you're actually doing things, you don't have time for hang-ups.
>
> *1977*

I come last to what many would put first. The Rule of Law. The first people to uphold the law should be governments. It is tragic that the Socialist Government, to its lasting shame, should have lost its nerve and shed its principles over the People's Republic of Clay Cross. And that a group of the Labour Party should have tried to turn the Shrewsbury pickets into martyrs. On both occasions the law was broken. On one, violence was done. No decent society can live like that. No responsible party should condone it. The first duty of Government is to uphold the law. If it tries to bob and weave and duck around that duty when it's inconvenient, if government does that, then so will the governed, and then nothing is safe—not home, not liberty, not life itself.

There is one part of this country where tragically defiance of the law is costing life day after day. In Northern Ireland our troops have the dangerous and thankless task of trying to keep the peace and hold the balance. We are proud of the way they have discharged their duty. This Party is pledged to support the unity of the United Kingdom. To preserve that unity and to protect the people, Catholic and Protestant alike, we believe that our armed forces must remain until a genuine peace is made. Our thoughts are with them, and our pride is with them too.

I have spoken of the challenges that face us here in Britain. The challenge to recover economically. The challenge to recover our belief in ourselves. I have shown our potential for recovery. I have dealt with some aspects of our strength and approach. And I have tried to tell you something of my personal vision, my belief in the standards on which this nation was greatly built, on which it greatly thrived, and from which in recent years it has greatly fallen away. We are coming, I think, to yet another turning point in our long history. We can go on as we have been going and continue down. Or we can stop—and with a decisive act of will we can say "Enough".

Let us, all of us, here today and others, far beyond this hall who believe in our cause make that act of will. Let us proclaim our faith in a new and better future for our Party and our people. Let us resolve to heal the wounds of a divided nation. And let that act of healing be the prelude to a lasting victory.

SPEECH ON SOCIALISM

Kensington Town Hall, 19 January 1976

I stand before you tonight in my Red Star chiffon evening gown. *(Laughter, Applause)*, my face softly made up and my fair hair gently waved *(Laughter)*, the Iron Lady of the Western world. A cold war warrior, an amazon philistine, even a Peking plotter. Well, am I any of these things? (No!) Well yes, if that's how they ...*(Laughter)*... Yes I am an iron lady, after all it wasn't a bad thing to be an iron duke, yes if that's how they wish to interpret my defence of values and freedoms fundamental to our way of life.

And by they, I mean that somewhat strange alliance between the comrades of the Russian Defence Ministry—and our (own) [Roy Mason] Defence Minister.

They're welcome to call me what they like if they believe that we should ignore the build-up of Russian military strength, and that we should not disturb their dreams of detente by worrying over the communist presence in Angola.

But I happen to believe that what is at stake is important and is crucial to our future both in this country and in the world as a whole.

We're waging a battle on many fronts.

We must not forget the guns and missiles aimed at us—but equally we must not let them blind us to the insidious war on words which is going on.

> Choice is the essence of ethics. If there were no choice there would be no ethics, no good, no evil. Good and evil only have meaning in so far as man is free to choose.
>
> *1977*

It is not just a matter of hurling insults—where he who hurls loudest, hurls last—that is the final resort of the man who has already lost the argument.

No, this is not such a war.

The war is a true war of words, where meanings get lost in a mist of revolutionary fantasy; where accuracy is slipped quietly under the carpet; and where truth is twisted and bent to suit the latest propagandist line.

That is what we are up against. And we have to fight it if only because we find it totally alien to our notions of freedom and truth. To illustrate what I mean, let us take that last sentence. It contains in it two words which, together, are among the most abused in the language of the struggle.

Freedom and Fight.

The Marxist has applied the description of freedom fighter to one who helps to bring about Marxism, a system which denies basic freedoms. In other words, that so-called freedom fighter is a man who helps to destroy freedom. Such is the corruption of the language they use. Necessary in their eyes because they know freedom is an appealing word.

The men of the Khmer Rouge whose first act on "liberating"—

as they put it—Cambodia last year, was brutally to drive a large part of the population out of the capital Phnom Penh. Yet they were called "freedom fighters".

The men who tried to reverse the clear wishes of the people of Portugal—as expressed through the ballot box—in Marxist vocabulary they were "freedom fighters" too. This surely must have been one of the most blatant attempts at subversion we have seen in recent times. So do not let us be misled by their abuse of these words. But the fallacies of the present propaganda war come nearer to home than this.

I'm not as posh as I sound. I'm not grand at all.

Daily Mirror, February 1977

Let us look at another word being just a subtly corrupted in the litany of the left. The word is "Public". We use it many times a day. It is with us all the time—because we are the public. All of us. Yet the word has become distorted. Take for example "Public Ownership." In theory: We own the mines. We own the railways. We own the Post Office. But in practice we don't really own anything.

"Public ownership" should mean that you and I own something, that we have some say in how it is run, that it is accountable to us. But the fact is that the words "public ownership" have come to mean the very, very private world of decisions taken behind closed doors, and of accountability to no-one.

How good for us all public ownership is presented as being. What a glimpse of socialist heaven it offers. The Socialists tell us that there are massive profits in a particular industry and they should not go to the shareholders—but that the public should reap the benefits. Benefits? What benefits? When you take into public ownership a profitable industry, the profits soon disappear. The goose that laid the golden eggs goes broody. State geese are not great layers.

The steel industry was nationalised some years ago in the public interest—yet the only interest now left to the public is in witnessing the depressing spectacle of their money going down the drain at a rate of a million pounds a day.

Socialists then shift the ground for taking industries into "public ownership". They then tell us that some industries cannot survive any longer unless they are taken into public ownership, allegedly to protect the public from the effects of their collapse. It all sounds so cosy, and so democratic.

But is it true? No, of course it isn't. The moment ownership passes into the name of the public is the moment the public ceases to have any ownership or accountability, and often the moment when it ceases to get what it wants. But it is invariably the moment when the public starts to pay. Pays to take the industry over.

Pays the losses by higher taxes. Pays for inefficiencies in higher prices. Outside many pits in the country is a notice which says: "Managed on behalf of the people." But will the people ever get to know who was responsible for the massive losses sustained since the mining industry was nationalised in 1947?

If these are public industries, then surely the public has a right to know? The more so, because they are monopoly industries. In fact, publicly owned authorities are usually the most private imaginable. We need to revise our vocabulary and call something public only when ordinary members of the public are in actual control.

The fact is that the British public more truly own firms like Marks & Spencer and others, than they do any of our nationalised industries. Some of them directly own shares in M&S. This gives them the right to ask questions about its management—its successes, its failures, and if they are not satisfied, they can sell their shares and invest their money elsewhere.

Many more have an indirect share in it through pension funds at their own work. The managers of those funds are paid to ask the very questions which keep the company on its toes. And millions of us use the option every year of voting with our feet on the success of St. Michael. We can choose whether to buy there or somewhere else.

That is real public ownership—and if the public ceased to

benefit, then M & S would cease to exist. What is it, then, that keeps them going? It is their incentive to satisfy their customers—you and me—the public. Despite what the Socialists would have you think, theirs is not an unusual story.

It is reflected in thousands of firms throughout the land. Successful firms, proving by their results that today's crisis is not one of free enterprise, but one caused by Socialism. Despite the handicaps imposed upon them, the taxation, the restrictions—they are still managing to give the public what it wants.

These are the fallacies in the use of the word "public". We must not let them get away with the deceptions and the half—truths which swarm around their dogma. Whenever we see the word "public" we must question it. How do the public benefit?

What choice does the public have? Choice is crucial in this. When a man moves his family into a Council house, we must make sure he has the chance of buying it. The ambition to own the roof over your head is a totally natural one—and judging by the way the present Cabinet indulges in it—a pretty strong instinct it is, too.

Why, then, do these so-called socialists work so actively to prevent home ownership in the Council estates? The answer is that if you give the ambitious man in the Council house the chance to buy it, you lose control over him.

A socialist system which has penetrated so far in its control over people that it can dictate the colour of their front doors is a system which will never let go control of the whole house. People might paint their doors a different colour, for a start.

We have always been the party of home ownership. Home ownership not only means security for the individual, it also means security and continuity for society as well. Security because people who work hard to buy their own homes have learned the responsibility of property and have a respect for other people's property as well.

Continuity because the ownership of a house is not just for one generation—its value is in more ways than one passed on to the next, and the next. The only way for the majority of people to have any real say in where they live and how they live is by extending home ownership.

> There are still people in my party who believe in consensus politics. I regard them as Quislings, as traitors... I mean it.
>
> *1978*

When we came to power in 1951, home ownership was only 29 per cent. In 1964 it was 45 per cent. By the time we had left Office in 1974 it was 52 per cent. And with our policies the figure will go even higher. Housing policy shows that the Conservative way really does work for the public in the true sense of the word.

When parents send their children to school, and I am talking about local authority schools—not fee paying schools—we must also see that some choice is available. In no field has the exclusion of the public been so severe as in the schools they nominally own, in whose name they are nominally run.

I do not wish to get embroiled here in the controversy currently raging about the running of William Tyndale School. It would be quite wrong for me to comment while the inquiry is still sitting. But there is one observation of fact about it, which can be made. That is that matters came to a head when the numbers of ordinary parents withdrawing their children from the school reached alarming proportions.

That was the only way they could make their views felt. They voted with their feet—just as surely as people would vote with their feet if Marks and Spencer ceased to provide value for money. Nobody wants to see a school shut down—no more than they want to see a firm put out of business.

That is why from the start we must make them more responsive to parents' wishes. That is why there must be choice of the type of education our children are given. It is true that some children flower quickly in the atmosphere of what is called the "progressive" classroom.

Others need the more organised structure of the traditional system. But parents should not be told which their children are going to get, and denied any choice at all. We believe people are not mere cyphers to be ordered this way and that, into this job or that, into this house or that, their children sent to this school or that.

Socialists believe people are not to be trusted with choice. I suppose because we might learn to use it. And enjoy it. And then where would it all end? Socialism is the denial of choice, the denial of choice for ordinary people in their everyday lives. There is a will in Britain to work and build up the future for our children. But Socialists don't trust the people. Churchill did. We do.

INTERVIEW ON DESERT ISLAND DISCS

BBC Radio 4, 18 February 1978
(questions from Roy Plomley annotated for copyright reasons)

Roy Plomley: How much does music matter to you?

MT: It's what I go to when I want to take refuge in something completely different, when I really want to get away from worries and go from a very logical life that I've lived and I've always been trained to live, really to a different depth of experience.

Roy Plomley: You play the piano?

MT: Yes, but I don't play any longer. I didn't get time enough to practise and I couldn't bear hearing myself play badly. Or, what happens to you after a time is you never learn anything new, you go on playing the things which you learned as a young person and never play anything new, so I'm afraid I just don't play at all now. One day when I've retired I'll take it up again.

Roy Plomley: You sang too?

MT: Not solo parts. All my family were musical. My father had a lovely bass voice and therefore we were accustomed to singing at home. We had to make our own entertainment and amusements in those days and we did. So I used to join choirs and I joined the Bach Choir when I was at Oxford and loved it.

Roy Plomley: Would you manage as a castaway? Did you ever camp?

MT: No, I, I haven't had much experience of camping and I just am a little bit worried about how I'm going to manage, but I am pretty practical.

Roy Plomley: Could you build some sort of shelter?

MT: Oh I think so. I do like doing things with my hands, so I think I would just about be all right. I'm quite a fast learner.

Roy Plomley: Would you attempt to escape?

MT: I don't think so because a desert island just all sounds very much of an island and I'm cautious by nature, and I would just hope that someone would come and rescue me, my dreams would go that way.

Roy Plomley: You were born in Grantham, a small town?

MT: A small town, yes, very much a community there, living in a town where everyone knew everyone else. I loved it.

Roy Plomley: You lived in a flat above your father's grocery shop …

MT: That's right...on the Great North Road.

Roy Plomley: Not an only child?

MT: No, *fortunately*! I have an older sister, for which I'm eternally grateful. You know blood *is* thicker than water. When you've got problems there's nothing like close relatives.

Roy Plomley: You've said your upbringing was rather puritan.

MT: Well it was very strict. We went to church twice on Sundays and to Sunday School twice. We were never allowed any amusements on Sundays. We did have people in and we talked. Er, I think wartime changed our ideas quite a lot because you had to do all sorts of different things on Sundays. But I can remember, I think the toughest thing of my childhood was that my father taught me *very firmly indeed*: you do not follow the crowd because you're afraid of being different. You decide what to do yourself. If necessary, you lead the crowd but you never just follow. Oh, it was very hard indeed but my goodness me, it stood me in good stead.

Roy Plomley: During holidays you sometimes helped in the shop?

MT: Oh yes, yes, and this is where one learned to see and talk to so many people and talk easily. I loved it, there were always people coming in and my father was a local councillor and they'd often come in to have a word with him about something.

Roy Plomley: Your father was a councillor, alderman and mayor. He described himself as an Independent. Which side was he on politically?

MT: Well they were Conservative but in those days, you know, we didn't fight local councils as party politicians. It wasn't the done thing. But we always helped the Conservative candidate and I can remember my first experience of politics was the 1935 election. I was only ten, but I do remember it, very vividly, and we used to go to the Committee Room and help, and the only way in which I could help run between the committee room and the polling station to get the lists of the numbers of people who'd voted and go and check them off. And I remember, it seems to strange to me now, you know it was quite a thrill for those of us working in the committee room when the candidate, Victor Warrender, then the Member of Parliament, came round and talked to us. And of course it never occurred to me that I'd been in the same position.

Roy Plomley: Did you ever think you would become leader?

MT: Never.

Roy Plomley: All very sudden. Had you organized supporters? How did you do it?

MT: No, I hadn't an organized group of supporters at all. Some of them came to me and said "Look, if you'll stand, we'll back you" and that was really ... so I knew that I had quite a bit of backing. But it all really happened rather suddenly. It was quite clear that there was going to be an election for the leadership and then it looked as if no one would put for the leadership. Oh I remember very vividly saying well, if no one else will do it, I *will*. And the moment I said it I never had a *moment's* hesitation about it. I knew it was absolutely the right thing to do, I wasn't worried that I'd said it. I wasn't worried that I'd made the decision, the decision was *made*. And then we just had to do the best we could and take what came.

SPEECH TO GLASGOW CONSERVATIVES – 'WRECKERS IN OUR MIDST'

City Hall, Glasgow. 19th January 1979

I hadn't thought to be talking to you under the conditions in our country that exist today. And people are understandably fearful about the future when they see a Government which claimed to have a unique relationship with the Trade Union movement unwilling to rise to the seriousness of the situation.

We Conservatives believe—that Parliament is the supreme forum of the nation; that it represents all our people equally; that the essence of a democracy is that no outside group, however strong, should be more powerful than the elected representatives of the people. —that freedom can only exist under a rule of law, impartially administered; and that no-one can be punished except in a properly authorised court.

> There are a few times when I get home at night and everything has got on top of me when I shed a few tears, silently, alone.
>
> *1978*

—that each individual has certain fundamental rights which no government or organisation is entitled to take away, and those include the right to go about one's lawful business without interference. —that democracy flourishes, not only because it represents a majority, but because that majority recognises that we each have a moral obligation to others. Without that, civilised society could not long survive.

We take these things for granted, but look at what is happening today.

Even the Prime Minister has finally concluded that our troubles are serious—a full, long and anxious week after he told us that it was unpatriotic to talk of crisis.

We did not need telling of the crisis. In Scotland you did not need telling; as you saw control pass to the pickets and the "strike committees", as you saw businessmen queueing up to get "permission" from the strike committee to move their own goods. You did not need telling as you saw men afraid to drive across picket lines or when you saw "flying pickets" in action. You did not need telling as you saw "protection" money extorted as the price of moving essential food supplies, the price of saving starving animals; or as you saw the sick, the elderly and the disabled become the victims of the heartless action of others.

What sort of society is this which breeds such selfish callousness?

They seem to know somehow exactly which factories to go to to cause maximum dislocation. They seem to have a speed and efficiency which came not only from—doubtless the belief of many of them—that they have a thoroughly worthy cause. But also, I think, it came from a ruthless determination from a few men to create mounting chaos. Now these few men are the wreckers in our midst. They're not the mass of trade unionists, but there are a few militants who are the wreckers. And I think they do as much damage to the decent name of trade unionism as they do to our economy. They seek to use freedom in order to destroy freedom.

What sort of a Government is this which sees its authority pass to strike committees?

You will have noted the speed and efficiency with which the pickets went into action.

Again and again we see sensible Trade Unionists pushed by militants in a way they do not want to go. They know they cannot protect their own families from food shortages, or collapsed public services. They too suffer hardships. So we have Trade Unionist against Trade Unionist. Society against itself. This picture of tyranny and tragedy is not the true Britain.

Let me say what I believe are the rights of lorry drivers and indeed the rights of employees and employers in this dispute.

Those who do not wish to support the lorry-drivers strike have an absolute right to collect or deliver goods of any kind, whether they are essential supplies or not. No picket has a right to stop them, if they don't want to stop, no picket has a right to demand money, and no picket has the right to threaten repercussions. Any such action is a flagrant breach of the law. And yet intimidation and blackmail are commonplace events today. Those who do not wish to support the strike are entitled to the protection of the Government in the exercise of their lawful rights.

Private employers can play their part in ensuring that they and their employees can exercise their rights, thereby protecting the jobs of those employees and the supplies of the nation.

They are trying to get their goods through. If their drivers are stopped against their will, threatened, blackmailed or intimidated in any way, they should instantly report the matter to the police. If such action continues, they should realise that the law can be invoked within a matter of hours. They should take urgent advice on the possibility of getting an interim injunction or interdict to restrain flagrantly unlawful action. If they do so, they will be acting in the interests of their workforce, their customers and all the people.

> I think it means that people are really rather afraid that this country might be rather swamped by people with a different culture and, you know, the British character has done so much for democracy, for law and done so much throughout the world that if there is any fear that it might be swamped people are going to react and be rather hostile to those coming in.
>
> *Granada TV, January 1978*

It is up to us to proclaim the rights of our fellow citizens and up to our fellow citizens to reassert them wherever they can.

How did all this come about? Not suddenly but over the years. Gradually the powers of Unions were increased. Great power requires great responsibility in its use. But as their power grew, something else was happening—the extreme left were gradually getting themselves into more and more influential positions in Trade Unions. Harold Wilson recognised this and introduced a policy called "In Place of Strife". Mr Callaghan soon saw that into the wastepaper basket.

When it came to power again, a majority Labour Government pushed through a mass of legislation on industrial relations, including the closed shop, which made up what amounts to a militants charter.

The legislation was the price paid for Union cooperation under the "Social Contract" The cooperation has ceased. The legislation remains. The fault lies not in this Government's stars but in its surrenders.

The law on where and when picketing can occur, the Closed

Shop, Secret Ballots—these are the things which need action, and I doubt whether a code of practice will be enough. It is strange that when asked to legislate to reduce Union power, the Government argues that these things can't be done by law. But it never hesitates to use the law to increase Union power—indeed that is the source of some of our troubles.

I offered, and the offer stands, to support the Prime Minister if he would introduce legislation on these matters, legislation which I believe the vast majority of our people, including most Trade Unionists, want.

But the reforms I put to him would mean changing exactly those laws which this Government has enacted. Would he or the Labour Party make amendments to the Closed Shop legislation which they introduced? Would he or they take away the new legal immunities they gave to Trade Unions? Would he or they really stop secondary picketing? Alas, I doubt it.

What were the great principles I started with?

Parliament supreme?—Not with the power in the hands of strike committees

Rule of Law?—The rule of lawlessness would be a better description of some of the things we have seen.

Individual rights?—Neither for Trade Unionists in a closed shop nor for those who only want to go about their daily business as they have every right to do.

Moral obligations?—Not when a minority hold to ransom the rest of the community who are in no way involved in their grievance.

We have to restore the standards and values in which we passionately believe—or else the way of life we have known will not survive. It is the way of life for which we were renowned. It was we who stood against tyranny. But for us, night would have over-taken civilisation. The enslaved peoples of Europe found in our defiance and in our resistance hope that one day their liberty would be restored to them—and it was.

Now we have to fight and win the conflicts within. And with

the same resolution, the same commitment, the same faith in our cause—the cause of liberty under the law in a Parliamentary Democracy...

...Britain used to be one of the 'top nations'. I don't claim we could have stayed 'top nation' forever, or that we can realistically aspire to that position today. But we should be able to hold and develop the place that we used to have before the rise of the Empire—a place once described as that of the smallest of the great powers and the greatest of the small.

To get from here to there, to break out from being classified as a less prosperous country, we need to become a less over-governed country.

I'm not laying all the blame for our decline at the feet of the Labour Party. But there are three quite specific ways in which it has made things worse.

First, I would single out the Labour Party's attitude to the creation of wealth. The Labour Left have never accepted the role of profits in a free economy. They have never understood that if you "crib and confine a nation's economic freedoms it cannot produce the wealth on which social progress so largely depends."

How can a country become more prosperous, with a Party in Government some of whose members regard the crippling of free enterprise as their principal political objective and others whose response to success is envy and an attempt to take away the hard-won earnings?

The second way in which Labour have helped to increase the rate of decline is by their attitude to the State and the individual. Year by year the State has interfered more and more. It has interfered in everyone's life from the cradle to the grave, from the class-room to the boardroom to the factory floor. The cost of that interference has grown so immeasurably that today the crushing burden of heavy direct taxes deters equally those at the bottom of the ladder and those at the top.

As a result a stagnant and shrinking economy has to carry a larger bureaucracy; businessmen find that it makes more sense to stand still, or to cut back, than to grow; standards in education—on which both the material and spiritual health of the nation so largely depend—are given second place to trying to engineer a spurious equality, preached but seldom practised by Socialist politicians.

Marxists get up early to further their cause. We must get up even earlier to defend our freedom.

Daily Mail, May 1978

The third main Labour contribution to decline has been something to which I have already referred, the way they have fed and nourished the worst instincts in the Trade Union movement so that what originally sprang from deep and genuine fellow-feeling for the brotherhood of man is today disliked and feared throughout the land, and does more damage to our country than ever before in its history.

Unless something radical is done, a harsher future lies ahead. For decline feeds on itself. A firm or a country cannot become less competitive year after year without eventually facing the threat not just of decline relative to the performance of others, but of absolute decline.

All those things have happened in Labour Britain. They reflect the sour face of Socialist failure.

Can we do better?

Yes, I believe we can, the Conservative Party believes we can, not because we think we have all the answers, but because we think we have the one answer that matters most—that Britain can and will succeed if we set the British people free to do so.

Despite the bleak and barren years of Labour we're not really an "LPC"—a third rate country heading downhill for the scrap-heap. We have great natural riches—the coal beneath our feet, the oil and gas in the sea around our shores.

What a bonus those energy resources give us, faced as we are with increases in the price of oil from abroad. How much more worried we would be about the competition from Japan, Germany and France if they could draw on the natural supplies of energy with which we are blessed.

We also have great human resources. We are the same people who down the years won innumerable commercial, diplomatic and cultural triumphs. We still have engineers, managers, inventors, artists of the highest talent. We still have great firms and industries—from agriculture to high technology—whose workers can perform as well as any in the world.

What we do not have is the climate for success. What we do not have is a stable framework within which excellence of every kind is stimulated and rewarded.

The Government promises drift: we need purpose. It promises more Socialism: we need less. It promises restriction: we need liberty.

Do you ever, in a quiet moment, find yourself thinking what your country means to you? Do you ever have in your mind an image of the ideal Britain? The country you would like to live in? I do.

Now is this Britain just an impossible dream? I don't think so. It can be brought about, in time, but the necessary steps will be resisted ruthlessly by those elements in our society who reject my vision of Britain totally, and who are working for the grey and grimy all-powerful state in which the freedom under the law I have described simply will not exist.

When I look back over the roll-call of the Leaders of our great Party—Alec Home, Harold Macmillan, Bonar Law, Arthur Balfour—as a mere Englishwoman I almost begin to feel an interloper. Scotland's genius has been Britain's inspiration for more than two hundred and fifty years. We need you more than ever in the dangerous eighties and nineties. Rather let us work together to build the Britain of our dreams.

SPEECH TO CONSERVATIVE LOCAL GOVERNMENT CONFERENCE ON DEVOLUTION

Caxton Hall, London. 3rd March 1979

Yesterday was a great day for the United Kingdom. Tomorrow—and it can't be far off—will be even better. For two years this Government have laboured night and day to drive the Scotland and Wales Acts through Parliament.

They insisted that their plans were a response to the clamour for Assemblies in Scotland and Wales, but even with that argument, the legislation would never have passed if the Cabinet had not been compelled to hold Referendums.

Nor would it have survived without the 40% rule. But with total cynicism they've tried to whip up emotions which just weren't there. And all that to appease the few whose votes they needed in Parliament.

On Thursday, the people of Wales voted overwhelmingly against the Assembly by a majority of 8 to 1. Every county voted NO.

In Scotland, of those who voted, almost as many were opposed to the Assembly as favoured it.

And if you count the abstentions as NO votes—and that's how Labour were describing them in the campaign—then you can only conclude that the Scottish people rejected Labour's plans decisively.

Dumfries and Galloway said NO. Shetland said NO. Orkney said NO. The Borders said NO. Tayside said NO. Grampian said NO.

There is no sound or honourable basis for the great constitutional change which Labour have proposed, and the final insult would be for this dying government to try to bend our constitution to keep themselves in power for a few more wretched weeks.

Clement Attlee wouldn't have done it. Hugh Gaitskell wouldn't have done it. We wouldn't do it.

Does what has happened affect the timing of the Election? You'd better ask the Prime Minister and the minor parties. Our opposition to Socialism has never been in doubt.

> Now is the time for truth and courage. The age of alibis and deception is over.
>
> If someone is confronting our essential liberties, if someone is inflicting injuries and harm, by God I'll confront them!
>
> *1979*

It wasn't in doubt in Knutsford. It wasn't in doubt at Clitheroe. And the people were in no doubt at all.

Labour has been the government now for exactly five years this weekend. They have been long and hard years for the British people. Five years of decline. What was the phrase?—five wasted years.

During these years, the Conservative Party has been greatly helped by all of you in local government which you know—who better—is about providing services and fulfilling human needs.

It is about giving genuine choice and variety in Education, about the drive to make home ownership a reality. About cutting out waste so that everyone benefits from the lower prices and costs which competition brings. About involving small business in the work of house repairs and house improvement. About helping those who can, to help themselves, so that we can do more for those who need it most. About Nottingham selling its 5000th Council House. About Northampton County Council letting out school bus services to private enterprise.

About East Sussex setting up a task force to encourage local industry. About Leeds cutting the time to process household planning applications to 28 days. About Hickley and Bosworth cutting its rates three years in succession. About Wandsworth holding the rates this year—which the Labour Councils—Hackney, Lambeth, Southwark, Camden and the rest are about to raise them sky-high—20, 30, 40%—perhaps even more.

You have shielded your people from the worst effects of Labour government. We are grateful for all that you have done. We've worked with you in Opposition. We shall go on working with you in government. Good government rests on a partnership between Whitehall and Town Hall.

We are going to give back to you more of the responsibility for running your own affairs. And we will talk with you about how those affairs can be run on the same principles of good government that will shape our policies at the centre.

I'm speaking about the future. But there may of course still be some way to go before we can roll up our sleeves and get down to business.

People are already asking me—"What will the Conservatives do as Labour wriggle this way and that to avoid their inevitable rendezvous with the voters"? I will tell you.

We shall continue to put to the people the great issues which will determine whether this country can succeed in the 1980's where it has failed for the last fifteen years—the issues which will decide whether we can survive at all as a society of which we are all justly proud and in which we want to bring up our children.

We cannot go on as we have been. We can and must halt and reverse the decline. We have the skill ability and resources to do better—much better—provided that we have a government that works with and not against the grain of human nature.

The Conservative approach to Britain's problems is based on four clear principles. First, we believe that the power of the State has been increased far too much. We intend to reduce it and give power back to the people. That is genuine devolution.

Second, we believe that the interests of all groups and people in a nation are ultimately the same. Labour's philosophy of setting one group against another in an increasingly bitter struggle for larger shares in a declining economy destroys confidence, self-respect and any chance of progress.

Third, we believe that the rule of law is the basis of a civilised society. A great political party can't be neutral on this question.

We have no time for so-called Labour moderates like the Education Minister [Shirley Williams] who is prepared to bring in new laws to destroy good schools, but won't use the existing law to keep open those schools that are hit by industrial action.

And fourth, we believe that the time has come when we must strike a reasonable balance between the powers and responsibilities of the trade union movement.

Those are our principles. They are not shared by Labour. All they have to offer is more of the policies that have led to our present troubles. The Labour Party is at a dead end. It is quite simply incapable of giving this country the leadership that it is crying out for.

What will be Labour's strategy, as the government rots away to its inevitable end? Well, Ministers have made no bones about it. The first plank is the concordat, announced two weeks ago with so much ballyhoo, and broken before the ink was dry on the paper. That deal was concluded with the explicit purpose of saving Labour's bacon, not Britain's future. Its basis is all too familiar.

In return for the promise of more Socialism—direction of savings in pension funds and in insurance, more planning agreements, legislation on industrial democracy,—the union leaders undertook (if that's not too strong a word) to do—something or other. Exactly what that amounts to, exactly what is on their side of the bargain, is not too clear.

Take picketing, for example. We are now assured that there is a code of practice which will prevent the abuses of the last few months. But it's a code which endorses secondary picketing, and even in some unspecified cases, wider picketing still; it's a code which is actually less strong than the code which we were told was being operated by the Transport and General Workers' Union during the weeks of the road haulage dispute. You remember that was the time when the government of Britain was handed over to the pickets and strike committees. Not much comfort there.

Or look at what is said on the closed shop. I've got one simple test for the effectiveness of what is proposed. Let Ministers and union leaders urge the reinstatement of those who have lost their jobs, lost their livelihoods with not a penny of compensation under Labour's closed shop law.

I can tell them where to start. They can begin with the British Rail men who've been thrown out of work. The day they do that, we might start believing in their good intentions.

Or take another example—the proposal that there should be no industrial action before an agreement has expired. What difference has that made to the civil service stoppages?

The truth is that the concordat doesn't begin to provide the sensible framework of law on industrial relations that this country needs and wants. It is no more and no less than its authors meant it to be—a life-line for a sinking government. The real job of encouraging—indeed insisting upon—responsible trade union behaviour will be one for the next Conservative government.

The other plank in Labour's strategy, we're told, is to have a long campaign so that they can—and I'm only paraphrasing their argument—"nail that woman". *(Laughter)* I imagine that is a reference to me. *(Laughter)* They seem to think that in a long campaign I'd make a lot of mistakes.

Well, no one's perfect and I can't make any guarantees. But I promise to try not to go to Guadeloupe next winter. *(Laughter and applause)* And if I do, I promise not to give a press conference at the airport when I come back. *(Laughter)*

People want to get, and have a right to expect, the best possible value for the money that is taken away from them in taxes and rates. We've seen elsewhere—in California for example—the rebellion against excessive property taxes. If we cannot give the ratepayers in Britain a better deal, we will face a similar rebellion here.

So if you're pressed at great cost to the rates to concede big pay increases in the guise of comparability with private industry, I suggest that your comparability study includes comparability on productivity, comparability on manning levels, comparability on job security and comparability on inflation—proofed pensions. That is the right way to run a Town Hall—or a government department for that matter.

We can certainly pay people more if they do more. But as a trade union leader, Frank Chapple, said the other day, "it is no good having an emotional involvement with the cause of low paid workers if this means paying three people to do one man's job."

That argument lies at the heart of the economic reality which we have to face up to in this country. But reality is almost the last thing that Labour are prepared to accept.

Only one thing has been worse than the quality of their economic policy making since they came to power in 1974. That is the dishonesty with which their policy has been justified.

Ministers have continually pointed to the contrast between what they describe as the harsh, inhuman monetarist policies proposed by Conservatives and the wholly benevolent policies which they claim are being pursued by Labour.

But when you look a little more closely, the harsh policies turn out to be Labour's, not ours. Interest rates are already up. If Labour clings to office, taxes will soon rise too, and so will prices. The Government's much vaunted single-figure inflation looks as though it could turn out to be a nine-month wonder. Higher taxes and higher interest rates will lead to a new recession.

British business, which is already producing less than it did in 1973, will produce less still as the recession bites. Mr Callaghan and Mr Healey are wrong, and of course they know it, when they claim that rates of interest would have been higher and the crisis deeper had our Party been in power, pursuing those "wicked" monetarist policies. The Prime Minister and the Government have encouraged both their supporters and the public, to believe that monetarism is a dirty word.

Yet they knew all the time that a monetarist policy was vital, that sound money—and that is what "monetarism" means—is essential to our economic recovery. The country is suffering because Labour has been pursuing not a comprehensive monetarist policy, but a half-baked one.

There are two basic tests of any economic policy. First, is it internally consistent and comprehensive? Second, has it been carefully explained to everyone, since everyone has a part to play in making it succeed? Labour's policy meets neither of these tests.

They boast about their firm resolve to curb the money supply. But that claim is never matched by an equally firm determination to cut government spending.

Yet all of us know that Government spending has got to be brought down to a level that can be financed, not only today but in the future, by taxation and rates which is at tolerable levels and by borrowing which is at acceptable rates of interest.

> Tony Benn is a skilful politician. He knows when to keep quiet.
>
> *1979*

Unless this is done, the money supply will accelerate again and with it inflation. Nor has the Government tried seriously to put its policy across either to the trade unions or to the general public. It has failed to make clear that inflationary expectations in general, and trade union pay demands in particular, must be brought down as the money supply comes down. If they are not, unemployment will rise, output will fall, and interest rates will increase. This is in danger of happening now.

A bad economic policy has been converted by a lack of frankness into a disastrous one. In the Labour movement, the dissembling are leading the credulous. As a Party we have consistently emphasised that it is the failure of so many to face the truth, that is largely responsible for today's crisis.

Under Labour, both Government and people have too often accepted the glib solution; taken the short cut; chosen the easy option. That is why the prosperity Labour promised has proved to be not a miracle but a mirage. If we are to escape from the endless cycle of recurring crises that we have endured in recent years, we must first face up to the underlying economic realities.

I want today to point to three of these. The first reality is that there is an inescapable link between prosperity and productivity. Since 1979 began, scarcely a week has passed without some group calling for higher pay: tanker drivers, lorry drivers, grave diggers, hospital workers, school caretakers…You can complete the list as easily as I can.

Everyone, or so it seems, is demanding more pay as though this were the automatic guarantee of a higher standard of living. Listening to the chorus of pay demands, you could easily be forgiven for imagining that a one-hundred per cent pay rise for everyone in the country would solve all our economic problems.

Yet the reality is that doubled pay that is not earned would before long mean doubled prices. The key to prosperity lies not so much in higher pay as in higher productivity. The reason why Britain is today the third poorest nation in the EEC, classed with Italy and Ireland, has little to do with pay; it has everything to do with productivity. Trade union leaders hanker after a West German standard of living. But they fail to recognise you can't have a West German standard of living with a British level of output per person.

We may state a truism—West German pay plus British productivity equals inflation. Read any international study of productivity and you will find that in most industries we produce less goods per head than the countries whose standard of living we envy—the USA, Switzerland, France, Germany.

Only when we stop being obsessed with pay and start to be obsessed with productivity are we going to prosper. Our government will cut direct taxes and increase incentives so that we release the latent energy and enterprise of the nation. We can put the ball at people's feet. Only they can kick it.

We also need a change of attitude if we are to do better. The clamour for more pay shows conclusively that people want a higher standard of living. That is as it should be. But if we are to get it, we must put pay second and productivity first. We must talk productivity and think productivity. We must become as insistent on higher productivity as we are now on higher pay.

It is the duty of a government to provide an economic climate in which increasing productivity leads to expansion, not to fewer jobs and more unemployment. But we should not be too depressed about the chances of achieving that objective so long as our goods are competitive.

So, the first economic reality is that only increased productivity will give us increased prosperity. Any policy which promises greater prosperity without higher productivity stands automatically condemned.

The second reality is this. Until we have increased productivity, individuals can take more of what the nation earns only at the expense of other people. In recent years we have become a jealous and divided society. A major reason is that for more than six years there has been no increase in the amount of wealth that the country produces.

We have failed to increase our standard of living either as individuals or as groups in the only way we can—by increasing output. Many people have therefore resorted to attempts to increase their pay at the expense of their fellows and these people, in their turn, have done the same. Well-intentioned attempts to increase the incomes of the low paid have foundered against the resistance of the higher paid. Unions like the NUR and ASLEF struggle to outbid each other in leapfrogging pay claims.

We each quote examples—real or not—of those with whom we compare ourselves and who, we say, are paid more than we are. The result is a society with little pity, racked by strikes where no quarter is given. Strong unions may in theory believe in greater equality of incomes, but not in practice. They want to have their cake and eat ours too. They demonstrate the second reality. If output stagnates, there is a temptation to take a larger share for ourselves even though that means less for others.

Our dependence on each other expresses itself not in a virtuous circle of cooperation and generosity but in a vicious circle of division and selfishness. There is, or if there is not, there should be, an old American proverb:

A lot you can share; nothing you can't.

That sums up precisely the second economic reality. A lot you can share. Since we have little, the result is that we are not one nation; we are not even two nations; we are a host of squabbling factions; and we are encouraged to fight and quarrel by Labour's philosophy and Labour's economic failure.

The third reality is that we are bound to suffer from the problems of a divided society so long as the emphasis is on what we can get out of the economy in pay by strikes and not on what we can put into it through productive effort.

> Let us make this country safe to work in. Lets us make this country safe to walk in. Let us make it a country safe to grow up in. Let us make it a country safe to grow old in.
>
> *In a Party Political Broadcast, 30 April 1979*

Division is inevitable because while our ambition steadily increases, output is held down. The myth that we have to demolish is that somewhere there is a crock of gold—owned by some unnecessary and underserving group—which we can raid whenever we want to increase our own standard of living without hurting anyone else.

Those who receive dividends are the prime example. The Left continually calls for tough price control in order to reduce profits and the dividends paid by business and, they wrongly assume, to raise substantially the welfare of the mass of the population. But this imagined crock of gold does not exist.

If all dividends were confiscated and shared out equally, that would raise average incomes by a mere two pence in the pound. In other words, to get rid of all dividends would be like the country putting in for a two per cent pay claim.

And, these days, even the Government's suggested five per cent pay rise is greeted with scorn. Look at the consequences that would follow from such a step. Pension schemes—in both public and private industries—would be decimated. The retired would suffer. Investment would be hit. Unemployment would rise. Our decline would steepen. The painful truth is that there is no crock of gold.

We can improve our position as a nation only by working together to create greater wealth. We cannot do it by each fighting for a bigger share of the existing cake. The cake is too small; the fight too damaging; and the result, impoverishment, cynicism, and conflict. It will be the job of the next Conservative Government to set the economy on a new course of expansion.

But our policy will only work if men and women use the opportunities we create. We must face the reality that we cannot, as individuals or as a nation, live beyond our means without disaster. We must work for greater productivity, not simply agitate for higher pay. We must not be diverted from this by a fruitless attempt to improve our personal position at the expense of each other. Nor must we imagine that there is somewhere some stock of wealth that we can confiscate to give ourselves instant prosperity without the need to work for it.

Those are the lessons of the last five years. We ignore them at our peril. We shall need all your help in local government to bring this country face to face with that truth. That must be our goal in the weeks and months that lie ahead. While the disreputable last act of this government is played out, while they lose their last shreds of self-respect in the struggle to cling to power, we must not be diverted from the task of showing that there is a more honest and rewarding way of running our affairs.

PARTY ELECTION BROADCAST

30 April 1979

We're coming to the moment of decision. As the tumult and the shouting of the last few weeks die away and you sit at home wondering what to do on Thursday I can well imagine you saying to yourselves, "If only the politicians would be quiet. If only we could sit peacefully for a few minutes and think about our country and its future and the decision you're asking us to make."

I know how you feel. The decision is crucial. The problems facing Britain are very grave. I can't remember when our people have approached an election quite as thoughtfully as this one.

We've tried to fight an honourable campaign; to put before you truthfully the choice this country faces. That choice will decide who governs Britain for the next five years. It may also decide what sort of country our children and grandchildren grow up in. When all the other questions have been argued and debated in the papers, on radio and on television, there's only one that really matters in the end. What's best for Britain?

Whichever party we belong to, or even if we belong to no party at all, most of us would agree that things have not gone well for our country in the last few years. Oh, there's still plenty to be proud of, plenty to admire and to cherish. But a lot of things we used to take for granted seem to be in danger of disappearing. Money that keeps its value. Real jobs that last. Paying our way in the world. Feeling safe in our streets—especially if you're a woman. Hospitals that long to give the service that they used to; schools which gave children from modest backgrounds, like my own, the chance to get on in life as far as we were able.

So much has been threatened lately. So much that used to be sure is sure no longer. So when our opponents say, "The Conservatives want to change things," I answer, "Yes, we do. And for the better." If ever there was a need for change it's now. I don't mean sudden change and I'm not talking about trying to bring back some nostalgic version of the past. I don't want to look back tonight anymore than you'll be looking back when you vote on Thursday. You'll be thinking of the future and how it can be better, and which of the parties is more likely to make it so.

Let me tell you how I see it. I've never believed that this country is a naturally socialist country. We're an independent people; we don't take easily to having more and more of our lives decided for us by the State. We don't take kindly to being pushed around. We're good neighbours, concerned for the welfare of others. We regard it as a privilege to say to the old, the sick, the needy and the disabled—"Don't worry, we'll look after you." But we believe that those who are strong and healthy and active should be encouraged to get on and make a success of things for themselves. Many of our troubles stem from the fact that in recent years we haven't been true to ourselves; true to our tradition of independence—largely because we've been encouraged not to be. It hasn't paid to work harder or try to do better for the family. Sometimes it hasn't paid to work at all.

That's had its effect right through the country, so instead of sharing out the proceeds of success, we've taken to fighting over how much we can afford from failure. Now none of us is so naive as to believe that cutting taxes will, by itself, suddenly transform everything and make our country prosperous overnight. But what we do believe is that there's all the difference in the world between creating a society in which it pays to work and creating one which it doesn't. Only by becoming prosperous again can Britain become a genuinely caring society, which is why we think that our way—not our opponents'—is truly "the better way."

I think that most of you who know their record know that too. There's a long tradition in this country that everyone is equal under the law. Indeed, a lot of our history has been about seeing that those who acquire great power are not allowed to abuse it. Trade unions today have a lot of rights, but not enough duties. I don't think that many people can take an honest look at our industrial relations and say that we can go on year after year tearing ourselves apart. I am sorry that our offer of support for the limited but essential union reforms was turned down by the Government last winter. So we shall have to carry them through ourselves. Our proposals are modest and strongly supported by the nation, including the vast majority of trade union members. I've no doubt whatever that no matter what they may say during an election the unions will accept the democratic will of the people, especially when the moderate majority make their voice heard, as I hope they will on Thursday.

> Unless we change our ways and our direction, our greatness as a nation will soon be a footnote in the history books, a distant memory of an offshore island, lost in the mist of time like Camelot, remembered kindly for its noble past.
>
> *2 May 1979*

We want to create a society which is open and free, but to protect that freedom in a more and more dangerous world we've got to keep up our guard. Surely if the 1930s taught us anything they taught us that? The right response to increasing Soviet strength is not increasing British weakness. We shall make sure that Britain's defences are up to strength and that the first duty of any government—the defence of the realm—is ensured.

Now, no one in my position, asking for your support, your understanding, could be unaware of the responsibility that I am asking you to give me at this moment of decision for our country. To that I should perhaps add the fact—and if I don't a lot of others will—that this is the first time in our history that a woman could, after Thursday, be holding the highest political office in our national life. It's never happened before. And I know that despite all the changes in our society there are some who still feel a little bit uncertain about it. I also know that there are others who would welcome it. I've always believed that what matters in politics, as in the rest of life, is not who you are, or where you come from, but what you believe and what you want to do with your life. What matters are your convictions.

> Communism never sleeps, never changes its objectives. Nor must we.
>
> *Financial Times, May 1979*

So, as we approach the end of this campaign, I want to tell you the thoughts and feelings that will guide me in government if you place your confidence in the Conservative Party on Thursday. Let me give you my vision. Somewhere ahead lies greatness for our country again; this I know in my heart. Look at Britain today and you may think that an impossible dream. But there's another Britain which may not make the daily news but which each one of us knows. It's a Britain of thoughtful people, oh, tantalisingly slow to act yet marvellously determined when they do. It's their voice which steadies each generation. Not by oratory or argument but by a word here or there; a sudden flash of truth which makes men pause and think and say, "That makes sense to me." That's how the foundations of fairness have been built up in this country, brick by brick, layer upon layer. In that way the law has grown, bringing to each age what seems reasonable and wise and true. Today, if you listen, you can hear that voice again. It calls not for upheaval or conflict or division; it calls for balance; for a land where all may grow, but none may grow oppressive. It's message is quiet but insistent. It says this: Let us make this a country safe to work in; let us make this a country safe to walk in; let us make it a country safe to grow up in; let us make it a country safe to grow old in. And it says, above all, may this land of ours, which we love so much, find dignity and greatness and peace again.

PART THREE

First Term

1979–83

Any woman who understands the problems of running a home will be near to understanding the problems of running a nation.

Observer, 8 May 1979

We should not underestimate the enormity of the task which lies ahead. But little can be achieved without sound money. It is the bedrock of sound government.

May 1979

REMARKS ON THE STEPS OF 10 DOWNING STREET

London, 4th May 1979

Question: How do you feel at this moment?

MT: Very excited, very aware of the responsibilities. Her Majesty The Queen has asked me to form a new administration and I have accepted. It is, of course, the greatest honour that can come to any citizen in a democracy. (Cheering) I know full well the responsibilities that await me as I enter the door of No. 10 and I'll strive unceasingly to try to fulfil the trust and confidence that the British people have placed in me and the things in which I believe. And I would just like to remember some words of St. Francis of Assisi which I think are really just particularly apt at the moment. 'Where there is discord, may we bring harmony. Where there is error, may we bring truth. Where there is doubt, may we bring faith. And where there is despair, may we bring hope' ...and to all the British people—howsoever they voted—may I say this. Now that the election is over, may we get together and strive to serve and strengthen the country of which we're so proud to be a part. And finally, one last thing: in the words of Airey Neave whom we had hoped to bring here with us, 'There is now work to be done.'

Question: Prime Minister, could I ask you if you would tell us what sort of administration you would like to have over the next five years?

MT: Well, we shall be going inside and we shall be getting on with that as fast as we can ... but I think the first job is to try to form a Cabinet. We must get that done. We can't really just ...

Question: How soon do you think you'll be able to name your Cabinet?

MT: Well, certainly not today. I hope to have some news by tomorrow evening. It's a very important thing. It's not a thing that should be suddenly rushed through. It's very important.

Question: And what will you be doing for the rest of today?

MT: I shall be here working.

Question: Have you got any thoughts, Mrs Thatcher, at this moment about Mrs Pankhurst and your own mentor in political life—your own father?

MT: Well, of course, I just owe almost everything to my own father. I really do. He brought me up to believe all the things that I do believe and they're just the values on which I've fought the election. And it's passionately interesting for me that the things that I learned in a small town, in very modest home, are just the things that I believe have won the election. Gentlemen, you're very kind. May I just go…

SPEECH TO THE CONSERVATIVE PARTY CONFERENCE

Brighton, 10 October 1980

At our party conference last year I said that the task in which the Government were engaged—to change the national attitude of mind—was the most challenging to face any British Administration since the war. Challenge is exhilarating. This week we Conservatives have been taking stock, discussing the achievements, the set-backs and the work that lies ahead as we enter our second parliamentary year. As you said Mr Chairman our debates have been stimulating and our debates have been constructive. This week has demonstrated that we are a party united in purpose, strategy and resolve. And we actually like one another.

When I am asked for a detailed forecast of what will happen in the coming months or years I remember Sam Goldwyn 's advice: "Never prophesy, especially about the future..."

(Interruption from a heckler on the floor) Never mind, it is wet outside. I expect that they wanted to come in. You cannot blame them; it is always better where the Tories are. And you—and perhaps they—will be looking to me this afternoon for an indication of how the Government see the task before us and why we are tackling it the way we are. Before I begin let me get one thing out of the way.

This week at Brighton we have heard a good deal about last week at Blackpool. I will have a little more to say about that strange assembly later, but for the moment I want to say just this.

Because of what happened at that conference, there has been, behind all our deliberations this week, a heightened awareness that now, more than ever, our Conservative Government must succeed. We just must, because now there is even more at stake than some had realised.

There are many things to be done to set this nation on the road to recovery, and I do not mean economic recovery alone, but a new independence of spirit and zest for achievement.

It is sometimes said that because of our past we, as a people, expect too much and set our sights too high. That is not the way I see it. Rather it seems to me that throughout my life in politics our

> We believe in a free Europe but not a standardised Europe. Diminish that variety within the Member States, and you impoverish the whole Community. We insist that the institutions of the European Community are managed so that they increase the liberty of the individual throughout our continent. These institutions must not be permitted to dwindle into bureaucracy. Whenever they fail to enlarge freedom the institutions should be criticised and the balance restored.
>
> *July 1979*

ambitions have steadily shrunk. Our response to disappointment has not been to lengthen our stride but to shorten the distance to be covered. But with confidence in ourselves and in our future what a nation we could be!

> Pennies don't fall from heaven; they have to be earned on earth.
>
> *Sunday Telegraph, November 1979*

In its first seventeen months this Government have laid the foundations for recovery. We have undertaken a heavy load of legislation, a load we do not intend to repeat because we do not share the Socialist fantasy that achievement is measured by the number of laws you pass. But there was a formidable barricade of obstacles that we had to sweep aside. For a start, in his first Budget Geoffrey Howe began to rest incentives to stimulate the abilities and inventive genius of our people. Prosperity comes not from grand conferences of economists but by countless acts of personal self-confidence and self-reliance.

Under Geoffrey's stewardship, Britain has repaid $3,600 million of international debt, debt which had been run up by our predecessors. And we paid quite a lot of it before it was due. In the past twelve months Geoffrey has abolished exchange controls over which British Governments have dithered for decades. Our great enterprises are now free to seek opportunities overseas. This will help to secure our living standards long after North Sea oil has run out. This Government thinks about the future. We have made the first crucial changes in trade union law to remove the worst abuses of the closed shop, to restrict picketing to the place of work of the parties in dispute, and to encourage secret ballots.

Jim Prior has carried all these measures through with the support of the vast majority of trade union members. Keith Joseph, David Howell, John Nott and Norman Fowler have begun to break down the monopoly powers of nationalisation. Thanks to them British Aerospace will soon be open to private investment. The monopoly of the Post Office and British Telecommunications is being diminished. The barriers to private generation of electricity for sale have been lifted. For the first time nationalised industries and public utilities can be investigated by the Monopolies Commission—a long overdue reform.

Free competition in road passenger transport promises travellers a better deal. Michael Heseltine has given to millions—yes, millions—of council tenants the right to buy their own homes.

It was Anthony Eden who chose for us the goal of "a property-owning democracy". But for all the time that I have been in public affairs that has been beyond the reach of so many, who were denied the right to the most basic ownership of all—the homes in which they live.

They wanted to buy. Many could afford to buy. But they happened to live under the jurisdiction of a Socialist council, which would not sell and did not believe in the independence that comes with ownership. Now Michael Heseltine has given them the chance to turn a dream into reality. And all this and a lot more in seventeen months.

The Left continues to refer with relish to the death of capitalism. Well, if this is the death of capitalism, I must say that it is quite a way to go.

But all this will avail us little unless we achieve our prime economic objective—the defeat of inflation. Inflation destroys nations and societies as surely as invading armies do. Inflation is the parent of unemployment. It is the unseen robber of those who have saved.

> John Hoskyns [Head of Number Ten Policy Unit]: If there is ever to be any sort of U-turn on policy you absolutely must think about it now.
>
> Margaret Thatcher: You know, I would rather go down than do that, so forget it.
>
> *1980*

No policy which puts at risk the defeat of inflation—however great its short-term attraction—can be right. Our policy for the defeat of inflation is, in fact, traditional. It existed long before Sterling M3 embellished the Bank of England Quarterly Bulletin, or "monetarism" became a convenient term of political invective.

But some people talk as if control of the money supply was

a revolutionary policy. Yet it was an essential condition for the recovery of much of continental Europe.

Those countries knew what was required for economic stability. Previously, they had lived through rampant inflation; they knew that it led to suitcase money, massive unemployment and the breakdown of society itself. They determined never to go that way again.

> I don't mind how much my Ministers talk, as long as they do what I say.
>
> *1980*

Today, after many years of monetary self-discipline, they have stable, prosperous economies better able than ours to withstand the buffeting of world recession.

So at international conferences to discuss economic affairs many of my fellow Heads of Government find our policies not strange, unusual or revolutionary, but normal, sound and honest. And that is what they are.

Their only question is: "Has Britain the courage and resolve to sustain the discipline for long enough to break through to success?"

Yes, Mr Chairman, we have, and we shall. This Government are determined to stay with the policy and see it through to its conclusion. That is what marks this administration as one of the truly radical ministries of post-war Britain. Inflation is falling and should continue to fall.

Meanwhile we are not heedless of the hardships and worries that accompany the conquest of inflation.

Foremost among these is unemployment. Today our country has more than 2 million unemployed.

Now you can try to soften that figure in a dozen ways. You can point out—and it is quite legitimate to do so—that 2 million today does not mean what it meant in the 1930s; that the percentage of unemployment is much less now than it was then.

You can add that today many more married women go out to work.

You can stress that, because of the high birthrate in the early

1960s, there is an unusually large number of school leavers this year looking for work and that the same will be true for the next two years.

You can emphasise that about a quarter of a million people find new jobs each month and therefore go off the employment register.

And you can recall that there are nearly 25 million people in jobs compared with only about 18 million in the 1930s. You can point out that the Labour party conveniently overlooks the fact that of the 2 million unemployed for which they blame us, nearly a million and a half were bequeathed by their Government.

But when all that has been said the fact remains that the level of unemployment in our country today is a human tragedy. Let me make it clear beyond doubt. I am profoundly concerned about unemployment. Human dignity and self respect are undermined when men and women are condemned to idleness. The waste of a country's most precious assets—the talent and energy of its people- makes it the bounden duty of Government to seek a real and lasting cure.

If I could press a button and genuinely solve the unemployment problem, do you think that I would not press that button this instant? Does anyone imagine that there is the smallest political gain in letting this unemployment continue, or that there is some obscure economic religion which demands this unemployment as part of its ritual? This Government are pursuing the only policy which gives any hope of bringing our people back to real and lasting employment. It is no coincidence that those countries, of which I spoke earlier, which have had lower rates of inflation have also had lower levels of unemployment.

I know that there is another real worry affecting many of our people. Although they accept that our policies are right, they feel deeply that the burden of carrying them out is falling much more heavily on the private than on the public sector. They say that the public sector is enjoying advantages but the private sector is taking the knocks and at the same time maintaining those in the public sector with better pay and pensions than they enjoy.

I must tell you that I share this concern and understand the resentment. That is why I and my colleagues say that to add to public spending takes away the very money and resources that industry needs to stay in business let alone to expand. Higher public spending, far from curing unemployment, can be the very vehicle that loses jobs and causes bankruptcies in trade and commerce. That is why we warned local authorities that since rates are frequently the biggest tax that industry now faces, increases in them can cripple local businesses. Councils must, therefore, learn to cut costs in the same way that companies have to.

> It was then that the iron entered my soul.
>
> *On the Heath Government, 1980*

That is why I stress that if those who work in public authorities take for themselves large pay increases they leave less to be spent on equipment and new buildings. That in turn deprives the private sector of the orders it needs, especially some of those industries in the hard pressed regions. Those in the public sector have a duty to those in the private sector not to take out so much in pay that they cause others unemployment. That is why we point out that every time high wage settlements in nationalised monopolies lead to higher charges for telephones, electricity, coal and water, they can drive companies out of business and cost other people their jobs.

If spending money like water was the answer to our country's problems, we would have no problems now. If ever a nation has spent, spent, spent and spent again, ours has. Today that dream is over. All of that money has got us nowhere but it still has to come from somewhere. Those who urge us to relax the squeeze, to spend yet more money indiscriminately in the belief that it will help the unemployed and the small businessman are not being kind or compassionate or caring.

They are not the friends of the unemployed or the small business. They are asking us to do again the very thing that caused the problems in the first place. We have made this point repeatedly.

I am accused of lecturing or preaching about this. I suppose it is a critic's way of saying "Well, we know it is true, but we have to carp at something." I do not care about that. But I do care about the future of free enterprise, the jobs and exports it provides and the independence it brings to our people. Independence? Yes, but let us be clear what we mean by that. Independence does not mean contracting out of all relationships with others. A nation can be free but it will not stay free for long if it has no friends and no alliances. Above all, it will not stay free if it cannot pay its own way in the world. By the same token, an individual needs to be part of a community and to feel that he is part of it. There is more to this than the chance to earn a living for himself and his family, essential though that is.

Of course, our vision and our aims go far beyond the complex arguments of economics, but unless we get the economy right we shall deny our people the opportunity to share that vision and to see beyond the narrow horizons of economic necessity. Without a healthy economy we cannot have a healthy society. Without a healthy society the economy will not stay healthy for long.

> The adrenalin flows when they really come out fighting at me, and I fight back and I stand there, and I know. Now come on Maggie, you are wholly on your own. No one can help you. And I love it!
>
> *1980*

But it is not the State that creates a healthy society. When the State grows too powerful people feel that they count for less and less. The State drains society, not only of its wealth but of initiative, of energy, the will to improve and innovate as well as to preserve what is best. Our aim is to let people feel that they count for more and more. If we cannot trust the deepest instincts of our people we should not be in politics at all. Some aspects of our present society really do offend those instincts.

Decent people do want to do a proper job at work, not to be restrained or intimidated from giving value for money. They believe that honesty should be respected, not derided. They see crime and violence as a threat not just to society but to their own orderly way of life. They want to be allowed to bring up their children in these beliefs, without the fear that their efforts will be daily frustrated in the name of progress or free expression. Indeed, that is what family life is all about.

> I love argument, I love debate. I don't expect anyone just to sit there and agree with me, that's not their job.
>
> *The Times, 1980*

There is not a generation gap in a happy and united family. People yearn to be able to rely on some generally accepted standards. Without them you have not got a society at all, you have purposeless anarchy. A healthy society is not created by its institutions, either. Great schools and universities do not make a great nation any more than great armies do. Only a great nation can create and involve great institutions—of learning, of healing, of scientific advance. And a great nation is the voluntary creation of its people—a people composed of men and women whose pride in themselves is founded on the knowledge of what they can give to a community of which they in turn can be proud.

If our people feel that they are part of a great nation and they are prepared to will the means to keep it great, a great nation we shall be, and shall remain. So, what can stop us from achieving this? What then stands in our way? The prospect of another winter of discontent? I suppose it might.

But I prefer to believe that certain lessons have been learnt from experience, that we are coming, slowly, painfully, to an autumn of understanding. And I hope that it will be followed by a winter of common sense. If it is not, we shall not be—diverted from our course.

To those waiting with bated breath for that favourite media catchphrase, the "U" turn, I have only one thing to say. "You turn if you want to. The lady's not for turning." I say that not only to you but to our friends overseas and also to those who are not our friends.

In foreign affairs we have pursued our national interest robustly while remaining alive to the needs and interests of others. We have acted where our predecessors dithered and here I pay tribute to Lord Carrington. When I think of our much-travelled Foreign

Secretary I am reminded of the advert, you know the one I mean, about "The peer that reaches those foreign parts that other peers cannot reach."

Long before we came into office, and therefore long before the invasion of Afghanistan I was pointing to the threat from the East. I was accused of scaremongering. But events have more than justified my words.

Soviet marxism is ideologically, politically and morally bankrupt. But militarily the Soviet Union is a powerful and growing threat.

Yet it was Mr Kosygin who said "No peace loving country, no person of integrity, should remain indifferent when an aggressor holds human life and world opinion in insolent contempt." We agree. The British Government are not indifferent to the occupation of Afghanistan. We shall not allow it to be forgotten. Unless and until the Soviet troops are withdrawn other nations are bound to wonder which of them may be next. Of course there are those who say that by speaking out we are complicating East-West relations, that we are endangering detente. But the real danger would lie in keeping silent. Detente is indivisible and it is a two-way process.

The Soviet Union cannot conduct wars by proxy in South-East Asia and Africa, foment trouble in the Middle East and Caribbean and invade neighbouring countries and still expect to conduct business as usual. Unless detente is pursued by both sides it can be pursued by neither, and it is a delusion to suppose otherwise. That is the message we shall be delivering loud and clear at the meeting of the European Security Conference in Madrid in the weeks immediately ahead.

But we shall also be reminding the other parties in Madrid that the Helsinki Accord was supposed to promote the freer movement of people and ideas. The Soviet Government's response so far has been a campaign of repression worse than any since Stalin 's day. It had been hoped that Helsinki would open gates across Europe. In fact, the guards today are better armed and the walls are no lower. But behind those walls the human spirit is unvanquished.

The workers of Poland in their millions have signalled their determination to participate in the shaping of their destiny. We salute them.

Marxists claim that the capitalist system is in crisis. But the Polish workers have shown that it is the Communist system that is in crisis. The Polish people should be left to work out their own future without external interference.

At every Party Conference, and every November in Parliament, we used to face difficult decisions over Rhodesia and over sanctions. But no longer. Since we last met the success at Lancaster House, and thereafter in Salisbury—a success won in the face of all the odds—has created new respect for Britain. It has given fresh hope to those grappling with the terrible problems of Southern Africa. It has given the Commonwealth new strength and unity. Now it is for the new nation, Zimbabwe, to build her own future with the support of all those who believe that democracy has a place in Africa, and we wish her well.

We showed over Rhodesia that the hallmarks of Tory policy are, as they have always been, realism and resolve. Not for us the disastrous fantasies of unilateral disarmament, of withdrawal from NATO, of abandoning Northern Ireland.

The irresponsibility of the Left on defence increases as the dangers which we face loom larger. We for our part, under Francis Pym 's brilliant leadership, have chosen a defence policy which potential foes will respect.

We are acquiring, with the co-operation of the United States Government, the Trident missile system. This will ensure the credibility of our strategic deterrent until the end of the century and beyond, and it was very important for the reputation of Britain abroad that we should keep our independent nuclear deterrent as well as for our citizens here.

We have agreed to the stationing of Cruise missiles in this country. The unilateralists object, but the recent willingness of the Soviet Government to open a new round of arms control negotiations shows the wisdom of our firmness.

We intend to maintain and, where possible, to improve our conventional forces so as to pull our weight in the Alliance. We have no wish to seek a free ride at the expense of our Allies. We will play our full part.

In Europe we have shown that it is possible to combine a vigorous defence of our own interests with a deep commitment to the idea and to the ideals of the Community.

The last Government were well aware that Britain's budget contribution was grossly unfair. They failed to do anything about it. We negotiated a satisfactory arrangement which will give us and our partners time to tackle the underlying issues. We have resolved the difficulties of New Zealand's lamb trade with the Community in a way which protects the interests of the farmers in New Zealand while giving our own farmers and our own housewives an excellent deal, and Peter Walker deserves to be congratulated on his success. Now he is two-thirds on his way to success in making important progress towards agreement on a common fisheries policy. That is very important to our people. There are many, many people whose livelihoods depend on it.

> I couldn't live without work. That's what makes me so sympathetic to these people who are unemployed. I don't know how they live without working.
>
> *News of the World, 4 May 1980*

We face many other problems in the Community, but I am confident that they too will yield to the firm yet fair approach which has already proved so much more effective than the previous Government's five years of procrastination.

With each day it becomes clearer that in the wider world we face darkening horizons, and the war between Iran and Iraq is the latest symptom of a deeper malady. Europe and North America are centres of stability in an increasingly anxious world. The Community and the Alliance are the guarantee to other countries that democracy and freedom of choice are still possible. They stand for order and the rule of law in an age when disorder and lawlessness are ever more widespread.

The British Government intend to stand by both these great institutions, the Community and NATO. We will not betray them.

The restoration of Britain's place in the world and of the West's confidence in its own destiny are two aspects of the same process. No doubt there will be unexpected twists in the road, but with wisdom and resolution we can reach our goal. I believe we will show the wisdom and you may be certain that we will show the resolution.

In his warm hearted and generous speech, Peter Thorneycroft said that, when people are called upon to lead great nations they must look into the hearts and minds of the people whom they seek to govern. I would add that those who seek to govern must in turn be willing to allow their hearts and minds to lie open to the people.

This afternoon I have tried to set before you some of my most deeply held convictions and beliefs. This Party, which I am privileged to serve, and this Government, which I am proud to lead, are engaged in the massive task of restoring confidence and stability to our people.

I have always known that that task was vital. Since last week it has become even more vital than ever. We close our Conference in the aftermath of that sinister Utopia unveiled at Blackpool. Let Labour's Orwellian nightmare of the Left be the spur for us to dedicate with a new urgency our every ounce of energy and moral strength to rebuild the fortunes of this free nation.

If we were to fail, that freedom could be imperilled. So let us resist the blandishments of the faint hearts; let us ignore the howls and threats of the extremists; let us stand together and do our duty, and we shall not fail.

> We have to get our production and our earnings in balance. There's no easy popularity in what we are proposing, but it is fundamentally sound. Yet I believe people accept there is no real alternative.
>
> *Conservatives Women's Conference, 22 May 1980*

SPEECH ON THE INVASION OF THE FALKLAND ISLANDS

House of Commons, 3rd April 1982

The Prime Minister (Mrs Margaret Thatcher): The House meets this Saturday to respond to a situation of great gravity. We are here because, for the first time for many years, British sovereign territory has been invaded by a foreign power. After several days of rising tension in our relations with Argentina, that country's armed forces attacked the Falkland Islands yesterday and established military control of the islands.

Yesterday was a day of rumour and counter-rumour. Throughout the day we had no communication from the Government of the Falklands. Indeed, the last message that we received was at 21.55 hours on Thursday night, 1 April. Yesterday morning at 8.33am we sent a telegram which was acknowledged. At 8.45am all communications ceased. I shall refer to that again in a moment. By late afternoon yesterday it became clear that an Argentine invasion had taken place and that the lawful British Government of the islands had been usurped.

I am sure that the whole House will join me in condemning totally this unprovoked aggression by the Government of Argentina against British territory. *[Hon. Members: "Hear, hear."]* It has not a shred of justification and not a scrap of legality.

It was not until 8.30 this morning, our time, when I was able to speak to the governor, who had arrived in Uruguay, that I learnt precisely what had happened. He told me that the Argentines had landed at approximately 6am Falkland's time, 10am our time. One party attacked the capital from the landward side and another from the seaward side. The governor then sent a signal to us which we did not receive.

Communications had ceased at 8.45am our time. It is common for atmospheric conditions to make communications with Port Stanley difficult. Indeed, we had been out of contact for a period the previous night.

The governor reported that the Marines, in the defence of Government House, were superb. He said that they acted in the best traditions of the Royal Marines. They inflicted casualties, but those defending Government House suffered none. He had kept the local people informed of what was happening through a small local transmitter which he had in Government House. He is relieved that the islanders heeded his advice to stay indoors. Fortunately, as far as he is aware, there were no civilian casualties. When he left the Falklands, he said that the people were in tears. They do not want to be Argentine. He said that the islanders are still tremendously loyal. I must say that I have every confidence in the governor and the action that he took.

I do love an argument.

Daily Mail, February 1980

I must tell the House that the Falkland Islands and their dependencies remain British territory. No aggression and no invasion can alter that simple fact. It is the Government's objective to see that the islands are freed from occupation and are returned to British administration at the earliest possible moment.

Argentina has, of course, long disputed British sovereignty over the islands. We have absolutely no doubt about our sovereignty, which has been continuous since 1833. Nor have we any doubt about the unequivocal wishes of the Falkland Islanders, who are British in stock and tradition, and they wish to remain British in allegiance. We cannot allow the democratic rights of the islanders to be denied by the territorial ambitions of Argentina.

Over the past 15 years, successive British Governments have held a series of meetings with the Argentine Government to discuss the dispute. In many of these meetings elected representatives of the islanders have taken part. We have always made it clear that their wishes were paramount and that there would be no change in sovereignty without their consent and without the approval of the House.

The most recent meeting took place this year in New York at the end of February between my hon. Friend the Member for Shoreham, (Mr Luce) accompanied by two members of the islands council, and the Deputy Foreign Secretary of Argentina. The atmosphere at the meeting was cordial and positive, and a communiqué was issued about future negotiating procedures. Unfortunately, the joint communiqué which had been agreed was not published in Buenos Aires.

There was a good deal of bellicose comment in the Argentine press in late February and early March, about which my hon. Friend [Richard Luce] the Minister of State for Foreign and Commonwealth Affairs expressed his concern in the House on 3 March following the Anglo-Argentine talks in New York. However, this has not been an uncommon situation in Argentina over the years. It would have been absurd to dispatch the fleet every time there was bellicose talk in Buenos Aires. There was no good reason on 3 March to think that an invasion was being planned, especially against the background of the constructive talks on which my hon. Friend had just been engaged. The joint communiqué on behalf of the Argentine deputy Minister of Foreign Affairs and my hon. Friend read:

"The meeting took place in a cordial and positive spirit. The two sides reaffirmed their resolve to find a solution to the sovereignty dispute and considered in detail an Argentine proposal for procedures to make better progress in this sense."

There had, of course, been previous incidents affecting sovereignty before the one in South Georgia, to which I shall refer in a moment. In December 1976 the Argentines illegally set up a scientific station on one of the dependencies within the Falklands group—Southern Thule. The Labour Government attempted to solve the matter through diplomatic exchanges, but without success. The Argentines remained there and are still there.

Two weeks ago—on 19 March—the latest in this series of incidents affecting sovereignty occurred; and the deterioration in relations between the British and Argentine Governments which culminated in yesterday's Argentine invasion began. The incident appeared at the start to be relatively minor. But we now know it was the beginning of much more.

The commander of the British Antartic Survey base at Grytviken on South Georgia—a dependency of the Falkland Islands over which the United Kingdom has exercised sovereignty since 1775 when the island was discovered by Captain Cook—reported to us that an Argentine navy cargo ship had landed about 60 Argentines at nearby Leith harbour. They had set up camp and hoisted the Argentine flag. They were there to carry out a valid commercial contract to remove scrap metal from a former whaling station.

The leader of the commercial expedition, Davidoff, had told our embassy in Buenos Aires that he would be going to South Georgia in March. He was reminded of the need to obtain permission from the immigration authorities on the island. He did not do so. The base commander told the Argentines that they had no right to land on South Georgia without the permission of the British authorities. They should go either to Grytviken to get the necessary clearances, or leave. The ship and some 50 of them left on 22 March. Although about 10 Argentines remained behind, this appeared to reduce the tension.

In the meantime, we had been in touch with the Argentine Government about the incident. They claimed to have had no prior knowledge of the landing and assured us that there were no Argentine military personnel in the party. For our part we made it clear that, while we had no wish to interfere in the operation of a normal commercial contract, we could not accept the illegal presence of these people on British territory.

We asked the Argentine Government either to arrange for the departure of the remaining men or to ensure that they obtained the necessary permission to be there. Because we recognised the potentially serious nature of the situation, HMS "Endurance" was ordered to the area. We told the Argentine Government that, if they failed to regularise the position of the party on South Georgia or to arrange for their departure, HMS "Endurance" would take them off, without using force, and return them to Argentina.

This was, however, to be a last resort. We were determined that this apparently minor problem of 10 people on South Georgia in pursuit of a commercial contract should not be allowed to escalate and we made it plain to the Argentine Government that we wanted to achieve a peaceful resolution of the problem by diplomatic means. To help in this, HMS "Endurance" was ordered not to approach the Argentine party at Leith but to go to Grytviken.

But it soon became clear that the Argentine Government had little interest in trying to solve the problem. On 25 March another Argentine navy ship arrived at Leith to deliver supplies to the 10 men ashore. Our ambassador in Buenos Aires sought an early response from the Argentine Government to our previous requests that they should arrange for the men's departure. This request was refused. Last Sunday, on Sunday 28 March, the Argentine Foreign Minister sent a message to my right hon. and noble Friend [Lord Carrington] the Foreign Secretary refusing outright to regularise the men's position. Instead it restated Argentina's claim to sovereignty over the Falkland Islands and their dependencies.

> I said at the start I shall get things right in the end, and I shall.
>
> *Daily Express, August 1980*

My right hon. and noble Friend the Foreign and Commonwealth Secretary then sent a message to the United States Secretary of State asking him to intervene and to urge restraint.

By the beginning of this week it was clear that our efforts to solve the South Georgia dispute through the usual diplomatic channels were getting nowhere. Therefore, on Wednesday 31 March my right hon. and noble Friend the Foreign Secretary proposed to the Argentine Foreign Minister that we should dispatch a special emissary to Buenos Aires.

Later that day we received information which led us to believe that a large number of Argentine ships, including an aircraft carrier, destroyers, landing craft, troop carriers and submarines, were heading for Port Stanley. I contacted President Reagan that evening and asked him to intervene with the Argentine President directly. We promised, in the meantime, to take no action to escalate the dispute for fear of precipitating—*[Interruption]*—the very event that our efforts were directed to avoid. May I remind Opposition Members—*[Interruption]*—what happened when, during the lifetime of their Government—

Mr J. W. Rooker (Birmingham, Perry Barr): We did not lose the Falklands.

The Prime Minister: —Southern Thule was occupied. It was occupied in 1976. The House was not even informed by the then Government until 1978, when, in response to questioning by my hon. Friend the Member for Shoreham (Mr Luce), now Minister of State, Foreign and Commonwealth Office, the hon. Member for Merthyr Tydfil (Mr Rowlands) said:

"We have sought the resolve the issue though diplomatic exchanges between the two Governments. That is infinitely preferable to public denunciations and public statements when we are trying to achieve a practical result to the problem that has arisen."—[*Official Report,* 24 May 1978; Vol. 950, c. 1550–51.]

Mr Edward Rowlands (Merthyr Tydfil): The right hon. Lady is talking about a piece of rock in the most southerly part of the dependencies, which is completely uninhabited and which smells of large accumulations of penguin and other bird droppings. There is a vast difference—a whole world of difference—between the 1,800 people now imprisoned by Argentine invaders and that argument. The right hon. Lady should have the grace to accept that.

The Prime Minister: We are talking about the sovereignty of British territory—*[Interruption]*—which was infringed in 1976. The House was not even informed of it until 1978. We are talking about a further incident in South Georgia which—as I have indicated—seemed to be a minor incident at the time. There is only a British Antarctic scientific survey there and there was a commercial contract to remove a whaling station. I suggest to the hon. Gentleman that had I come to the House at that time and said that we had a problem on South Georgia with 10 people who had landed with a contract to remove a whaling station, and had I gone on to say that we should send HMS "Invincible", I should have been accused of war mongering and sabre rattling.

Information about the Argentine fleet did not arrive until Wednesday. Argentina is, of course, very close to the Falklands—a point that the hon. Member for Merthyr Tydfil cannot and must not ignore—and its navy can sail there very quickly. On Thursday, the Argentine Foreign Minister rejected the idea of an emissary and told our ambassador that the diplomatic channel, as a means of solving this dispute, was closed. President Reagan had a very long telephone conversation, of some 50 minutes, with the Argentine President, but his strong representations fell on deaf ears. I am grateful to him and to Secretary Haig for their strenuous and persistent efforts on our behalf.

I want my money back!

Dublin EC summit, November 1980

On Thursday, the United Nations Secretary-General, Mr Perez De Cuellar, summoned both British and Argentine permanent representatives to urge both countries to refrain from the use or threat of force in the South Atlantic. Later that evening we sought an emergency meeting of the Security Council. We accepted the appeal of its President for restraint. The Argentines said nothing. On Friday, as the House knows, the Argentines invaded the Falklands and I have given a precise account of everything we knew, or did not know, about that situation. There were also reports that yesterday the Argentines also attacked South Georgia, where HMS "Endurance" had left a detachment of 22 Royal Marines. Our information is that on 2 April an Argentine naval transport vessel informed the base commander at Grytviken that an important message would be passed to him after 11 o'clock today our time. It is assumed that this message will ask the base commander to surrender.

Before indicating some of the measures that the Government have taken in response to the Argentine invasion, I should like to make three points. First, even if ships had been instructed to sail the day that the Argentines landed on South Georgia to clear the whaling station, the ships could not possibly have got to Port Stanley before the invasion. *[Interruption.]* Opposition Members may not like it, but that is a fact.

Secondly, there have been several occasions in the past when an invasion has been threatened. The only way of being certain to prevent an invasion would have been to keep a very large fleet close to the Falklands, when we are some 8,000 miles away from base. No Government have ever been able to do that, and the cost would be enormous.

Jim Prior: I read in my paper you had developed a sexy voice.

Margaret Thatcher: Jim, what makes you think I wasn't sexy before?

1981

Mr Eric Ogden (Liverpool, West Derby): Will the right hon. Lady say what has happened to HMS "Endurance"?

The Prime Minister: HMS "Endurance" is in the area. It is not for me to say precisely where, and the hon. Gentleman would not wish me to do so.

Thirdly, aircraft unable to land on the Falklands, because of the frequently changing weather, would have had little fuel left and, ironically, their only hope of landing safely would have been to divert to Argentina. Indeed, all of the air and most sea supplies for the Falklands come from Argentina, which is but 400 miles away compared with our 8,000 miles.

That is the background against which we have to make decisions and to consider what action we can best take. I cannot tell the House precisely what dispositions have been made—some ships are already at sea, others were put on immediate alert on Thursday evening.

The Government have now decided that a large task force will sail as soon as all preparations are complete. HMS "Invincible" will be in the lead and will leave port on Monday.

I stress that I cannot foretell what orders the task force will receive as it proceeds. That will depend on the situation at the time. Meanwhile, we hope that our continuing diplomatic efforts, helped by our many friends, will meet with success.

The Foreign Ministers of the European Community member States yesterday condemned the intervention and urged withdrawal. The NATO Council called on both sides to refrain from force and continue diplomacy.

The United Nations Security Council met again yesterday and will continue its discussions today. [*Laughter.*] Opposition Members laugh. They would have been the first to urge a meeting of the Security Council if we had not called one. They would have been the first to urge restraint and to urge a solution to the problem by diplomatic means. They would have been the first to accuse us of sabre rattling and war mongering.

Mr Tam Dalyell (West Lothian): The right hon. Lady referred to our many friends. Have we any friends in South America on this issue?

The Prime Minister: Doubtless our friends in South America will make their views known during any proceedings at the Security Council. I believe that many countries in South America will be prepared to condemn the invasion of the Falklands Islands by force.

We are now reviewing all aspects of the relationship between Argentina and the United Kingdom. The Argentine chargé d'affaires and his staff were yesterday instructed to leave within four days.

As an appropriate precautionary and, I hope, temporary measure, the Government have taken action to freeze Argentine financial assets held in this country. An order will be laid before Parliament today under the Emergency Laws (Re-enactments and Repeals) Act 1964 blocking the movement of gold, securities or funds held in the United Kingdom by the Argentine Government or Argentine residents.

As a further precautionary measure, the ECGD has suspended new export credit cover for the Argentine. It is the Government's earnest wish that a return to good sense and the normal rules of international behaviour on the part of the Argentine Government will obviate the need for action across the full range of economic relations.

We shall be reviewing the situation and be ready to take further steps that we deem appropriate and we shall, of course, report to the House.

The people of the Falkland Islands, like the people of the United Kingdom, are an island race. Their way of life is British; their allegiance is to the Crown. They are few in number, but they have the right to live in peace, to choose their own way of life and to determine their own allegiance. Their way of life is British; their allegiance is to the Crown. It is the wish of the British people and the duty of Her Majesty's Government to do everything that we can to uphold that right. That will be our hope and our endeavour and, I believe, the resolve of every Member of the House.

REMARKS ON THE RETAKING OF SOUTH GEORGIA

Downing Street, 25th April 1982

MT: Ladies and gentlemen. The Secretary of State for Defence has just come over to give me some very good news and I think you'd like to have it at once.

John Nott: The message we have got is that British troops landed on South Georgia this afternoon, shortly after 4 pm London time. They have now successfully taken control of Grytviken; at about 6 pm London time, the white flag was hoisted in Grytviken beside the Argentine flag. Shortly afterwards, the Argentine forces there surrendered to British forces. The Argentine forces offered only limited resistance to the British troops. Our forces were landed by helicopter and were supported by a number of warships, together with a Royal Fleet Auxiliary. During the first phase of this opinion, our own helicopters engaged the Argentine submarine, *Santa Fé*, off South Georgia. This submarine was detected at first light and was engaged because it posed a threat to our men and to the British warships launching the landing. So far, no British casualties have been reported. At present we have no information on the Argentine casualty position. The Commander of the operation has sent the following message: "Be pleased to inform Her Majesty that the White Ensign flies alongside the Union Jack in South Georgia. God save the Queen."

> My politics are based...on things I and millions like me were brought up with. An honest day's work for an honest day's pay; live within your means; put by a nest egg for a rainy day; pay your bills on time; support the police.
>
> *1981*

Press: What happens next Mr Nott ? What's your reaction ...?

MT: Just rejoice at that news and congratulate our forces and the marines. *[MT answers emphatically then turns towards the door of No.10].* Goodnight. *[Begins walking back to the door of No. 10]*

Press: Are we going to war with Argentina Mrs Thatcher?

MT: *[pausing on the doorstep of No. 10]* Rejoice.

STATEMENT ON THE ARGENTINEAN SURRENDER

House of Commons, 14th June 1982

The Prime Minister (Mrs Margaret Thatcher): On a point of order, Mr Speaker. May I give the House the latest information about the battle of the Falklands? After successful attacks last night, General Moore decided to press forward. The Argentines retreated. Our forces reached the outskirts of Port Stanley. Large numbers of Argentine soldiers threw down their weapons. They are reported to be flying white flags over Port Stanley. Our troops have been ordered not to fire except in self-defence. Talks are now in progress between General Menendez and our Deputy Commander, Brigadier Waters, about the surrender of the Argentine forces on East and West Falkland. I shall report further to the House tomorrow.

Hon. Members: Hear, hear!

Mr Michael Foot (Ebbw Vale): Further to that point of order, Mr Speaker. First, may I thank the right hon. Lady for coming to the House to give us the news, particularly because the news is so good for all concerned, especially because it appears from what she has been able to tell us that there will be an end to the bloodshed, which is what we have all desired. There will be widespread, genuine rejoicing—to use the word that the right hon. Lady once used—at the prospect of the end of the bloodshed. If the news is confirmed, as I trust it will be, there will be great congratulations from the House tomorrow to the British forces who have conducted themselves in such a manner and, if I may say so, to the right hon. Lady. *[Hon. Members: "Hear, hear."]* I know that there are many matters on which we shall have to have discussions, and perhaps there will be arguments about the origins of this matter and other questions, but I can well understand the anxieties and pressures that must have been upon the right hon. Lady during these weeks. I can understand that at this moment those pressures and anxieties may have been relieved, and I congratulate her on that.

I believe that we can as a House of Commons transform what has occurred into benefits for our country as a whole. I believe that that is the way in which we on the Opposition Benches will wish to proceed. There are many fruitful lessons in diplomacy and in other matters that we can draw from this occasion, and that will be the Opposition's determination.

Mr David Steel (Roxburgh, Selkirk and Peebles): *rose*——

Dr David Owen (Plymouth, Devonport): *rose*——

Mr Speaker: Order. I shall call both right hon. Members in turn.

Hon. Members: Why?

Mr David Steel: Further to the point of order, Mr Speaker. Will the Prime Minister accept that this is an occasion when the whole House should rejoice and congratulate both the Government and the forces involved on bringing this sad matter to a satisfactory and peaceful conclusion?

The Lord President of the Council and Leader of the House of Commons (Mr John Biffen): *rose*——

Dr Owen: *rose*——

Mr Speaker: I call the right hon. Member for Plymouth, Devonport (Dr Owen). *[Hon. Members: "Why?"]*

Dr Owen: Further to the point of order, Mr Speaker. May I join the Leader of the official Opposition and the Leader of the Liberal

Party in conveying the congratulations of the whole House to the Royal Navy, the Army, the Royal Air Force and the Royal Marines, and to the Government and all the Ministers who played a crucial role in the achievement of an extremely successful outcome? I wish all well, especially—thinking of those who have lost their lives—those families who are currently grieving tonight for their sacrifice. The sacrifice of their loved ones was a sacrifice which was necessary for all.

REMARKS ON THE ECONOMY – 'FRIT'

House of Commons, 19th April 1983

The Prime Minister (Mrs Margaret Thatcher): Assuming that the forecasts on inflation are reasonable—I know that our inflation forecasts have been wrong for a long time—even if inflation were to go up a bit in the coming months, and even if prices were to increase a little in the year—*[Interruption.]*

Mr Healey: Cut and run.

The Prime Minister: The right hon. Gentleman is afraid of an election, is he? Afraid? Frightened? Frit? Could not take it? Cannot stand it? If I were going to cut and run, I should have gone after the Falklands. Frightened! Right now inflation is lower than it has been for 13 years—a record which the right hon. Gentleman could not begin to touch.

Mr Foot: If the right hon. Lady is now to join the Chancellor of the Exchequer in favour of the cut-and-run election that will make excellent news throughout the country, because we are certainly happy to have it whenever they wish. *[Interruption.]* I just want, if I can, to ask the right hon. Lady—whether or not she goes for the election; even if she decides to stick it out and face the figures and the facts—to try to give the correct figures to the country. Will she acknowledge that she inherited from the Labour Government a much lower inflation figure than the one she left us when she was a member of the Government of the right hon. Member for Sidcup (Mr Heath)? I know that she never likes to defend anything that she did in that Government, but she had better do so now.

REMARKS DURING VISIT TO THE FALKLAND ISLANDS

Town Hall, Port Stanley, 10 January 1983

Sir Rex Hunt, Civil Commissioner: Prime Minister, ladies and gentlemen

This is a great moment in the history of the Falkland islands. For me personally it is probably the greatest moment of my life. It was here in Stanley Town Hall on the second of April that I told General Garcia that he had landed illegally on British territory and I ordered him and his troops to remove themselves forthwith. In reply General Garcia said that they were taking back what was rightfully theirs, and that they would be here forever. But for our distinguished guest they might well have been. *(cheers)* thank *[words missing]* we sent out a task force. It landed here after coming 8,000 miles at San Carlos, yomped across from San Carlos to Stanley and defeated the Argentines in ten and a half weeks. *(cheers)* To do all that in ten and a half weeks was an incredible achievement. I know that for those of you who were here throughout that period it seemed like a lifetime, and I should like to hand over now to one of you who was here through all that time, a senior member of the Falkland islands government, your financial secretary who has a few words to say for all of you islanders.— Harold Rowlands.

The hon Harold Rowlands, OBE, financial secretary: Prime Minister, ladies and gentlemen it is the greatest moment of my life here today. I am very pleased to be able to thank Mrs Thatcher in person for the liberation of the Falkland islands. Not only the liberation but also the rehabilitation and now the development of the islands. We look forward to the development of these islands, that the battle was not wasted, that the men whose lives were lost will be remembered. We will make sure that it was worthwhile. I am sure that the majority of people will be looking forward to a great future, and to start it off in 1983. I think it's fantastic that we start our 150th celebrations in advance *(cheers)*.

Prime Minister, I have now the pleasure and the honour to present the freedom of the Falkland Islands. *(cheers)* I would like to mention that it was not planned. The councillors did not know of Mrs Thatcher's arrival here. Spontaneously, yesterday all councillors unanimously agreed on your behalf, the people of the Falklands. The people that are in this hall tonight, the people that are on duty. That are sick, unable to attend the meeting tonight, also the people *[line missing]* on behalf of them with great pleasure. I should like to read you what is in it, and we must congratulate our Attorney General on having guided us on this matter, and also to our printer who did a marvellous bit of printing at the last moment. It says: "freedom of the Falkland islands. Whereas we the people of the Falkland islands have recently suffered armed invasion of our beloved islands, and whereas but for the support and aid given to us by the people of the United Kingdom of Great Britain and Northern Ireland we would still be under foreign domination today, now we the undersigned representatives of the people of the Falkland islands, in acknowledgement of our humble and sincere gratitude and appreciation of the courageous steadfast and unyielding leadership

The election of a man [Ronald Reagan] committed to the cause of freedom and renewal of America's strength has given encouragement to all those who love liberty.

February 1981

of Margaret Hilda Thatcher, Prime Minister of the United Kingdom, throughout the campaign for our freedom of Stanley and all townships and settlements throughout the Falkland Islands." (*cheers*)

The Prime Minister (Mrs Margaret Thatcher): Mr Rowlands, that's the most marvellous honour you could have conferred upon me, and I am deeply happy to accept it. Each of us has our own memories of the period through which we've lived. Somehow history is something that happens to other people, and then all of a sudden we found ourselves making history here in these islands. I will never forget, and nor will the Governor [Rex Hunt] —forgive me if I still use the old name (*cheers*)—the night that information came through that there was a fleet that looked as if it was heading for the invasion of Port Stanley. We had to contact the governor, we contacted the President of the United States hoping that he would be able to stop it. It was not to be. For two days we carried a few of us that knowledge that maybe the Falklands were going to be invaded, and help was a very very long way away. You know what happened, and I am very happy to report as you know that the whole British people were outraged that such an invasion should have occurred, and promptly set about remedying the situation of throwing the invader off the islands. And as I said in the House of Commons, restoring British sovereignty and British administration to a people of British stock who were British, were loyal British, and wished to remain British in a British island. *(cheers)*. And so with the total support of the British people the task force sailed. It must have been an agonising time for you. It was for us as the campaign was shaped and planned, and we faced the worry of more and more Argentine soldiers being put upon these islands, a worry which you saw in practical terms at this end. Then we were able in a magnificent campaign to retake South Georgia, and that of itself was a very famously fought battle. And we learned the difficulties of the weather in this part of the world, because I will tell you what happened when those forces arrived in South Georgia. They arrived to a force 11 gale. You can imagine the worries that that gave us. You have I understand experienced many force 11 gales. In spite of that they took South Georgia, and I understand that that was a tremendous boost to morale on these islands. It was then you realised we really were coming to regain the Falklands for British sovereignty and British administration.

> Failure? The possibilities don't exist.
>
> *On the Falklands War, 1982*

We wondered how precisely it would come about, and there was so much planning going on, and we didn't know the precise shape of the campaign. We knew we had the finest professional forces devoted and dedicated to the cause of freedom and justice the world over (*cheers*). In them we put our faith and our trust. Then one dark winter's night a silent armada put ashore British forces on what was then a hostile enemy coast, but full of loyal devoted British citizens, that was in San Carlos. I remember I was in my own constituency that day. I knew the night it was going to happen. I was worried stiff as you may imagine, but I had a full day's engagements in my own constituency of Finchley near London, and I knew if I didn't go and carry out the lot someone would know something was up. So I went and smiled my way through the day. I'm not quite sure to this moment what I said except that somehow I had a speech to make, and I said please would they understand that my mind wasn't wholly on the party politics of Britain, it was really 8000 miles away which was a long way geographically but at that moment it was only a heartbeat away. And at the end of that day in my constituency I was able to say that the Union Jack was once again flying on the Falkland Islands (*cheers*). To a reception like this, as they too rose and cheered like that.

There were many difficult worrying days to follow, and many difficult battles to fight, and it is one thing that troubles us all that at times of national danger it is always the young people who have to bear the brunt of the fighting and make great sacrifices, and I have today been paying our tribute to those who gave their lives in battle that we might live in freedom *(applause).* But it was a tremendous inspiration to the youth, British youth everywhere, to know that when the call came their generation was not found wanting but on the contrary added lustre to the battles which Britons have fought the world over *(applause).* And we owe it to them to build our lives remembering the sacrifices that they made for us. And therefore I am confident that you in this famous city of Port Stanley, and many others in the famous townships throughout these islands, will strive again and again to build a better life for your families for the future, the better because of the sacrifices that have been made for us because we are a people that cannot live without breathing the air of freedom and justice (*cheers*).

You will understand that perhaps the most emotional night of my life was when the news came in that the Argentine troops were retreating from Tumbledown mountain past Mount William into Port Stanley. We weren't quite sure. And I waited until ten o'clock in the evening London time—rather differently your time—to go down to the House of Commons, to stand at the despatch box and say the reports are that white flags are flying over Port Stanley (*cheers*).

Today again the Union Jack flies over Port Stanley, and may it ever fly there (*cheers*). So we in the Falkland Islands and in Great Britain re-dedicate our lives to the cause of freedom and justice of people here and everywhere. We have given an example to the world, and hope to many of those who do not enjoy these great qualities. May we also act as a beacon of hope to them, that so long as we defend that which is ours now, they too one day may enjoy these great things.

The hon. H. T. Rowlands: Ladies and gentlemen, I would like to call for three cheers for the incomparable Margaret Thatcher (*three cheers*) (*more cheers*).

SPEECH TO THE SCOTTISH CONSERVATIVE CONFERENCE. CITY HALL

Perth, 13th May 1983

The problems that confronted us when we came to office were daunting. Labour had borrowed and left Britain bowed down by debt. We were shocked by the winter of discontent. Shop stewards usurped the role of management and sometimes seemed more powerful than the Government itself. Britain's defences were undermined and our police demoralised. Inflation was taking off again. In short, we were a nation which had all too plainly lost its way, and almost abandoned hope of finding it again. And we found a world poised on the brink of the worst recession since the 1930s.

It was, without a doubt, the bleakest prospect facing any newly elected government in Britain since the War. We could have bought a little time with short-term soft options. But too many previous Governments had done that—you elected us to tackle the real problem. And we've had the courage to do it.

And so we set in hand a programme to cure the nation's sickness and restore its health and reputation. We had to break the habit of inflation once and for all, before the habit became an addiction. We had to set about repaying the debts Labour left behind. We had to restore worthwhile rewards for leadership and enterprise and give them room to breathe again and put out shoots of healthy long-term growth. We had to restore to management responsibility to manage, and to employees their right to be consulted by the union that claimed to represent them. We had to uproot the thickets of bureaucracy and controls in Whitehall and the town halls. We had to rebuild the nation's ability to defend itself in an increasingly dangerous world. We had to increase the numbers and the authority of the police and let them know that they had a Government which would back them to the hilt in enforcing the law.

We had to give council tenants the opportunity to buy their own homes. We had to get a fairer balance of benefits and payments in the European Community. We had to prove to friend and foe that those who looked to us for their defence would find once again that our word is our bond.

These things we have done. What we could not do—for it is not in the power of any Government—was to shift overnight the ingrained habits of half a lifetime. Had both sides of industry realised that in future they had to take responsibility for their own actions, and that they would not automatically be bailed out regardless of their performance, hundreds of thousands of worthwhile and productive jobs would have survived the recession.

> Economics are the method. The object is to change the heart and soul.
>
> *Sunday Times, 3 May 1981*

But the convictions that a pay rise every year was each man's birthright, and that jobs had somehow nothing to do with satisfying the customer, died hard. When proof arrived that times had changed, it was often too late.

And there is something else that we have done. We have exploded those scare stories with which our opponents tried so hard to cling to power in the 1979 election.

Let me remind you of a few of them.

They said we would cut pensions. Instead, we've raised them by two-thirds—well ahead of prices.

They said we'd dismantle the National Health Service. Instead, we have nearly doubled spending on the Health Service here in Scotland—and today there are many more doctors, dentists, and nurses—almost 6,000 of them—in your Scottish hospitals and health centres, than when we took office.

They said we'd cripple education. Instead expenditure per child is at an all-time record, and so is the proportion of teachers to pupils; and a higher proportion of our young men and women are going on to full-time further education than ever before.

They said we'd be the dear-food party. Just let's look at the record. When they were in power, food prices more than doubled. What you got for £10 at the beginning cost you £22 at the end. Under this Government, what you could buy for £10 when we took office would cost you £13.50 today. Not good enough, but getting better. And in the last year food prices have risen by less than a penny in the pound.

When you stop a dictator there are always risks, but there are great risks in not stopping a dictator. My generation learned that long ago.

1982

And may I remind you that inflation—now at 4.6% and going down is at its lowest level for 15 years? That is an achievement of which we can be justly proud, and for which we have every reason to be grateful to Geoffrey Howe.

They said we would starve the Scottish Development Agency of funds and let it die. Instead we have nearly doubled the cash it has had to spend productively in Scotland.

I remind you of these scares because in the next three weeks there will be plenty more.

There will be plenty more because if there's one thing our opponents don't want to talk about, it is their own policies. So you must see to it that every home in Scotland understands precisely what they stand for:

First, this Labour Party wants us to abandon our own independent nuclear deterrent; a deterrent which has helped to keep the peace for nearly 40 years; a deterrent which has been endorsed by every Labour Leader— Attlee, Gaitskell, Wilson and Callaghan —but not this one.

And they want us to do it without a corresponding reduction from the Soviet Union. As Mr Andropov put it when asked whether he would agree to one-sided disarmament, "We are not a naive people."

And as if that was not enough, they want to serve notice to quit on every American nuclear base in Britain, many of which have been here for 30 years and which are part of NATO defence.

Not exactly the action of a reliable ally. Nor does it recognise the tremendous contribution made by the United States to the defence of free Europe.

This Labour Party would take Britain out of the Common Market—putting at risk 50,000 Scottish jobs and millions of £s of new investment.

This Labour Party has adopted a deliberate policy of inflation in spite of everything we've suffered from rising prices in the last ten years.

This Labour Party would take away the council tenant's right to buy his own home which has transformed the lives of half a million families.

This Labour Party would put Britain back under the dominance of the Trade Unions. They would repeal our legislation which has helped to restore the balance between the unions and the community and given individual rights to union members.

This Labour Party would take over control of how your pension fund invests the money you have entrusted to it for your retirement.

Without a shadow of a doubt, this Labour Party has the most extreme and most damaging programme ever placed before the British electorate. No wonder they usually try to talk of anything but that.

But voting Labour is not the only way of putting Labour in.

When Labour came to power in 1974, they did so on their smallest post-War vote to date. And who put them in? The Liberals and the Nationalists in Scotland. And do you remember what happened in 1976 when the Labour Government was tottering? Who came to the rescue? It was those self-same Liberals with the notorious Lib-Lab Pact who propped up the most illiberal Government of modern times.

Today the Liberals have new allies: the S D P: the very men (and women) who, when members of the Labour Government, destroyed our direct grant and grammar schools, who undermined respect for the family in the name of a misleading permissiveness, and who nationalised still more of our industries.

It would be a final irony if the votes they received this time were to put back into office the very party which they themselves had abandoned.

Mr President, when we met in Perth last year it was in the shadow of great events then taking place on the other side of the world. Not for the first time in our history, the courage, skill and sheer professionalism of the armed forces of the Crown, went on to earn for them the admiration of the world. And if today we walk a little taller—and I believe we do—then it is those brave young men who deserve the praise. But they have achieved something even more important: their deeds have made the world a safer place for all of us.

That truth is worthy of a moment's reflection. In recent months we have heard a lot about the protest lines at Holy Loch and Greenham Common—and elsewhere in Western Europe. Now I do not doubt the sincerity and indeed the idealism of many of these people. The real aims of some of them is another matter. But if a hostile Government was tempted to pursue its demands by armed aggression, which example would be more likely to make it pause: the renunciation of the means of national self-defence which the banners call for? Or the swift and sure response of our young men in the South Atlantic just a year ago?

As Lord Home said only a few weeks ago: "I can find nothing in Christian teaching that forbids me to defend myself when faced with an evil aggressor who aims to destroy my religion and all the values which I treasure."

And that is why on June 9th we will ask the people of Scotland and the rest of the United Kingdom to treat the Nation's defence as the first call on the Nation's resources.

It is not only in international affairs that this Government has strenuously upheld the rule of law. We have done so with great determination at home, not least here in Scotland.

To the criminal, the greatest deterrent is the certainty that he will be detected and punished. In the war against crime, our police are in the front line. In that war they can be confident, and our people can be confident that this Government gives them total support.

The Left would openly seek to make the police instruments of socialism, because they (the Left) set little store on a truly free society.

We believe in a police force that is well-manned, well-paid, well-equipped, one which in carrying out its duties is fair, independent, and impartial, one that is devoted to conserving the essential freedoms of our society.

We have proved this belief in our police not only by word but also by action. When we came to office, we immediately made substantial improvements in their pay, condition and equipment. Last year we spent twice as much on the Scottish police as Labour did.

> If they are invaded, we have to get them back.
>
> *To John Nott on the Falklands, 2 April 1982*

But the police need more than money: they need to be equipped with effective powers to seek out the criminal and bring him to justice. The Scottish police now have the powers they need to deal with the scourge of violent crime. We found the great cities of Scotland scarred by the violence of the stick the knife and the razor.

Too often what might have passed off as a drunken disturbance became a mob murder because such weapons were being carried.

We legislated to give the police power to stop and search those whom they suspected of carrying such weapons. This power, so necessary for the protection of our people, was bitterly opposed by all the other political parties in Scotland. It has been used responsibly and effectively. One third of those searched have been found to have offensive weapons. This legislation is a real step forward in crime prevention.

Nor did we forget the victims of crime. We brought in for the first time in Scotland a comprehensive scheme to require criminals to pay compensation to their victims.

Sport was not forgotten in this reform either. So often a

Saturday afternoon's entertainment at a Scottish football match had been marred by the drunken and violent behaviour of a hooligan minority. This disruption was threatening the very life of the game at which the Scots have so often excelled. The crowds dwindled. Some responsible fans stayed away.

We took firm action. Its success is plain. The cans and bottles left after a match are now no more than a handful. The disruptive behaviour has strikingly diminished.

And spectators can enjoy the game again—and we all enjoyed Aberdeen's triumph in Europe this week.

Vandalism is the acid which corrodes and destroys the quality of life for so many. Vandalism has destroyed schools in Strathclyde and ratepayers have a bill of £1,000 per day just to repair broken windows. All over Scotland new houses suffer damage even before they are occupied.

Mindless destruction and drunken violence have made life a waking nightmare for those who live in some of Scotland's housing schemes. For them our resolute approach to law and order holds out most hope. Theirs is a misery which no one should have to bear.

We support the police unswervingly. We support the bobby on the beat. We are alert to take every opportunity to win the war against crime. We shall not rest until the bullies, who prey on the elderly, on the lonely widow, on the disabled, are brought to justice.

But a better police force is only one part of the Conservative approach to law and order. That approach has an even more positive side. Our whole philosophy is built on respect for the traditional moral values which are the cornerstones of a free society. All our policies are designed to encourage personal responsibility, personal initiative, self respect and respect for others and their property.

We have provided for many families for the first time the exciting opportunity to own their own homes; to have a property in the maintenance of which they can take pride.

The transformation which home ownership can make is perhaps nowhere more clearly illustrated than in the experiment carried out in the Easterhouse area of Glasgow where the local authority had a neighbourhood so devastated by vandalism that nobody wanted to live in it. The houses were made available to private purchasers, and now each home is privately owned and the transformation is miraculous.

We have to tackle and reverse the tragedy of unemployment, and to do it at a difficult time when world recession has coincided with a technological revolution, a time when new industries in the Far East compete in our markets both at home and abroad.

But these things have happened. And there is little point in bemoaning them. They merely raise the hurdles higher. But we still have to jump them.

New jobs come from new businesses and new products. Some of today's jobs in Scotland did not exist 10 years ago.

What can Government do to help with this industrial rebirth? It can create the climate in which industry can flourish. It can keep inflation down. This Government has—and we shall get it down further. It can help cut overheads in industry. This Government has—we have cut the National Insurance Surcharge—that tax on jobs imposed by Labour. In doing so we have returned £2,000 million to the private sector.

It can cut its own bureaucracy. This Government has—we have announced today that we now have the smallest Civil Service for 20 years.

> We have ceased to be a nation in retreat. We have instead a new-found confidence—born in the economic battles at home and tested and found true 8,000 miles away. That confidence comes from the re-discovery of ourselves, and grows with the recovery of our self-respect. And so today, we can rejoice at our success in the Falklands and take pride in the achievement of the men and women of our Task Force. But we do so, not as at some last flickering of a flame which must soon be dead. No—we rejoice that Britain has re-kindled that spirit which has fired her for generations past and which today has begun to burn as brightly as before. Britain found herself again in the South Atlantic and will not look back from the victory she has won.
>
> *3 July 1982*

It can legislate for more balanced Trades Union Laws. This Government has—We have passed two Acts in this Parliament and will put through more in the next Parliament.

It can provide tax incentives to good management. This Government has—We have cut the tax rates, especially on middle and top management. Their talents are in demand internationally. We need them here.

It can provide help through lower taxes and loan guarantees for small business. This Government has—we have the best range of constructive measures for small business to be found anywhere.

> The spirit has stirred and the nation has begun to assert itself. Things are going to be the same again.
>
> *On the Falklands War, 1982*

It can help inventors and young people with ideas to launch new products. This Government has—any high technology firm with a suitable invention can get a grant to cover one third of the costs of bringing the product to the market.

It can help with research into new technology to put us ahead of the rest of the world. This Government has—in response to the Alvey Report, we have recently announced an ambitious scheme in which Government, universities and industry collaborate on the next generation of computers and beyond. £200 million comes from Government and £150 million from private industry. This is really investing in the future.

It can help through public purchasing. This Government has—some 90% of our defence supplies and equipment come from British firms. There are at present defence orders for £1850 million in Britain's shipyards.

It can help with training young people to ensure that they have the skills which the new jobs will require. This Government has—We have the biggest and most exciting training programme for young people in our history. We have known the need for years. This Government is tackling it.

That is what Government can do.

But of course nothing can replace the enterprise of individuals or the drive and pressure of the market place. The strategy which I have outlined is a strategy for genuine jobs.

Conservative Governments have never been laissez faire.—That label belonged to the Liberals.

Conservatives believe that Government must be strong to do those tasks which only Governments can perform. Equally, we are wise to leave to industry and to individual endeavour those things in which only they can succeed.

I think in their hearts people know that our way is the one that will produce results. No glib talk; no gimmicks, no reckless expenditure, no false promises. Just effort, inventiveness, quality, efficiency, and reliability. Then we've got to go out and sell

It is not easy, but then our forebears who created the industrial revolution did not have it easy either. But they did not say we must wait for the upturn to come. They went out and created the upturn.

And so prosperity spread. And the standard of living rose. Even though Departments of Industry didn't exist.

In four short years, Britain has recovered her confidence and her self-respect. We have regained the regard and admiration of other nations. We are seen today as a people with integrity, resolve and the will to succeed. This is no small achievement.

Mr President, this is a historic election. For the choice facing the nation is between two totally different ways of life.

And what a prize we have to fight for: no less than the chance to banish from our land the dark divisive clouds of Marxist socialism and bring together men and women from all walks of life who share a belief in freedom and who have the courage to uphold it.

So tonight we go forth from Perth to battle. Great things are expected of us.

If we keep our standards and our vision bright, what we have begun here tonight in Perth, will end not only in victory for our Party, but in fulfilment, of our nation's destiny.

SPEECH AT CONSERVATIVE YOUTH RALLY

Wembley Conference Centre, 5th June 1983

Mr Chairman, fellow Young Conservatives. What a super start to this marvellous rally, and may I thank the superstars for their splendid contribution, which means such a lot personally to me, and such a lot to the cause which we are all here to support this afternoon.

This really is a remarkable and invigorating start to the last week of the election campaign.

And I believe that this Youth Rally shows the world what we in the Conservative Party already know—Britain's young people want another Tory Government.

That's marvellous, but there is quite a lot to come yet and I don't want you to have sore throats before the end. That's the sort of reception we want at the end. You've already demonstrated that there's an excitement and an enthusiasm which is the envy of all other parties.

And this great hall, filled to capacity with young people who want to live your own lives, in the way you choose, with a style which is on your own within the law. *[sic]* Young people want to stay free.

Could Labour have managed a rally like this? *["No"]*

Well, in the old days perhaps. But not now. For they are the party of yesterday. And tomorrow is ours.

We are all here to state our faith in Britain's future and our determination to keep her strong and free.

And this rally isn't going to duck the issues. There'll be no fudging, and no manifesto-changing here.

We are here to talk about the programme of the *next* Government. We are here to make sure that it is a Conservative Government.

So let me start with the most difficult issue of our time, because we Conservatives don't duck the difficult issues. We face them determined to overcome them.

And the most difficult issue is the growing unemployment with which our world is faced.

Over 26 million out of work in the OECD countries alone.

Behind those unemployment figures lie the individual tragedies and the dashing of family hopes which make us determined to fight to rid our nation of this evil.

Twenty three and a half million jobs—that's what we have in Britain.

Twenty six and a half million jobs—that's what we would need to eliminate unemployment.

It's been, it's been hard work, you know, safeguarding those twenty three and a half million jobs in these last four years. Hard work in the teeth of a world recession that was not Britain's fault. But hard work, too, because of past failures of past governments to deal with the root causes of Britain's problems. They preferred to take the easy way.

> There are forces more powerful and pervasive than the apparatus of war. You may chain a man, but you cannot chain his mind. You may enslave him, but you will not conquer his spirit. In every decade since the war Soviet leaders have been reminded that their pitiless ideology only survives because it is maintained by force. But the day will come when the anger and frustration of the people is so great that force cannot contain it. Then the edifice cracks; the mortar crumbles; one day, liberty will dawn on the other side of the wall.
>
> *In Berlin, 19 October 1982*

Let's just have a quick look at some of those failures which are causing us so much trouble now.

—The failure in the past to keep our prices down. You remember when inflation reached 27 per cent in November 1975? No, you wouldn't, but some of us do. But it was ..it's appalling when you think of it. Twenty seven per cent in one year, in 1975. That cost Britain thousands of jobs—jobs taken by countries where goods where cheaper than ours.

—The failure to push up efficiency. We just didn't keep up with our competitors. So they got the orders and we lost the jobs. Overmanning which was started years ago, to try to keep jobs finished up, pathetically, by losing us whole companies and whole industries and thousands of jobs.

—The failure to build new businesses and to use to new and latest technology. You know how many companies put it in, but they weren't allowed to use it to great advantage because some of the trade unions insisted that the manning levels were still those that belonged to the old machinery. We taxed people too much and discouraged enterprise. So many of our able people went abroad, those who could create wealth, those who could create new industries, those who could design well, those who could build the new technology. So other countries scooped the pool and too many of our people were made redundant.

> I am painted as the greatest little dictator, which is ridiculous – you always take some consultations.
>
> *The Times, 1983*

Mr Chairman, those days of failure are over. At last Britain is taking the measures which have started us on the road to success.

Success first in keeping costs down, because government can help in that way. And inflation at four per cent makes us among the best in the industrialised world, and the best for fifteen years in this country.

Success too in getting productivity up. Britain is showing that we can produce as efficiently as anyone else in the world.

And there's success in new enterprise—20,000 more new companies were born than we lost in the last two years—and great success in new technologies. Because the way in which we are moving into the new science-based industries gives this country a new opportunity and a new phase of development. We've always been best at research, we've always been most inventive, but until now we haven't been able to translate that research and inventiveness into profits and industrial success and jobs. And that's what we're going to do under Conservative Government.

The age of the microchip has dawned in Britain, and we're determined to see that the sun rises here too. And with the help of those behind us *[looks at guests on platform behind her]* we'll get it to high noon as well.

You don't remember *High Noon*? We remember it don't we Monty [Monty Modlyn]? The most marvellously successful film of all time. One of the most successful films.

But the new electronics industries are producing the new jobs as they train and take on new people.

Now that is a successful start on our strategy for jobs.

There is no magic cure to genuine jobs. *[sic]* If there had been both we and other governments would have gone there before now.

But ours is a true cure, and it is born of supreme effort to produce the best in Britain and to excel (whether in the services, in the sciences, or in the arts)—to excel in everything we do. That's the kind of Britain I want to see.

And what about the alternative government—the Labour Party?

Well, we know the main thrust of their proposals. It is a matter of spending what you haven't earned, and that would lead to the inevitable financial crisis as we have to be bailed out by other countries.

And Labour's legacy from the last Labour Government, the legacy to the young people of today was an overseas debt of $22 billion. And so far even though we have been in a deep world recession, Britain under a Tory government has paid off $10 billion of that debt.

Under Conservatives we pay our debts and we honour our obligations.

But it's worse than that. Because Labour would put people out of work if their manifesto policies were ever put into practice when they came into power.

Over two million jobs depend upon our exports to the rest of the European Community, as the whole of our industry has geared up to our membership of that community and to sell our exports to them. Two million jobs at risk. And Labour would leave that Common Market within the first Parliament with no second thoughts of a referendum.

Then I don't know whether you looked at their defence policy? No, I'm not talking about the nuclear aspect, though I'll have a word about that later. I'm talking about some of the smaller print. Because there's a little bit of it which says "and we are going to reduce our expenditure on defence to the average proportion spent by European countries". That would mean reducing expenditure on defence by £4.5 billion, or by the amount equal to what we spend on the Royal Navy. And that would lose a fantastic number of jobs as we could no longer afford the conventional forces or the conventional equipment which perform and defend us so magnificently the world over.

And that's only part of it. I've been through their manifesto, this thing ... *[holds up Labour manifesto; audience boos]* ... In politics *know your enemies.* They don't want you to read it. That's why we've had all these leaks and scares. Ridiculous. Because they don't want you to read what was in their manifesto because they knew if you did know you'd totally and utterly reject it. And so will the majority of our people.

> I was brought up by a Victorian grandmother. We were taught to work jolly hard. We were taught to prove yourself; we were taught self reliance; we were taught to live within our income. You were taught that cleanliness is next to Godliness. You were taught self respect. You were taught always to give a hand to your neighbour. You were taught tremendous pride in your country. All of these things are Victorian values. They are also perennial values.
>
> *LBC Radio, April 1983*

Well' I've been through it and I've counted at least forty seven new ways of controlling and confining Britain within a Socialist straitjacket; controlling us. Just listen to some of the things they are planning to do.

There is a section in here which would enable them to take over any company in Britain at any time, either permanently or temporarily, of they so choose.

There's a section which says, "if the banks don't cooperate, any bank which refused to do what they wanted with your money, they'd be nationalised too. *[boos]* Oh yes.

There's a section which goes on to say it's going to close down private employment agencies, although they find and provide the jobs. And also there's another section, which talks about stopping your right to buy your own council house.

I'll tell you something else: they don't stop at the front door.

Listen to this: *[opens manifesto to read; laughter and applause]*

"Men and women should be able to share the rights and responsibilities of paid employment and domestic activities, so that job segregation within and outside the home is broken down."

They're going to see if Denis does his share of the washing up.

More seriously, it's a list of proposals aimed at destroying the spirit of enterprise and the chance to display and develop your talent, your ability, your excellence whatever it may be, and wherever you choose to develop it. They think it's attractive to offer to the young a future wholly controlled by the operation of the Socialist state. What is their message? To each his own pigeon-hole. From each, total conformity. We utterly reject it.

That sort of society is not fit for Britons. And we here today are determined it shall never come about.

So as I read through that document it occurred to me—and from what I've heard they've been saying, which I haven't liked very much either, that Labour is the pessimistic party. It spreads its gloom wherever it goes. There is no joyous acceptance of what is right or determination to improve what is wrong. There is no pride in Britain's achievements.

Instead, there is a compulsive concentration on failure and a kind of envy which resents success.

And it's that kind of sourness which has made them a party which has given up hope. They have no hope that British industry can ever compete, so they can take cover behind import controls. We believe British industry *can* compete and so we're going to give it the opportunity.

They have no hope and no determination to achieve multilateral disarmament, disarmament on all sides, so they go in for one-sided abandonment of our deterrent, while they leave nuclear weapons in the hands of our sworn enemies.

They've no hope that Britain can make her way in Europe, so they want to pull out of the Common Market.

They have no hope of real jobs for our people so they go in for false jobs—whatever the cost.

Labour has no hope for Britain, and it offers no hope to Britain. They have no faith in the British people.

What a contrast with us. Where Labour's pessimistic, we are full of hope. Where they are bitter, we are determined to succeed. Where they *fear* the future, we rise to the challenge and the excitement and the adventure.

But then *ours* in the British way. This is a nation built on the success of merchant ventures. Men who were willing to sail out into the unknown to carry our trade and bring back wealth to our people. Men who took our ways of freedom and law to countries who would never otherwise have known them and some who would wish they still have them.

Imagine what Labour would have done to them, those brave seafarers who risked all on the chance of success. Just imagine, had they been in power in those days.

First, those merchant venturers who went out in the time of the first Elizabeth, they would have to be registered. Then they would have to enter into a planning agreement with the relevant Government department. After that there would be meetings with the Minister of Trade to decide which merchant would be allowed to venture and where.

Then the National Investment Bank would have to decide who, if anyone, was allowed to invest in the fitting-out of the ship. And which pension fund was to be expected to risk its money. And then the TUC would have nominated fifty per cent of the representatives of any governing body to decide on a division of the profits, if there were any, after tax.

The merchant venturer could then leave Britain, as long as he had cleared the voyage with the Foreign Investment Unit and satisfied the shop stewards that there were no non-union cabin boys on board.

No wonder under Labour no-one ventures. And friends if no-one ventures, no-one else gains. And that's why the economy foundered for years. And it's not only the economy. We said a council tenant should be able to buy his own home. They too should have the chance to be freeholders, heirs to Runnymede.

But Labour can't stomach it. They would stop all council house sales at present prices. They'd take away the discounts you get for years of rent paying. And they'd allow local councils to stop sales altogether.

But that's not enough for them. They would fix a fetter on the freehold of the people who have already bought. They would limit your power to sell what is yours—they'd limit your freehold.

Do you remember Kipling's famous verse?

"At Runnymede, at Runnymede,
Your rights were won at Runnymede!
No freeman shall be fined or bound,
Or dispossessed of freehold ground."

Well, you would under Labour.

We Conservatives believe passionately in giving a chance to those who have never had one before—in giving a chance to be independent of government and not dependent on every political whim whether of national or local government.

Conservatives give you the chance to choose. For Conservatives believe in freedom. And notice that I say *freedom*, not license—there's no "devil take the hindmost" philosophy here. We are committed to a civilized society, where the poor and the sick, the disabled and the elderly, are properly cared for. Cared for by the community, cared for by their families, and cared for by voluntary agencies. And one thing our opponents *hate* is the excellent record of this government in both pensions and in the National Health Service, in spite of the most difficult world recession we've been through.

Because the facts are that after the last four years of Tory

Government the retirement pension now buys more than ever it did under Labour. And the facts are that despite the recession and despite the scares we had last time, there are now 56,000 more nurses and 7,000 doctors in the National Health Service, which is now able to treat two million more patients a year. Take those facts and shout them from the housetops. Because that is how Conservatives care.

Oh yes, we believe in the welfare state. But we don't stop there. We believe also in voluntary effort and family support. They march hand in hand to achieve the best possible life for the needy and the disadvantaged.

That's effective Conservative care.

Yet Mr Chairman we know that freedom cannot survive without personal responsibility. And a very famous quotation, which I repeated one day in the House of Commons, which I said: "Do you remember who it was said 'freedom incurs responsibility, that's why so many people fear it'?" "Who?" they yelled. Well, they're always yelling at Question Time. "Who?" they yelled, thinking they'd caught me out, I couldn't remember. Well, as a matter of fact it was George Bernard Shaw. But it's absolutely right. Freedom incurs responsibility. Because we know that freedom depends upon us all regaining that sense of discipline and duty upon which the free society depends.

And we think that freedom is worth defending—even though it be challenged eight thousand miles away.

For at home, without a framework of just law, impartially administered, freedom becomes anarchy. And without order it degenerates into the tyranny of the strong. And abroad freedom can only flourish if our dedication to it is *never* in doubt.

Mr Chairman, there are powerful dictators and powerful countries who would snuff it out. Nations whose ambitions would deny freedom to others as they deny freedom gtheir own people. Dictators who cannot bear to be opposed.

They must know beyond all doubt that we in Britain have the capacity and the will to secure and to defend our own way of life.

It was Pericles of Athens, 2500 years ago, who gave our civilisation an understanding of that need. He said to his fellow citizens: "Freedom is the sweetest possession of those alone who have the courage to defend it."

Mr Chairman we in the Conservative Party and in the Conservative Government have the courage to lead our people to defend it. The fact is that our policies have kept the peace in Europe for more than thirty eight years. And that is a prize above all others and we must not put it at risk now.

> The SDP MPs should have stayed within the Labour Party and fought from within it. But they hadn't got the guts.
>
> *1 June 1983*

And our determination to defend freedom, and to retain the capacity to deter, marks the great divide between Conservatives and our opponents. After years of wrangling and strife, the Labour left has won and Labour is committed to abandoning nuclear weapons while leaving them in the hands of our enemies.

Mr Foot says—and I quote—"If you vote Labour, you are voting for a Britain...without nuclear weapons."

Of course he also says we'd still be strong, free and loyal to our friends. But nothing could be further from the truth. If we had no nuclear deterrent the balance between East and West would be upset. Britain would be wide open to blackmail. Because without a missile being fired, the Russians could demand of us to do what they will. And we would have no alternative but to surrender.

Is that freedom? Is that strength? In my book that would be serfdom. And that's no fit state for Britain. A Conservative victory on June 9th makes peace with freedom and justice more sure. It sends a message to the world: That Britain is still a bastion of liberty and law. That Britain is still a staunch and reliable ally.

Doesn't that give real hope to your generation? A solid base upon which to build your lives. Most of you here are going to live a long time into the 21st century. We've all got to see to it that you'll have that great heritage of liberty that our forebears won for us. And we've got to see that it's our responsibility to hand on our heritage to future generations and to add our contribution to it.

Ladies and gentlemen, it is your future which is at stake.

And that future starts on Thursday. What we do in these next five years will set the course for your lifetime.

Oh, Britain could make futile gestures and hope that the Soviet Union would reciprocate— Do you believe they would? *["No"]* Ask the Czechs. Ask the Hungarians. Ask the Poles. Ask the Afghans.

And Britain could try quack cures for unemployment—But that couldn't produce the jobs. Britain could let down her friends and desert her allies—But that wouldn't build a secure and stable Britain. Britain could do all of those things—either with Labour or Labour's former allies—the Alliance. But if we were to do those things we'd regret it all our lives—and that's far too long for anyone here.

And that's why there are not going to be any regrets. Because in the next few days we're going to do everything in our power to see that a Conservative Government is returned on Thursday.

To see —That Britain votes for her future —That Britain votes for jobs and that Britain votes for peace with freedom and justice.

That's why we ask you to make sure that next Thursday Britain votes decisively for the Government that has restored her confidence and rekindled her pride.

PART FOUR

Second Term

1983–87

Power is a trust and we must exercise it in that way.

9 June 1983

We intend freedom and justice to conquer. Yes, we do have a creed and we wish others to share it. But it is not part of the policy to impose our beliefs by force or threat of force.

September 1983

We got really good consensus during the last election. Consensus behind my convictions.

1984

SCRIPT OF A SKETCH PERFORMED BY MARGARET THATCHER WITH NIGEL HAWTHORNE AND PAUL EDDINGTON AT AN AWARDS CEREMONY FOR THE NATIONAL VIEWERS & LISTENERS ASSOCIATION

20 January 1984

SCRIPT:

Prime Minister: Ah, good morning Jim, Sir Humphrey. Do come in and sit down. How's your wife? Is she well?

Jim Hacker: *[Puzzled]* Oh yes, fine, Prime Minister. Fine. Thank you. Yes, fine.

PM: Good. So pleased. I've been meaning to have a word with you for some time. I've got an idea.

JH: *[Brightening visibly]* An idea, Prime Minister? Oh good.

Sir Humphrey: *[Guardedly]* An idea, Prime Minister?

PM: Well, not really an idea. It's gone beyond that actually. I've given it quite a bit of thought and I'm sure you, Jim, are the right man to carry it out. It's got to do with a kind of institution and you are sort of responsible for institutions, aren't you?

SH: *[Cautiously]* Institutions, Prime Minister?

JH: *[Decisively]* Oh yes, institutions fall to me. Most definitely. And you want me to set one up, I suppose?

PM: Set one up? Certainly not. I want you to get rid of one.

JH: *[Astonished]* Get rid of one, Prime Minister?

PM: Yes. It's all very simple. I want you to abolish economists.

JH: *[Mouth open]* Abolish economists, Prime Minister?

PM: Yes, abolish economists ... quickly.

SH: *[Silkily]* All of them, Prime Minister?

PM: Yes, all of them. They never agree on anything. They just fill the heads of politicians with all sorts of curious notions, like the more you spend, the richer you get.

JH: *[Coming around to the idea]* I see your point, Prime Minister. Can't have the nation's time wasted on curious notions, can we? No.

SH: *[Sternly]* Minister.

PM: Quite right, Jim. Absolute waste of time. Simply got to go.

JH: *[Uncertain]* Simply got to go?

PM: *[Motherly]* Yes Jim. Don't worry. If it all goes wrong I shall get the blame. But if it goes right - as it will - then you'll get the credit for redeploying a lot of underused and misapplied resources. Probably get promotion too.

SH: *[Indignantly]* Resources? Resources, Prime Minister? We're talking about economists.

PM: Were, Sir Humphrey. Were.

JH: *[Decisively]* Yes Humphrey, were. We're going to get rid of them.

PM: Well, its all settled then. I'll look forward to receiving your plan for abolition soon. Tomorrow, shall we say? I'd like you to announce it before it all leaks.

JH: *[Brightly]* Tomorrow then, Prime Minister.

PM: Yes. Well, go and sort it out. Now, Sir Humphrey ... what did you say your degree was?

SH: *[Innocently]* Degree, Prime Minister?

PM: *[Firmly]* Yes, Sir Humphrey, degree. Your degree. You have one, I take it - most Permanent Secretaries do, or perhaps two?

SH: *[Modestly]* Er, well actually, Prime Minister, a double first.

PM: Congratulations, Sir Humphrey, but what in?

SH: *[Weakly]* Politics ... er ... and er ... economics.

PM: *[Soothingly]* Capital, my dear Sir Humphrey. You'll know exactly where to start.

SH: *[Bleakly]* Yes, Prime Minister.

[**Exit** Jim Hacker and Sir Humphrey]

REMARKS FOLLOWING THE IRA BOMBING IN BRIGHTON

Brighton Police Station. 12th October 1984

John Cole, BBC: How are you Prime Minister?

MT: Very well, thank you very much. Our worry is whether there's anyone under that rubble because I don't know whether you've seen it, but it's pretty awful.

JC: Have you seen your other cabinet colleagues?

MT: Yes indeed. Geoffrey Howe is here with us and Leon [Leon Brittan] is here with us, the Home Secretary. Uh, we were all very, very fortunate, very fortunate indeed.

JC: Were you asleep at the time, Prime Minister?

MT: Uh, the, I'm not quite sure the Chancellor of the Exchequer … No, I was up working. The bomb went off somewhere between quarter to three and three, I know that because I looked up when I'd finished something at quarter to three, and I just turned to do one final paper and then, em, it went off. My husband was in bed and all the windows went and the bathroom's extremely badly damaged.

JC: In your own room?

Protection Officer: I think that's enough, Prime Minister.

Denis Thatcher: Yes. Yes.

MT: Yes. We were very lucky.

Unidentified journalist: Will you be giving your speech this afternoon, Prime Minister?

MT: Of course. Of course.

In the Conservative Party we have no truck with outmoded Marxist doctrine about class warfare. For us it is not who you are, who your family is or where you come from that matters, but what you are and what you can do for your country that counts.

1984

JC: Have you any message for people at breakfast time about the atrocity?

MT: I can only say, as usual, the police are there very quickly, or immediately, they're on the scene there. We've very worried about the policemen who were on duty outside. The firemen came extremely quickly and were marvellous. We were very, very fortunate. We're anxiously awaiting news of other people. Em, you hear about these atrocities, these bombs, you don't expect them to happen to you. But life must go on, as usual.

JC: And your conference will go on?

MT: The Conference will go on. The Conference … *[MT pauses as if unsure whether the camera was running. Camera lights brighten.]* All right, all right John. The conference will go on, *as usual.*

JC: Thank you Prime Minister.

SPEECH TO THE 1984 CONSERVATIVE PARTY CONFERENCE

Brighton, 12th October 1984

The bomb attack on the Grand Hotel early this morning was first and foremost an inhuman, undiscriminating attempt to massacre innocent unsuspecting men and women staying in Brighton for our Conservative Conference. Our first thoughts must at once be for those who died and for those who are now in hospital recovering from their injuries. But the bomb attack clearly signified more than this. It was an attempt not only to disrupt and terminate our Conference; It was an attempt to cripple Her Majesty's democratically-elected Government. That is the scale of the outrage in which we have all shared, and the fact that we are gathered here now—shocked, but composed and determined—is a sign not only that this attack has failed, but that all attempts to destroy democracy by terrorism will fail.

I should like to express our deep gratitude to the police, firemen, ambulancemen, nurses and doctors, to all the emergency services, and to the staff of the hotel; to our ministerial staff and the Conservative Party staff who stood with us and shared the danger.

As Prime Minister and as Leader of the Party, I thank them all and send our heartfelt sympathy to all those who have suffered.

And now it must be business as usual. We must go on to discuss the things we have talked about during this Conference; one or two matters of foreign affairs; and after that, two subjects I have selected for special consideration—unemployment and the miners' strike.

This Conservative Conference—superbly chaired, and of course, our Chairman came on this morning with very little sleep and carried on marvellously,—and with excellent contributions from our members, has been an outstanding example of orderly assembly and free speech. We have debated the great national and international issues, as well as those which affect the daily lives of our people. We have seen at the rostrum miner and pensioner, nurse and manager, clergyman and student. In Government, we have been fulfilling the promises contained in our election manifesto, which was put to the people in a national ballot.

> What we've got is an attempt to substitute the rule of the mob, for the rule of the law. It must not succeed.
>
> *On the miners' strike, 1984*

This Government, Mr President, is reasserting Parliament's ultimate responsibility for controlling the total burden of taxation on our citizens, whether levied by central or local government, and in the coming session of Parliament we shall introduce legislation which will abolish the GLC and the Metropolitan County Councils.

In the quest for sound local government, we rely on the help of Conservative councillors. Their task should never be underestimated and their virtues should not go unsung. They work hard and conscientiously in the true spirit of service and I pay special tribute to the splendid efforts of Conservative councils up and down the country in getting better value for money through greater efficiency and putting out work to competitive tender. This is privatization at the local level and we need more of it.

At national level, since the General Election just over a year ago, the Government has denationalized five major enterprises, making a total of thirteen since 1979. Yesterday, you gave Norman Tebbit a standing ovation; today, our thoughts are with him and his family.

Again and again, denationalization has brought greater motivation to managers and workforce, higher profits and rising investment, and what is more, many in industry now have a share in the firm for which they work. We Conservatives want every owner to be an earner and every earner to be an owner.

Soon, we shall have the biggest ever act of denationalization with British Telecom and British Airways will follow; and we have not finished yet. There will be more to come in this Parliament.

And just as we have stood by our pledge on denationalization, it is our pride that despite the recession, we have kept faith with 9 million pensioners and moreover, by keeping inflation down, we have protected the value of their savings. As Norman Fowler told the Conference on Wednesday, this Government has not only put more into pensions, but has increased resources for the National Health Service. Our record for last year, to be published shortly, will show that the Health Service today is providing more care, more services and more help for the patient than at any stage in its history. That is Conservative care in practice. And I think it is further proof of the statement I made in Brighton in this very hall two years ago—perhaps some of you remember it—that the National Health Service is safe with us.

Now Mr President and Friends, this performance in the social services could never have been achieved without an efficient and competitive industry to create the wealth we need. Efficiency is not the enemy, but the ally, of compassion.

In our discussions here, we have spoken of the need for enterprise, profits and the wider distribution of property among all the people. In the Conservative Party, we have no truck with outmoded Marxist doctrine about class warfare. For us, it is not who you are, who your family is or where you come from that matters. It is what you are and what you can do for our country that counts. That is our vision. It is a vision worth defending and we shall defend it. Indeed, this Government will never put the defence of our country at risk.

No-one in their senses wants nuclear weapons for their own sake, but equally, no responsible prime minister could take the colossal gamble of giving up our nuclear defences while our greatest potential enemy kept theirs.

Policies which would throw out all American nuclear bases—bases which, mind you, have been here since the time of Mr Attlee, Mr Truman and Winston Churchill—would wreck NATO and leave us totally isolated from our friends in the United States, and friends they are. No nation in history has ever shouldered a greater burden nor shouldered it more willingly nor more generously than the United States. This Party is pro-American.

And we must constantly remind people what the defence policy of the Opposition Party would mean. Their idea that by giving up our nuclear deterrent, we could somehow escape the result of a nuclear war elsewhere is nonsense, and it is a delusion to assume that conventional weapons are sufficient defence against nuclear attack. And do not let anyone slip into the habit of thinking that conventional war in Europe is some kind of comfortable option. With a huge array of modern weapons held by the Soviet Union, including chemical weapons in large quantities, it would be a cruel and terrible conflict. The truth is that possession of the nuclear deterrent has prevented not only nuclear war but also conventional war and to us, peace is precious beyond price. We are the true peace party. And the nuclear deterrent has not only kept the peace, but it will continue to preserve our independence. Winston Churchill's warning is just as true now as when he made it many many years ago. He said this: "Once you take the position of not being able in any circumstances to defend your rights against aggression, there is no end to the demands that will be made nor to the humiliations that must be accepted." He knew, and we must heed his warning.

I am always on the job.

Interview on Aspel and Co, 1984

And yet, Labour's defence policy remains no Polaris, no Cruise missiles in Britain, no United States nuclear bases in Britain, no Trident, no independent nuclear deterrent.

There is, I think, just one answer the nation will give. No defence—no Labour Government.

Now, Mr President, we had one of the most interesting debates of this Conference on unemployment, which we all agree is the scourge of our times.

To have over 3 million people unemployed in this country is bad enough, even though we share this tragic problem with other nations, but to suggest, as some of our opponents have, that we do not care about it is as deeply wounding as it is utterly false. Do they really think that we do not understand what it means for the family man who cannot find a job, to have to sit at home with a sense of failure and despair? Or that we do not understand how hopeless the world must seem to a young person who has not yet succeeded in getting his first job? Of course, we know, of course we see, and of course, we care. However could they say that we welcome unemployment as a political weapon? What better news could there be for any Government than the news that unemployment is falling and the day cannot come too soon for me.

Others, while not questioning our sincerity, argue that our policies will not achieve our objectives. They look back forty years to the post-war period, when we were paused to launch a brave new world; a time when we all thought we had the cure for unemployment. In that confident dawn it seemed that having won the war, we knew how to win the peace. Keynes had provided the diagnosis. It was all set out in the 1944 White Paper on Employment. I bought it then; I have it still. My name is on the top of it. Margaret H. Roberts. One of my staff took one look at it and said: "Good Heavens! I did not know it was as old as that!"

> I came to office with one deliberate intent – to change Britain from a dependent to a self reliant society, from a give it to me to a do it for yourself nation, to a get and go instead of a sit back and wait Britain.
>
> *The Times, 8 February 1984*

Now, we all read that White Paper very carefully, but the truth was that politicians took some parts of the formula in it and conveniently ignored the rest. I re-read it frequently. Those politicians overlooked the warning in that Paper that government action must not weaken personal enterprise or exonerate the citizen from the duty of fending for himself. They disregarded the advice that wages must be related to productivity and above all, they neglected the warning that without a rising standard of industrial efficiency, you cannot achieve a high level of employment combined with a rising standard of living.

And having ignored so much of that and having ignored other parts of the formula for so much of the time, the result was that we ended up with high inflation and high unemployment.

This Government is heeding the warnings. It has acted on the basic truths that were set out all those years ago in that famous White Paper. If I had come out with all this today, some people would call it "Thatcherite" but, in fact, it was vintage Maynard Keynes. He had a horror of inflation, a fear of too much State control, and a belief in the market.

We are heeding those warnings. We are taking the policy as a whole and not only in selected parts. We have already brought inflation down below 5% Output has been rising steadily since 1981 and investment is up substantially. But if things are improving, why—you will ask—does unemployment not fall?

And that was the question one could feel throughout that debate, even though people know there is always a time lag between getting the other things right and having a fall in unemployment. Why does unemployment not fall?

May I try to answer that question?

Well, first, more jobs are being created. As Tom King pointed out, over the last year more than a quarter of a million extra jobs have been created, but the population of working age is also rising very fast as the baby boom of the 1960s becomes the school-leavers of the 1980s; so although the number of jobs are rising, the population of working age is also rising, and among the population of working age a larger proportion of married women are seeking work, and so you will see why we need more jobs just to stop unemployment rising and even more jobs to get it falling.

Now, on top of that, new technology has caused redundancy in many factories, though it has also created whole new industries providing products and jobs that only a few years ago were undreamed of.

So it has two effects: the first one redundancies, the second and slightly later, new jobs as new products become possible. This has happened in history before.

A few days ago I visited York, where I saw the first railway engine, Stevenson's "Rocket". I thought of the jobs, the prospects and the hope that the new steam engines and the railways then brought to many people. Communities queued up to be on a railway line, to have their own station. Those communities welcomed change and it brought them more jobs.

I confess I am very glad we have got the railways, but if we were trying to build those same railways today, I wonder if we would ever get planning permission—it sometimes takes so long. And that is one thing that can sometimes delay the coming into existence of jobs.

"Employment cannot be created by Act of Parliament or by Government action alone. The success of the policy outlined in this Paper will ultimately depend on the understanding and support of the community as a whole and especially on the efforts of employers and workers in industry."

May I turn now to the coal industry?

For a little over seven months we have been living through an agonising strike. Let me make it absolutely clear the miners' strike was not of this Government's seeking nor of its making.

We have heard in debates at this Conference some of the aspects that have made this dispute so repugnant to so many people. We were reminded by a colliery manager that the NUM always used to accept that a pit should close when the losses were too great to keep it open, and that the miners set great store by investment in new pits and new seams, and under this Government that new investment is happening in abundance. You can almost repeat the figures with me. £2 million in capital investment in the mines for every day this Government has been in power, so no shortage of capital investment.

We heard moving accounts from two working miners about just what they have to face as they try to make their way to work. The sheer bravery of those men and thousands like them who kept the mining industry alive is beyond praise. "Scabs" their former workmates call them. Scabs? They are lions! What a tragedy it is when striking miners attack their workmates. Not only are they members of the same union, but the working miner is saving both their futures, because it is the working miners, whether in Nottinghamshire, Derbyshire, Lancashire, Leicestershire, Staffordshire, Warwickshire, North Wales or Scotland, it is the working miners who have kept faith with those who buy our coal and without that custom thousands of jobs in the mining industry would be already lost.

> I can cope with nine of them, so they ought to be able to stand one of me. They could end the tiresomeness and stubbornness by giving me what I want.
>
> *The Times, 10 April 1984*

And then we heard—unforgettably—from the incomparable Mrs Irene McGibbon—who told us what it is like to be the wife of a working miner during this strike. She told us of the threats and intimidation suffered by herself and her family and even her 11-year-old son, but what she endured only stiffened her resolve. To face the picket line day after day must take a very special kind of courage, but it takes as much—perhaps even more—to the housewife who has to stay at home alone. Men and women like that are what we are proud to call "the best of British" and our police who upheld the law with an independence and a restraint perhaps only to be found in this country are the admiration of the world.

To be sure, the miners had a good deal and to try to prevent a strike the National Coal Board gave to the miners the best ever pay offer, the highest ever investment and for the first time the promise that no miner would lose his job against his will. We did this despite the fact that the bill for losses in the coal industry last year was bigger than the annual bill for all the doctors and dentists in all the National Health Service hospitals in the United Kingdom.

Let me repeat it: the losses—the annual losses—in the coal industry are enormous. £1.3 billion last year. You have to find that money as tax-payers. It is equal to the sum we pay in salaries to all the doctors and dentists in the National Health Service.

Mr President, this is a dispute about the right to go to work of those who have been denied the right to go to vote, and we must never forget that the overwhelming majority of trade unionists, including many striking miners, deeply regret what has been done in the name of trade unionism. When this strike is over—and one day it will be over—we must do everything we can to encourage moderate and responsible trade unionism so that it can once again take its respected and valuable place in our industrial life.

> I think that was an assassination attempt, don't you?
>
> *To speechwriter Ronnie Millar a few minutes after the IRA bomb went off in Brighton, October 1984*

Meanwhile, we are faced with the present Executive of the National Union of Mineworkers. They know that what they are demanding has never been granted either to miners or to workers in any other industry. Why then demand it? Why ask for what they know cannot be conceded? There can only be one explanation. They did not want a settlement; they wanted a strike. Otherwise, they would have balloted on the Coal Board's offer. Indeed, one-third of the miners did have a ballot and voted overwhelmingly to accept the offer.

Mr President, what we have seen in this country is the emergence of an organized revolutionary minority who are prepared to exploit industrial disputes, but whose real aim is the breakdown of law and order and the destruction of democratic parliamentary government. We have seen the same sort of thugs and bullies at Grunwick, more recently against Eddie Shah in Stockport, and now organized into flying squads around the country. If their tactics were to be allowed to succeed, if they are not brought under the control of the law, we shall see them again at every industrial dispute organized by militant union leaders anywhere in the country.

One of the speakers earlier in this Conference realized this fact, realized that what they are saying is: "Give us what we want or we are prepared to go on with violence," and he referred to Danegeld. May I add to what that speaker said.

"We never pay anyone Danegeld, no matter how trifling the cost, for the end of that gain is oppression and shame, and the nation that plays it is lost." Yes, Rudyard Kipling. Who could put it better?

Democratic change there has always been in this, the home of democracy. But the sanction for change is the ballot box.

It seems that there are some who are out to destroy any properly elected government. They are out to bring down the framework of law. That is what we have seen in this strike, and what is the law they seek to defy?

It is the Common Law created by fearless judges and passed down across the centuries. It is legislation scrutinized and enacted by the parliament of a free people. It is legislation passed through a House of Commons, a Commons elected once every five years by secret ballot by one citizen, one vote. This is the way our law was fashioned and that is why British justice is renowned across the world.

"No government owns the law. It is the law of the land, heritage of the people. No man is above the law and no man is below it. Nor do we ask any man's permission when we require him to obey it. Obedience to the law is demanded as a right, not asked as a favour." So said Theodore Roosevelt.

Mr President, the battle to uphold the rule of law calls for the resolve and commitment of the British people. Our institutions of justice, the courts and the police require the unswerving support of every law-abiding citizen and I believe they will receive it.

The nation faces what is probably the most testing crisis of our time, the battle between the extremists and the rest. We are fighting, as we have always fought, for the weak as well as for the strong. We are fighting for great and good causes. We are fighting to defend them against the power and might of those who rise up to challenge them. This Government will not weaken. This nation will meet that challenge. Democracy will prevail.

INTERVIEW WITH DIANE SAWYER, CBS NEWS

12 February 1985 (broadcast 18 February)

Diane Sawyer: Is there a difference in being a woman? Is there something that makes it different?

Prime Minister: Well, I cannot tell you the difference between a woman prime minister and a man prime minister, because I have only ever been a woman prime minister, and therefore I do not notice. But I do think this about women in general: they are very practical; they do always have to cope. Come what may, they cope. They have to, and I think therefore they do take a very practical attitude, and I have noticed over the years something else. I noticed it from university on. A woman with the same amount of ability as a man will have much less self-confidence than a man; much less self-confidence about getting up and speaking, doing public speaking; much less self-confidence about giving their views. I think it is gradually changing, but whether in the United States or here, we have far too few women coming into public life and I think that that still is a factor. They get on with doing the practical work, but do not find it so easy to get up and give their views or to come into debating and discussion. Don't you find that?

DS: Ronald Reagan's personality has proven to be a kind of buffer for him when times get hard. Do you envy that?

PM: No. I think [Ronald Reagan] he is marvellous. As I told you, I am his greatest fan. We each have our own style. You cannot change it! I have not the slightest intention of changing mine! After all, it has not done me so badly so far!

DS: I read a quote once—I am full of quotes today—I read a quote once where your father said: "Margaret is 99.5% perfect—the half percent that could be a little bit warmer!"

PM: I am not quite sure where you heard these quotes from at all. That is the first time I have ever heard that. I do not think you will find my family ever said that I was cold and I think it is quite an advertisement for anyone that they have such a close family life as we have.

DS: Do you like television as a medium? There has been much discussion this political season in the United States about the effects of television on personalities and people and I read once that you said you think that television interviews often take the life's blood out of real people.

PM: Well, they do. They are flat. I mean, that when I go about people find me very different from television. I do not know why, because I never watch myself on television, and it is highly selective. You know, you ask a few questions. It is so selective. But it has brought a great deal of richness to life, a great deal of knowledge to life, but I am always nervous of it, of course, very nervous.

DS: Are there times when you just want to pack it in?

PM: No. No, no, no. No, I don't. I never want to pack it in. Of course, I will have to one day. Of course I will have to, but I do not want to pack it in for quite a time yet. I still think, maybe you don't like her style, but I still think a firm hand is needed.

DS: Did it wound you when Oxford University decided not to give you an honorary degree as they had done other Oxford-educated prime ministers, saying that you had been bad for education?

PM: Well, I am afraid that their arguments were not very good because as some of the newspapers pointed out, in fact, the resources for education in fact had been increased and the number in higher education is at an all-time record, etc., but those are the statistics and I am afraid their case in logic was not a very good one. But when the Council of the University asked for my name to go forward I knew that I would probably meet this opposition, because that is the way the socialists work. We Conservatives at University would never have dreamed of opposing Harold Wilson as a Labour Prime Minister for an honorary degree...

DS: ...but this was a faculty vote wasn't it...not socialists?

PM: Yes, it is a political vote. It is a political vote. So I was not surprised. I think other people were perhaps more surprised than I was. I was not surprised. Their arguments were not terribly good, but I was most certainly not surprised. But when the Council asked me to let my name go forward, yes. I said yes, of course, and it was indicated that there might be a vote. Well so what?

DS: Did it wound you?

PM: No, it did not wound me, because I know Oxford.

DS: Once you said this to the Soviet Union ... I wanted to ask you about it ... you said that the Russians are bent on world dominance; that they know they are a super power only in one sense, the military sense; they are a failure in human and economic terms.

PM: Well that is what I really rather indicated earlier when I said now that we have seen communism in practice for so many years, as distinct from in writing in the books, we have seen the kind of society which it creates. It gives neither dignity to man nor does it bring prosperity. When they turn round to help other people, other countries, they do not help them with civil aid as the United States does and we do—they help them with armaments.

Ethiopia is a typical example. A communist country with communist leaders. The Soviet Union sell them armaments...with which to prosecute a civil war. [They] did not turn round and say: "Feed your people!"

After the United States left Vietnam, a communist country then, turned round and attacked Cambodia. Did not say "Let us turn round and look after the wellbeing of the people!" Oh no, it was the West who had to go in and say: "Look, you are selling armaments to them; we will give them food! We will help them!"

You find that the world over. Three out of four dollars that the United States spends on Central America goes to civil programmes, goes to helping with food, goes to help them to pull themselves up—not so the Soviets. Oh no, take your measure of them. We have to deal with them.

DS: That is why people were sort of perplexed when they heard you say of Mr Gorbachev, "I like Mr Gorbachev!"

PM: I liked him as a personality. I can do business with him, because I accept certain things. Communism is going to stay in the Soviet Union and its satellites for a long time. It is the most rigid doctrine I have ever come across. It has not built in the means to adapt. It is very different from Chinese communism. They have built in the means to adapt their society. The Soviet communism has not. But the fact is it is going to stay there for a very long time and the government of the Soviet Union and the governments of the Western World have one thing in common—we neither of us wish ever to see a war breaking out or a conflict developing and it is in both our interests to see that it does not. In our interest, because democracies and lovers of freedom do not pursue their aims by war. They like, they love peace. We are defensive organisations. They—they are prepared to pursue their aims by military means, and we have to see that we are strong enough to stop them, but I do believe this: that there is a generation in power in the Kremlin who remembers the terrors and horrors of the last War and they would be very slow to embark on another major war. We have got to use that. I believe President Reagan understands that and it is this common interest in no conflict that means we have to negotiate. So you have to negotiate on armaments; get the numbers down and, you know, you do negotiate better when you have more contacts and understand the personalities you are dealing with.

So, yes, we did get on. We did not have what I call the minuets of diplomacy. You know, the set pieces. We sat down and talked—rather as I am talking to you—Now, let us talk about the things that really matter, and [Mikhail Gorbachev] he was prepared to talk. And so yes, we have to do business, and I can do business and I am glad he came!

DS: But it does seem there is a difference between you and Ronald Reagan on one issue at least, namely, you have said, after Grenada, that you simply do not think countries should go in and liberate other people's countries. I think he would probably argue—and certainly those who support him would argue—that you are really saying by that that you do not believe that an oppressed people should ever be rescued by military force.

PM: No, certainly one is not saying that. Do you think we would have carried on in war-time, when the whole of Europe had collapsed, if we thought that?

DS: ...Grenada...

PM: You have to be very very careful before you use military force. To anyone who dares compare Afghanistan and Grenada, I would be the first to say do not be so absurd. The United States went in, did what she had to do, and then came out. I had something very very important to do at that time; that was to get Cruise missiles sited in Britain. I was doing it against a background that they were saying to me: "The President of the United States would not consult you about their use" and I was saying: "Yes, of course [Ronald Reagan] he will and that is part of the understanding between us!" Along comes Grenada, which I thought could have been dealt with by other means, and then I am told "Well, he did not consult you over that; why should he consult you over Cruise?" and there was one really big issue in world context to get solved during that time and that was to get Cruise sited and I was pilloried for not being consulted. It did not bother me, because I have every sympathy with anyone in charge who if they are going to embark on a military operation, keeps it as tightly to themselves as they possibly can, because that is to your armed forces' best advantage. Nevertheless, I did carry out my role and we were the first to do it, and if I had not, an awful lot would have collapsed.

> I am an ally of the United States. We believe the same things, we believe passionately in the same battle of ideas; we will defend them to the hilt. Never try to separate me from them.
>
> *To Mikhail Gorbachev at their first meeting in 1984*

I thought Grenada could have been dealt with by different means. The President took a different view. Maybe in his sphere he was right, in mine I was right. But he went in and then came out. My goodness me, I wish to goodness that the Russians would do the same in Afghanistan!

DS: Last October—October of 1984—terrorists tried to kill you. The IRA claimed responsibility. Do you believe that those in the United States who support Irish relief funds and who send money into Northern Ireland are supporting terrorism?

PM: Oh yes, they are! Those who send money to NORAID are supporting the supply of guns and ammunition with which to kill British soldiers, British policemen, innocent British citizens, not only in Northern Ireland, and also to damage and injure sometimes some Americans who are over here.

After I went round the hospitals after the Harrods' bomb, one of the first persons I saw was an American who had been injured. Oh yes, that is what they are doing.

DS: Is President Reagan going to help you prevent that?

PM: The President and the Friends of Ireland in Congress and Garret FitzGerald, the Taoiseach of the Republic, have been superb, each and every one of them, in totally and utterly condemning terrorism and utterly condemning the IRA, because the IRA is out for a rule of the gun; it is out against democracy; it is often run by Marxist Leninists and Garret FitzGerald, the Taoiseach, will say as firmly as I do they are not only trying to change the situation in Northern Ireland against the wish of the people, but they are against democracy in the Republic, and people who contribute to NORAID are contributing to terrorism and to terrorists who are trying to overturn democracy not only in Northern Ireland but in the Republic of Ireland too. I think your Friends of Ireland in Congress have been marvellous about totally condemning terrorism and so has the President. If you believe in democracy, you cannot believe in terrorism. Every single person in Northern Ireland has the right to vote either for local councils or to the Parliament in Westminster or to their Assembly. They have all the same civil rights. You cannot believe in the ballot and then resort to the bullet!

DS: Does it haunt you, that day? This is the last question.

PM: Yes, to some extent, because I lost some very very dear friends that day and the things that you thought could not happen did happen and we can never get those friends back. But having said that, we were so determined that it would not make any difference to the way in which we carried on and we showed our determination and I went into the Conference immediately the following morning, 9.30am. Ironically enough we were discussing Northern Ireland as I walked on to the platform. There were not many people in the hall, because the security to get in was enormous, but the applause that broke out was terrific and at our mass meeting in the afternoon every seat was full; 6,000 people came to say: "You will not have any effect on us! We shall carry on!" That was their message, and it was marvellous that the gun could not stop British democracy. It would never win.

DS: You said you realised that they did not intend for you to see another day.

PM: Look! Every person in politics in the Western world takes that risk and you just carry on and we do not really think of it. We are deeply grateful to those who protect us. One day it may happen. My goodness me, the gunman is not going to stop us from carrying out the business of democracy—ever! He will fail and people must help him to fail by cutting off the money and supplies of armaments he needs!

SPEECH TO A JOINT SESSION OF CONGRESS. US HOUSE OF REPRESENTATIVES

Washington DC, 20 February 1985

Mr Speaker, Mr President, Distinguished Members of Congress:

On this, one of the most moving occasions of my life, my first words must be to say thank you for granting me this rare privilege of addressing a Joint Meeting of the United States Congress.

My thoughts turn to three earlier occasions when a British Prime Minister, Winston Churchill, has been honoured by a call to address both Houses. Among his many remarkable gifts, Winston held a special advantage here. Through his American mother, he had ties of blood with you. Alas, for me, these are not matters we can readily arrange for ourselves!

Those three occasions deserve to be recalled, because they serve as lamps along a dark road which our people trod together, and they remind us what an extraordinary period of history the world has passed through between that time and ours; and they tell us what later generations in both our countries sometimes find hard to grasp: why past associations bind us so closely.

Winston Churchill 's vision of a union of mind and purpose between the English-speaking peoples was to form the main spring of the West. No-one of my generation can forget that America has been the principal architect of a peace in Europe which has lasted forty years. Given the shield of the United States, we have been granted the opportunities to build a concept of Europe beyond the dreams of our fathers; a Europe which seemed unattainable amid the mud and slaughter of the First World War and the suffering and sacrifice of the Second.

> I like Mr Gorbachev. We can do business together.
>
> *On Mikhail Gorbachev, December 1984*

When, in the Spring of 1945, the guns fell silent, General Eisenhower called our soldiers to a Service of Thanksgiving. In the order of service was a famous prayer of Sir Francis Drake :

"Oh Lord God, when Thou givest to Thy Servants to endeavour any great matter, grant us to know that it is not the beginning but the continuing of the same until it be thoroughly finished, which yieldeth the true glory!"

On this day, close to the 40th anniversary of that service and of peace in Europe—one of the longest periods without war in all our history—I should like to recall those words and acknowledge how faithfully America has fulfilled them. For our deliverance from what might have befallen us, I would not have us leave our gratitude to the tributes of history. The debt the free peoples of Europe owe to this nation, generous with its bounty, willing to share its strength, seeking to protect the week, is incalculable. We thank and salute you!

Of course, in the years which separate us from the time when Winston Churchill last spoke to Congress, there have been disappointments as well as hopes fulfilled: the continued troubles in the Middle East; famine and oppression in Africa; genocide in South East Asia; the brutal occupation of Afghanistan; the undiminished agony of tortured Poland; and above all, the continued and continuing division of the European continent.

From these shores, it may seem to some of you that by comparison with the risk and sacrifice which America has borne through four decades and the courage with which you have shouldered unwanted burdens, Europe has not fully matched your expectations. Bear with me if I dwell for a moment on the Europe to which we now belong.

It is not the Europe of ancient Rome, of Charlemagne, of Bismarck. We who are alive today have passed through perhaps the greatest transformation of human affairs on the Continent of Europe since the fall of Rome. In but a short chapter of its long history, Europe lost the position which it had occupied for two thousand years—and it is your history as much as ours.

For five centuries, that small continent had extended its authority over islands and continents the world over.

For the first forty years of this century, there were seven great powers: United States, Great Britain, Germany, France, Russia, Japan, Italy. Of those seven, two now tower over the rest—United States and the Soviet Union.

To that swift and historic change Europe—a Europe of many different histories and many different nations—has had to find a response. It has not been an easy passage to blend this conflux of nationalism, patriotism, sovereignty, into a European Community, yet I think that our children and grandchildren may see this period—these birth pangs of a new Europe—more clearly than we do now. They will see it as a visionary chapter in the creation of a Europe able to share the load alongside you. Do not doubt the firmness of our resolve in this march towards this goal, but do not underestimate what we already do.

Today, out of the forces of the Alliance in Europe, 95% of the divisions, 85% of the tanks, 80% of the combat aircraft, and 70% of the fighting ships are provided, manned and paid for by the European Allies and Europe has more than three million men under arms and more still in reserve. We have to. We are right in the front line. The frontier of freedom cuts across our continent.

Members of Congress, the defence of that frontier is as vital to you as it is to us.

It is fashionable for some commentators to speak of the two

super powers—United States and the Soviet Union—as though they were somehow of equal worth and equal significance. Mr Speaker, that is a travesty of the truth! The Soviet Union has never concealed its real aim. In the words of Mr Brezhnev, "the total triumph of all Socialism all over the world is inevitable—for this triumph we shall struggle with no lack of effort!" Indeed, there has been no lack of effort!

Contrast this with the record of the West. We do not aim at domination, at hegemony, in any part of the world. Even against those who oppose and who would destroy our ideas, we plot no aggression. Of course, we are ready to fight the battle of ideas with all the vigour at our command, but we do not try to impose our system on others. We do not believe that force should be the final arbiter in human affairs. We threaten no-one. Indeed, the Alliance has given a solemn assurance to the world—none of our weapons will be used except in response to attack.

In talking to the Soviet Union, we find great difficulty in getting this message across. They judge us by their ambitions. They cannot conceive of a powerful nation not using its power for expansion or subversion, and yet they should remember that when, after the last War, the United States had a monopoly of nuclear weapons, she never once exploited her superiority. No country ever used such great power more responsibly or with such restraint. I wonder what would have befallen us in Western Europe and Great Britain if that monopoly had been in Soviet hands!

Mr Speaker [Tip O'Neill], wars are not caused by the build-up of weapons. They are caused when an aggressor believes he can achieve his objectives at an acceptable price. The war of 1939 was not caused by an arms race. It sprang from a tyrant's belief that other countries lacked the means and the will to resist him. Remember Bismarck 's phrase: "Do I want war? Of course not! I want victory!"

Our task is to see that potential aggressors, from whatever quarter, understand plainly that the capacity and the resolve of the West would deny them victory in war and that the price they would pay would be intolerable. That is the basis of deterrence and it is the same whatever the nature of the weapons, for let us never forget the horrors of conventional war and the hideous sacrifice of those who have suffered in them.

Our task is not only to prevent nuclear war, but to prevent conventional war as well.

No-one understood the importance of deterrence more clearly than Winston Churchill, when in his last speech to you he said: "Be careful above all things not to let go of the atomic weapon until you are sure and more than sure that other means of preserving peace are in your hands!" Thirty-three years on, those weapons are still keeping the peace, but since then technology has moved on and if we are to maintain deterrence—as we must—it is essential that our research and capacity do not fall behind the work being done by the Soviet Union. That is why I firmly support President Reagan 's decision to pursue research into defence against ballistic nuclear missiles—the Strategic Defence Initiative. Indeed, I hope that our own scientists will share in this research.

United States and the Soviet Union are both signatories to the 1972 Anti-Ballistic Missile Treaty, a treaty without any terminal date. Nothing in that treaty precludes research, but should that research—on either side—lead to the possible deployment of new defence systems, that would be a matter for negotiation under the treaty.

Mr Speaker, despite our differences with the Soviet Union, we have to talk with them, for we have one overriding interest in common—that never again should there be a conflict between our peoples. We hope too that we can achieve security with far fewer weapons than we have today and at lower cost, and thanks to the skilful diplomacy of Secretary Shultz, negotiations on arms control open in Geneva on the 12th March. They will be of immense importance to millions. They will be intricate, complex and demanding, and we should not expect too much too soon.

We must recognise that we have faced a Soviet political offensive designed to sow differences among us; calculated to create infirmity of purpose; to impair resolve, and even to arouse fear in the hearts of our people.

Hope is such a precious commodity in the world today, but some attempted to buy it at too high a price. We shall have to resist the muddled arguments of those who have been induced to believe that Russia's intentions are benign and that ours are suspect, or who would have us simply give up our defences in the hope that where we led others would follow. As we learned cruelly in the 1930s, from good intentions can come tragic results!

Let us be under no illusions. It is our strength and not their goodwill that has brought the Soviet Union to the negotiating table in Geneva.

Mr Speaker, we know that our alliance—if it holds firm—cannot be defeated, but it could be outflanked. It is among the unfree and the underfed that subversion takes root. As Ethiopia demonstrated, those people get precious little help from the Soviet Union and its allies. The weapons which they pour in bring neither help nor hope to the hungry. It is the West which heard their cries; it is the West which responded massively to the heart-rending starvation in Africa; it is the West which has made a unique contribution to the uplifting of hundreds of millions of people from poverty, illiteracy and disease.

But the problems of the Third World are not only those of famine. They face also a mounting burden of debt, falling prices for primary products, protectionism by the industrialised countries. Some of the remedies are in the hands of the developing countries themselves. They can open their markets to productive investment; they can pursue responsible policies of economic adjustment. We should respect the courage and resolve with which so many of them have tackled their special problems, but we also have a duty to help.

How can we help? First and most important, by keeping our markets open to them. Protectionism is a danger to all our trading partnerships and for many countries trade is even more important than aid. And so, we in Britain support President Reagan 's call for a new GATT round.

The current strength of the dollar, which is causing so much difficulty for some of your industries, creates obvious pressures for special cases, for new trade barriers to a free market. I am certain that your Administration is right to resist such pressures. To give in to them would betray the millions in the developing world, to say nothing of the strains on your other trading partners. The developing countries need our markets as we need theirs, and we cannot preach economic adjustment to them and refuse to practise it at home.

> If they do not wish to confer honour, I am the last person who would wish to receive it.
>
> *On Oxford University's decision not to give her an honorary degree, 1985*

And second, we must remember that the way in which we in the developed countries manage our economies determines whether the world's financial framework is stable; it determines the level of interest rates; it determines the amount of capital available for sound investment the world over; and it determines whether or not the poor countries can service their past loans, let alone compete for new ones. And those are the reasons why we support so strongly your efforts to reduce the budget deficit.

No other country in the world can be immune from its effects—such is the influence of the American economy on us all.

We in Europe have watched with admiration the burgeoning of this mighty American economy. There is a new mood in the United States. A visitor feels it at once. The resurgence of your self-confidence and your national pride is almost tangible. Now the sun is rising in the West. For many years, our vitality in Britain was blunted by excessive reliance on the State. Our industries were nationalised controlled and subsidised in a way that yours never were. We are having to recover the spirit of enterprise which you never lost. Many of the policies you are following are the policies we are following. You have brought inflation down. So have we. You have declared war on regulations and controls. So have we. Our Civil Service is now smaller than at any time since the War and controls on pay, prices, dividends, foreign exchange, all are gone.

You have encouraged small business—so often the source of tomorrow's jobs. So have we. But above all, we are carrying out the largest programme of denationalisation in our history.

Just a few years ago, in Britain, privatisation was thought to be a pipe dream. Now it is a reality and a popular one. Our latest success was the sale of British Telecommunications. It was the largest share issue ever to be brought to the market on either side of the Atlantic—some 2 million people bought shares.

Members of Congress, that is what capitalism is—a system which brings wealth to the many and not just to the few.

The United Kingdom economy is in its fourth year of recovery. Slower than yours, but positive recovery. We have not yet shared your success in bringing down unemployment, although we are creating many new jobs, but output, investment and standard of living are all at record levels and profits are well up. And the pound? It is too low! For whatever the proper international level of sterling, it is a marvellous time for Americans not only to visit Britain but to invest with her and many are!

America is by far the largest direct investor in Britain and I am delighted to say that Britain is the largest direct investor in the United States.

The British economy has an underlying strength and like you, we use our strength and resolve to carry out our duties to our allies and to the wider world.

We were the first country to station Cruise missiles on our territory. Britain led the rest. In proportion to our population, we station the same number of troops as you in Germany. In Central America, we keep troops stationed in Belize at that government's request. That is our contribution to sustaining democracy in a part of the world so vital to the United States. We have troops in Cyprus and in the South Atlantic and at your request a small force in Sinai, and British servicemen are now on loan to some thirty foreign countries. We are alongside you in Beirut; we work with you in the Atlantic and in the Indian Ocean; our navy is on duty across the world. Mr Speaker, Britain meets her responsibilities in the defence of freedom throughout the world and she will go on doing so.

Members of Congress, closer to home there is a threat to freedom both savage and insiduous. Both our countries have suffered at the hands of terrorists. We have both lost some of our best young lives and I have lost some close and dear friends. Free, strong, democratic societies will not be driven by gunmen to abandon freedom or democracy. The problems of the Middle East will not be solved by the cold blooded murder of American servicemen in Lebanon, nor by the murder of American civilians on a hi-jacked aircraft. Nor will the problems of Northern Ireland be solved by the assassin's gun or bomb.

Garret FitzGerald and I—and our respective governments—are united in condemning terrorism. We recognise the differing traditions and identities of the two parts of the community of Northern Ireland—the Nationalist and the Unionist. We seek a political way forward acceptable to them both, which respects them both. So long as the majority of people of Northern Ireland wish to remain part of the United Kingdom, their wishes will be respected. If ever there were to be a majority in favour of change, then I believe that our Parliament would respond accordingly, for that is the principle of consent enshrined in your constitution and in an essential part of ours.

There is no disagreement on this principle between the United Kingdom Government and the Government of the Republic of Ireland. Indeed, the four constitutional nationalist parties of Ireland, north and south, who came together to issue the New Ireland Forum Report, made clear that any new arrangements could only come about by consent, and I welcome too their outright condemnation and total rejection of terrorism and all its works.

Be under no illusions about the Provisional IRA. They terrorise their own communities. They are the enemies of democracy and of freedom too. Don't just take my word for it. Ask the Government of the Irish Republic, where it is an offence even to belong to that organisation—as indeed it also is in Northern Ireland.

I recognise and appreciate the efforts which have been made

by the Administration and Congress alike to bring home this message to American citizens who may be misled into making contributions to seemingly innocuous groups. The fact is that money is used to buy the deaths of Irishmen north and south of the border and 70% of those killed by the IRA are Irishmen—and that money buys the killing and wounding even of American citizens visiting our country.

Garret FitzGerald —and I salute him for the very brave thing he did yesterday in passing a special law to see that money did not get to the IRA— Garret FitzGerald and I will continue to consult together in the quest for stability and peace in Northern Ireland and we hope we will have your continued support for our joint efforts to find a way forward.

Distinguished Members of Congress, our two countries have a common heritage as well as a common language. It is no mere figure of speech to say that many of your most enduring traditions—representative government, habeas corpus, trial by jury, a system of constitutional checks and balances—stem from our own small islands. But they are as much your lawful inheritance as ours. You did not borrow these traditions—you took them with you, because they were already your own.

Human progress is not automatic. Civilisation has its ebbs and flows, but if we look at the history of the last five hundred years, whether in the field of art, science, technology, religious tolerance or in the practise of politics, the conscious inspiration of it all has been the belief and practise of freedom under law; freedom disciplined by morality, under the law perceived to be just.

I cannot conclude this address without recalling words made immortal by your great President Abraham Lincoln in his second Inaugural Address, when he looked beyond an age when men fought and strove towards a more peaceful future.

"With malice towards none, with charity for all, with firmness in the right that God gives us to see the right. Let us strive on to finish the work we are in, to do all which may achieve and cherish a just and lasting peace among ourselves and with all nations!"

Members of Congress, may our two kindred nations go forward together sharing Lincoln 's vision, firm of purpose, strong in faith, warm of heart, as we approach the third millenium of the Christian era.

Mr Speaker, thank you!

INTERVIEW WITH DR MIRIAM STOPPARD (EXTRACTS), FOR YORKSHIRE TV'S *WOMAN TO WOMAN*

2 October 1985

Dr Stoppard: Do you think that your upbringing prepared you for the kind of life that you have to lead?

Margaret Thatcher: All my upbringing was to instil into both my sister and I a fantastic sense of duty, a great sense of whatever you do you are personally responsible for it. You do not blame society. Society is not anyone. You are personally responsible and just remember that you live among a whole lot of people and you must do things for them, and you must make up your own mind. That was very very strong, very strong. I remember my father sometimes saying to me if I said: "Oh so and so is doing something; can't I do it too?" You know, children do not like to be different. "You make up your own mind what you are going to do, never because someone else is doing it!" and he was always very stern about that. It stood one in good stead.

DS: You have referred to the importance of your upbringing, to your politics and your philosophy. Can you tell me a little bit about your home? What was it like?

MT: Well, home really was very small and we had no mod cons and I remember having a dream that the one thing I really wanted was to live in a nice house, you know, a house with more things than we had.

DS: When you say "no mod cons" what do you mean?

MT: We had not got hot water. We only had a cold water tap. We had to heat all the hot water in a copper. There was an outside toilet. So when people tell me about these things, I know about them, but everything was absolutely clean, bright as a new pin and we were taught cleanliness was next to godliness, and yes, I often used to get down and polish the floor. We had lino on the floor, because both the floor and the old-fashioned mahogany furniture had to be clean. It was absolutely imperative and yes, everything had to be washed and washed and washed again. And we did a bake twice a week. My mother was very busy. This is why I learned to be busy. And my father was very busy. We used every hour of every day. We used to bake twice a week, a big bake, twice a week.

DS: What did you actually do when you baked?

MT: Baking, you baked your own bread, you baked your own pastry, you did quite a lot of steam puddings, you would do quite a number of pies; you would always bottle fruit; you would do about twenty Christmas puddings just before Christmas and they would last you until Easter, you know, one or two a week. Oh yes, we had no such thing as a refrigerator. I only knew one person in our circle who had a refrigerator. We had no such thing as a vacuum cleaner—dustpan and brush all the time. No such things as sprays in those days, no hard polishing, but cleanliness was vital. Washday Monday, ironing Tuesday. Washday, no washing machine. Washed it in a great big dolly tub with a dolly and a great big mangle and then everything was very nicely mangled. A great big ironing day Tuesday, and so one was brought up really in a very regular way and my mother did all of that. She made our clothes. We would paint and redecorate our own rooms and she would work in the shop, and I was always used to being in and out of the shop, so that is where I got used to talking to almost anyone and everyone.

But I was used to my mother working hard and of course, she took over when my father went out to do voluntary things, and we did. We were very prominent in the church. We did things for the church; we did things for National Savings; we did things for what in those days was called the League of Pity … these days it is the NSPCC. You were taught to take part. You were part of something and you were taught to take part. And whenever we did a bake, then we always took out either a few loaves or some home-made cakes for someone who was not well. That was just part of doing the ordinary bake.

> We must try to find ways to starve the terrorist or the hijacker of the oxygen of publicity on which they depend.
>
> *Speech to the American Bar Association, 15 July 1985*

DS: Can you tell me a little bit about your father?

MT: My father left school when he was 13... 12, 13...he really was very bright. In these days, he would gone to university, but in those days there weren't the opportunities and he went to work in a local grocer's shop and then he got a chance to better himself as you referred to in those days, and he came to Grantham because he was born in Northamptonshire, and worked in a grocer's shop that was still there in my time. And I remember him telling me he earned 14 shillings a week and 12 shillings went to digs, the cost of digs; the next priority was one shilling to be saved, and then you spent the next shilling. But note, one shilling had to be saved. You did not save what you have got left; there was a priority to save.

And then he saved and saved, and then my mother was a dressmaker and she saved and saved, and gradually they bought their own grocery business and I was born, and in those days you did not always go into hospital to be born. So I was born at home, and do you know, when I became Prime Minister, I had a lovely letter, right out of the blue, and it started off: "I have perhaps a special reason to write to you and perhaps more right than almost anyone else, because I delivered you when you were born." Wasn't that marvellous?

DS: How extraordinary!

MT: Wasn't that marvellous?

DS: Have you met the lady?

MT: The gentleman was Dr Tate. I think he is no longer with us, but I was so pleased to receive this letter. Activity always and we worked. My father read a great deal and therefore we read. Every Saturday, I used to go up to the public library, every Saturday morning, to get two books. One would be about the current affairs of the day. It might have been a biography, it might have been about politics; and one would have been perhaps a novel for my mother; and we always read those books, as I got older. We read the books and we always talked about them, every single Saturday, and the librarian knew I would come and say: "Oh I have saved this for your father and you to read!"

In those days, you know, the shop was open until 9 o'clock on a Saturday night, 8 o'clock on Friday night, and people would come in, and a grocer's shop was not just a place where you bought groceries. You talked. And so we talked about the affairs of the day and I can remember talking about the rise of Hitler and how worrying it was. Now, this is in a grocer's shop in a small town and when I hear politicians saying people will not understand that, I say: "Don't you believe it!" We understood it all and we talked about it. So really it was the most fantastic upbringing.

I was the youngest and I loved talking to people about things which were the important matters of the day. Yes, we did talk about the terrible plight of people who were unemployed. Of course, some of them were customers to our shop. We knew some of them. We all helped one another in those days. Life was not something we did not know about. We were right in it.

DS: Can I just go back to your father again, because he was a strong influence on your life. Can you tell me any kind of examples that he set you, lessons that you remember? You have already mentioned a few, but do you have other things that he impressed on you?

MT: I can remember some incidents really of how practical he was. First, when it came into the local council, whether the parks should be open on Sunday for swimming and for tennis. Now, he felt very strongly that you ought not to do those things on Sunday, and I think he voted against it. But then, along came war and we had a lot of people stationed in Grantham, a lot of Air Force men were stationed near Grantham and a lot of soldiers, and I can remember my father saying: "Now, I am going to take a different view. Those people must not on Sunday just walk around and have nothing to do. Yes, the swimming pool must be open. Yes, the tennis courts must be open. Yes, the cinema must be open. Yes, we must have canteens and places open for them on Sunday to come to and we must run some of the canteens for them." And it was really astonishing that he could look at things and say: "Look! It is the lesser of two problems, that they have somewhere to go. No, I do not approve of people doing these things on Sunday, but nevertheless they must have something to do and it is better that they are able to do those things!" And it really was a very good practical lesson. His principles did not change at all. I mean, we did sew on Sundays, but there were playing cards in our house. You would never have played rummy or anything like that on a Sunday. But things have changed tremendously. You would never have done that.

DS: Where do you think your father got his ideas from?

MT: Well, he was brought up very much in a family. They all very much went to church and we went to church, and he was a local preacher and I have still got some of the notes that he made in making up sermons.

He was a very staunch believer in Methodism; a very staunch believer in John Wesley and I knew some of the big names of those times: Leslie Weatherhead, Donald Soper; these were common names to me and we met some of them.

I knew about overseas missions because we used to have some of the overseas missionaries from Africa coming and talking to us about it. We lived an astonishingly international life for people in a small town, but if you believe in things, you do. I mean, just look now. You have Oxfam, you have Christian Aid. You also have overseas missions. But this was all a part of our life.

We were also a very musical family and we loved the hymns of John and Charles Wesley. We also had oratorios in our church. Music is a fantastic part of Methodism. And so we had the great big oratorios which we all practised for; and then we would get the big singers coming down and they would stay, because you could not afford to put them up in a hotel, with members of the congregation, and so we all met them.

DS: What were, though, some of the faults that he criticised? What did he not like to see in other people?

MT: Well, you always had to stand up for what you believed in. This was the most important thing. You did not compromise. You stood up for what you believed in and you decided what you believed in.

He was always very strong, I remember, on one thing: if you thought something was wrong or people were not having a fair deal—I remember him saying to me: "It is not enough! You do not get up in the market place and make a speech about it. That is not carrying out your responsibility. That is running away from your responsibility. That is running away from your responsibility. The question is: what are you prepared yourself to do about it?" So you can imagine some of the arguments we used to have between those people on the council who were of a different political complexion from us.

That was it. If you feel strongly about something, do not go and wave a banner to protest. That is not enough. You do something about it yourself.

DS: Thank you. What good qualities do you think you inherited or learned from him?

MT: I suppose this kind of integrity. You first sort out what you believe in. You then apply it. You then must argue your case, but you do not say: "Well I am going to do it because someone else did it!" and always you do not compromise on things that matter. That is something you never compromise on; other things you do.

Sometimes I am called inflexible. I am inflexible about certain things. You are inflexible in defence of freedom. You are inflexible that the rule of law must be applied; otherwise there is chaos or anarchy. You help the police, because the police cannot do their job unless they get back-up. We ... demonstrate. You do not strike. You discuss things. You pay your tax on time, and so on. Because this is how society is run. Very ordinary people like us made their contribution by living up to certain standards and doing certain things and you always always lend a hand to someone who needs it. You always are first to go and help, and you are always prepared to get involved. I mean, if by any chance there an accident...I can remember seeing an accident happen…we lived on cross-roads...a motor accident...yes, you must be prepared to go and give evidence as a witness.

You see, so many people these days say: "Oh, I did not want to get involved!" and do you know, that is how you miss so many things. If you do not get involved, well you are not really doing your duty.

DS: Do you think you inherited any of his faults?

MT: I suppose I have a lot of faults. We all have. I think I inherited so much that was good from him. The other thing is, my goodness me, you never buy anything you cannot afford to buy, never. You save up for it first. If you get yourself into debt you never get yourself out of it.

I will tell you, you learn an awful lot in a shop, particularly a shop which ran accounts. You would see some people get themselves into debt and the worst thing is to get yourself into debt with something you have eaten. You know, never get yourself into debt with something that has disappeared, and sometimes you would find people who could not pay their bills. I'll tell you who always paid cash on the nail. It was the old-age pensioners, because they never had enough to get into debt with. You know, if they got into debt they would not have enough to get out of it, and they were some of the best managers. They could make ten shillings a week, it was then, stretch further than anyone else, and they would never never get behind. So you learned you have a duty to be a good manager. Some housewives are good managers, some not, but you live according to your means.

Many many is the time I can remember saying, when I said: "Oh my friends have got more," "Well we are not situated like that!" One kicked against it, of course one kicked against it. They had more things than we did. Of course one kicked against it but when you grow up yourself and have a family and your children want things that others have, I can still hear my mother: "Well we are not situated like that!"

Or when you went out to buy something and you were going to actually have new covers for the settee. That was a great event; to have new covers for a settee was a great expenditure and a great event, so you went out to choose them, and you chose something that looked really rather lovely, something light with flowers on. My mother: "That is not serviceable!" And how I longed for the time when I could buy things that were not serviceable! I find myself now thinking, when I buy new covers, goodness me that will show the dirt too much. You know, you have had just exactly the same things.

DS: Reaction, yes. Did your father teach you to argue?

MT: Oh we did argue. This was the great thing. You see television—we are on television now—gives you fantastic opportunities, but it stops so much. So often I think that people sit their children in front of television when they come home from school and they have got to get them a meal and the telephone is going and then you have got to get supper and you do not talk to them. Do you know the most important thing with a family is to have time for them, to talk to them, to listen to their problems. It is not money. Do you know, people think money will solve things; it will not. It is time. It is interest. It is letting them know that they matter; that they matter more than anything else. We mattered more than anything else in the world really to my father. My children matter more than anything else to me. But they always had time, however busy.

We learn things from talking to others, but we discussed the things of the day and, as I say, we always had these books and we talked about things. So I was a natural debater at school. The common arguments were natural and we always used to listen to talks on the radio. Sunday night, after the 9 o'clock news, throughout all wartime, there were talks given at 9.15. A.P. Herbert gave some talks, J.B. Priestley gave talks; there was a man called Quentin Reynolds gave talks and took Hitler's original name and called him Mr Schicklgruber; and we used to listen to these, and then [Winston Churchill] Winston sometimes would give talks and we used to talk about them, because our greatest pleasure then, and it still is now, was to have to people in to supper on Sunday evening after chapel. People came in to supper or we went out to supper. So yes, we talked and we talked across generations and one of the dangers, I think, today is that young people talk only in their age group. You talk to your fellow pupils. You do not talk so much to an older generation. Of course, grannies lived with us in those days and there used to be other relatives sometimes about. Grannies lived with us and grannies had time.

I can remember every evening, granny always used to put us to bed. My mother was busy. And do you know, one did not want so much stories. I always used to say to granny: "What happened when you were a girl?" and she would tell us. You know, the visit to the baker, of the carts that went round in the streets drawn by horses and there were still some; and of the great events of the time and how they heard about them. And you heard them over and over and over again.

DS: In your house, how lively was the discussion? Did you actually argue with your father? Did you stand up for yourself?

MT: Oh yes. Oh yes, we argued and we were taught to argue. This was part of it. Yes. Never forget you must make up your own mind. You must learn to examine things; you must learn to think about them. Oh yes, we were taught to argue, and we did. Sometimes it finished up with: "Well, you will learn!" and that is the worst thing you can ever say to a child because you feel very resentful then, and occasionally you find yourself saying them to your own children. "Well I cannot quite explain to you but you will learn!" "Why do I have to be in so early at night? Other people don't!" "Well it is better that you should!" "Well why is it better that you should?" "Well you will learn!" Of course, I sometimes wish now that parents would be a little bit more careful about what time their children came in, because there are so many more dangers about now. We were protected from them by parents who said: "Well now, who are you going out with and where are you going?" and you used to kick against it. You used to resent it. It was for your protection, and we did not realise it then.

DS: You are very nationalistic I suppose. You are very proud ...

MT: Very patriotic.

DS: You were a patriotic family, were you?

MT: Immensely patriotic, but so were the people...look, we were patriotic. Everyone was patriotic. It did not matter how little you had.

DS: During war-time ...

MT: No, no. One of the first things I remember was the great Silver Jubilee of 1935. The Silver Jubilee of King George V and Queen Mary and our town was decorated with blue and yellow streamers, which was the colour of our town, and with red, white and blue, and we all listened in to the great service at St. Paul's. We heard the great commentaries of the great things going to St. Paul's. Everyone took part, and there was a great bonfire, and I remember a great occasion, because who should come to our town but a film star. Now this was quite something. A film star who was called Carl Brisson—I remember it to this day—and he knew Jack Buchanan. Carl Brisson, and we all gathered round listening and talking to a film star, and my father was on the council so we went in and we were lucky enough to meet him. We just listened to his experiences and then we went up and we lit the bonfire. Just the same when our Queen had her jubilee and we lit the bonfire. But it was everyone together.

You see, in a small town there were always things like that. There were sports among all the schools on the playing fields and you all went together. And I remember that our job, our little primary school, Huntingtower Primary School—and I still have letters from pupils who were with me—was to form the M of the Grantham. One school did the G, another did the R; we did the M, and we had to get it absolutely right, and we rehearsed.

But you see, there were always things going on, always things, so we were never bored.

Oh, do you know, I am so glad I was brought up that way. It

is a much more wholesome upbringing. You know, you were not a spectator society; you were doers. You took part and you were a part of.

I have always hoped that I gave my children as much as my parents gave me in their time and in what was right and what was wrong, and that you must go out and do something yourself if you believe in something, and always to involve people.

DS: Do you find a natural bent always to do something for your country as well because of this kind of early upbringing you had when you were so proud?

MT: Oh yes, yes. We were so proud of our country. We really were and we knew about Canada, we knew about Australia, and we knew about South Africa, we knew about New Zealand and we knew about India. I had an ambition as a child. I told you all the missionaries used to come and people used to come from India. I had an ambition. I wanted to be part of the Indian Civil Service, because our Civil Service was the best in the world.

Now, we were brought up that Britain was the best in the world because she had standards of honesty and integrity and law. The best in the world and the Indian Civil Service was part of our Civil Service and it was the best in the world and it was to do things for the Indians and it was to help them. I said: "I think, Daddy, if I manage to get to university"—if, it was a fantastic privilege in those days, a fantastic privilege—"If I manage to get to university, I think I'd like to go in the Indian Civil Service, because I will be able to do something for them!" I remember my father saying—this was before the War—"I do not think there will be one by the time you are grown up."

DS: Really?

MT: Wasn't that prophetic? But you see he was well in … don't you find you give your own children dubellip; try to give your own children what you have not had. For us, it was rather a sin to enjoy yourself by entertainment. Do you see what I mean? Life was not to enjoy yourself. Life was to work and do things. My father had not had an education because as I told you, he had to go out early, but he was the best-read man I ever knew. We used to have something in our house called the "Hibbert Journal", a very very learned journal. I used to read it. So he tried to give me all the education we could possibly have.

I was taught to play the piano at the age of 5 because I was musical and therefore I must be given every opportunity and they sacrificed to get me the best teacher. Tell you something else! Do you know at five I remember going with my music case to my first music teacher, Miss Tatham ... a little person ... and I went and I looked and I could read. I looked at the piano and on the piano was the name "Made by J. Roberts". I said: "That is my great uncle" and it was. My great uncle in Northamptonshire made his living by making pianos and he had got his own business and made his name so I started to learn to play the piano on a piano made by my great uncle. How did we get here?

My father gave me all the education in the world, really self-education. When a string quartet came to Grantham we went to listen to it; when a singer came to Grantham we went to listen to it. There were current affairs lectures, university extensions on a Thursday night. He took me. We asked questions; we learned to listen. He gave me the education ... self-education ... he had never had.

I tried to give my children, as well as the education, a little more amusement, a little bit more to play every sport so that everywhere they went they could play sports. We were notallowed to go to theatre very much. Well, that was one's upbringing.

DS: Can I just talk about your mother for a minute?

MT: Mother was marvellous, yes, go on. She was very practical. You see, daddy taught me...we discussed with my father...I have always thought...again, there is a poem of Kipling called "The

Mary and the Martha", based on Christianity. Mary was the one who listened at the feet of Jesus and always was interested in what was going on and Martha was the one who always went "Now is there enough to eat?" "Do you want fresh clothes?" "Would you like to lie down?" "Would you like to wash?" This was my mother. Everything in the house, everything practical, and she was. I still retain it, because I can still make clothes and when we moved to a house, we had not very much money, when we moved to a big house and I started to cover the things which gave me enormous pleasure.

But she was very very practical and we gained a lot from her, but she worked. You say I work. I do, but so did my mother. We all worked.

DS: The kind of education that your father was giving you, did she take an equal part in that?

MT: No, not so much. Mummy did not get involved in the arguments. She had probably gone out in the kitchen to get the supper ready, so that when we had finished we had the supper. But she did play the piano and she had quite a good contralto voice, and my father had a very good bass voice, and so all the songs, you know "Just a Song at Twilight" I knew…"My Sweet Little Alice Blue Gown"…all the old-age pensioners will tell you. and we used to go out sometimes in concert parties...Again in war-time…to sing. You took part.

DS: What example did your mother set you, as opposed to your father?

MT: Oh Mummy backed up Daddy in everything as far as you do what is right. She was terribly proud. I mean, she would just say to me sometimes: "Your father had a very difficult day in council standing up for his principles!" This again I knew. And he was Chairman of the Finance Committee and my goodness our town never got into debt. My goodness me, every money was spent carefully, nothing spent extravagantly. He was on the council for such a long time and eventually became an alderman. We do not have aldermen now. And eventually, when the political complexion changed they threw him off being an alderman…it was such a tragedy.

DS: Did your mother serve to protect him though?

MT: Yes. He always got maximum support from his family. I remember when my father was turned off that council making a speech for the last time, very emotional: "In honour, I took up this gown; in honour, I lay it down!" That is how he felt.

DS: When you were 17/18 you were preparing to go to Oxford, you were going to leave your home behind. Did you as early as that have a very clear view that politics was what you wanted to do?

MT: No, because it was not possible in those days. You remember Members of Parliament were not paid very much. I was also going to have to earn my own living and so it just did not open up as a possibility. It was not really until Members of Parliament got enough to keep them that I could possibly have thought of becoming an MP. Although I remember vividly on one occasion when we were at university and home for the Christmas Recess and one of my school-friends was also at Oxford and we had a party in her house and after the party—you know, that stage when you always go into the kitchen and sit down and just talk about things—I remember one person, having been talking to me about politics, just saying: "What you would really like to do is be an MP, wouldn't you?" and I said "Yes, but I do not know whether it is possible!" But that was the first time, and I can remember it vividly. It sort of clicked immediately. Yes, that is what I would really like to do. But even then, I did not think it was possible, because I was just going to have to earn my own living and there was not enough in politics in those days. I think it was paid £400 a year and for that all your expenses had to be paid out and it was not possible.

DS: But you did put a lot of energy, didn't you, into the work?

MT: Yes, a fantastic amount, because I was fascinated with it. People say: "Are you interested in politics?" "Were you interested in politics then?" I was more than interested in it. It was a kind of fascination and it was partly because we had done all of this reading and discussing, partly because they were cataclysmic times with the rise of Hitler and that war and how could it be that having learned so much from history, a tyrant had still come to power and we still had to enter upon war to beat him? So it was a total fascination. I could not get away from it. That is much more the real thing.

DS: Did you have a clear idea of the sort of man that you wanted to marry?

MT: No, no. I wonder if one ever does or is it just that it is so long ago? A clear idea. No, don't you meet someone and fall in love with them? I do not think there is any point in going round with a specification, six feet two inches tall, nice dark curly hair, brown velvet voice, kind, tall, lean, athletic. That is no good. It is the person, the personality you fall in love with. Specification is no good.

DS: You say "fall in love with". Was it love at first sight?

MT: No, no, no. Denis and I knew one another a very long time I met him in my political work. I can tell you the exact night. I was adopted as a candidate for Dartford when I was 23, they having met me at the party conference, a friend of mine said to the Chairman of Dartford: "If you are seeking a candidate, would you consider a woman?" "Oh no, no, no. A woman would not do for Dartford at all!" "Well, would you meet her?" and so I was met at the party conference there on Llandudno pier and the long and short of it is that I went down, along with about twenty others, and I was chosen, and I was adopted. There was a meeting and I had to get back to London from the meeting and so I had supper with some of the helpers and they also had a man called Denis Thatcher to supper who had a business locally and who had a car and who would drive me back to London. That is how I met him, but it was three years before we decided to get married. So it was very much a communality of interests and was something that grew.

DS: Do you think he was rather unusual in taking you on?

MT: Perhaps very brave.

DS: It was kind of new to have a woman doing all those things and a lot of men said: "Oh, we want the little woman to stay at home!" so I suppose he was.

MT: I think perhaps in those times he was. Do not forget we had come through a war-time period when women did a lot, and then you tended to get a reaction after the war that women should go home and do more in the home. But there had been tremendous periods when women had been able to do both. Do not forget a lot of women had to go out to work really as part of the family income. There were the mill girls in Lancashire. They did a lot of the factory work.

So yes, in one way it was unusual, but in another way it was very much part of life. But it was unusual, I think, for a professional man with women who also had a profession, to do it.

DS: Because of the public attendance that your appearance gets—your hair, your clothes—do you ever get annoyed that that is something you have to attend to as well really which a man would not, when you have to get on with running the country?

MT: Again, it has just become part of the job, although I think men should sometimes give a little bit of attention to theirs, you know. I can remember, there have been occasions, when perhaps one or two of our people have ... quite a long time ago I had to go to great big international exhibitions and I tell you something one learns in politics. The Russians, when they go out always come out in the most beautifully tailored suits and there is very considerable criticism if our men politicians are not in nicely tailored suits, nice ties, nice shirts. And they should, because they are representing their country. So theirs matters to me. Once you are representing your country it matters.

Now it has just become second nature. Yes, you do have to watch. That is why I told you this radar bowl of a hat was not really quite right. But what you do is decide the clothes in which you are comfortable. You must be comfortable. You are going to a great occasion. It must be a style that you are comfortable in. Must be a fabric that you are comfortable in, that hangs well, and you must know that you look appropriate for the occasion. Never flashy, just appropriate, well-tailored, and it is not unfeminine to be well-tailored. Indeed, it often perhaps concentrates on what you are going to say if you have got well-tailored things on because people no longer look at your clothes.

DS: Do you ever find that makes it difficult for you then, that maybe you do have an emotional response to a situation, maybe it might even be such that you want to cry, but you feel that because you are a woman in a man's world you just cannot do that, you have got to be stiffer than the stiffest upper lip?

MT: While there is a crisis on you will get on with it. Haven't you always noticed, no matter what the crisis, you can cope while it is on. You can keep going day and night and day and night. You can keep going through big conferences even if there is a crisis. It is when it is over that all of a sudden you feel tired and feel "Oh, goodness me!" but you can cope during a crisis.

I have often said it is the ordinary daily load which in a way can take more out of you than a crisis because in a crisis the adrenalin flows and the test is whether you can take the ordinary daily responsibility and that in the end is what you have to do here, and I am always very pleased when people say to me that "there have been many many men who have come in and they have looked a bit more worn and torn after six years than you do!" and again, I think, well, if you have been looking after children when you are young and keeping a house going and everything else you do just keep going. And there is a difference between men and women in that way. Just be proud of it.

DS: You did say that there are moments when the crisis is over or when the work has taken its toll that you do think "Oh, I am very tired!" What do you do in those situations?

MT: Well you just come in and you just flop down and you just talk to your family. When Falklands was over, never will I forget that night. You did not realise the enormity of the burden until it was over.

DS: One of your most famous sayings is that you thought there would never be a female prime minister in your time.

MT: That is quite right. I did. I could not see people choosing a woman Prime Minister, but you know, we talk far too much about labels. They never choose a man Prime Minister. They choose John Smith or Alfred Bloggins. They do not choose a woman Prime Minister. They choose a personality and I never thought I would have the opportunity, but I never thought I would have the opportunity to serve in a Cabinet. As I said originally, I never thought I would have the chance to be a Member of Parliament.

In life, you know, some people try to map out their lives. I can remember some of my young contemporaries at Oxford saying: "I am going to be Prime Minister!" That was the one thing I never said, because I did not think I would have the chance.

You just take what opportunities are available to you and grasp them with both hands.

REMARKS ON THE ANGLO IRISH AGREEMENT

Hillsborough Castle, Co. Down. 15th November 1985

Dr FitzGerald and I have today signed a serious and solemn agreement, which signifies the way ahead in relations between our two countries and towards peace and reconciliation in Northern Ireland.

The Agreement has three main elements:

a preamble which includes our total rejection of violence and our recognition of the validity of both traditions in Northern Ireland;

an article in which the two governments affirm that any change in the status of Northern Ireland would only come about with the consent of a majority of people of Northern Ireland, which recognises that the present wish of a majority is for no change and declares that if in the future a majority formally consent to a united Ireland, the two governments will support legislation accordingly; and the third element: articles establishing a new intergovernmental conference concerned both with Northern Ireland and with relations between the two parts of Ireland.

The Irish Republic will be able to put forward views and proposals in the conference on stated aspects of Northern Ireland affairs, and determined efforts will be made to resolve any differences.

We shall also be putting forward views, in particular on cross-border cooperation and security, but also on economic, social and cultural matters, including the enhancement of cross-border cooperation in combatting terrorism.

Full responsibility for the decisions and administration of government will remain with the United Kingdom north of the border and with the Republic south of the border.

The conference will be serviced by a secretariat on a continuing basis.

We have also issued today a communique on our meeting which says that the new intergovernmental conference will concentrate in its initial meetings on relations between the security forces and the minority community in Northern Ireland, on ways of improving security cooperation between the two governments, and on seeking measures which would underline the importance of public confidence in the administration of justice.

By promoting peace and stability and by enhancing our cooperation against terrorism, the agreement will bring benefits to all the people of Northern Ireland. I hope that it will also open the way for moves towards devolution in Northern Ireland.

On behalf of the United Kingdom, I went into this agreement because I was not prepared to tolerate a situation of continuing violence. I want to offer hope to young people particularly that the cycle of violence and conflict can be broken.

I believe in the Union and that it will last as long as the majority so wish. I point out that the legitimacy of the Unionist position has been recognised by the Republic in a formal international agreement.

Cooperation in the intergovernmental conference is a two-way street. We shall wish to pursue matters affecting the Republic in the interests of the people of Northern Ireland, for instance, improved security cooperation and economic cooperation. The spirit of the agreement is not one of each interfering in the other's affairs; it is of both sides working together on problems which affect both the North and the Republic.

The agreement is a positive incentive to devolve government in Northern Ireland, because if a system of devolved government acceptable to both communities can be devised, then the matters with which the developed government deals will be taken out of the hands of the intergovernmental conference. We shall be doing our utmost to achieve that devolved government.

To sum up: we entered into this agreement to defeat the men of violence and to bring peace and stability. We enter into this agreement in good faith. We shall do everything to make it succeed. Whether it works will depend also on the will of the people and I hope that they will seize the chance which the agreement gives. Indeed, we call on all people of good will to join us in building peace and stability in Northern Ireland.

SPEECH ON THE WESTLAND AFFAIR

House of Commons. 23rd January 1986

With permission, Mr Speaker, I wish to make a statement on the outcome of the inquiry into the disclosure of certain information in my hon. and learned Friend the Solicitor-General's letter of 6 January.

As the House knows, the chairman of Westland plc, Sir John Cuckney, wrote to me on 30 December 1985 asking whether Westland would no longer be considered a European company by the Government if a minority shareholding in the company were held by a major international group from a NATO country outside Europe.

This question was of fundamental importance to the company in making its decision as to what course it was best to follow in the interests of the company and its employees. It was therefore essential to be sure that my reply should be in no way misleading to anyone who might rely upon it in making commercial judgments and decisions.

The reply was accordingly considered among the Departments concerned, and the text of my letter of 1 January 1986 was agreed in detail by my right hon. and learned Friend the Secretary of State for Trade and Industry [Leon Brittan], my right hon. Friends the then Secretary of State for Defence [Michael Heseltine] and the Chief Secretary to the Treasury [John MacGregor], and finally by my hon. and learned Friend the Solicitor-General. My letter was made public.

Two days later, on 3 January, my right hon. Friend the then Secretary of State for Defence replied to a letter of the same date from Mr Horne of Lloyds Merchant Bank asking him a number of questions, covering some of the same ground as my own reply to Sir John Cuckney. The texts of the letters became public that same day.

My right hon. Friend's reply was not cleared or even discussed with the relevant Cabinet colleagues. Moreover, although the reply was also material to the commercial judgments and decisions that would have to be made, my hon. and learned Friend the Solicitor-General was not invited to scrutinise the letter before it was issued.

On the morning of 6 January, my hon. and learned Friend the Solicitor-General wrote to my right hon. Friend the then Secretary of State for Defence. He said—and I quote:

"It is foreseeable that your letter will be relied upon by the Westland Board and its shareholders.

Consistently with the advice I gave to the Prime Minister on 31 December, the Government in such circumstances is under a duty not to give information which is incomplete or inaccurate in any material particular."

The letter continued:

"On the basis of the information contained in the documents to which I have referred, which I emphasise are all that I have seen, the sentence in your letter to Mr Horne does in my opinion contain material inaccuracies in the respects I have mentioned, and I therefore must advise that you should write again to Mr Horne correcting the inaccuracies."

That is the end of the quotation.

I have quoted extensively from the letter which, as hon. Members will know, was published a week ago. As I have already indicated, it was especially important in this situation for statements made on behalf of the Government, on which commercial judgments might be based, to be accurate and in no way misleading.

That being so, it was a matter of duty that it should be made known publicly that there were thought to be material inaccuracies which needed to be corrected in the letter of my right hon. Friend. the Member for Henley (Mr Heseltine) of 3 January, which, as the House will recall, had already been made public. Moreover, it was urgent that it should become public knowledge before 4 pm that afternoon, 6 January, when Sir John Cuckney was due to hold a press conference to announce the Westland board's recommendation to shareholders of a revised proposal from the United Technologies Corporation-Fiat consortium.

These considerations were very much in the mind of my right hon. and learned Friend the Secretary of State for Trade and Industry when the copy of the Solicitor-General's letter was brought to his attention at about 1.30 pm that afternoon of 6 January. He took the view that the fact that the Solicitor-General had written to the then Secretary of State for Defence, and the opinion he had expressed, should be brought into the public domain as soon as possible. He asked his officials to discuss with my office whether the disclosure should be made, and, if so, whether it should be made from 10 Downing street, as he said he would prefer.

My right hon. and learned Friend made it clear that, subject to the agreement of my office, he was giving authority for the disclosure to be made from the Department of Trade and Industry, if it was not made from 10 Downing street. He expressed no view as to the form in which the disclosure should be made, though it was clear to all concerned that in the circumstances it was not possible to proceed by way of an agreed statement.

My office were accordingly approached. They did not seek my agreement: they considered—and they were right—that I should agree with my right hon. and learned Friend the Secretary of State for Trade and Industry that the fact that the then Defence Secretary's letter of 3 January was thought by the Solicitor-General to contain material inaccuracies which needed to be corrected should become public knowledge as soon as possible, and before Sir John Cuckney's press conference. It was accepted that the Department of Trade and Industry should disclose that fact and that, in view of the urgency of the matter, the disclosure should be made by means of a telephone communication to the Press Association. *[Interruption.]* Had I been consulted, I should have said that a different way must be found of making the relevant facts known.

The report finds, in the light of the evidence, that the Department of Trade and Industry acted in good faith in the knowledge that it had the authority of its Secretary of State and cover from my office for proceeding. An official of the Department accordingly told a representative of the Press Association of the letter by my hon. and learned Friend the Solicitor-General and material elements of what it said. The company was also informed. The information was on the Press Association tapes at 3.30 pm.

> Has he resigned or has he gone for a pee?
>
> *To Cabinet colleagues on Michael Heseltine's resignation, January 1986*

My right hon. and learned Friend the Secretary of State for Trade and Industry was, in my judgment, right in thinking that it was important that the possible existence of material inaccuracies in the letter of 3 January by the then Secretary of State for Defence should become a matter of public knowledge, if possible before Sir John Cuckney's press conference at 4 pm that day. In so far as what my office said to the Department of Trade and Industry was based on the belief that I should have taken that view, had I been consulted, it was right.

My right hon. and learned Friend the Attorney-General [Sir Michael Havers] has authorised me to inform the House that, having considered the report by the head of the Civil Service, and on the material before him, he has decided after consultation with, and with the full agreement of, the Director of Public Prosecutions and senior Treasury counsel, that there is no justification for the institution of proceedings under the Official Secrets Act 1911 in respect of any of the persons concerned in this matter.

In order that there should be no impediment to co-operation in the inquiry, my right hon. and learned Friend had authorised the head of the Civil Service to tell one of the officials concerned, whose testimony would be vital to the inquiry, that he had my right hon. and learned Friend's authority to say that, provided that he received full co-operation in his inquiry, the official concerned would not be prosecuted in respect of anything said during the course of the inquiry.

The head of the Civil Service did, indeed, receive full co-operation not only from that official but from all concerned. My right hon. and learned Friend tells me that he is satisfied that that in no way interfered with the course of justice: on the facts as disclosed in the inquiry there would have been no question of proceeding against the official concerned

SPEECH AT THE SIGNING OF THE CHANNEL TUNNEL FIXED LINK TREATY

Chapter House, Canterbury Cathedral. 12th February 1986

Mr President, Your Excellencies, Ladies and Gentlemen:

This is an historic occasion. Our meeting today and the signature of the Channel Fixed Link Treaty has brought to the brink of fruition a project that has challenged engineers, entrepreneurs and governments on both sides of the Channel for generations.

One could say that the first Channel Link Promoter was Napoleon Bonaparte. His engineers presented him, in 1802, with a plan involving two tunnels, a mid-channel artificial island, a paved roadway, ventilation shafts and oil lamps. This particular project, for reasons which are not entirely clear, did not enjoy the wholehearted support of the British Government. Indeed, I understand that there was some relief on their part when it was abandoned!

An illustrious predecessor of mine was also a Channel Link

supporter. Sir Winston Churchill, when he was First Lord of the Admiralty in 1914, wrote a paper indicating his support for a Channel tunnel, but only provided it came to surface half a mile from the English coast. He insisted that the remaining distance be covered by a bridge with a drawbridge in one of the spans. In times of tension, the lifting of the drawbridge, coupled with a warning to suspend traffic, would afford a time for complete security.

Times change and I shall not be asking the representatives of the Channel Tunnel Group and France Manche who are here today to include a similar device in their plans!

Mr President, I hope that after all these years the link will at last be built and that it will change the lives of people on both sides of the Channel.

When we met last month, on that magnificent day in Lille, attention was understandably focussed on the benefits the Link will bring to the people of Northern France. As we meet today, in this ancient city of Canterbury, in the very heart of the region of Britain most directly affected by the Link, I should like to address a few words to the people of Kent.

Many of you are concerned about the consequences the Link will have for the local environment and for employment in the area. Let me assure you the Government is alive to your concerns. Environmental impact is one of the factors which we took particularly into account in our selection of the Channel Tunnel Group Scheme, and we shall ensure that everything possible is done to mitigate the environmental consequences.

We are also determined to do whatever is necessary to improve the local road network, so that there can be rapid and uncongested access to the Link. We shall, for instance, look sympathetically at proposals for such help from the Kent County Council, and we shall ensure that there is the fullest consultation between the Government and Local Authorities.

I would urge the people of Kent, a number of whose elected representatives are in the audience today, to treat the Link as an opportunity; an opportunity that will bring long-term and lasting benefits—tourism, industry and jobs—to the region and to the United Kingdom as a whole.

Mr President, the Chapter House in which we now meet was once part of a great Benedictine monastery, revived and reorganised in the 11th century by Archbishop Lanfranc, the first and greatest of the Norman Archbishops of Canterbury.

Much of the work on the Cathedral, which you have just seen, was carried out by another Frenchman, William of Sens the most talented architect of his age.

> I always cheer up immensely if an attack is particularly wounding because I think, well, if they attack me personally it means they have not a single political argument left.
>
> *TV Interview for Italian Television, 1986*

The Cathedral itself was built of stone brought from France, from Caen in Normandy, and is to this day regularly restored with French stone.

Our surroundings are thus rich in associations with France, stretching back over centuries. What more fitting place could there be to sign this treaty, which takes those associations forward into the 21st Century?

(Now speaks in French—simultaneous translation follows.)

This treaty is an important event, not only for relations between our two countries, but also for the whole of Europe, and will open up a new chapter in industrial cooperation between France and Great Britain, based on private enterprise and the competence of our heads of industry and businesses, and this will also give a unique opportunity to our businessmen and finance in order to show what they can do. This endeavour will create jobs in the building industry and will stimulate the achievements and, what is perhaps the most important thing, this will in a way bear witness to the spirit of enterprise and invention of our own generation, and this will in fact demonstrate that we can be as bold as our predecessors when required to do so and this will encourage our successors to effort and creativity.

SPEECH TO THE 1986 CONSERVATIVE CENTRAL COUNCIL

Spa Pavilion, Felixstowe, 15th March 1986

Mr Chairman, we come to this conference confident in your support, confident in our policies, confident in the future of our country. Of course, there are the professional grumblers who will always complain whatever we do. And if they ever got to the Pearly Gates, they'd grumble there. Because the gates squeaked; or they weren't pearly enough. And St. Peter didn't bow low enough after all they'd done—or should I say, after all they had left undone.

Mr Chairman, if we let the grumblers have their way, we would be bending and turning with every twist in the opinion polls. That is not this Government's style, nor this Prime Minister's. Our style is to decide what is right for the country, not what is temporarily convenient. Applause dies with the day. Belief lives on. We look to the future, for we are more than a one generation society.

Soon we will enter our eighth year of Government. We are a free people: free to choose our way of life; free because of the rule of law. But that freedom can never be taken for granted. From one age to another, threats to its precious qualities come stealthily by different paths.

Seven years ago, that freedom was challenged by the Winter of Discontent. And the will of a Labour Government bowed to the might of the trade unions. More recently, it was challenged again by the miners' strike. But a Conservative Government stood firm.

This Government has, step by step, diminished the industrial and political power of centralised trade unionism and restored strength to the hands of their own members. That battle for freedom wasn't won by the faint hearts but by the stout hearts. There are some things on which you can never give way. Today, Mr Chairman, there is a whole new atmosphere in industrial relations.

There can be no better example than here in the Port of Felixstowe where we see trade unionists and employers equally committed to their enterprise. They know that if you work together, then the team can achieve great things. Pull apart and you perish. Pull together and you succeed.

Mr Chairman, a nation will not long remain free if its currency is debased. Money does not buy freedom; but misuse of money, the filching of its value by the State, can swiftly diminish freedom. We have restored honest money. And by so doing we have given more confidence to men and women that what they give to their work, they will harvest.

And we have recovered much of the freedom of the individual from the socialist concept of the corporate state. Not only in home-ownership, where the most remarkable increase has been among manual workers and among young people in their twenties.

We have also dismantled state industries and spread their ownership. In Jaguar, Cable and Wireless, Amersham, British Telecom, and many more such as National Freight. And I always like to see, on the National Freight vehicles, the slogan: "Now we're in the driving seat." Not the Government. Not the bureaucrats. Not the bosses. Not the militant unions. But the workers and management working together.

Seven years ago, who would have dared forecast such a transformation of Britain. This didn't come about because of consensus. It happened because we said: this we believe, this we will do. It's called leadership. Conservative policies are winning the day; and even the grudging support of a few politicians elsewhere.

Yet, at the time, they fought us tooth and nail. Today, they can see our success, and they want to claim it as their own. But does anyone seriously think that Conservative achievements would be safe in their hands? So I warn you:

—Don't take it for granted that inflation will stay low. If it weren't for the Tories, pensioners would have to watch out. Inflation destroys your savings.

—Don't take it for granted that mortgage interest relief will continue. If it weren't for the Tories, many young people wouldn't be able to buy their own home.

—Don't take it for granted that trade unionists will continue to have a vote in their union. If it weren't for the Tories, they wouldn't have one today.

—Don't take it for granted that you'll be allowed to keep all your shares. Nationalisation lies right at the heart of Labour's policy.

—And don't take it for granted that this country will always have the defences we need. If it weren't for the Tories, far from being defended, Britain would be defenceless against any nuclear power in the world.

—Don't take any of these things for granted, Mr Chairman. Conservative achievements are safe only in Conservative hands.

Now let's look ahead a little. There has been the odd report recently that Thatcherism has run its course, and is on its way out. As an informed source close to Downing Street, I have to report that those reports are eyewash. We're only just beginning. We've barely got past the stage of excavation, let alone of topping out!

You may feel that the first seven years of Conservative Government have produced some benefits for Britain. And so they have. But the next seven are going to produce more—many more. And the next seven after that, more still. Let me tell you why.

Conservatism is not some abstract theory. It's a crusade to put power in the hands of ordinary people. And a very popular crusade it is proving. Tenants are jumping at the opportunity to buy their own council houses.

Workers are jumping at the opportunity to buy shares in their own privatised companies. Trade unionists are jumping at the opportunity, which the ballot box now gives them, to decide "who rules" in their union. And the rest of Britain is looking on with approval. For popular capitalism is biting deep. It used to be Socialists who talked of crusades. Well, let them launch a new one on the old Socialist lines. What about a Socialist crusade to rehabilitate that old favourite, the municipal landlord, and to lure home owners back into becoming council tenants? Or a socialist crusade to re-nationalise Vickers, and take back the workers' shares. Or a Socialist crusade to abolish bothersome union ballots and get back to the good old days of Big Brother.

After all, these aims are the very heartbeat of Socialism. But you may have noticed how muted nowadays are the trumpets for such Socialist crusades. For popular capitalism, which is the economic expression of liberty, is proving a much more attractive means for diffusing power in our society.

> No one would remember the Good Samaritan if he'd only had good intentions. He had money as well.
>
> *1986*

Socialists cry "Power to the people", and raise the clenched fist as they say it. We all know what they really mean—power over people, power to the State. To us Conservatives, popular capitalism means what it says: power through ownership to the man and woman in the street, given confidently with an open hand. Mr Chairman, today the climate for British industry is better than it has been for 30 years.

Last year investment was at an all-time record of £60 billion—new roads, modern factories, the latest equipment. That augurs well for the future. Industry is more profitable than it has been for twenty-five years. Since 1980 productivity in manufacturing industry has risen faster than in France, faster than in Germany. And, for the last six years, Britain has had a balance of payments surplus.

This economic success story does not always get the credit it deserves. Some people carry British understatement and self-criticism too far. The renaissance of enterprise and the renewal of our national fabric often go unsung. Maybe we feel about our industry as we feel about our weather: it is never quite right, the prospects are too often cloudy or overcast. Yet it is our weather, about which we always complain, which gives us our green and pleasant land.

What is it that now gives us such optimism for the future? First, oil. Only a year ago a single barrel of oil cost around $25 to buy. Today it costs about $13. To read some reports you'd think we all ought to go into mourning to mark the death of expensive oil. Yes, of course, it will lose us some revenue and some exports. But all those who thought the oil price explosion of the 1970s did harm to our industry and slowed our growth rate were right. Falling oil prices are, on the whole, good news. There's more money to spend on other things. The spending power in the nation's pockets and purses is rising.

Industry's costs are being cut. All this is a bit like a tax cut, but one for which, alas, the Government cannot take credit. Last year's Central Council came just after the budget. This year it's 3 days before.

Can you hear me Nigel [Lawson]? Don't worry. I'm not going to give away any budget secrets.

Second, interest rates. In the last few weeks the cost of borrowing money in several major countries has fallen. That too is good for the world economy and helps our own companies trading overseas.

We are living at a time which calls for more partnership and co-operation, both between countries and between companies. We have to work together. Moreover, Britain receives a tidy income from our overseas investments—and will continue to do so long after North Sea Oil is a thing of the past.

Third, exchange rates. Every industrialist I speak to has a different view of the exchange rate he wants. Markets, not governments, set exchange rates; and it's just not possible to satisfy everyone all of the time. But the agreement reached last year between the five major industrial nations has contributed to a welcome change in the pattern of exchange rates.

And that benefits all of us—and brings great opportunities. But I must repeat my constant message to all industrialists. Exchange rates go up and down. Success comes from your own efforts and your own efficiency. Never rely on the exchange rate to beat your rivals.

Mr Chairman, I have already mentioned the reform of trade union law, privatisation, employee shareholdings, and lower inflation. And there have been a number of tax reforms. In this favourable climate new jobs are coming—700,000 in under 3 years—more than in any other country in Europe.

We need jobs in both manufacturing and services. What's the point of making a television set if there are no programmes to show on it? Who would want to buy a car if there were no garages to sell petrol and service it? What's the use of making radiators if there are no plumbers to install central heating?

We need a well-serviced economy, which buys British—because British is best. I recently held a meeting of businessmen at Number Ten, called "Better Made in Britain". The purpose was to see how British-made goods could win a bigger share of the home market and so create more jobs.

It's humbug to complain about unemployment if you drink French mineral water and drive an imported car. This Government is backing business with a dynamic policy for enterprise. We're training people in the skills they need—high technology, design, marketing and engineering.

We're strengthening competition and small business. We're battling for Britain in the export markets of the world. And we're going for more privatisation, less regulation and wider share ownership. And it's not only happening in Britain.

Privatisation is on the agenda in Turkey, Malaysia, Japan, Mexico and Canada. And China too is striving to create free enterprise. People are no longer worried about catching the British disease. They're queueing up to obtain the new British cure. Mr Chairman, we've done better for the health service than any previous government. I could reel off facts and figures to prove it.

I do so regularly in the House of Commons, although the Opposition try to stop me. That's because when they don't like the truth, they do everything they can to drown it. But there's something you must often have asked yourselves.

Why aren't we better at getting our excellent message across? This Government hasn't cut investment in health—we've increased it.

—Yes, over 40 major hospital schemes have already been completed.

—and yes, a further 150 of varying sizes are under way.

—yes, there are 11,500 new hospital beds; over 100 new X-ray departments; and nearly 200 new operating theatres.

—yes, there are more doctors, dentists and nurses.

—and yes, we can now treat more patients.

These are not just achievements of Government. We owe a debt to all those in the health and social services who look after others with such commitment and dedication. Yet, despite all these increases in the health service, people still talk of cuts, Why? We live in a television age—and television is selective.

One camera shot of a pretty nurse helping an elderly patient out of an empty hospital ward speaks louder than all the statistics in Whitehall and Westminster. Never mind that the hospital is being closed because it's out of date. Never mind that, a few miles away, a spanking new hospital is being opened—with brighter wards, better operating theatres and the very latest equipment.

In today's world, selective seeing is believing. And in today's world, television comes over as truth. I remember myself opening a beautiful new hospital. Virtually the only publicity was a demonstration outside—about cuts. And there's something else. Medical science is advancing so fast that now there's almost no limit to how much we could spend.

A responsible society is one in which people do not leave it to the person next door to do the job. It is one in which people help each other. Where parents put their children first. Friends look out for the neighbours, families for their elderly members. That is the starting point for care and support—the unsung efforts of millions of individuals, the selfless work of thousands upon thousands of volunteers. It is their spirit that helps to bind our society together... Caring isn't measured by what you say: It's expressed by what you do.

Conservative Women's Conference, 1986

Indeed the Royal Commission on the National Health Service which reported in 1979 said:

We had no difficulty in believing...that we can easily spend the whole of the Gross National Product" on the National Health Service.

> There is no such thing as Society. They are individual men and women, and there are families.
>
> *1987*

The opportunities for spending money on health may not be limited, but taxpayers' money is.

There are other deserving causes: the Police, education, pensions and defence. Yet we have ploughed more money into the health service, precisely to bring these medical advances within reach of more and more people.

And that is also the reason why we have prescription and health charges. Together they bring in £500 million. That £500 million can pay the salaries of some 60,000 nurses or buy half a million operations. There are always difficult choices to be made. We choose to give priority to the Health Service, as you can see from one final statistic. When we came into Office, spending on the National Health Service was £7½ billion a year. This year it will be £17½ billion—an increase which goes way above inflation. The Opposition can keep on turning out their propaganda. But it can't alter facts. And it can't dislodge all the new doctors and dentists or destroy all the new hospitals.

Mr Chairman, I spoke earlier of freedom. In the eyes of many of our people, the freedom most at risk today is freedom to walk in the street without fear; freedom to answer the door without fear; freedom to be safe and secure in your own home.

The recent crime figures for England and Wales have appalled us all, with their record of brutality, violence and rape. The Lord Chief Justice has described rape as "a violation which obliterates the personality of victims." I'm sure you applaud the lead he has given in proposing sentences up to life imprisonment for this, one of the most savage of crimes.

Central and Local Government carry, as they have for years, a duty to protect the citizen:

—to provide and equip police forces

—to make by statute laws which will deter and punish the criminal

—to support and if necessary augment the numbers of those who administer justice.

More police—we've seen to that. Better equipment—they have it. Another Criminal Justice Bill—it's in preparation. But when crime is rife and people are troubled, they must not be passive. A free people must share the burden of law and order, not remit it all to the State. There are many tasks to be shared.

To check wrongdoing in home and school. To take practical measures of crime prevention. Not to shrug shoulders when crime is committed under our nose. Not to shield the offender. Not to resist being a witness. Never to turn away but to help the victims of crime to come through their traumatic experience.

And I would like to pay tribute here to Victim Support Schemes that last year helped 125,000 victims of crime. They do wonderful voluntary work.

Mr Chairman, glancing back along the road we have come, and despite all the problems we have yet to face, I believe there are solid grounds for encouragement, to lift the spirit. We are no longer seen by our friends abroad as Europe's poor relation. Indeed, when I read what is written about us in other lands, I am tempted to think we are sometimes seen in higher regard than we see ourselves.

In seven short years we have changed the face of this country of ours. But I am only too well aware that there is always another hill to climb, another battle to be won. In a nation of our history, in a Party of our traditions, it is the lamp at the top of the hill. To which the leader must always be drawn, must never lose sight of, must strive with might and main to keep alight.

Amid all the tasks before us, and the obstacles—and the distractions, which we shall surmount—for this Party, this

Government, this Nation, the lamp on the hill shines like a beacon. From that lamp our eye must not, and shall not, waver.

SPEECH ON THE BOMBING OF LIBYA

House of Commons, 15th April 1986

With permission, Mr Speaker, I shall make a statement about Libya. Before I do so, may I first say that my right hon. Friend the Leader of the House [John Biffen] will shortly be making a business statement indicating that there will be a full day's debate on this matter tomorrow.

The House is aware that last night United States forces made attacks on specific targets in Libya.

The Government have evidence showing beyond dispute that the Libyan Government have been and are directly involved in promoting terrorist attacks against the United States and other Western countries, and that they had made plans for a wide range of further terrorist attacks.

The United Kingdom has itself suffered from Libyan terrorism. The House will recall the murder of WPC Fletcher in St. James's Square. There is no doubt, moreover, of the Libyan Government's direct and continuing support for the Provisional IRA, in the form of money and weapons.

Two years ago, we took certain measures against Libya, including the closure of the Libyan people's bureau in London, restrictions on the entry of Libyans into the United Kingdom, and a ban on new contracts for the export to Libya of defence equipment. Yesterday the Foreign Ministers of the European Community reaffirmed their grave concern at Libyan-inspired terrorism and agreed on new restrictions against Libya.

Since we broke off diplomatic relations with Libya, we have had no choice but consistently to advise British nationals living and working there that they do so on their own responsibility. Our interests there have been looked after by the Italian Government. Our representative in the British interests section of the Italian Embassy will continue to advise the British community as best he can.

The United States has tried by peaceful means to deter Colonel Gaddafi and his regime from their promotion of terrorism, but to no effect.

President Reagan informed me last week that the United States intended to take military action to deter further Libyan terrorism. He sought British support for this action. He also sought agreement, in accordance with our long-standing arrangements, to the use in the operation of some United States aircraft based in this country. This approach led to a series of exchanges including a visit by Ambassador Walters on Saturday, 12 April.

> I exercise my right as a free citizen to spend my own money in my own way, so that I can go out on the day, the time, to the doctor I choose and get out fast.
>
> *On why she chooses to use private healthcare, causing a political storm during the General Campaign, June 1987*

Article 51 of the UN charter specifically recognises the right to self-defence. In view of Libya's promotion of terrorism, the failure of peaceful means to deter it and the evidence that further attacks were threatened, I replied to the President that we would support action directed against specific Libyan targets demonstrably involved in the conduct and support of terrorist activities; and, further, that if the President concluded that it was necessary, we would agree to the deployment of United States aircraft from bases in the United Kingdom for that purpose.

I reserved the position of the United Kingdom on any question of further action which might be more general or less clearly directed against terrorism.

The President assured me that the operation would be limited to clearly defined targets related to terrorism, and that the risk of collateral damage would be minimised. He made it clear that use of F111 aircraft from bases in the United Kingdom was essential, because by virtue of their special characteristics they would provide the safest means of achieving particular objectives with the lowest possible risk both of civilian casualties in Libya and of casualties among United States service personnel.

Terrorism is a scourge of the modern age. Libya has been behind much of it and was planning more. The United Kingdom itself has suffered from Libya's actions. So have many of our friends, including several in the Arab world.

The United States, after trying other means, has now sought by limited military action to induce the Libyan regime to desist from terrorism. That is in the British interest. It is why the Government support the United States action.

PART FIVE

Third Term

1987–90

We were told our campaign wasn't sufficiently slick. We regard that as a compliment.

1987

SPEECH TO THE COLLEGE OF THE EUROPE

Bruges Belfrey, Bruges, 20 September 1988

Prime Minister, Rector, Your Excellencies, Ladies and Gentlemen:

First, may I thank you for giving me the opportunity to return to Bruges and in very different circumstances from my last visit shortly after the Zeebrugge Ferry disaster, when Belgian courage and the devotion of your doctors and nurses saved so many British lives.

And second, may I say what a pleasure it is to speak at the College of Europe under the distinguished leadership of its Rector [Professor Lukaszewski]. The College plays a vital and increasingly important part in the life of the European Community.

And third, may I also thank you for inviting me to deliver my address in this magnificent hall. What better place to speak of Europe's future than a building which so gloriously recalls the greatness that Europe had already achieved over 600 years ago.

Your city of Bruges has many other historical associations for us in Britain. Geoffrey Chaucer was a frequent visitor here. And the first book to be printed in the English language was produced here in Bruges by William Caxton.

Mr Chairman, you have invited me to speak on the subject of Britain and Europe. Perhaps I should congratulate you on your courage. If you believe some of the things said and written about my views on Europe, it must seem rather like inviting Genghis Khan to speak on the virtues of peaceful coexistence!

I want to start by disposing of some myths about my country, Britain, and its relationship with Europe and to do that, I must say something about the identity of Europe itself. Europe is not the creation of the Treaty of Rome. Nor is the European idea the property of any group or institution.

We British are as much heirs to the legacy of European culture as any other nation. Our links to the rest of Europe, the continent of Europe, have been the dominant factor in our history. For three hundred years, we were part of the Roman Empire and our maps still trace the straight lines of the roads the Romans built.

Our ancestors—Celts, Saxons, Danes—came from the Continent. Our nation was—in that favourite Community word—"restructured" under the Norman and Angevin rule in the eleventh and twelfth centuries.

This year, we celebrate the three hundredth anniversary of the glorious revolution in which the British crown passed to Prince William of Orange and Queen Mary. Visit the great churches and cathedrals of Britain, read our literature and listen to our language: all bear witness to the cultural riches which we have drawn from Europe and other Europeans from us. We in Britain are rightly proud of the way in which, since Magna Carta in the year 1215, we have pioneered and developed representative institutions to stand as bastions of freedom. And proud too of the way in which for centuries Britain was a home for people from the rest of Europe who sought sanctuary from tyranny. But we know that without the European legacy of political ideas we could not have achieved as much as we did.

From classical and mediaeval thought we have borrowed that concept of the rule of law which marks out a civilised society from barbarism. And on that idea of Christendom, to which the Rector referred—Christendom for long synonymous with Europe—with its recognition of the unique and spiritual nature of the individual, on that idea, we still base our belief in personal liberty and other human rights. Too often, the history of Europe is described as a series of interminable wars and quarrels. Yet from our perspective today surely what strikes us most is our common experience. For instance, the story of how Europeans explored and colonised—and yes, without apology—civilised much of the world is an extraordinary tale of talent, skill and courage.

But we British have in a very special way contributed to Europe. Over the centuries we have fought to prevent Europe from falling under the dominance of a single power. We have fought and we have died for her freedom. Only miles from here, in Belgium, lie the bodies of 120,000 British soldiers who died in the First World War.

Had it not been for that willingness to fight and to die, Europe would have been united long before now—but not in liberty, not in justice. It was British support to resistance movements throughout the last War that helped to keep alive the flame of liberty in so many countries until the day of liberation.

Tomorrow, King Baudouin will attend a service in Brussels to commemorate the many brave Belgians who gave their lives in service with the Royal Air Force—a sacrifice which we shall never forget. And it was from our island fortress that the liberation of Europe itself was mounted. And still, today, we stand together.

Nearly 70,000 British servicemen are stationed on the mainland of Europe. All these things alone are proof of our commitment to Europe's future. The European Community is *one* manifestation of that European identity, but it is not the only one. We must never forget that east of the Iron Curtain, people who once enjoyed a full share of European culture, freedom and identity have been cut off from their roots.

We shall always look on Warsaw, Prague and Budapest as great European cities. Nor should we forget that European values have helped to make the United States of America into the valiant defender of freedom which she has become.

This is no arid chronicle of obscure facts from the dust-filled libraries of history. It is the record of nearly two thousand years of British involvement in Europe, cooperation with Europe and contribution to Europe, contribution which today is as valid and as strong as ever [sic].

Yes, we have looked also to wider horizons—as have others—and thank goodness for that, because Europe never would have prospered and never will prosper as a narrow-minded, inward-looking club.

The European Community belongs to *all* its members. It must reflect the traditions and aspirations of *all* its members. And let me be quite clear. Britain does not dream of some cosy, isolated existence on the fringes of the European Community. Our destiny is in Europe, as part of the Community. That is not to say that our future lies only in Europe, but nor does that of France or Spain or, indeed, of any other member. The Community is not an end in itself. Nor is it an institutional device to be constantly modified according to the dictates of some abstract intellectual concept. Nor must it be ossified by endless regulation.

> We have become a grandmother.
>
> *To reporters outside 10 Downing Street, 1989*

The European Community is a practical means by which Europe can ensure the future prosperity and security of its people in a world in which there are many other powerful nations and groups of nations. We Europeans cannot afford to waste our energies on internal disputes or arcane institutional debates. They are no substitute for effective action.

Europe has to be ready both to contribute in full measure to its own security and to compete commercially and industrially in a world in which success goes to the countries which encourage individual initiative and enterprise, rather than those which attempt to diminish them.

This evening I want to set out some guiding principles for the future which I believe will ensure that Europe does succeed, not just in economic and defence terms but also in the quality of life and the influence of its peoples.

My first guiding principle is this: willing and active cooperation between independent sovereign states is the best way to build a successful European Community. To try to suppress nationhood and concentrate power at the centre of a European conglomerate would be highly damaging and would jeopardise the objectives we seek to achieve.

Europe will be stronger precisely because it has France as France, Spain as Spain, Britain as Britain, each with its own customs, traditions and identity. It would be folly to try to fit them into some sort of identikit European personality. Some of the founding fathers of the Community thought that the United

States of America might be its model. But the whole history of America is quite different from Europe. People went there to get away from the intolerance and constraints of life in Europe. They sought liberty and opportunity; and their strong sense of purpose has, over two centuries, helped to create a new unity and pride in being American, just as our pride lies in being British or Belgian or Dutch or German.

I am the first to say that on many great issues the countries of Europe should try to speak with a single voice. I want to see us work more closely on the things we can do better together than alone. Europe is stronger when we do so, whether it be in trade, in defence or in our relations with the rest of the world. But working more closely together does not require power to be centralised in Brussels or decisions to be taken by an appointed bureaucracy.

Indeed, it is ironic that just when those countries such as the Soviet Union, which have tried to run everything from the centre, are learning that success depends on dispersing power and decisions away from the centre, there are some in the Community who seem to want to move in the opposite direction.

We have not successfully rolled back the frontiers of the state in Britain, only to see them re-imposed at a European level with a European super-state exercising a new dominance from Brussels.

Certainly we want to see Europe more united and with a greater sense of common purpose. But it must be in a way which preserves the different traditions, parliamentary powers and sense of national pride in one's own country; for these have been the source of Europe's vitality through the centuries. My second guiding principle is this: Community policies must tackle present problems in a *practical* way, however difficult that may be.

If we cannot reform those Community policies which are patently wrong or ineffective and which are rightly causing public disquiet, then we shall not get the public support for the Community's future development. And that is why the achievements of the European Council in Brussels last February are so important.

It was not right that half the total Community budget was being spent on storing and disposing of surplus food. Now those stocks are being sharply reduced. It was absolutely right to decide that agriculture's share of the budget should be cut in order to free resources for other policies, such as helping the less well-off regions and helping training for jobs.

It was right too to introduce tighter budgetary discipline to enforce these decisions and to bring the Community spending under better control. And those who complained that the Community was spending so much time on financial detail missed the point. You cannot build on unsound foundations, financial or otherwise, and it was the fundamental reforms agreed last winter which paved the way for the remarkable progress which we have made since on the Single Market.

But we cannot rest on what we have achieved to date. For example, the task of reforming the Common Agricultural Policy is far from complete. Certainly, Europe needs a stable and efficient farming industry. But the CAP has become unwieldy, inefficient and grossly expensive. Production of unwanted surpluses safeguards neither the income nor the future of farmers themselves.

We must *continue* to pursue policies which relate supply more closely to market requirements, and which will reduce over-production and limit costs. Of course, we must protect the villages and rural areas which are such an important part of our national life, but not by the instrument of agricultural prices. Tackling these problems requires political courage. The Community will only damage itself in the eyes of its own people and the outside world if that courage is lacking.

My third guiding principle is the need for Community policies which encourage enterprise. If Europe is to flourish and create the jobs of the future, enterprise is the key. The basic framework is there: the Treaty of Rome itself was intended as a Charter for Economic Liberty. But that it is not how it has always been read, still less applied. The lesson of the economic history of Europe in the 70s and 80s is that central planning and detailed control do not work and that personal endeavour and initiative do.

That a State-controlled economy is a recipe for low growth and that free enterprise within a framework of law brings better results. The aim of a Europe open to enterprise is the moving force behind the creation of the Single European Market in 1992. By getting rid of barriers, by making it possible for companies to operate on a European scale, we can best compete with the United States, Japan and other new economic powers emerging in Asia and elsewhere.

And that means action to *free* markets, action to *widen* choice, action to *reduce* government intervention. Our aim should *not* be more and more detailed regulation from the centre: it should be to deregulate and to remove the constraints on trade. Britain has been in the lead in opening its markets to others.

The City of London has long welcomed financial institutions from all over the world, which is why it is the biggest and most successful financial centre in Europe. We have opened our market for telecommunications equipment, introduced competition into the market services and even into the network itself—steps which others in Europe are only now beginning to face.

In air transport, we have taken the lead in liberalisation and seen the benefits in cheaper fares and wider choice. Our coastal shipping trade is open to the merchant navies of Europe. We wish we could say the same of many other Community members.

Regarding *monetary matters*, let me say this. The key issue is not whether there should be a European Central Bank. The immediate and practical requirements are:

—to implement the Community's commitment to free movement of capital—in Britain, we have it;

—and to the abolition through the Community of exchange controls—in Britain, we abolished them in 1979;

—to establish a genuinely free market in financial services in banking, insurance, investment;

—and to make greater use of the ECU.

This autumn, Britain is issuing ecu-denominated Treasury bills and hopes to see other Community governments increasingly do the same. These are the real requirements because they are what the Community business and industry need if they are to compete effectively in the wider world.

> I am extraordinarily patient – provided that I get my own way in the end.
>
> *1989*

And they are what the European consumer wants, for they will widen his choice and lower his costs. It is to such basic practical steps that the Community's attention should be devoted. When those have been achieved and sustained over a period of time, we shall be in a better position to judge the next move.

It is the same with *frontiers* between our countries. Of course, we want to make it easier for goods to pass through frontiers. Of course, we must make it easier for people to travel throughout the Community. But it is a matter of plain common sense that we cannot totally abolish frontier controls if we are also to protect our citizens from crime and stop the movement of drugs, of terrorists and of illegal immigrants. That was underlined graphically only three weeks ago when one brave German customs officer, doing his duty on the frontier between Holland and Germany, struck a major blow against the terrorists of the IRA.

And before I leave the subject of a single market, may I say that we certainly do not need new regulations which raise the cost of employment and make Europe's labour market less flexible and less competitive with overseas suppliers. If we are to have a European Company Statute, it should contain the minimum regulations. And certainly we in Britain would fight attempts to introduce collectivism and corporatism at the European level—although what people wish to do in their own countries is a matter for them.

My fourth guiding principle is that Europe should not be protectionist. The expansion of the world economy requires us to continue the process of removing barriers to trade, and to do so in the multilateral negotiations in the GATT. It would be a betrayal if, while breaking down constraints on trade within Europe, the Community were to erect greater external protection.

We must ensure that our approach to world trade is consistent with the liberalisation we preach at home. We have a responsibility to give a lead on this, a responsibility which is particularly directed towards the less developed countries. They need not only aid; more than anything, they need improved trading opportunities if they are to gain the dignity of growing economic strength and independence.

My last guiding principle concerns the most fundamental issue—the European countries' role in defence. Europe must continue to maintain a sure defence through NATO. There can be no question of relaxing our efforts, even though it means taking difficult decisions and meeting heavy costs.

It is to NATO that we owe the peace that has been maintained over 40 years. The fact is things *are* going our way: the democratic model of a free enterprise society *has* proved itself superior; freedom is on the offensive, a peaceful offensive the world over, for the first time in my life-time.

We must strive to maintain the United States' commitment to Europe's defence. And that means recognising the burden on their resources of the world role they undertake and their point that their allies should bear the full part of the defence of freedom, particularly as Europe grows wealthier.

Increasingly, they will look to Europe to play a part in out-of-area defence, as we have recently done in the Gulf. NATO and the Western European Union have long recognised where the problems of Europe's defence lie, and have pointed out the solutions. And the time has come when we must give substance to our declarations about a strong defence effort with better value for money.

It is not an institutional problem. It is not a problem of drafting. It is something at once simpler and more profound: it is a question of political will and political courage, of convincing people in all our countries that we cannot rely for ever on others for our defence, but that each member of the Alliance must shoulder a fair share of the burden.

We must keep up public support for nuclear deterrence, remembering that obsolete weapons do not deter, hence the need for modernisation. We must meet the requirements for effective conventional defence in Europe against Soviet forces which are constantly being modernised. We should develop the WEU, not as an alternative to NATO, but as a means of strengthening Europe's contribution to the common defence of the West. Above all, at a time of change and uncertainly in the Soviet Union and Eastern Europe, we must preserve Europe's unity and resolve so that whatever may happen, our defence is sure.

At the same time, we must negotiate on arms control and keep the door wide open to cooperation on all the other issues covered by the Helsinki Accords. But let us never forget that our way of life, our vision and all we hope to achieve, is secured not by the rightness of our cause but by the strength of our defence. On this, we must never falter, never fail.

Mr Chairman, I believe it is not enough just to talk in general terms about a European vision or ideal. If we believe in it, we must chart the way ahead and identify the next steps. And that is what I have tried to do this evening. This approach does not require new documents: they are all there, the North Atlantic Treaty, the Revised Brussels Treaty and the Treaty of Rome, texts written by far-sighted men, a remarkable Belgian—Paul Henri Spaak—among them.

However far we may want to go, the truth is that we can only get there one step at a time. And what we need now is to take decisions on the next steps forward, rather than let ourselves be distracted by Utopian goals. Utopia never comes, because we know we should not like it if it did.

Let Europe be a family of nations, understanding each other better, appreciating each other more, doing more together but relishing our national identity no less than our common European endeavour. Let us have a Europe which plays its full part in the wider world, which looks outward not inward, and which preserves that Atlantic community—that Europe on both sides of the Atlantic—which is our noblest inheritance and our greatest strength.

May I thank you for the privilege of delivering this lecture in this great hall to this great college.

SPEECH TO THE GENERAL ASSEMBLY OF THE CHURCH OF SCOTLAND

Assembly Hall, The Mount, Edinburgh, 21 May 1988

Moderator: I am greatly honoured to have been invited to attend the opening of this 1988 General Assembly of the Church of Scotland; and I am deeply grateful that you have now asked me to address you.

I am very much aware of the historical continuity extending over four centuries, during which the position of the Church of Scotland has been recognised in constitutional law and confirmed by successive Sovereigns. It sprang from the independence of mind and rigour of thought that have always been such powerful characteristics of the Scottish people, as I have occasion to know. It has remained close to its roots and has inspired a commitment to service from all people.

I am therefore very sensible of the important influence which the Church of Scotland exercises in the life of the whole nation, both at the spiritual level and through the extensive caring services which are provided by your Church's department of social responsibility. And I am conscious also of the value of the continuing links which the Church of Scotland maintains with other Churches.

Perhaps it would be best, Moderator, if I began by speaking personally as a Christian, as well as a politician, about the way I see things. Reading recently, I came across the starkly simple phrase:

"Christianity is about spiritual redemption, not social reform."

Sometimes the debate on these matters has become too polarised and given the impression that the two are quite separate. But most Christians would regard it as their personal Christian duty to help their fellow men and women. They would regard the lives of children as a precious trust. These duties come not from any secular legislation passed by Parliament, but from being a Christian.

But there are a number of people who are not Christians who would also accept those responsibilities. What then are the distinctive marks of Christianity?

They stem not from the social but from the spiritual side of our lives, and personally, I would identify three beliefs in particular:

First, that from the beginning man has been endowed by God with the fundamental right to choose between good and evil. And second, that we were made in God's own image and, therefore, we are expected to use all our own power of thought and judgement in exercising that choice; and further, that if we open our hearts to God, He has promised to work within us. And third, that Our Lord Jesus Christ, the Son of God, when faced with His terrible choice and lonely vigil *chose* to lay down His life that our sins may be forgiven. I remember very well a sermon on an Armistice Sunday when our Preacher said, "No one took away the life of Jesus, He chose to lay it down."

I think back to many discussions in my early life when we all agreed that if you try to take the fruits of Christianity without its roots, the fruits will wither. And they will not come again unless you nurture the roots.

But we must not profess the Christian faith and go to Church simply because we want social reforms and benefits or a better standard of behaviour;but because we accept the sanctity of life, the responsibility that comes with freedom and the supreme sacrifice of Christ expressed so well in the hymn:

"When I survey the wondrous Cross, On which the Prince of glory died, My richest gain I count but loss, And pour contempt on all my pride."

May I also say a few words about my personal belief in the relevance of Christianity to public policy—to the things that are Caesar's?

The Old Testament lays down in Exodus the Ten Commandments as given to Moses, the injunction in Leviticus to love our neighbour as ourselves and generally the importance of observing a strict code of law. The New Testament is a record of the Incarnation, the teachings of Christ and the establishment of the Kingdom of God. Again we have the emphasis on loving our neighbour as ourselves and to "Do-as-you-would-be-done-by."

I went to Oxford University, but I've never let that hold me back.

Conservative Party Conference, October 1989

I believe that by taking together these key elements from the Old and New Testaments, we gain: a view of the universe, a proper attitude to work, and principles to shape economic and social life.

We are told we must work and use our talents to create wealth. "If a man will not work he shall not eat" wrote St. Paul to the Thessalonians. Indeed, abundance rather than poverty has a legitimacy which derives from the very nature of Creation.

Nevertheless, the Tenth Commandment—Thou shalt not covet—recognises that making money and owning things could become selfish activities. But it is not the creation of wealth that is wrong but love of money for its own sake. The spiritual dimension comes in deciding what one does with the wealth. How could we respond to the many calls for help, or invest for the future, or support the wonderful artists and craftsmen whose work also glorifies God, unless we had first worked hard and used our talents to create the necessary wealth? And remember the woman with the alabaster jar of ointment.

I confess that I always had difficulty with interpreting the Biblical precept to love our neighbours "as ourselves" until I read some of the words of C.S. Lewis. He pointed out that we don't exactly love *ourselves* when we fall below the standards and beliefs we have accepted. Indeed we might even hate ourselves for some unworthy deed.

None of this, of course, tells us exactly what kind of political and social institutions we should have. On this point, Christians will very often genuinely disagree, though it is a mark of Christian manners that they will do so with courtesy and mutual respect. What is certain, however, is that any set of social and economic arrangements which is not founded on the acceptance of individual responsibility will do nothing but harm.

I am what I am.

29 November 1989

We are all responsible for our own actions. We can't blame society if we disobey the law. We simply can't delegate the exercise of mercy and generosity to others. The politicians and other secular powers should strive by their measures to bring out the good in people and to fight down the bad: but they can't create the one or abolish the other. They can only see that the laws encourage the best instincts and convictions of the people, instincts and convictions which I'm convinced are far more deeply rooted than is often supposed.

Nowhere is this more evident than the basic ties of the family which are at the heart of our society and are the very nursery of civic virtue. And it is on the family that we in government build our own policies for welfare, education and care.

You recall that Timothy was warned by St. Paul that anyone who neglects to provide for his own house (meaning his own family) has disowned the faith and is "worse than an infidel".

We must recognise that modern society is infinitely more complex than that of Biblical times and of course new occasions teach new duties. In our generation, the only way we can ensure that no-one is left without sustenence, help or opportunity, is to have laws to provide for health and education, pensions for the elderly, succour for the sick and disabled.

But intervention by the State must never become so great that it effectively removes personal responsibility. The same applies to taxation; for while you and I would work extremely hard whatever the circumstances, there are undoubtedly some who would not unless the incentive was there. And we need their efforts too.

Moderator, recently there have been great debates about religious education. I believe strongly that politicians must see that religious education has a proper place in the school curriculum.

In Scotland, as in England, there is an historic connection expressed in our laws between Church and State. The two connections are of a somewhat different kind, but the arrangements in both countries are designed to give symbolic expression to the same crucial truth: that the Christian religion—which, of course, embodies many of the great spiritual and moral truths of Judaism—is a fundamental part of our national heritage. And I believe it is the wish of the overwhelming majority of people that this heritage should be preserved and fostered. For centuries it has been our very life blood. And indeed we are a nation whose ideals are founded on the Bible.

Also, it is quite impossible to understand our history or literature without grasping this fact, and that's the strong practical case for ensuring that children at school are given adequate instruction in the part which the Judaic-Christian tradition has played in moulding our laws, manners and institutions. How can you make sense of Shakespeare and Sir Walter Scott, or of the constitutional conflicts of the 17th century in both Scotland and England, without some such fundamental knowledge?

But I go further than this. The truths of the Judaic-Christian tradition are infinitely precious, not only, as I believe, because they are true, but also because they provide the moral impulse which alone can lead to that peace, in the true meaning of the word, for which we all long.

To assert absolute moral values is not to claim perfection for ourselves. No true Christian could do that. What is more, one of the great principles of our Judaic-Christian inheritance is tolerance. People with other faiths and cultures have always been welcomed in our land, assured of equality under the law, of proper respect and of open friendship. There's absolutely nothing incompatible between this and our desire to maintain the essence of our own identity. There is no place for racial or religious intolerance in our creed.

When Abraham Lincoln spoke in his famous Gettysburg speech of 1863 of "government of the people, by the people, and for the people", he gave the world a neat definition of democracy which has since been widely and enthusiastically adopted. But what he enunciated as a form of government was not in itself especially Christian, for nowhere in the Bible is the word democracy mentioned. Ideally, when Christians meet, as Christians, to take counsel together their purpose is not (or should not be) to ascertain what is the mind of the majority but what is the mind of the Holy Spirit—something which may be quite different.

Nevertheless I am an enthusiast for democracy. And I take that position, not because I believe majority opinion is inevitably right or true—indeed no majority can take away God-given human rights—but because I believe it most effectively safeguards the value of the individual, and, more than any other system, restrains the abuse of power by the few. And that *is* a Christian concept.

But there is little hope for democracy if the hearts of men and women in democratic societies cannot be touched by a call to something greater than themselves. Political structures, state institutions, collective ideals—these are not enough.

We Parliamentarians can legislate for the rule of law. You, the Church, can teach the life of faith.

But when all is said and done, the politician's role is a humble one. I always think that the whole debate about the Church and the State has never yielded anything comparable in insight to that beautiful hymn "I Vow to Thee my Country." It begins with a triumphant assertion of what might be described as secular patriotism, a noble thing indeed in a country like ours:

"I vow to thee my country all earthly things above; entire, whole and perfect the service of my love."

It goes on to speak of "another country I heard of long ago" whose King can't be seen and whose armies can't be counted, but "soul by soul and silently her shining bounds increase". Not group by group, or party by party, or even church by church—but soul by soul—and each one counts.

That, members of the Assembly, is the country which you chiefly serve. You fight your cause under the banner of an historic Church. Your success matters greatly—as much to the temporal as to the spiritual welfare of the nation. I leave you with that earnest hope that may we all come nearer to that other country whose "ways are ways of gentleness and all her paths are peace."

INTERVIEW WITH *WOMAN'S OWN*, (THERE IS NO SUCH THINGS AS SOCIETY)

23 September 1987

I think we have gone through a period when too many children and people have been given to understand "I have a problem, it is the Government's job to cope with it!" or "I have a problem, I will go and get a grant to cope with it!" "I am homeless, the Government must house me!" and so they are casting their problems on society and who is society? There is no such thing! There are individual men and women and there are families and no government can do anything except through people and people look to themselves first. It is our duty to look after ourselves and then also to help look after our neighbour and life is a reciprocal business and people have got the entitlements too much in mind without the obligations, because there is no such thing as an entitlement unless someone has first met an obligation and it is, I think, one of the tragedies in which many of the benefits we give, which were meant to reassure people that if they were sick or ill there was a safety net and there was help, that many of the benefits which were meant to help people who were unfortunate— "It is all right. We joined together and we have these insurance schemes to look after it." That was the objective, but somehow there are some people who have been manipulating the system and so some of those help and benefits that were meant to say to people:"All right, if you cannot get a job, you shall have a basic standard of living!" but when people come and say:"But what is the point of working? I can get as much on the dole!" You say:"Look" It is not from the dole. It is your neighbour who is supplying it and if you can earn your own living then really you have a duty to do it and you will feel very much better!"

There is also something else I should say to them:"If that does not give you a basic standard, you know, there are ways in which we top up the standard. You can get your housing benefit."

But it went too far. If children have a problem, it is society that is at fault. There is no such thing as society. There is living tapestry of men and women and people and the beauty of that tapestry and the quality of our lives will depend upon how much each of us is prepared to take responsibility for ourselves and each of us prepared to turn round and help by our own efforts those who are unfortunate. And the worst things we have in life, in my view, are where children who are a great privilege and a trust—they are the fundamental great trust, but they do not ask to come into the world, we bring them into the world, they are a miracle, there is nothing like the miracle of life—we have these little innocents and the worst crime in life is when those children, who would naturally have the right to look to their parents for help, for comfort, not only just for the food and shelter but for the time, for the understanding, turn round and not only is that help not forthcoming, but they get either neglect or worse than that, cruelty.

How do you set about teaching a child religion at school, God is like a father, and she thinks "like someone who has been cruel to them?" It is those children you cannot … you just have to try to say they can only learn from school or we as their neighbour have to try in some way to compensate.

This is why my foremost charity has always been the National Society for the Prevention of Cruelty to Children, because over a century ago when it was started, it was hoped that the need for it would dwindle to nothing and over a hundred years later the need for it is greater, because we now realise that the great problems in life are not those of housing and food and standard of living.

When we have got all of those, when we have got reasonable housing when you compare us with other countries, when you have got a reasonable standard of living and you have got no-one who is hungry or need be hungry, when you have got an education system that teaches everyone—not as good as we would wish—you are left with what? You are left with the problems of human nature, and a child who has not had what we and many of your readers would regard as their birthright—a good home—it is those that we have to get out and help, and you know, it is not only a question of money as everyone will tell you; not your background in society. It is a question of human nature and for those children it is difficult to say:"You are responsible for your behaviour!" because they just have not had a chance and so I think that is one of the biggest problems and I think it is the greatest sin.

SPEECH TO THE 1989 CONSERVATIVE PARTY CONFERENCE

Winter Gardens, Blackpool, 13th October 1989

Mr President [William Whitelaw], Friends, I can think of no more fitting Chairman for this final session of our Conference than you, Mr President, the greatest team player in British politics, a straight bat at the wicket, steady on the green, mighty in the scrum. Your role in Government was invaluable: always wise, often witty, and just occasionally...wily.

Mr President, this Conference, as distinct from last week's little exercise in shadow-boxing in Brighton, has addressed, head-on, the real issues of the day. Which is what you would expect from a Party and a Government of real beliefs. Not for us, disposable ideals. Not for us, throwaway conviction. Not for us, rent-a-principle. We Conservatives know what we believe, say what we believe, and stand by what we believe.

Mr President, what a fantastic year this has been for freedom.

Nineteen eighty-nine will be remembered for decades to come as the year when half the people of half our continent began to throw off their chains. The messages on our banners in 1979—freedom, opportunity, family, enterprise, ownership—are now inscribed on the banners in Leipzig, Warsaw, Budapest and even Moscow.

For decades, East Germans had risked their lives to claw their way through the barbed wire to freedom. Now they come, not by the brave handful but by the cheerful thousand. Hungary, turning day by day more confidently towards freedom and dignity, dismantles Communism and opens her borders to the West. In Poland, the freely elected representatives of a courageous people, move resolutely into the seats of government. And let us never forget Poland's contribution to our own Finest Hour.

What happened in Russia in 1917 wasn't a revolution. It was a coup d'etat. The true revolution is what is happening in Russia and Eastern Europe today.

In 1979, we knew that we were starting a British revolution; in fact, we were the pioneers of a world revolution. So it's ironic that as enterprise and liberty rise from the dead ashes of State Control, the Labour Party here is still trying to blow life into those old embers. Imagine a Labour canvasser talking on the doorstep to those East German families when they settle in, on freedom's side of the wall. "You want to keep more of the money you earn?

I'm afraid that's very selfish. We shall want to tax that away. You want to own shares in your firm? We can't have that. The state has to own your firm. You want to choose where to send your children to school? That's very divisive. You'll send your child where we tell you."

Mr President, the trouble with Labour is that they're just not at home with freedom. Socialists don't like ordinary people choosing, for they might not choose Socialism. That's why Labour wants the State to take more and more of the decisions. "But that's all changed," we're told.

If you believe the reports, Brighton last week was the scene of an unprecedented mass conversion. Nothing like it, since the Chinese General who baptised his entire army with a hosepipe.

Isn't it amazing? The Party which fought to stop council tenants having the right to buy their homes now tells us it is the Party of home ownership. The Party which called for one-sided nuclear disarmament now says it stands for strong defence. The Party which took us to the IMF, like some Third World Country, now primly poses as a model of financial rectitude. And it's all happened, as dear old Tommy Cooper used to say: "Just like that."

Would you believe it? Well no; actually I wouldn't.

You see one can't help wondering: "If it's that easy for the Labour Leader to give up the principles in which he does believe, won't it be even easier for him to give up the principles in which he does not believe?" The truth is: nothing has really changed. Labour just wants power at any price and they'll say anything to get it. Labour's real prescription for Britain is the disease half the world is struggling to cure.

And as for the leaders of the former Alliance parties, I will say no more than this: They have never learned what every woman knows:- you can't make a soufflé rise twice.

Mr President, it is no accident that Socialism has failed. Nor that the democracies and free enterprise economies of the West have prospered. These results are the inevitable consequences of two quite different approaches. It's not a question of a little less planning here or a little less regulation there, or of a fraction more private capital in this sector or a touch more competition in that.

Socialism is not just about economics. Its central dogma is to make the State the ultimate authority for the whole of life. It's based on coercion. It denies the dignity of people. It is a secular creed which has utterly failed. The ruins that remain of Socialism in Europe today are physical shortages, a corrupt bureaucracy, growing unrest, and the urgent cry of those refugees, "We want to get out."

Our creed never set out to dominate the whole of life. At the heart of our belief is the principle of freedom, under a rule of law. Freedom that gives a man room to breathe, to take responsibility, to make his own decisions and to chart his own course. Remove man's freedom and you dwarf the individual, you devalue his conscience and you demoralise him. That is the heart of the matter.

Some talk as if we should be ashamed of harnessing men's talents to the common good. They paint wealth as selfishness, a better standard of living as greed. But only by creating wealth can you relieve poverty. It's what you do with your wealth that counts. In these ten Conservative years, voluntary giving has doubled. Individuals and companies contribute unprecedented sums to rejuvenate the inner cities and support great charitable causes. Others give their time and their effort.

Of course, there are people who are selfish. There are people who are downright evil. Human wickedness is always with us—but you'll find it's not in this Party that crime and hooliganism are excused. For the most part, freedom enables and moves men and women to be warm-hearted and generous.

For every Pharisee our system produces, you will find at least three good Samaritans.Ten years ago, we set out together on a great venture. To provide a new lexicon for prosperity. To replace "It can't be done," with "I'll have a go". And we succeeded. Yes, there are still serious problems to tackle—and I'll come to them in a moment. But let us set them against the massive achievements of our period in office.

— industry: modernised at a pace unrivalled in the post-war years:

— productivity in manufacturing: gains far exceeding those in Europe and North America

— profits: the best for twenty years leading to investment at record levels

> I am not one who, to quote an American author, believes that democracy and enterprise have finally won the battles of ideas – that we have therefore arrived at the end of history, and there is nothing left to fight for. That would be unutterably complacent, indeed foolish. There will always be threats to freedom, not only from frontal assaults, but more insidiously by erosion from within.
>
> *Independent, 14 November 1989*

— jobs: more people in work in Britain than ever before

— living standards: higher than we have ever known

— reducing the national debt: not piling it up for our children to repay

— privatisation: five industries that together were losing over £2 million a week in the public sector, now making profits of over £100 million a week in the private sector

That is the measure of our achievements. But if you really want to see how the economy is doing, look at the newspapers. No, I didn't say read them. Just count the ones that didn't exist before 1979—and weigh the ones that did. And if you're still not satisfied, talk to the Americans and Japanese. They are investing more in Britain than in any other European country. Moreover, for the first time in years there are as many British as there are German companies in the top one hundred in Europe. And, further, of these, six of the seven top earners are British or part-British. And, with all these achievements under our belt, who presumes to advise us on inflation? Labour—who hold the record for the highest inflation for fifty years: 27 percent.

Mr President, all inflation is painful. So is reducing it. But in 1982, we got it down to 5 per cent and by 1986 to 3 per cent. Today, inflation is 7.6 per cent. For a Conservative Government that's far too high. We must get it down again. And we will. But I know what a worry inflation is especially for pensioners. We have always promised that whatever the rise in inflation, the retirement pension will be fully protected against it. This month's figure for inflation which came out this morning, is the one used for the pension increase next April. That means that the single pension next April will go up by £3.30 and the married pension by £5.30. This Government keeps its promises.

I also know what a worry high interest rates are for families with mortgages and for those involved in farming and other small businesses. But when the choice is between high rates now or persistent higher inflation later, with all the damage that would do, the choice is clear. Inflation will come down through the use of high interest rates, as it has in the past. And so it must, for the rest of the world isn't standing still. America, Japan, West Germany—they're all investing, modernising, and cutting costs.

To stay competitive, we must do the same. As Nigel Lawson made clear, industry must not expect to find refuge in a perpetually depreciating currency. Only by steadily improving efficiency will we win and keep our share of the world's markets. Britain's economy is strong. When inflation is beaten—and it will be—Britain will be stronger still. Mr President, we Conservatives have extended ownership of homes, shares and pensions to more people than ever before. We've created that democracy of ownership upon which political democracy depends.

We've laid the economic foundations of a decent and prosperous future. None of this would have been possible without the two finest Chancellors of the Exchequer since the War—Geoffrey Howe and Nigel Lawson. Their achievements have enabled us to provide more resources where they were needed—for schools, for hospitals, for pensioners and disabled people.

But money can't achieve everything. We have to make sure that public services meet the needs of the public and not just the convenience of those who work in them. It would be wholly wrong if people could only exercise choice in the private sector, and were given no choice in the public sector—if they had simply to take it or leave it. If patients had no choice where they were to be treated, they'd be left on waiting lists—long waiting lists.

If parents couldn't choose their children's school, they'd have to go where the local authority sent them. If tenants had no say in the way their estates were run, they would be under the thumb of their council landlords. What could be more democratic than to give people a direct say in these things? What could be more arrogant than to deny it to them?

That's why choice matters so much, choice for the less well-off as much for the comfortably off.

Mr President, in every year since I became Prime Minister,

more money has been spent on the Health Service, in every year more doctors and nurses have been recruited and in every year more patients have been treated.

These are the actions of a Government determined to make the Health Service one of the best in the world. The advances in the last ten years have—by any standards—been remarkable. At the same time people rightly worry about waiting lists for operations and also about the time that outpatients have to wait before being seen. The time taken to treat patients can be weeks in one area and years in another. There are some who say that the only way to improve the NHS further is to give it more money. So we have. Two billion pounds more this year than last. But the truth is that money on its own is not the answer. That's why we are looking at other ways of improving the service to the patient.

We want those hospitals and doctors who carry the heaviest burden of work to be rewarded for it. We want people to be able to choose where they can get the best and quickest hospital care. In view of some of the false impressions that have been created, let me emphasise one simple point:

—The National Health Service will not be privatised. The National Health Service was never going to be privatised. No matter what the emergency, accident or disease; no matter how long or complicated the treatment, the Health Service is there, the Health Service will always be there, to provide the finest care. There to heal, there to cure and there to tend the needs of the patient.

Mr President, we all want our children to have more opportunity than we had ourselves. We know their individual strengths and capacities. We wish everyone to be able to explore the limits of their own abilities and to find their place in the world. And we fervently believe that parents are the best people to judge what is right for their children.

Socialists, however, are obsessed with equal outcomes at the expense of equal opportunities. Time and again, we erected ladders for children to climb; time and again, the Socialist politicians climbed them, and having done so, they tried to kick them away. They did it with Grammar Schools. They did it with Direct Grant Schools. They want to do it with Assisted Places and Grant Maintained Schools. Mr President, they haven't changed.

Let me tell you what I found when I opened a new school in Nottingham a fortnight ago. It was a City Technology College. The local Labour controlled council had told an eleven year old girl that she would be thrown out of the Council's Music School if she attended the CTC where she's been accepted.

To deprive an eleven year old of her music classes because she goes to a school that the Council doesn't control—there's Socialist compassion for you. In the teeth of fierce Labour opposition, we have enlarged the choice of schools for parents and children and brought in major education reforms. We've brought in a National Curriculum of ten subjects which all children have a right and need to know: with mathematics, English, and science at their core.

Who now argues that we were wrong? They know that we were right:

— right to insist on higher standards in the classroom

— right to establish a curriculum which gives children the skills for work and the knowledge for a full life

— right to pass on the best of our heritage and scholarship to the next generation.

— and right to establish wider opportunities throughout the entire education system.

But there are still too many ways in which opportunity after school can be blocked. For instance, there are prejudices about the age at which people can begin a new career. Well, I started being Prime Minister at the age of fifty-three. I'd never been a Prime Minister before. But I adapted to the work.

I did my best. And my employers have twice asked me to stay on. Then again, some people find a lot of jobs blocked to them because they don't have the right qualifications. I went to Oxford University, but I've never let it hold me back. Let there be no mistake, skills, degrees, diplomas, qualifications—these are necessary in the modern industrial world. But opportunity mustn't be cut short at eighteen. We must make sure it lasts a lifetime.

We have already set up the first training scheme that's open to all young people—and a new adult training scheme for the long-term unemployed. Incidentally it's the best of its kind in Europe. Other people come here to see how we do it. But we also need to remove those obstacles and disincentives which government itself has erected. That's why I'm proud that this month we abolished the earnings rule for pensioners.

We must take with us into the 1990s the lessons of the decade we are leaving behind. And the overwhelming lesson is that Socialism has failed.

January 1990

Income Tax and National Insurance can also be an obstacle to those starting work—especially the low-paid. So, again, I'm proud that this Government has cut income tax at all levels. And this very month we have cut the national insurance contributions by up to £3 a week. And thanks to the Chancellor, from next April, married women will be taxed separately—giving them complete privacy in their tax affairs.

And then, Mr President, in 1992 the professions will have the freedom to move throughout Europe. That will open up a much wider vista for all young people. These and other changes are passports, passports that will enable their holders to overcome a false start in early life, passports with no expiry date, passports to the Conservative world of opportunity.

Mr President, when I spoke to the Royal Society about the environment over a year ago, I spoke about the global threat of climate change. I set out the magnitude of the challenge we face. Until recently, we have always thought that whatever progress humanity makes, our planet would stay much the same. That may no longer be true. The way we generate energy. The way we use land. The way industry uses natural resources and disposes of waste. The way our populations multiply. Those things taken together are new in the experience of the earth. They threaten to change the atmosphere above us and the sea around us. That is the scale of the global challenge.

We have to work to solve these problems on a sound scientific basis so that our remedies will be effective. It is no good proposing that we go back to some simple village life and halve our population by some means which have not yet been revealed, as if that would solve all our problems.

> I do wish I had brought my cheque book. I don't believe in credit cards.
>
> *At the Ideal Home Exhibition, March 1990*

Indeed, some of the Third World's primitive farming methods created the deserts and denuded the forests. And some of Eastern Europe's crude technologies polluted the skies and poisoned the rivers. It's prosperity which creates the technology that can keep the earth healthy.

We are called Conservatives with good reason. We believe in conserving what is best—the values of our way of life, the beauties of our country. The countryside has shaped our character as a nation. We have a special responsibility not to let the towns sprawl into it. We will keep the Green Belt green. And to make Britain cleaner, we shall bring in a new Environment Bill to give us much tougher controls on pollution, litter and waste.

Next month, I shall be going to the United Nations to set out our view on how the world should tackle climate change. We have proposed a global convention—a sort of good conduct guide to the environment for all the world's nations on problems like the greenhouse effect. Britain has taken the lead internationally and we shall continue to do so. This is not only a question of acting responsibly, though we do. There is something deeper in us, an innate sense of belonging, of sharing life in a world that we have not fully understood.

As Voyager 2, on its remarkable twelve year flight, raced through the solar system to Neptune and beyond, we were awe-struck by the pictures it sent back of arid, lifeless planets and moons. They were a solemn reminder that our planet has the unique privilege of life. How much more that makes us aware of our duty to safeguard our world. The more we master our environment, the more we must learn to serve it. That is the Conservative approach.

Mr President, there are always new dangers to be faced, new battles to be fought. We are at war against drugs: — against those who produce drugs, against those who peddle drugs, against those who launder the profits of the drug trade. Drugs stunt young lives, they break up families, they injure babies before they are even born. There are those in Britain who say we should legalise certain drugs. As though burglary could be defeated by legalising theft. How typical of the muddled thinking of the so-called progressives. In fact, such action would expose many more of our young people to the danger of drugs. We must continue to protect them with the full force of the law. The police and customs officers deserve our thanks for all they do.

We also face a continuing battle against the terrorists and those who take hostages. We think of Terry Waite, Brian Keenan, John McCarthy—and of their families and friends who endure so much.

Any government which has influence over those who hold hostages should be ready as a matter of course to use that influence to bring about their release. A country cannot support terrorism and still expect to be treated as a member of the international community. To take hostages is to exclude yourself from the civilised world.

In Germany in the last few weeks we have seen the IRA gun down a young army wife sitting alone in her car. And in Britain, we have seen them bomb the young musicians in the Royal Marines Band. Some can't wait to put the blame on security arrangements, as though they were somehow responsible for these appalling crimes. Let us pin the responsibility to where it belongs: on the common murderers of the IRA.

We thank our servicemen and women and the police for their courage and dedication. Mr President, in today's rapidly changing world you never know where conflict may arise. In the last ten years, we have seen the Soviet invasion of Afghanistan, the Iran/Iraq war, Vietnam's occupation of Cambodia, conflicts in Africa and Central America, attacks on shipping in the Gulf, one crisis after another in the Lebanon and the Middle East. And for us, the battle for the freedom of the Falklands.

Times of great change are also times of uncertainty and even danger. The lesson is that you must always keep your defences strong so that you are prepared for any situation. Some among us remember all too well what happened in the 1920s and 1930s when we allowed our hopes for a peaceful world to outrun our judgements on the need for defence. And the world paid a terrible price.

We know now that it's strong defence which protects peace, and it's weakness which brings war. So we have kept our defences strong and we have kept the peace in Europe. Yes, we are ready to negotiate to reduce the levels of weapons on both sides. But only so long as it can be done without jeopardising our security. President Gorbachev understands that principle very well. From our very first meeting he has always told me that he would never do anything to put the Soviet Union's security in danger—and he knows that I would never endanger our security, nor would the Government I lead.

Yet that's just what Labour would do. Endanger our security. Last week the Labour Party voted overwhelmingly to cut Britain's defence budget by a quarter—almost equivalent to the entire Royal Navy. Of course, Labour says that they would keep our nuclear deterrent. But what for? Not to defend or deter, certainly not. Only to negotiate it away as quickly as possible in return for a small cut in the Soviet Union's vast nuclear arsenal.

We would give up all our nuclear weapons while the Soviet Union would keep most of theirs. What a bargain! Labour's supposed conversion to multilateralism is no more than a confidence trick to try to make Labour electable. It's still unilateral disarmament—unilateral disarmament by agreement with the Soviet Union. That isn't a defence policy to see Britain through the 1990s; it's a form of words to see Labour through the next election.

How does one explain the Labour leader's contortions? Is he being false to his convictions? Or true to his character? Mr President, politicians come in many colours, but if you aspire to lead this nation:

"This, above all, to thine own self be true." You don't reach Downing Street by pretending you've travelled the road to Damascus when you haven't even left home.

It will be our job to expose Labour's defence policy and make sure no-one is taken in. It is Government's responsibility to safeguard our defence. Today, as for the past ten years, only a Conservative Government can be trusted to do that.

Mr President, I spoke to you first as Leader of our Party here in Blackpool, on this platform, at our Party Conference in 1975. I remember it so well. It was not the height of our political fortunes. Nor the height of Britain's. Freedom was in retreat. The countries of Eastern Europe seemed crushed for ever under the communist heel. But I said then that we were coming up to a turning point in our history. Few believed it—but that turning point came in 1979. For we Conservatives were the pathfinders. We did not know it at the time but the torch we lit in Britain, which transformed our country—the torch of freedom that is now the symbol of our Party—became the beacon that has shed its light across the Iron Curtain into the East.

Ken Clarke: Isn't it terrible about losing to the Germans at our national sport?
Prime Minster Margaret Thatcher: I shouldn't worry too much – we've beaten them twice this century at theirs.

Following England's loss to Germany in the 1990 Football World Cup semi-final

Today that beacon shines more strongly than at any time this century. You can see it reflected in the faces of the young people from the Communist countries who have reached the West. Like most young people the world over they are resolved to make their own way; to achieve success by their own efforts; to live the life they choose as part of a free world—a free world they have never known.

They are re-telling the story of our history. We cannot know the direction in which free nations in the future will progress. But this we do know—and dare not forget. Only those whose commitment to free enterprise and opportunity is a matter of conviction, not convenience have the necessary strength to sustain them. Only those who have shown the resolve to defend the freedom of the West can be trusted to safeguard it in the challenging, turbulent and unpredictable times that lie ahead.

Mr President, the decade and the century which open up before us must see the lasting triumph of liberty, our common cause. The world needs Britain—and Britain needs us—to make that happen.

SPEECH TO THE 1990 CONSERVATIVE PARTY CONFERENCE

Bournemouth International Centre 12th October 1990

I want to begin on a personal note and I think you will understand why.

Since we met last year, I have lost the best of friends, Ian Gow, and we have all lost one of our wisest and bravest colleagues. Before he was murdered by the IRA, Ian taught us how a civilised community should respond to such an outrage. This is what he said:

"The message that should go out from all decent people—and 99 per cent of the people in Northern Ireland and 99 per cent of people in Great Britain are decent people—is that we will never, never surrender to people like this."

Let us pledge to Ian 's memory that we will never waver from the steadfast courage he showed in defence of our fellow citizens in Ulster, their rights and their liberties. Ian was a brave man. And it is brave men and women who will ensure that democracy triumphs over darkness.

Mr President, this year the world seems to have relived the opening sentence of *A Tale of Two Cities* "It was the best of times, it was the worst of times." The worst of times as a tyrant struck down a small country that stands at the gate-way to the Gulf; the best of times as tyranny crumbled and freedom triumphed across the continent of Europe. The toppling of the Berlin Wall. The overthrow of Ceausescu by the people he had so brutally oppressed. The first free elections in Eastern Europe for a generation. The spread of the ideas of market freedom and independence to the very heart of the Soviet Leviathan.

Who could have foreseen all this? Who will ever forget the testimonies of courage we heard yesterday in this very hall? Our friends from Eastern Europe reminded us that no force of arms, no walls, no barbed wire can for ever suppress the longing of the human heart for liberty and independence. Their courage found allies. Their victory came about because for forty long, cold years the West stood firm against the military threat from the East. Free enterprise overwhelmed Socialism.

This Government stood firm against all those voices raised at home in favour of appeasement. We were criticised for intransigence. Tempted repeatedly with soft options. And reviled for standing firm against Soviet military threats. When will they learn? When will they ever learn?

Now again in the sands of the Middle East, principle is at stake. Mr President, dictators can be deterred, they can be crushed—but they can never be appeased. These things are not abstractions. What changed the world and what will save the world were principle and resolve.

Our principles: freedom, independence, responsibility, choice—these and the democracy built upon them are Britain's special legacy to the world. And everywhere those who love liberty look to Britain. When they speak of parliaments they look to Westminster. When they speak of justice they look to our common law. And when they seek to regenerate their economies, they look to the transformation we British have accomplished. Principles and resolve: They are what changed Britain a decade ago. They are what the Conservative Party brings to Britain. And they alone can secure her freedom and prosperity in the years ahead.

Mr President, a decade ago we revived this country by setting out in a new Conservative direction. We didn't seek a more comfortable way of muddling through, some means of making socialism work in a less destructive way. We too had learned what our Polish guest had experienced far more bitterly: that Socialism can't be improved, it has to be removed.

> If we let Iraq succeed, no small country can ever feel safe again. The law of the jungle takes over.
>
> *August 1990*

So we cut taxes, reduced controls, denationalised state industries, widened share ownership. And we put the union bosses in their rightful place—under the control of their own members. It wasn't easy. And it was only possible because we had faith in the country's enterprise and talent—and because we had the tenacity to see our policies through—indeed, the strength to succeed.

Remember the strikes that were supposed to bring Britain to a halt? The steel strike ten years ago—backed by Labour. The violent coal strike, which lasted a year—backed by Labour. And a host of other strikes—backed by Labour. *We stood firm*. And last year in Britain there were fewer strikes than at any time since the war.

And there's a record number of people in jobs. Yesterday's jobs have been replaced by new jobs. Better jobs. Cleaner jobs. In modern industries. And young people now face a brighter working future. Our scientific research is second to none. Our universities, our polytechnics, our colleges of further education—they're doing a superb job.

So industry now has a new underlying strength. As a recent survey shows, of the 50 most successful European companies, the French have 8, Germany has 2, and 28 are British. It can be and often is better made in Britain.

Mr President, exactly a week ago, John Major dropped one of his quiet surprises on an unsuspecting press. Well, they surprise us sometimes too. He announced that interest rates would be cut by 1 per cent and that Britain would enter the Exchange Rate Mechanism. Of course, we have long been committed to joining the ERM—but only when our own policies of firm financial discipline were seen to be working.

The signs are clear that our policies to bring down inflationary pressures are succeeding and that monetary growth is back within its limits. It was this which enabled us to cut interest rates. Inflation announced this morning is 10.9 per cent. But it will soon begin to decline. And joining the ERM will reinforce our own financial discipline against it. And it will require industry to remain competitive. Inflation is still too high. But it must and will be beaten.

Mr President, our entry into the ERM has been warmly welcomed by our Community partners. But as John Major made absolutely clear yesterday, this Government has no intention of agreeing to the imposition of a single currency. That would be entering a federal Europe through the back-Delors. Any such proposal involves a loss of sovereignty which Parliament would not accept.

I hope that the Community will agree to John Major's important proposals for a common currency, to be used alongside existing national currencies. Europe works better when we respect one another's different national and Parliamentary traditions.

But meanwhile we must continue the prudent policies of successive Tory Chancellors. They have enabled us, out of the budget surpluses of the last three years, to repay twenty six thousand million pounds of the national debt. It is a large sum. It amounts to well over one thousand pounds for every household in the land.

We have kept control of public finances but we have also honoured our pledge to protect the value of pensions against inflation. And we will continue to do so. It means that next April the single pension will go up by £5.10 to £52 a week, and the married pension by £8.15 to £83.25 a week. This Party keeps its promises.

Last week, Mr President, I seemed to hear a strange sound emanating from Blackpool. And I thought at first it was seagulls. Then I remembered that Labour was holding its annual Conference there. And I realised it wasn't seagulls, it was chickens — chickens being counted before they were hatched — except for Labour's call to enter the ERM and cut interest rates. That was a case of counting chickens after they'd flown the coop.

Then, I heard voices getting all worked up about someone they kept calling the "Prime Minister in Waiting". It occurs to me, Mr President, that he might have quite a wait.

I can see him now, like the people queuing up for the Winter sales. All got up with his camp bed, hot thermos, woolly balaclava, CND badge ... Waiting, waiting, waiting ...And then when the doors open, in he rushes—only to find that, as always, there's *"that woman"* ahead of him again. I gather there may be an adjective between "that" and "woman" only no-one will tell me what it is.

But, I'll tell you this, "that man" is going to trip over his promises in the rush if he's not careful.

There is his promise, for example, not to cut taxes "for many years to come." That's the one Labour promise it's safe to believe. Indeed the Labour leader was being unduly modest. He wouldn't cut taxes ever. Why? Because he's a socialist—and they just don't like the idea. In government, they put taxes up and in opposition, they fight our proposals to bring taxes down.

And taxes would go up and up if Labour spends as much of your money as they've promised. But they say "we're reformed characters, next time it will be different, we've paid our debt to society." If that were true, it would be the first ever debt Labour has ever paid. We Conservatives say that society must be protected from such a persistent offender —and a sentence of eleven years in opposition is nowhere near enough. Then Labour say they're going to introduce "freedom and fairness" in trade union law.

In other words, freedom to force their members out on strike against their will. Freedom to organise secondary strikes against third party employers, other workers and the general public. And freedom to give wings to flying pickets to go round the country and bring it to a halt. Those aren't freedoms. They're powers to hurt others; and there's nothing fair about them.

Labour's third pledge is to replace the Community Charge by the unfairness of rates with all the additional horrors of a revaluation. What Labour wants is for local authorities to be accountable not to the citizen but to its own Left-wing.

For years council after council has been hijacked by socialist extremists. The residents wanted litter-free zones, but what they got was nuclear-free zones. The Community Charge is making them more accountable and less electable. No wonder Labour councillors don't want it.

Then there's this plan of Labour's for smaller, more decentralised government—which would contain two brand new ministries, a couple of new departments of state, nine different bodies in each region, a hundred new committees, heaven knows how many councils and commissions on top, and a great herd of great herd of quangos thundering up Whitehall. A mere 2012 new bureaucratic bodies in all.

It's the oldest law of politics: government tends to expand and socialist government expands absolutely.

Mr President, that's four impossible pledges so far. And I could go on for hours quoting from Labour's lexicon of logical contradictions. There is its pledge to cut emissions of carbon dioxide—by burning more coal. And its promise to improve educational standards—by phasing out tests.

But the really remarkable thing about Labour is, they want you to swallow that they're now a party of moderation. Labour's Blackpool Conference was the amateur dramatics of the season, a grand masquerade at which militants and trots peeped out from behind a painted smile. Glenda [Jackson] had given them a few professional tips. The audience had learnt its lines. The rehearsals had gone splendidly. Ron Todd gave a dazzling performance as Mr Moderation.

Alas, on the night, the extras got everything mixed up and voted the wrong way—to emasculate defence, to bump up public spending, to ditch our electoral system, and to deselect moderate MPs.

The audience applauded like mad. Only Dennis Skinner remained glued to his seat. The theatre of the absurd was clearly not for him. Well, Mr President, they can produce all the assurances in the world. They can say that they never read their own manifestos or understood their own speeches.

But there's one thing they can't do. They can't tell the nation why it should trust a Party whose only claim to office is that it has ditched its principles, disguised its policies and denied its past. And when a party does that, how could anyone trust its promises for the future?

Now, that brings me to the Liberal Party. I gather that during the last few days there have been some ill-natured jokes about their new symbol, a bird of some kind, adopted by the Liberal Democrats at Blackpool. Politics is a serious business, and one should not lower the tone unduly. So I will say only this of the Liberal Democrat symbol and of the party it symbolises.

This is an ex-parrot.

It is not merely stunned. It has ceased to be, expired and gone to meet its maker. It is a parrot no more. It has rung down the curtain and joined the choir invisible. This is a late parrot.

And now for something completely different ...

Mr President, most of us remember a time when although people saved for a rainy day they couldn't hope to leave what one might call a capital sum to their children. These days, it's different. Many more people have homes and shares and savings to pass on. Indeed, the average real value of what pensioners can leave to their children is almost twice what it was only ten short years ago.

So as time goes by capital passes from one generation of a family to another, bringing a wealth of opportunity and an opportunity for wealth. Labour's response to people's well-being is to sneer at it as materialism—when they are not denying it as myth. They relish class division. They depend on it. It's the root of all socialism.

We relish opportunity for all—through education, through training, through lower taxes, through ownership of homes and shares. So that people can make their own way by hard work and enterprise—and build up capital by saving and investment. We relish choice for all—in health, in schools, in housing. So that people get what they want, not what politicians want.

And the more we foster these things, the more we break down barriers—barriers between workers and bosses, skilled and unskilled, tenants and owners, barriers between private and public. That's the why we break them down. And that's the kind of open classless Britain I want to see. And it's the kind of opportunity Britain the Conservative Party stands for. A Britain where people begin by improving their own lives and end by helping to improve the lives of others. Much has been done. But more remains to be done.

So far we've slashed income tax; abolished seven taxes; and given married women their own separate tax allowance. That's good. But not good enough. So as soon as it's safe to do so, we'll cut income tax again. We've trebled the number of shareholders in Britain and privatised twenty major industries. That's good, but not enough.

We want more shareholders and more workers to own shares. So we'll privatise the major ports; then we'll tackle British Rail — with more to come.

We have enabled three million more people—half of them council tenants—to become new home-owners. Good—but not enough. So we'll introduce a pilot scheme in England to allow New Town tenants to turn their rents into mortgages—as we did with great success in Scotland and Wales. If this scheme succeeds like those, we'll extend it nationwide.

Mr President, children leaving school—and some adults who've missed out—deserve the chance to learn a skill. We need more flexible training. So we've put it into the hands of local businessmen, who know the skills needed for the future. That's good—but not enough. Now we're giving a brand new voucher to trainees in eleven pilot areas so they can use it to get the training they want. If that's a success, we shall make them available nationwide.

This training voucher gives real motivation and power to young people. And it's the first voucher scheme we've introduced—and I hope it won't be the last. Mr President, this Government has made education a top priority. By providing the framework for higher standards. By establishing a national curriculum. By spending more on each child than ever before. And by the smallest class sizes ever.

But, above all, by freedom, choice and competition. Some fifty grant maintained schools—that is, the new independent state schools—are the first to relish their freedom from local authority control and the extra resources that freedom brings. That's good, but it's not enough. I want to see far more schools becoming independent State schools.

And as John MacGregor announced on Wednesday, we shall give every primary and secondary school in the country the opportunity to have independent status. That way the money goes direct to the school and not to the administration. But let's be perfectly clear: governments can determine the structure of education. But they can't determine its soul.

It's for parents to use their new power to insist on the best. It's for teachers and heads to provide it. And it's for the examination boards and the Inspectorate to be rigorous in monitoring the results. Asking too little of our children is not only doing them an injustice, it's jeopardising our national future.

They tell us: "Spelling doesn't matter." It does if you're after a job. They say: "Grammar is old-fashioned." Not if you want to make sense. They add: "Doing sums is outdated." I'm glad nobody told me that when I was negotiating the return of our money from Europe. And then the education specialists tell us: "It depends what you mean by standards." Well, if they don't know that, what are they doing in education?

Let me give them some clues: we are open to new methods of

teaching. But not if they mean our children can't read. Yes, we do want more learning for work. But not at the cost of academic achievement for the most gifted children. Of course we want more examination successes. But not a confetti of meaningless qualifications. Employers will soon see that one, soon see through it.

A new battle for Britain is under way in our schools. Labour's tattered flag is there for all to see. Limp in the stale breeze of sixties ideology. But let's be fair. Labour wouldn't neglect education. They've promised us action. That's what alarms me:

—Action to close down the newly independent State schools, to close down the Grammar schools, to close down the City Technology Colleges.

—Action to stamp out choice for ordinary people, and to impose State uniformity.

—Action to rob parents of power and give it to Unions and administrators.

Labour is stuck fast in the egalitarian sands from which the rest of the world is escaping. We Conservatives have run up our flag. Choice, high standards, better teachers—a wider horizon for every child from every background. The Labour leader has chosen education to be his Party's battleground. So be it. We need have no fear of the result.

Mr President, I know the importance this Conference attaches to reducing crime. Crime and violence injure not only the victim, but all of us, by spreading fear and making the streets no-go areas for decent people.

Government has strengthened police numbers, improved police pay and revolutionised police technology. We've provided stiffer sentences for the men of violence. And when the courts hand down severe sentences for violent crimes they will receive this Government's unqualified support.

To be soft on crime is to betray the law-abiding citizen. And to make excuses for the criminal is to offer incentives to dishonesty and violence. Crime flourishes in a culture of excuses.We

Conservatives know, even if many sociologists don't, that crime is not a sickness to be cured—it's a temptation to be resisted, a threat to be deterred, and an evil to be punished.

Mr President, this year we celebrated the Fiftieth Anniversary of the Battle of Britain. We remembered "the few": and as the Hurricanes, the Spitfires and the lone Lancaster flew over London, we looked back to a time when our nation stood alone and showed its true mettle. That spirit is just as alive today. The world knows it can count on Britain to be staunch in defence. And that's why London was chosen for NATO's summit meeting last July, one of the most important ever held.

Now at last we can afford to reduce our forces in Europe. But we mustn't weaken our defence: we must adapt it to meet new threats—to prepare for the unexpected. Danger never sleeps. Governments which assume that there are no clouds on the horizon risk finding themselves at the heart of the storm.

When NATO Foreign Ministers met in Scotland in June, I warned: — that NATO must be ready to act beyond its boundaries — that our dependence on Middle Eastern oil will grow again in the next century — and that we must have the capacity to defend our trade routes.

Those warnings were more timely than I knew. Today in the Gulf we face an attempt to extinguish liberty and nationhood. Saddam Hussein took Kuwait by war, with no respect for her people, for property or for international law. And every day he remains is a new act of war.

This tyrant has taken our people hostage. And not a day goes by without our thinking of their plight and how we can bring them safely home to their families. Mr President, Saddam Hussein must withdraw from Kuwait and the legitimate government must be restored. As Winston Churchill said in the Thirties: "If you give in to aggression there will be no end to the humiliation you will have to suffer."

In times of great crisis, Britain and the United States stand as always together—and President Bush deserves our admiration and full support for the lead he has given. Sanctions are being drawn tighter and tighter and we most earnestly hope that they will work. If not, the military option is there and the build-up of forces continues. We must be ready for any contingency. Some people suggest there should be negotiations. What is there to negotiate about? You don't negotiate with someone who marches into another country, devastates it, killing whoever he...stands in his way. You get him out, make him pay and see that he is never in a position to do these things again.

> It seems like cloud cuckoo land ... If anyone is suggesting that I would go to Parliament and suggest the abolition of the Pound Sterling – no! ... We have made it quite clear that we will not have a single currency imposed upon us.
>
> *October 1990*

Saddam Hussein can't do these things without paying compensation. He and those who carry out his orders must be made answerable for their crimes. Never before have the nations of the world been so united in a single resolve: that aggression shall not pay. But if this Government had not kept Britain's defences strong, we would never have had the forces and the equipment to send to the Gulf: our Tornadoes, Jaguars, frigates, minesweepers, and the Desert Rats.

Our servicemen and servicewomen have already demonstrated their superb professionalism. Yet, even at a time when tyrants like Saddam Hussein are getting closer to having nuclear weapons of their own, Labour would still give up our nuclear deterrent.

Mr President, this government will maintain our nuclear deterrent, guardian of the peace for 40 years. We shall keep Britain strong and secure. We will never take risks with our defences.

Mr President, when the call came to send forces to the Gulf, it was independent nations—above all the United States and Britain—which took rapid and decisive action. Many other nations followed, especially in the Arab world. Nationhood remains the focus of loyalty and sovereignty in the modern world. The revolutions of 1989 in Eastern Europe showed how deep that feeling is. As the Eastern Europeans detach themselves from the aberration of Communism, they look to their own country and heritage.

So, too, do the people of newly united Germany. The speeches on the day of unification, echo and re-echo with references to sovereignty and independence. Europe cannot be built by ignoring or suppressing this sense of nationhood, by trying to turn us into regions rather than nations. The way forward lies in willing cooperation between independent sovereign states. Nor do we see the Europe of the future as a tight little inward-looking protectionist group which would induce the rest of the world to form itself into similar blocs. We want a Europe which is outward-looking, and open to all the countries of Europe once they are democratic and ready to join.

We do not judge how European you are by how much you want to increase the power of the unelected Commission. Intervention, centralisation and lack of accountability may appeal to socialists. They have no place in our Conservative philosophy. We shall resist unnecessary regulation and bureaucracy: but when rules have been agreed, our fellow members of the European Community will find that Britain has the best record for implementing them openly and honestly.

Mr President, we are careful about money and rightly so. We're the second biggest net contributor to Europe, paying over £2 billion a year. But—and it is a crucial but—we shall never accept the approach of those who want to use the European Community as a means of removing our ability to govern ourselves as an independent nation.

Our Parliament has endured for seven hundred years and has been a beacon of hope to the peoples of Europe in their darkest days. Our aim is to see Europe become the greatest practical expression of political and economic liberty the world over. And we will accept nothing less.

Mr President, this was the year when time ran out on Socialism. Marxist Socialism is not yet buried but its epitaph can now be written. It impoverished and murdered nations. It promoted lies and mediocrity. It persecuted faith and talent. It will not be missed.

We have entered an age in which the people increasingly yearn for the path of freedom, free enterprise and self reliance.

Even in the newly liberated East, they are not seeking some third way between free enterprise and Socialism: they know that if, they know if Labour doesn't that the third way leads only to the Third World.

Labour's vision has been shattered. Beneath its contrived self-confidence lies a growing certainty that the world and history have passed it by; and that if Britain rejects them yet again, as I believe it will, socialism must return for ever to its proper place—the reading room of the British Library where Karl Marx found it, Section: History of Ideas, Subsection 19th Century, Status Archaic.

The new world of freedom into which the dazzled Socialists have stumbled is not new to us. What to them is uncharted territory is to us familiar and well loved ground. For Britain has returned to those basic truths and principles which made her great—personal liberty, private property and the rule of law, on which democratic freedoms everywhere are based. Ours is a creed which travels and endures. Its truths are written in the human heart. It is the faith which once more has given life to Britain and offers hope to the world. We pledge in this Party to uphold these principles of freedom and to fight for them. We pledge it to our allies overseas. And we pledge it to this country which we are proud to serve.

STATEMENT ON THE ROME SUMMIT

House of Commons, 30th October 1990

With permission, Mr Speaker, I shall make a statement on the European Council held in Rome on 27 and 28 October, which I attended with my right hon. Friend the Foreign and Commonwealth Secretary [Douglas Hurd]. The conclusions of the Council have been placed in the Library of the House.

The Council had to deal in the first place with some urgent items of current business: namely, the Community's failure to agree a negotiating position on agriculture for the Uruguay round of trade negotiations; the situation in the Gulf, and the position of the foreign nationals held hostage in Iraq and Kuwait; and the problems which have arisen in Hungary.

Looking further ahead, the Council also dealt with the preparations for the two intergovernmental conferences, on economic and monetary union and also on institutional reform, which are due to begin in December. I shall report on the Council's business in that order.

The Uruguay round of trade negotiations is due to be completed before the end of this year. The outcome will decide whether world trade becomes steadily more open, or we repeat the mistakes of the past and relapse into protectionism.

The most difficult item is agriculture. All the major participants in the Uruguay round committed themselves to table negotiating offers by 15 October. All except the European Community have done so.

The Community has been discussing this problem since the round began in the autumn of 1986. It gave an unequivocal commitment in April last year to make substantial and progressive reductions in agricultural support. That commitment was repeated at the Houston economic summit in July this year.

The Commission has put forward a proposal for 30 per cent. reductions, backdated to 1986. So what has already been done by way of reduction of support since then will be set against that 30 per cent.

There have been six sessions of European Community Ministers to discuss the proposal. The most recent, lasting some 16 hours, was on Friday last week. But no agreement has been reached. The main opposition has come from France and Germany.

The Community's failure has harmed its reputation. Negotiations between the leading groups of countries cannot start until the Community's proposals have been tabled.

The European Council requested Ministers to meet again and put the Commission in a position to table a negotiating offer. The Netherlands Prime Minister suggested that the basis for this should be the position reached when Agriculture Ministers suspended their work early on 27 October. But President Mitterrand made it clear that France would continue to vote against those proposals.

It remains for Agriculture and Trade Ministers to try yet again to reach a conclusion. If we fail, it will give a signal to the world that the Community is protectionist.

Next, with regard to the Gulf and the position of the hostages, the European Council agreed a firm statement calling for Iraq's withdrawal from Kuwait and confirming Europe's absolute commitment to full implementation of the United Nations Security Council resolutions. The statement makes it clear that we shall consider further steps if Iraq does not comply. The message is that Saddam Hussein must not gain anything from his aggression.

The Council also strongly condemned Iraq for holding foreign nationals as hostages and for using them in an unscrupulous way. This is totally unacceptable. Moreover, Iraq is negotiating over the hostages with the purpose of trying to divide the international community. After considerable discussion, the Council affirmed our determination not to send representatives of our Governments in any capacity to negotiate with Iraq for the release of hostages, and to discourage others from doing so. I believe that the unity of the Twelve, and our determination not to allow Saddam Hussein to divide us on the question of hostages, will send a very powerful signal to Iraq.

The third point is assistance to Hungary. In the course of the Council, member states received appeals from the Government of Hungary for help in dealing with the serious problems that have arisen as a result of the reduction in the supply of oil from the Soviet Union. The consequent price rises have given rise to unrest. The Council issued a strong statement of support for Hungary in pursuing its path towards democratic and economic reforms and the rule of law. The Council also agreed, at the United Kingdom's suggestion, to bring forward and disburse rapidly the second instalment of the $1 billion Community loan for Hungary which we agreed last year. This will be of direct practical assistance.

Those were the urgent matters on which the Council had to act. Looking further to the future, we also discussed the preparations for the two intergovernmental conferences, or IGCs, which will start their work on 14 December.

For the conference on political union, the Council had before it a report by Foreign Ministers listing a wide range of possible institutional changes which the intergovernmental conference might consider. Heads of Government called for further work to be done on these proposals between now and December.

My right hon. Friend the Foreign Secretary and I argued that it would be wrong to prejudge the conclusions of the intergovernmental conference. We were on strong ground, since the Community's original decision to call the conference specified that it should set its own agenda. Nevertheless, others wished to give specific directions to the IGC. We therefore reserved the United Kingdom's position on, for example, extension of the Community's powers into new areas, greater powers for the European Parliament in the legislative sphere, defining European citizenship, and a common foreign and security policy. All these are issues for discussion at the intergovernmental conference itself rather than to be settled in advance.

On economic and monetary union, I stressed that we would be ready to move beyond the present position to the creation of a European monetary fund and a common Community currency which we have called a hard ecu. But we would not be prepared to agree to set a date for starting the next stage of economic and monetary union before there is any agreement on what that stage should comprise. And I again emphasised that we would not be prepared to have a single currency imposed upon us, nor to surrender the use of the pound sterling as our currency.

The hard ecu would be a parallel currency, not a single currency.

If, as time went by, people and Governments chose to use it widely, it could evolve towards a single currency. But our national currency would remain unless a decision to abolish it were freely taken by future generations of Parliament and people. A single currency is not the policy of this Government. I should like to offer four comments in conclusion.

First, the Community finds it more difficult to take the urgent, detailed decisions than to discuss longer-term concepts. Moreover, no one should underestimate the extent to which national interests prevail among those who most proclaim their Community credentials.

Secondly, Britain intends to be part of the further political, economic and monetary development of the European Community. That is what the great majority of member states want, too. When we come to negotiate on particular points, rather than concepts or generalities, I believe that solutions will be found which will enable the Community to go forward as Twelve. That will be our objective.

Thirdly, we are fighting in Europe for British farmers, for British consumers, for a new world trade agreement, for help to the newly democratic countries of eastern Europe, and for the interests and concerns of our people.

Fourthly, while we fully accept our commitments under the treaties and wish to co-operate more closely with other countries in the European Community, we are determined to retain our fundamental ability to govern ourselves through Parliament. I believe that that is the wish of this House, and we on this side will do our best to see that it is fulfilled.

Mr Neil Kinnock (Islwyn): I thank the right hon. Lady for that statement and welcome the summit statements on, first, the complete solidarity of the Governments of the Community countries against Saddam Hussein and, secondly, economic support for the Soviet Union, Hungary and other central and east European countries.

On the central matter discussed in Rome, is it not clear that last weekend the Prime Minister managed to unite the rest of the European Community against her, to divide her own party and, more importantly, further to weaken the influence that Britain needs in order properly to uphold our national interests in the European Community? Can the Prime Minister tell us why she was apparently taken by surprise by the proposals put by others in Rome? Does she not recall that in 1985 she whipped and guillotined the Single European Act through the House, in June 1989 at Madrid she formally agreed with other heads of Government to be determined to achieve the progressive realisation of economic and monetary union, and at the Dublin summit this year she agreed to intensify the process of European union in economic, monetary and political terms? Those were all steps which raised comment at the time. Did she not know what she was doing on those occasions, or was she living in cloud cuckoo land?

The Prime Minister says that the Government would not surrender the use of the pound sterling as our currency. Perhaps she will therefore tell us how she regards the advice of her fellow Conservative, Commissioner Brittan, when he said:

"You don't have to lose the pound sterling under the single currency plan. You can perfectly well have a note or a coin which states its value in pounds...and its fixed equivalent in ecu...It's been agreed that that would be possible."

On the connection between currency and sovereignty, can the Prime Minister, who abandoned her own Madrid conditions before she put sterling into the exchange rate mechanism, tell the House what will be her conditions now for putting sterling into the narrow banding of the ERM? The Prime Minister could come to a debate and explain all these things from the Dispatch Box if she was willing to do so.

When the Prime Minister conducts herself as she did in Rome this weekend, is it any wonder that she cannot even get agreement for the necessary reduction in farm subsidies? *[Interruption.]* She has no influence at all. When she conducts herself as she does, is it any wonder that some members of her own party believe that she has undermined the Chancellor's efforts to build support for the so-called hard ecu? Does she not realise that such an attitude makes the Heads of other Governments even less susceptible to listening to the sensible arguments that can be deployed in favour of sovereignty in the Community? Does she accept that it is reasonable to put the view that the determinants of the pace and direction of economic and monetary union should be the realities of economic performance and the degree of economic convergence, not arbitrary diary dates?

Does the Prime Minister not understand that, with her method of conducting affairs, she is throwing away that sound argument and losing both potential allies and necessary influence? Does she not appreciate that, even now, her tantrum tactics will not stop the process of change or change anything in the process of change? All they do is strand Britain in a European second division without the influence over change that we need, the financial and industrial opportunities that we need and the sovereignty that we need.

The Prime Minister: It is our purpose to retain the power and influence of this House, rather than denude it of many of its powers. I wonder what the right hon. Gentleman's policy is, in view of some of the things that he said. Would he have agreed to a commitment to extend the Community's powers to other supplementary sectors of economic integration without having any definition of what they are? One would have thought, from what he said, that he would. The Commission wants to extend its powers and competence into health matters, but we said no, we would not agree to that.

From what the right hon. Gentleman said, it sounded as though he would agree, for the sake of agreeing, and for being Little Sir Echo, and saying, "Me, too." Would the right hon. Gentleman have agreed to extending qualified majority voting within the Council, to delegating implementing powers to the Commission, to a common security policy, all without any attempt to define or limit them? The answer is yes. He does not have a clue about the definition of some of the things that he is saying, let alone securing a definition of others.

We have agreed to wait to give support to the Soviet Union until the IMF report is received. That is coming at the next summit.

It was not we who stopped unity on agriculture—it was France and Germany. Had the right hon. Gentleman even read the statement, which he had before I came in, he would have noticed—and had he even listened to the statement when I made it, he would have known—that it was Francois Mitterrand who said that he would not agree to the Commission's proposal. We are not to blame in any way for not reaching agreement on agriculture. But for the insistence of my right hon. Friend the Foreign and Commonwealth Secretary and me, the chair would not even have had the matter discussed, so urgent was it that it should be. I told the chair over a week ago that, if the farm Ministers did not reach agreement, we must discuss the matter, and I wrote to him. He did everything that he could to see that a matter so urgent was not discussed, but we succeeded in getting it discussed.

As to the right hon. Gentleman's strictures about economic and monetary union, that phrase was agreed by the European Community before we went in. It is one of those things that we inherited. It was agreed in 1972. When it came to defining it—*[Interruption.]* We went into the Community in 1973, and I had understood that most Labour Members were in favour of that. I wonder today if they are changing their stance for the sake of debating points.

Leon Brittan is a loyal member of the Commission. Yes, the Commission wants to increase its powers. Yes, it is a non-elected body and I do not want the Commission to increase its powers at the expense of the House, so of course we differ. The President of the Commission, Mr Delors, said at a press conference the other day that he wanted the European Parliament to be the democratic body of the Community, he wanted the Commission to be the Executive and he wanted the Council of Ministers to be the Senate. No. No. No.

Perhaps the Labour party would give all those things up easily. Perhaps it would agree to a single currency and abolition of the pound sterling. Perhaps, being totally incompetent in monetary matters, it would be only too delighted to hand over full responsibility to a central bank, as it did to the IMF. The fact is that the Labour party has no competence on money and no competence on the economy—so, yes, the right hon. Gentleman would be glad to hand it all over. What is the point of trying to get elected to Parliament only to hand over sterling and the powers of this House to Europe? Perhaps the right hon. Gentleman will understand his brief a little better next time.

SPEECH AT THE LORDS MAYOR'S BANQUET

Guildhall, City of London, 12 November 1990

May I begin by thanking you, My Lord Mayor, for your toast to Her Majesty's Ministers. May I thank you also for your splendid speech and congratulate you on being elected Lord Mayor.

Since I first went into bat eleven years ago, the score at your end has ticked over nicely, You are now the 663rd Lord Mayor. At the Prime Minister's end, we are stuck on 49. I am still at the crease, though the bowling has been pretty hostile of late. And in case anyone doubted it, can I assure you there will be no ducking the bouncers, no stonewalling, no playing for time. The bowling's going to get hit all round the ground. That is my style.

My Lord Mayor, it has always been the hallmark of the city that it has sought not only to promote commerce and trade, but to enrich the society of which it is a part. This has been especially so in education and training, to which you referred, and where the City and Guilds Certificates have been a byword for excellence and craftsmanship.

Nowhere is this tradition sustained more proudly than in your own livery company, the Mercers. Its history as an education charity dates back over five centuries, supporting such schools as Abingdon and St Paul's. That tradition will take on new form with the Mercers' plans to help establish a new City Technology College at Telford. Once again, the City is foremost in upholding standards—standards which are the key to Britain's success in the world of tomorrow.

My Lord Mayor, the Britain of twelve years ago had become bureaucratic, tightly controlled and reconciled to decline. It had lost all vitality. Such a society could not adapt, it could not respond to new opportunities—it was stuck in its own mould.

Only a free people and a free economy have the capacity to meet new challenges, create new activities and find new solutions. That is why in 1979 there had to be a clean break and we had to build opportunity Britain, where talent and the spirit of enterprise could succeed. And the British people responded magnificently.

Our growth in output and investment has been second to none of our principal competitors in Europe. Instead of trailing, we led. Most striking of all, for the last eight years we have maintained our share of world trade—ending the progressive decline that dates back to 1870. And we need to remind ourselves more often that, per person, Britain exports more than Japan—a very good record for our industry.

After nine consecutive years of growth, we needed to slow down. We are still paying the cost in high inflation of not recognising early enough the sheer strength and vitality of the expansion unleashed in Britain. There was too much borrowing. It would have been better if more people had heeded the advice from the Book of Ecclesiasticus:

"Be not made a beggar banqueting upon borrowing, when thou hast nothing in they purse."

For obvious reasons I hesitated to use that, but you, My Lord Mayor, are a Scot, you have not been doing the borrowing, you have been doing the lending and probably making a very good thing of it.

All the signs are that we are winning the fight against inflation and that monetary growth is back on track. It will not be long before the inflation figure starts to fall.

Other countries, too, have their problems. But unlike many of them, we have a budget surplus, not a massive deficit. Just a few days ago, the Chancellor published his Autumn Statement giving the results of the annual public spending negotiations. Before the Statement, we had been accused of letting rip; of abandoning fiscal discipline; of caving in to every special interest. My Lord Mayor, to coin a phrase: no, no, no.

Even old Treasury hands describe this as the most difficult and bruising round for years. But it has met our long-term goal of reducing the share of national income taken by the state. Two years ago at this Banquet I said we would bring public spending to below 40 per cent of national income for the first time in twenty years. We did. We will do so again this year, and keep it on a downward trend in the future.

> I fight on, I fight to win.
>
> *Upon leaving Downing Street for the Commons, 21 November 1990*

We have set standards of sound finance not seen for two generations. At last there has been a return to orthodox finance and an end to the post-war illusion that year after year one could go on spending more than one had. But we have done more than balance the books. For four years now, we have had a budget surplus, repaying £25 billion of Government debt. We are diminishing, not adding to, the burden of debt which our children will have to meet. We believe it is wrong for us to live at the expense of future generations.

Even so, we have been able to meet our commitments to pensioners; to give extra help to the disabled; and to increase the amount available for the Health Service. My Lord Mayor, to do that and still redeem debt, is truly the mark of good stewardship and the Chancellor and Chief Secretary deserve our thanks and congratulations.

So with our industry revitalised, with inflation set to come down, and public finances sound, we can face the 1990s with confidence.

My Lord Mayor, as you may have noticed, Europe has been in the news a bit lately. But the real news of these last two weeks was not the headlines: "Maggie Isolated." It was the breakthrough of the British and French tunnels deep below the Channel.

That was history in the making. For the first time in many thousands of years Britain and France are linked. Or as one of our more lively daily papers put it: "The Europeans are no longer cut off from merrie England."

It seems no time at all since President Mitterrand and I met in Lille in 1986 to sign the original agreement: and later in the Chapter House of Canterbury Cathedral to complete the formalities. All that since then. But that is the private sector for you. I believe the Tunnel will have a fundamental and beneficial effect on attitudes in this country to mainland Europe.

These two events—the headlines on the one hand, and the tunnel on the other—underline the difference between rhetoric and reality. The reality lies in getting things done: the practical steps which mean more trade, more travel, more cooperation of every sort between the Continent and the United Kingdom.

And as I have many times said, so much of our history has been in Europe and our destiny lies in Europe. But we tend to approach things in a rather different way from some of our partners in the European Community. Our common law, our democracy, our Parliamentary institutions and proceedings have developed and matured over many centuries. We believe that institutions are stronger when they grow and evolve. So we are cautions about grand designs and blue-prints. We like to be certain we can achieve something before we commit our good name to it.

That is very much our approach to the discussions on economic and monetary union. We don't readily understand why people insist on setting time-tables for future stages before they have decided on their content.

We look at the wide differences between countries in the Community:—at the differences in their living standards;—at the vastly different inflation rates, from 2½ per cent in one country to 22 per cent in another;—at the differences in their public finances, ranging from our budget surplus to a huge budget deficit in Italy;—we look at the continuing high subsidies to industries in many European countries, which make it difficult to have a genuine Single Market.

We look at all these things and ask: with such enormous disparities, is it really sensible to tie ourselves down now to specific commitments in the distant future before we can possibly know whether they can be achieved and what their consequences would be for each of our countries?

Isn't it better to follow an evolutionary approach, to make progress a step at a time? That's the course Britain has chosen, in proposing the hard Ecu as a common European currency alongside national currencies, so that people can choose which to use. Ours is the only fully worked-out proposal for the next stage which has been tabled and I pay tribute to the City's part in developing it.

And surely it is more sensible to see that every country fulfils its existing obligations before moving on to set new targets. In the City, you take pride that your word is your bond. That's Britain's approach to Europe. We don't make promises we can't keep. Whether on the Single Market, over the environment, in the GATT negotiations or in a host of other ways, the record clearly shows that when we say we'll do something, we do it *(applause)*.

We don't want Europe to be an exclusive and inward-looking club. That would risk pushing other groups of countries in Asia and in North America to form competing trade blocs. Nothing would more surely stifle the free exchange of goods and services worldwide on which the City and indeed Britain depend for their livelihood.

The City, My Lord Mayor, as you have said, is and must remain the pre-eminent financial centre in Europe. The success of a financial centre depends on willingness to take risks and make markets, on an ability to come up with new services to meet changing financial and industrial needs; and it depends on integrity. These things will remain true however Europe develops.

In Switzerland, Luxembourg and Hong Kong, the amount of

business done far exceeds that in their own national currency. In the same way, London is far more important as a place to issue bonds or trade foreign exchange than sterling alone would imply. Indeed, while sterling's role as a reserve currency declined, London's strength as a financial centre grew.

The qualities that have brought London to its present eminence rest ultimately on the people who work in its markets. Reputation and tradition built up over centuries will endure. London has what it takes to stay on top in Europe and the world—and London must and will stay on top *(applause)*.

My Lord Mayor, as we look around the world, what an astonishing change it has been, change more fundamental than at any time since the War. —Just twelve months since the Berlin Wall came down. —Twelve months in which democracy and the rule of law have begun to return to the countries of Eastern Europe. —Twelve months which have seen the most profound changes in the Soviet Union—and we don't yet know where they will end. —Twelve months in which the threat of military attack on Western Europe has been radically diminished—and that would never have happened but for our resolve to maintain a strong defence *(applause)*. And the changes have not been limited to Europe. —We have witnessed unprecedented reform in South Africa, as well as the release of Nelson Mandela. —The world has started to come to grips with the problem of climate change.

> Having consulted widely among colleagues, I have concluded that the unity of the Party and the prospects of victory in a General Election would be better served if I stood down to enable Cabinet colleagues to enter the ballot for the leadership. I should like to thank all those in Cabinet and outside who have given me such dedicated support. It is vital that we stand together. The unity of the Party is crucial and that's why I'm giving up. I couldn't bear all the things I have stood for over the past eleven years being rejected. The Cabinet must unite to stop Michael Heseltine.
>
> *Resignation statement to the Cabinet, 22 November 1990*

—We have seen what may be the greatest international coalition in history take shape: the uniting of many nations, races and faiths against Saddam Hussein and his brutal invasion and plunder of Kuwait.

—And we have seen a great and welcome increase in the influence of the United Nations.

There is much over which we can rejoice and give thanks. Those of us who have visited Eastern Europe and felt the new freedom in the air find it profoundly moving, as do those who have heard President de Klerk talk of his hopes for a non-racial future for South Africa.

And with the crumbling of Communism internationally, we no longer face the same dangers from subversion, nor the same risk that local conflicts will polarise into confrontation between East and West.

But we can't forget the darker side: the many victims of terrorism; the hostages in Beirut, particularly Terry Waite, John McCarthy and Jack Mann; the Kuwaiti people, the victims of Iraq's systematic cruelty and destruction; the British hostages in Iraq and Kuwait and the agony and uncertainty of their families who have to watch and wait; and isolated in the Embassy and surrounded by Iraqi guns, our Ambassador in Kuwait and his one remaining colleague are holding out. Their courage and fortitude are in the highest tradition of our Diplomatic Service. We are proud of them! *(applause)*

Some of you will have read a letter which appeared in one of our national newspapers the other day. It reminds us that—and I quote—"hundreds of Kuwaitis are being tortured and killed in some of the most horrible ways possible"; and the writer goes on to say—and I quote once more: "every visit by every politician, diplomat or envoy prolongs the agony of those of us under Iraqi occupation—it does not bring the Iraqi regime in Kuwait any nearer to its end."

That letter is from a British citizen trapped in Kuwait.

I have received a letter, too, from the mother of one of the hostages in Iraq in which she tells how he was allowed to telephone her the other day but had only one message: don't negotiate with the terrorists, with Saddam Hussein!

Such, My Lord Mayor, is the tremendous courage of the British people caught up in this appalling situation. We ourselves must not show one ounce less resolve than they do. We hope that sanctions will compel Iraq to withdraw soon but if not, Arab and Western forces will have no alternative but to free Kuwait by military means.

Make no mistake! Free Kuwait we shall! If we fail to act conclusively now, we should only bequeath the problem to future generations, who would indeed have cause to blame us and our hopes for a better world in which law and decency prevail would be destroyed. You cannot allow the sanction of force to remain in the hands of someone who has no moral scruples whatsoever!

My Lord Mayor, I can't remember a time when the demands upon us—upon Britain and the Western countries—have been greater: calls for help to sustain democracy and reform in the Soviet Union and in the countries of Eastern Europe; the call to help defend countries outside Europe threatened by aggression. Thank goodness we kept our defences strong so that we could respond to the crisis in the Gulf with our Tornados and our Royal Navy ships and the Desert Rats!

One lesson stands out: at times such as these—times of change, of hope and yet of danger—Britain's unique qualities are needed once again:—steadfastness in defence;—staunchness as an ally; and—willingness always to give a lead. Time after time, when put to the test in a just cause, these qualities have served Britain and the world well. They will do so again.

REMARKS AFTER THE FIRST LEADERSHIP ELECTION BALLOT

Courtyard of the British Embassy, Paris. 20 November 1990

John Sergeant, BBC: Mrs Thatcher, could I ask you to comment?

Margaret Thatcher: Just a moment. Good evening. Good evening gentlemen.

Bernard Ingham: *Pressing forward.* Where is the microphone?

John Sergeant, BBC: It is here. This is the microphone.

Sergeant holds microphone out towards MT

MT: I am naturally very pleased that I got more than half the Parliamentary Party and disappointed that it's not *quite* enough to win on the first ballot, so I confirm it is my intention to let my name go forward for the second ballot.

Peter Allen, ITN: Isn't the … isn't the vote against you, Mrs Thatcher, large enough for you to have to acknowledge …

MT: Look, I have …

Peter Allen, ITN: …that you no longer enjoy the confidence of the party?

MT: I have got more than half the votes of the Parliamentary Party. It was not quite the fifteen per cent above those of Mr Heseltine —I think it's about 14.6 per cent—so it means we have to go for a second ballot, so I confirm that I shall let my name go forward.

Journalists: *[speaking at once]* Prime Minister! Mrs Thatcher! Does that mean …

MT: I must go and do some telephone calls.

Journalist: Do you feel at all betrayed by some of the …

MT: Thank you very much, thank you.

Some minutes later Douglas Hurd also spoke to the press outside the Embassy

Douglas Hurd: I would just like to make a brief comment on the ballot result.
The Prime Minister continues to have my full support and I am sorry that this destructive, unnecessary contest should be prolonged in this way. Thank you

SPEECH IN THE CONFIDENCE DEBATE – "I'M ENJOYING THIS!"

House of Commons, 22 November 1990

The Prime Minister (Mrs Margaret Thatcher): It is, of course, the right and duty of Her Majesty's Opposition to challenge the position of the Government of the day. It is also their right to test the confidence of the House in the Government if they think that the circumstances warrant it. I make no complaint about that. But when the windy rhetoric of the right hon. Member for Islwyn (Mr Kinnock) has blown away, what are their real reasons for bringing this motion before the House? There were no alternative policies—just a lot of disjointed, opaque words.

It cannot be a complaint about Britain's standing in the world. That is deservedly high, not least because of our contribution to ending the cold war and to the spread of democracy through eastern Europe and Soviet Union—achievements that were celebrated at the historic meeting in Paris from which I returned yesterday.

It's a funny old world.

At a Cabinet meeting following her resignation, 27 November 1990

It cannot be the nation's finances. We are repaying debts, including the debts run up by the Labour party. It cannot be the Government's inability to carry forward their programme for the year ahead, which was announced in the Gracious Speech on 7 November. We carried that debate by a majority of 108.

The Opposition's real reason is the leadership election for the Conservative party, which is a democratic election according to rules which have been public knowledge for many years—one member, one vote. That is a far cry from the way in which the Labour party does these things. Two in every five votes for its leader are cast by the trade union block votes, which have a bigger say than Labour Members in that decision: precious little democracy there.

The real issue to be decided by my right hon. and hon. Friends is how best to build on the achievements of the 1980s, how to carry Conservative policies forward through the 1990s and how to add to three general election victories a fourth, which we shall surely win.

Eleven years ago, we rescued Britain from the parlous state to which socialism had brought it. I remind the House that, under socialism, this country had come to such a pass that one of our most able and distinguished ambassadors [Sir Nicholas Henderson] felt compelled to write in a famous dispatch, a copy of which found its way into *The Economist*, the following words: "*We talk of ourselves without shame as being one of the less prosperous countries of Europe. The prognosis for the foreseeable future*"

Conservative government has changed all that. Once again, Britain stands tall in the councils of Europe and of the world, and our policies have brought unparalleled prosperity to our citizens at home.

In the past decade, we have given power back to the people on an unprecedented scale. We have given back control to people over their own lives and over their livelihood—over the decisions that matter most to them and their families. We have done it by curbing the monopoly power of trade unions to control, even to victimise, the individual worker. Labour would return us to conflict, confrontation and government by the consent of the TUC. We have done it by enabling families to own their homes, not least through the sale of 1.25 million council houses. Labour opposes our new rents-to-mortgage initiative, which will spread the benefits of ownership wider still. We have done it by giving people choice in public services—which school is right for their children, which training course is best for the school leaver, which doctor they choose to look after their health and which hospital they want for their treatment.

Labour is against spreading those freedoms and choice to all our people. It is against us giving power back to the people by privatising nationalised industries. Eleven million people now own shares, and 7.5 million people have registered an interest in buying electricity shares. Labour wants to renationalise electricity, water and British Telecom. It wants to take power back to the state and back into its own grasp—a fitful and debilitating grasp.

Mr Martin Flannery (Sheffield, Hillsborough): The right hon. Lady says that she has given power back to the people, but more than 2 million of them are unemployed. Has she given power back to them? Inflation is 10.9 per cent. Is that giving power back to the people, compared with rates throughout the rest of Europe? Is the frittering away of £100 billion-worth of North sea oil, which no other country has had, giving power back to the people? Will she kindly explain that—and how pushing many people into cardboard boxes and taking power away from them is somehow giving power back to them?

The Prime Minister: Two million more jobs since 1979 represent a great deal more opportunity for people. Yes, 10.9 per cent.

inflation is much higher than it should be, but it is a lot lower than 26.9 per cent. under the last Labour Government. Yes, we have benefited from North sea oil. The Government have made great investments abroad that will give this country an income long after North sea oil has ceased. We have provided colossal investment for future generations. Labour Members ran up debts, which we have repaid. We are providing investment for the future; we do not believe in living at the expense of the future.

Mr Dave Nellist (Coventry, South-East): If things are as good as the Prime Minister is outlining, why are her colleagues not happy for her to continue in the job of defending that record?

The Prime Minister: These are the reasons why we shall win a fourth general election. We have been down in the polls before when we have taken difficult decisions. The essence of a good Government is that they are prepared to take difficult decisions to achieve long-term prosperity. That is what we have achieved and why we shall handsomely win the next general election.

I was speaking of the Labour party wanting to renationalise privatised industry. Four of the industries that we have privatised are in the top 10 British businesses, but at the very bottom of the list of 1,000 British businesses lie four nationalised industries. Labour's industries consume the wealth that others create and give nothing back.

Because individuals and families have more power and more choice, they have more opportunities to succeed—2 million more jobs than in 1979, better rewards for hard work, income tax down from 33p in the pound to 25p in the pound and no surcharge on savings income. Living standards are up by a third and 400,000 new businesses have been set up since 1979—more than 700 every week. There is a better future for our children, thanks to our hard work, success and enterprise. Our people are better off than ever before. The average pensioner——

Mr Simon Hughes (Southwark and Bermondsey): Will the right hon. Lady give way?

The Prime Minister: If the hon. Gentleman will just listen, he might hear something that he did not know. The average pensioner now has twice as much to hand on to his children as he did 11 years ago. They are thinking about the future. This massive rise in our living standards reflects the extraordinary transformation of the private sector.

Mr Hughes: There is no doubt that the Prime Minister, in many ways, has achieved substantial success. There is one statistic, however, that I understand is not challenged, and that is that, during her 11 years as Prime Minister, the gap between the richest 10 per cent. and the poorest 10 per cent. in this country has widened substantially. At the end of her chapter of British politics, how can she say that she can justify the fact that many people in a constituency such as mine are relatively much poorer, much less well housed and much less well provided for than they were in 1979? Surely she accepts that that is not a record that she or any Prime Minister can be proud of.

The Prime Minister: People on all levels of income are better off than they were in 1979. The hon. Gentleman is saying that he would rather that the poor were poorer, provided that the rich were less rich. That way one will never create the wealth for better social services, as we have. What a policy. Yes, he would rather have the poor poorer, provided that the rich were less rich. That is the Liberal policy.

Mr Hughes: No.

The Prime Minister: Yes, it came out. The hon. Member did not intend it to, but it did.

The extraordinary transformation of the private sector has created the wealth for better social services and better pensions—

it enables pensioners to have twice as much as they did 10 years ago to leave to their children.

We are no longer the sick man of Europe—our output and investment grew faster during the 1980s than that of any of our major competitors.

Several Hon. Members: *rose*——

The Prime Minister: If hon. Members would be a little patient, it would allow me to get a little further.

No longer a doubtful prospect, when American and Japanese companies invest in Europe, we are their first choice. Britain no longer has an overmanned, inefficient, backward manufacturing sector, but modern, dynamic industries.

The right hon. Gentleman referred to the level of inflation. Yes, in 1987 and 1988, the economy did expand too fast. There was too much borrowing, and inflation rose. That is why we had to take the tough, unpopular, measures to bring the growth of money supply within target. Inflation has now peaked and will soon be coming down. Inevitably, the economy has slowed, but we firmly expect growth to resume next year. For the fundamentals are right. Our industry is now enterprising. It has been modernised and restructured. In sector after sector, it is our companies which lead the world—in pharmaceuticals, in telecommunications and in aerospace. Our companies have the freedom and talent to succeed—and the will to compete.

Mr Sillars: The Prime Minister is aware that I detest every single one of her domestic policies, and I have never hidden that fact. *[Interruption.]*

Mr Speaker: Order.

Mr Sillars: However, it is always a greater pleasure to tackle a political heavyweight opponent than a lightweight Leader of the

Opposition—*[Interruption]*—who is afraid to explain why, after a lifetime of campaigning to get rid of nuclear weapons, he is going to plant three Trident missiles in my country.

Can I take the Prime Minister back to the question of the poor getting poorer? Does she not realise—even at this point, five minutes after midnight for her—that, because of the transfer of resources from the poor to the wealthy, the poll tax was unacceptable, and that it was because of the poll tax that she has fallen?

The Prime Minister: I think that the hon. Gentleman knows that I have the same contempt for his socialist policies as the people of east Europe, who have experienced them, have for theirs. I think that I must have hit the right nail on the head when I pointed out that the logic of those policies is that they would rather the poor were poorer. Once they start to talk about the gap, they would rather that the gap were that—*[indicating]*—down here, not this—*[indicating]*—but—*[indicating]*. So long as the gap is smaller, they would rather have the poor poorer. One does not create wealth and opportunity that way. One does not create a property-owning democracy that way.

Can I now get back to the subject of industry and an industrial policy from which Scotland has benefited so much, and from which it could never have benefited under the Government that the hon. Member for Glasgow, Govan Mr Sillars) used to support, and under the political policy that he espouses now?

Yes, our companies have the freedom and talent to succeed, and the will to compete. And compete we must. Our competitors will not be taking a break. There must be no hankering after soft options and no going back to the disastrous economic policies of Labour Governments. No amount of distance lends enchantment to the lean years of Labour, which gave us the lowest growth rate in Europe, the highest strike record and, for the average family, virtually no increase in take-home pay. Labour's policies are a vote of no confidence in the ability of British people to manage their own affairs. We have that confidence. Confidence in freedom and confidence in enterprise. That is what divides Conservatives from socialists.

Our stewardship of the public finances has been better than that of any Government for nearly 50 years. It has enabled us to repay debt and cut taxes. The resulting success of the private sector has generated the wealth and revenues which pay for better social services—to double the amount being spent to help the disabled, to give extra help to war widows, and vastly to increase spending on the national health service. More than 1 million more patients are being treated each year and there are 8,000 more doctors and 53,000 more nurses to treat them.

Mr Jack Ashley (Stoke-on-Trent, South): *rose*——

The Prime Minister: That is the record of eleven and a half years of Conservative Government and Conservative principles. All these are grounds for congratulation, not censure, least of all from the Leader of the Opposition, who has no alternative policies.

Mr Ashley: *rose*——

The Prime Minister: I shall give way to the right hon. Gentleman, but then I should like to move on to say something about Europe, because what the Leader of the Opposition said about it was, to say the least, opaque.

Mr Ashley: The Prime Minister mentioned disabled people, and as she is always anxious to be honest with the House, would she care to give a wider perspective about what has happened to disabled people under her Government? Would she care to confirm the official figures, which show that, in the first 10 years of her reign, average male earnings rose by 20 per cent. in real terms, whereas benefits for disabled people in that period rose 1 per cent. in real terms? How well did disabled people do out of that?

The Prime Minister: The right hon. Gentleman is very selective indeed. He knows full well that, in the past 11 years, we have spent twice as much on the disabled, over and above inflation—not twice as much in cash terms, but twice as much in terms of what the benefits will buy—especially in the mobility allowance and the Motability scheme. This has been quite outstanding and has been brought about because, under our policies, we have been able to create the wealth which created the resources to do that, among other things.

During the past 11 years, this Government have had a clear and unwavering vision of the future of Europe and Britain's role in it. It is a vision which stems from our deep-seated attachment to parliamentary democracy and commitment to economic liberty, enterprise, competition and a free market economy. No Government in Europe have fought more resolutely against subsidies, state aids to industry and protectionism; unnecessary regulation and bureaucracy and increasing unaccountable central power at the expense of national Parliaments. No Government have fought more against that in Europe than we have.

We have fought attempts to put new burdens and constraints on industry, such as the social charter which would take away jobs, in particular part-time jobs. For us part of the purpose of the Community is to demolish trade barriers and eliminate unfair subsidies, so that we can all benefit from a great expansion of trade both within Europe and with the outside world.

The fact is that Britain has done more to shape the Community over the past 11 years than any other member state. Britain is leading the reform of the common agricultural policy, getting surpluses down, putting a ceiling on agricultural spending. We have been the driving force towards the single market which, when it is completed, will be the most significant advance in the Community since the treaty of Rome itself. We have done more than any other Government to resist protectionism, keep Europe's market open to trade with the rest of the world, and make a success of the GATT negotiations.

We have worked for our vision of a Europe which is free and open to the rest of the world, and above all to the countries of eastern Europe as they emerge from the shadows of socialism. It would not help them if Europe became a tight-knit little club, tied up in regulations and restrictions. They deserve a Europe where there is room for their rediscovered sense of nationhood and a place to decide their own destiny after decades of repression.

All part of my vision of a wider Europe.

On the fall of the Berlin Wall, November 1990

With all this, we have never hesitated to stand up for Britain's interests. The people of Britain want a fair deal in Europe, particularly over our budget contribution. We have got back nearly £10 billion which would otherwise have been paid over to the EC under the arrangements negotiated by the Labour party when it was in power.

Indeed, what sort of vision does the Labour party have? None, according to the Leader of the Opposition. Labour Members want a Europe of subsidies, a Europe of socialist restrictions, a Europe of protectionism. They want it because that is how they would like to run—or is it ruin?—this country.

Every time that we have stood up and fought for Britain and British interests, Labour Front Bench spokesmen have carped, criticised and moaned. On the central issues of Europe's future, they will not tell us where they stand. Do they want a single currency? The right hon. Gentleman does not even know what it means, so how can he know?—*[Laughter.]*

Mr Kinnock: It is a hypothetical question.

The Prime Minister: Absolute nonsense. It is appalling. He says that it is a hypothetical question. It will not be a hypothetical question. Someone must go to Europe and argue knowing what it means.

Are Labour members prepared to defend the rights of this United

Kingdom Parliament? No, for all that the right hon. Gentleman said. For them, it is all compromise, "sweep it under the carpet", "leave it for another day", and "it might sort itself out", in the hope that the people of Britain will not notice what is happening to them, and how the powers would gradually slip away.

The Government will continue to take a positive and constructive approach to the future of Europe. We welcome economic and monetary co-operation: indeed, no other member state has gone further than Britain in tabling proposals for the next stage, including the hard ecu. But our proposals would work with the market and give people and Governments real choice.

We want the Community to move forward as twelve: and from my talks in Paris with other European leaders over the past few days, I am convinced that that is their aim too. Europe is strongest when it grows through willing co-operation and practical measures, not compulsion or bureaucratic dreams.

Mr Alan Beith (Berwick-upon-Tweed): Will the Prime Minister tell us whether she intends to continue her personal fight against a single currency and an independent central bank when she leaves office?

Mr Dennis Skinner (Bolsover): No. She is going to be the governor. *[Laughter.]*

The Prime Minister: What a good idea. I had not thought of that. But if I were, there would be no European central bank accountable to no one, least of all national Parliaments. The point of that kind of Europe with a central bank is no democracy, taking powers away from every single Parliament, and having a single currency, a monetary policy and interest rates which take all political power away from us. As my right hon. Friend the Member for Blaby (Mr Lawson) said in his first speech after the proposal for a single currency was made, a single currency is about the politics of Europe, it is about a federal Europe by the back door. So I shall consider the proposal of the hon. Member for Bolsover (Mr Skinner). Now where were we? I am enjoying this.

Mr Michael Carttiss (Great Yarmouth): Cancel it. You can wipe the floor with these people.

The Prime Minister: Yes, indeed—I was talking about Europe and the socialist ideal of Europe. Not for us the corporatism, socialism and central control. We leave those to the Opposition. Ours is a larger vision of a Community whose member states co-operate with one another more and more closely to the benefit of all.

Are we then to be censured for standing up for a free and open Britain in a free and open Europe? No. Our policies are in tune with the deepest instincts of the British people. We shall win the censure motion, so we shall not be censured for what is thoroughly right.

Under our leadership, Britain has been just as influential in shaping the wider Europe and the relations between East and West. Ten years ago, the eastern part of Europe lay under totalitarian rule, its people knowing neither rights nor liberties. Today, we have a Europe in which democracy, the rule of law and basic human rights are spreading ever more widely, where the threat to our security from the overwhelming conventional forces of the Warsaw pact has been removed: where the Berlin wall has been torn down and the cold war is at an end.

These immense changes did not come about by chance. They have been achieved by strength and resolution in defence, and by a refusal ever to be intimidated. No one in eastern Europe believes that their countries would be free had it not been for those western Governments who were prepared to defend liberty, and who kept alive their hope that one day east Europe too would enjoy freedom.

But it was no thanks to the Labour party, or to the Campaign for Nuclear Disarmament of which the right hon. Gentleman is still a member. It is this Government who kept the nuclear weapons which ensured that we could never be blackmailed or threatened. When Brezhnev deployed the SS20s, Britain deployed the cruise missiles and was the first to do so. And all these things were done in the teeth of the opposition of the hon. Gentlemen opposite—and their ladies. *[Laughter]* The SS20s could never have been negotiated away without the bargaining strength which cruise and Pershing gave to the west.

Should we be censured for our strength? Or should the Labour party be censured for its weakness? I have no doubt that the people of Britain will willingly entrust Britain's security in future to a Conservative Government who defend them, rather than to socialists who put expediency before principle.

Sir Eldon Griffiths (Bury St. Edmunds): May I offer my right hon. Friend one measurement of the immense international respect and affection that she enjoys as a result of her policies of peace through strength? An opinion poll published on the west coast of America last month—*[Laughter.]*

Mr Speaker: Order. This takes up a great deal of time. The hon. Gentleman is seeking to participate in the debate. Will he please ask a question?

Ladies and Gentlemen, we're leaving Downing Street for the last time after eleven and a half wonderful years, and we're very happy that we leave the United Kingdom in a very, very much better state than when we came here eleven and a half years ago. It's been a tremendous privilege to serve this country as Prime Minister—wonderfully happy years—and I'm immensely grateful to the staff who supported me so well, and may I also say a word of thanks to all the people who sent so many letters, still arriving, and for all the flowers. Now it's time for a new chapter to open and I wish John Major all the luck in the world. He'll be splendidly served and he has the makings of a great Prime Minister, which I'm sure he'll be in very short time. Thank you very much. Goodbye.

Remarks departing Downing Street, 28 November 1990

Sir Eldon Griffiths: The figures are Gorbachev 74 per cent., Bush 75 per cent. and Thatcher 94 per cent.

The Prime Minister: I am sure that they were quite right, too.

I wish to say a word or two about the situation in the Gulf, because it will dominate politics until the matter is resolved. It is principle which is at stake, as well as the rule of international law.

In my discussions with other Heads of Government at the CSCE summit in Paris, I found a unanimous and impressive determination that Iraq's aggression must not succeed. The resolutions of the United Nations must be implemented in full. That is the peaceful option, Mr Speaker, and it is there to be taken, if Saddam Hussein so chooses. There was also a widespread recognition among my colleagues in Paris that the time was fast approaching when the world community would have to take more decisive action to uphold international law and compel Saddam Hussein to leave Kuwait.

No one can doubt the dangers which lie ahead. Saddam Hussein has many times shown his contempt for human life, not least for the lives of his own people. He has large armed forces. They are equipped with peculiarly evil weapons, both chemical and biological.

Mr Tam Dalyell (Linlithgow): Will the Prime Minister give way?

The Prime Minister: No, not now.

Twice in my time as Prime Minister we have had to send our forces across the world to defend a small country against ruthless aggression: first to our own people in the Falklands and now to the borders of Kuwait. To those who have never had to take such decisions, I say that they are taken with a heavy heart and in the knowledge of the manifold dangers, but with tremendous pride in the professionalism and courage of our armed forces.

There is something else which one feels. That is a sense of this country's destiny: the centuries of history and experience which ensure that, when principles have to be defended, when good has to be upheld and when evil has to be overcome, Britain will take up arms. It is because we on this side have never flinched from difficult decisions that this House and this country can have confidence in this Government today.

PART SIX

Prime Minister Emeritus

1990–

I shan't be pulling the levers, but I shall be a very good back seat driver.

In her role following her departure from No. 10, 1990

One is an ordinary person, and don't you forget it!

To Eve Pollard, 1991

SPEECH ON EUROPE

House of Commons, 26th June 1991

Mrs Margaret Thatcher (Finchley)

The right hon. Member for Manchester, Gorton (Mr Kaufman) started his speech by making it clear that his party would vote against the Government tonight. He gave no justification for that course of action. He and his hon. Friends know full well that the hand of my right hon. Friend the Prime Minister would be greatly strengthened in Luxembourg if he had a really good vote behind him when he goes there on Friday. I hope that many people—*[Interruption.]* Not only did the right hon. Member for Gorton give no justification for that course of action: he gave virtually no positive proposals whatsoever. At one time, he seemed to advocate a policy of perpetual disagreement in the Community; then, having complained about unemployment, he launched into an attack against Japanese investment in this country. Many people in this country are very grateful for Japanese investment.

May I thank my right hon. Friend the Foreign Secretary for his clear exposition and for the way in which he puts things? I noted that, at Luxembourg, we shall not reach conclusions, but he will, I think, be the first to agree that we can influence the way in which things go at Maastricht by the arguments and proposals that we make. My right hon. Friend made it very clear that one of the difficulties of discussing the matter of the Community is that it is riddled with jargon and Eurospeak, and that words are used which do not have a precise meaning, such as the word "subsidiarity". It is a vague term which raises far more questions than it answers. When we use those terms, we should be careful to define them.

I do not wish to speak for very long, Mr Speaker, so may I therefore set the background, as I see it, to my remarks and then raise five points that I hope my right hon. Friends will consider in their deliberations in Luxembourg?

The issues that we are debating today are fundamental to the future role of this Parliament, and deserve to be treated seriously. They are fundamental to the kind of Europe in which our children will live and they are fundamental to our future relationship with the wider world, especially the eastern European states and the United States of America. The fact itself that we are debating these issues reminds us of the cardinal principle of our system of government—that Ministers are directly answerable to Parliament and that the buck stops here.

My right hon. Friend the Prime Minister has previously spoken eloquently of his wish to see Britain at the heart of Europe. He is right, and we have been. That is how we secured reform of the Community's finances. That is how we won reform of the common agricultural policy, although there is more to do, and that is how we started the creation of the single market. None of those things could have been achieved from the sidelines. We had to be in the midst of battle, and we were. We won many battles, and as we finished the battles, the position was far, far better for Britain than it was when we started. It is by staying in the centre that we can press the case for free trade through the general agreement on tariffs and trade and for reaching agreements with the countries of eastern Europe. My right hon. Friends have pursued those matters with vigour, and they are right to do so.

The summary of the documents for the forthcoming Luxembourg Council—I have not seen the full documents, because they came too late, and I share the views of those who protested that they were not available—reveals a quite different destiny for Europe from any that we were ever given to expect when we went in. They are proposals for a federal union. They call for a common foreign, security and, in due course, defence policy, in which majority voting would apply. They call for a great extension of Community powers and competence in energy, in health and over labour laws—again, often with majority voting.

We had some experience of the extension of majority voting in the Single European Act. I suggest that we are very careful before we consider extending majority voting any further. The fact is that majority voting means that we give the Community the right to impose on the British people laws with which the House—the elected representatives—may fundamentally disagree. That is a very, very serious step to take. The document also calls for a central bank to set monetary policy, leading to a single European currency. *The Times* has referred to all this as "supranationalism run riot". My right hon. Friend [John Major] the Prime Minister declared in the House on 18 June:

"A European super-state would not be acceptable to me or to the House—and in my judgment it would not be acceptable to the country."—[*Official Report*, 18 June 1991; Vol. 193, c. 142.]

Every Prime Minister needs a Willie.

On William Whitelaw, 1991

I wholeheartedly agree with both *The Times* and my right hon. Friend.

Few of us will forget what Mr Delors told Members of the European Parliament in 1988. He said:

"In 10 years time, 80 per cent. of economic legislation and perhaps even fiscal and social legislation will be of Community origin."

That is the road that he wants us to take, and it is the road that we must resist.

I understand that my right hon. Friends cannot reveal their full negotiating hand, but I hope that, in their negotiations in Luxembourg, they will keep in mind the following five points. First, the present debate in Europe touches issues more profound than any since the Community's foundation. It is of an entirely different order of magnitude and importance from the debate on the Single European Act. That made some important changes in the concept of majority voting to make it more difficult for countries that do not believe in free trade to block the completion of the Common Market. It repeated earlier commitments to economic and monetary union, while attempting to define it as only economic and monetary co-operation. What is now being considered is a massive extension of the Community's powers and competence into almost every area of our national life and that of other member states. It would be the greatest abdication of national and parliamentary sovereignty in our history.

Some people argue that the changes envisaged in the draft treaties on the table in Luxembourg would not happen for many years, so there is no need to worry. That is a very dangerous approach, because, once those powers were given away, they would never be given back. All the evidence indicates that, while our people want Britain to be actively involved in Europe—and of course, I was the Prime Minister who enabled the channel tunnel to get going, so I do believe in having more to do with Europe—our people do not want to see a massive extension of the powers of Brussels into every corner of national life even if it is dressed up as a step-by-step approach—a kind of federal Europe achieved by stealth. I fully support the firm stand that my right hon. Friends have taken.

I fully support the firm stand that my right hon. Friend the Foreign Secretary and my right hon. Friend the Prime Minister have taken against any commitment to a federal Europe. I would hope that most people in the House were against a federal Europe; otherwise, what is the point of people standing as candidates at the next election—to come back here and propose to hand over all their powers as representatives of constituents to another Parliament?

The second point—[Hon. Members: "The second point."] Thank you very much. The second point is that we should not let those who support a federal Europe pretend that they are somehow more European than the rest of us. They are not; they are just more federal. There is nothing specifically European about a federal structure—indeed, the opposite: it is the nation state which is European.

It has been the great achievement of the Community to bring about greater co-operation between those nation states—not to merge them. Instead of pouring distinctive nations into institutions and arrangements of the same mould, we should be encouraging different kinds and degrees of co-operation between European countries. My right hon. Friend the Foreign Secretary said as much in his speech on 31 May in Shropshire, and I heartily agree with him.

That sort of European co-operation is already developing—for example, in other European matters, France feels easiest with a different defence relationship with NATO than the rest of us, but in practice she contributes in important ways to the west's defence. No one says that France is isolated—they accept the difference.

The Schengen group of countries have been able to reduce their frontier controls because of their common borders. We recognise that that would not do for us in Britain, because considerations of security and immigration are quite different for an island nation. But that does not mean that they cannot reduce their borders because all their geography indicates that. These different relationships make sense for those who participate, but they are not a model for everyone. The true Europeans are those who base themselves on Europe's history and traditions rather than on constitutional blueprints.

Thirdly, we should not for one moment fall for attempts to argue that a federal Europe would mean a devolution of powers. If that were the case, why change what we have at present? Powers are devolved, in that they are held by national Parliaments and Governments, as they should be. For Mr Delors to say that his proposals would mean devolving powers is ridiculous. They are not his or the Community's to devolve.

Our sovereignty does not come from Brussels—it is ours by right and by heritage. We choose what we devolve to the Community—not the other way round.

The fourth consideration which I hope my right hon. Friends will have in mind is the danger of being drawn along by what start out as vague commitments but end up as highly specific and damaging proposals. There is a much greater willingness in some European countries than in Britain to sign up to great rhetorical statements and declarations, without worrying too much about what they will mean in practice; and it is welcome that, as some of the earlier declarations of intent have been committed to treaty language, a number of Governments—not just ours—have become more worried about the practical consequences. Such is the case with the social charter.

Moreover, some are now seeing that a single currency could not possibly work with the disparities between European economies as great as they are now—and that setting the goal of a single currency has no relevance to Europe's current economic problems. Moreover, to go to a single currency—

Moreover, to go to a single currency is not just a practical matter: it is a fundamental question of principle. It is not only a merger of currencies: it is to give up for all time the right of the Banks of England and of Scotland and our Treasury to issue our own currency, backed by our own economic policy, answerable to our own Parliament. That is why I do not believe in a single currency.

If, nevertheless, some other members of the European Community wish to agree to the idea of a single European currency—and not all of them belong to the exchange rate mechanism yet—they are entitled to go ahead and do so. Luxembourg is already linked to the Belgian franc, and the Dutch guilder is close to the deutschmark.

But unless legislation on a single currency were contained in a separate treaty, certain consequences could follow. I shall give three. First Britain, although not in a single currency herself, may be expected to contribute to the huge increases in structural funds required in order to allow the weaker member countries to participate in EMU.

Secondly, unforeseen consequences could arise as European Courts interpret the single currency provisions in the context of the full treaty of Rome.

Thirdly, there is no way in which the economies of the former communist states of eastern Europe could withstand the pressures

In my view dictators do not surrender. They have to be well and truly defeated.

Independent on Sunday, 20 January 1991

placed on their fragile industries by a single currency—witness what has happened to eastern Germany.

We have to complete the transformation of the countries of eastern Europe into free enterprise democracies, and enable them to join the European Community as soon as possible. They need an anchor to the west.

It is if one moves to a single locked currency that one gets enormous difficulties, because there is no latitude to vary the currency. Therefore, any difficulties in the monetary or economic system have to go either to increased inflation or to increased recession and increased unemployment. The 6 per cent. swing gives us some latitude, but I believe that joining the exchange rate mechanism gave us all we needed for stiffening against inflation, and I do not believe that it is necessary or desirable to go any further into stages 2 or 3.

Finally, looking beyond the borders of the European Community, we have to strengthen and develop Europe's trade with the United States and the rest of north America, Canada and Mexico, perhaps through moves to a transatlantic free trade area. Further, the European nations have to encourage the Soviet Union and its constituent republics as they struggle along the path of reform.

We shall not achieve any of that if we accept a centralised, inward-looking European community. In both Luxembourg and Maastricht, we must speak out and reach out to the wider world. In my right hon. Friend the Prime Minister we have a leader with the vision and sense of purpose to do just that. I wish my right hon. Friends well in their great task, and I give them my full support.

INTERVIEW WITH MICHAEL BRUNSON, ITN NEWS

Great College Street, Westminster, 28 June 1991

Margaret Thatcher: ...It was just very strange. Have you seen a situation slip away from you? I'm a politician. I know. I can feel it, I can sense it and when some people whom I expected to be absolutely staunch had very different views, said "Look, I will support you but I don't think that…it is a foregone conclusion, then – all right. No General can fight without a really good army behind. What went wrong was that we did not get a big enough majority on the first ballot. There was nothing I could do to cure that. That was the thing I couldn't get over. They said to me as I went to them, "You haven't been to ask us to vote for you. Other people have." And I said "Goodness me, do I, after eleven and a half years, have to go and ask personally for votes…"

…Um, one had not won and there had been a different leader and a different Prime Minister, you couldn't have gone forward united. You couldn't have done…a Prime Minister really should have the majority of a party clearly behind him.

Um, I got up early and things hadn't changed, so I decided to take the course of action which I did. And then I went into the House…*(MT drew her head back, looking upset)*

Michael Brunson: Could I just first of all ask you to recall what must have been a very difficult meeting of the Cabinet?

MT: Yes, of course it was, of course it was. You don't take a decision like that without it being difficult, without heartbreak. Heartbreak there may have been, but it was the right decision.

MB: The image that people will perhaps remember…so the Cabinet was extremely difficult. Then you had to come out into Downing Street and you had to face the cameras and in effect you had to face the world.

MT: Mm-hh. *[MT evidently upset, dabs her eyes with a white handkerchief.]*

MB: You had to come and make what was perhaps the statement of your life. *[Brunson also a bit emotional]* And then – we notice now that it is affecting you now – and it must have been…

MT: Yes…*[Smiles slightly.]* It is not affecting my voice now. It is not affecting my voice. You are thinking back to traumatic things. Um, but I managed to get through them. I managed to get through the television, I managed to get through the Cabinet, again because there was *something else to do* …

MB: And then the House …

MT: By that time I was back *fighting fit*. *[Pause]* As you saw.

…Wouldn't life be very much better if more people took responsibility for their families, and for building their own future, and building their own security? And when they do that – and have a little bit over to help people less fortunate than themselves – isn't that a good thing?

And aren't we trying to get the third world out of the poverty it is in, by building up its industries, and having some investment to go and help them with?

John Wesley answered the question you've just put: "Do not impute to money the faults of human nature."

It's not the money, it's not the wealth you create, it's what you *do* with it. And most people *do* want a better standard of living. Many many people use their money to…to to do more for arts, to see more, to enjoy more of the art great artistic works, whether it be music, whether it be art. Look at the fantastic *voluntary* effort in this country. It is enormous. No – those…look, 'greed', isn't it absurd. Trade unions mostly argue for higher wages, they argue for higher differentials. But they then come in and say – 'greed'. Some people are greedy. But people who want a better standard of living and a better way of life for their children are not. They are highly moral, they are highly valued citizens and they are usually those people who look after their houses and their families, look after their neighbourhoods, join in, doing things for their neighbourhood, community spirit. This is the real Thatcherism.

MB: sn't there always the danger that people might be seeing you still as trying to second guess the Prime Minister?

MT: Well, I hope they won't. I hope they won't. I did all my own first guessing, for fifteen years of what right to do – and it wasn't *guessing*, it was going back to the right principles and passionate belief. And you asked me recently what things I remember. I recall one thing very vividly. In 1980 one finance minister from another part of the world, who actually really rather believed in what I was doing but hadn't seen it put into practice before, and saying to me: "Look you are having difficulty. We are watching you very carefully, we are watching Britain very carefully" – that's good, they always pleased me when they are watching Britain – "because if you can roll back the frontiers of socialism and in Britain roll forward the frontiers of freedom, other people will follow you." What an extraordinary thing to say.

I knew I must keep doing. My goodness me I took a pounding. But we *did*. We did change trade union law. We did say to a company, look if you are going broke this is because you haven't got it right and we are not going to pour taxpayer's money to save you when in fact if there is any taxpayer's money it to be ought to be going to bringing to birth the new industries. And for the first time they had to take the consequences of their own action. What else is democracy and responsibility all about? We did. And we got people enthusiastic about enterprise. Do you know we have had more young people starting up on their own than ever before. It is a new spirit. That is the essence. To get the economy right, you have to understand human nature. There *is* a new spirit and we *did* get it right. And I'm not going to see it go.

MB: Just a final point on the whole business of the way your premiership ended. I think you've said that no Prime Minister really ought to have to leave in those circumstances. Of course, the counterargument is ... it's almost like that old phrase about "Be you never so high, the law is above you. " It's almost a sense, isn't it, in which you say "Be you never so high as Prime Minister, but you may be out of Downing Street tonight," and Prime Ministers ought to know that.

I have never been defeated by the people. It is my great pride.

Interview with Barbara Walters, February 1991

MT: Oh, if you are out for what I call constitutional reasons, of course. Slight pause. We were out for reasons of the rules made by the Conservative Party for leaders in Opposition. And that is very different. That is very different. The rules are still there. Uh, they are not rules that apply to the Labour Party or to any other party. This was the first time it had happened and ... uh, it happened. It happened, I took the right decision. I am now free to live another life of very practical use, both to the people of this country and internationally. I have a *passion* for Britain, for the spirit of the people, for their character. It's done wonders for the world in the past. It can still do wonders for the world into the future.

MB: And what is your Foundation going to do?

MT: It is going to embody all of those things I have explained and believed in. How to roll forward the frontiers of freedom, how to bring it about, educating people about what it is all about, giving practical help to the people in Eastern Europe who are trying to do it. They will want to know how to learn. We can give them scholarships, they can come over here. We can get people to go over there to advise them. We can hold conferences where they all get together and learn from one another and perpetuate the ideals. And also being very active in the environment and ... there is a good deal of work to do there on a scientific basis. It is partly education, it is partly practical, it is enlarging the frontiers of freedom, it is bringing more and more of the world to democracy, on the basis of what we in Britain have done. It is taking our leadership to others. They come in—I have telephone calls—"How can we do it?"—one can't give anything like the amount of money which governments can give, but one knows people who... you give them a helping hand, you put them in the way of grants, of scholarship, you teach them how to do it.

Most of the changes in the world are brought about by a few people who believe things, and don't give up. The Sakharovs, the Solzhenitsyns, knew what was needed. The next generation we have to teach how.

> I've been very quiet at home, which has been a very great effort on my part. A little less silence might be called for on my part.
>
> *Speaking about Europe, 22 June 1991*

And the young people have never been made servile or passive by the Communist system. The older people have. When I spoke to the young people in Moscow, in Leningrad, they are Thatcherites to a man, and woman. Isn't it marvellous! But they are ready, raring to go. We must help them with the how of it. The spirit of enterprise, the spirit...the character that is Britain. We are such a marvellous people, and we've done so much for Europe. We've done so much, we've taken to the far flung corners of the world our legal system, our common law—one of the best in the world—sound, uncorrupt administration, the spirit of enterprise. America practice it the other side. The best she learned from us. This...we must have a Foundation to make certain we have a centre through which it can continue. That is what I will do. The best of Britain to the best of the world.

SPEECH ON EUROPE

House of Commons, 20th November 1991

Mrs Margaret Thatcher (Finchley): I should like to make it clear at the outset of my remarks that tonight I shall support the motion in the name of my right hon. Friend. *[Interruption.]*

I congratulate my right hon. Friend on his speech and on the clear way in which he set out his views and indicated his way ahead. I know that he has difficult negotiations at Maastricht and that therefore he needs our support in those negotiations.

I for one am very grateful for this opportunity that has been given to right hon. and hon. Members seriously to put forward their views on what should be a very great and serious occasion. When my right hon. Friend is negotiating in Maastricht, it will undoubtedly be a very tense and hard negotiation. He has already said that there are some proposals which are quite unacceptable to the Government, and he pointed out which they were. His task will be to remove those proposals before he comes back to this House. *[Interruption.]* In my day, that would have required the occasional use of the handbag. Now it will doubtless be the cricket bat, but that is a good thing because it will be harder.

The Government will achieve their objectives only by putting our arguments vigorously and persistently, by refusing to be intimidated by deadlines and by making it clear that there are certain points on which we are not prepared to surrender. *[Interruption.]* Right hon. and hon. Members may be certain that I shall make my views clear, if I am given the opportunity to do so. It is not my custom to use coded messages.

My right hon. Friends have already shown that they can negotiate hard and that they have the courage to say no to proposals that are plainly not acceptable to the House. They have already explained why some measures should not be made by amending the treaty of Rome because that would bring them under the jurisdiction of the European Court, which has different methods of construing any proposal or legislation from those used by our courts.

I was astonished by the speech of the right hon. Member for Islwyn (Mr Kinnock). This is a very serious debate. There are enormously serious issues affecting the future rights of the House and its future responsibilities. When we are talking about the rights and responsibilities of the House, what we are really talking about are the rights of our constituents, and they need to be treated very seriously indeed.

May I make one or two more comments on the speech of the Leader of the Opposition? I came to the same conclusion from his speech as my right hon. Friend the Chancellor—that the right hon. Member for Islwyn was going to have a single currency willy-nilly. He has already made up his mind. The argument that he uses is that, if others have it, we must. That is an argument for a flock of sheep, not for people who are sent here to analyse the problem and to use our minds and our reason to say which course we should follow. If ever it is said that whatever they do we must follow, then they will put all kinds of things on the table which we shall have to fight very much harder.

I know full well that the Labour party made a commitment to a single currency and attached certain conditions. That commitment was made before the draft proposals were published. When they were published, as the right hon. Member for Bethnal Green and Stepney (Mr Shore) said, those conditions were not there. That should have made a difference to the Labour party's decision.

It is not surprising to some of us that the Labour party might wish to hand control of our financial and economic affairs to Europe, or indeed to almost anyone other than itself. It would suit it to get out of the responsibility and to pass it over to another body. That is not what we are here for. The fundamental issue—*[Interruption.]* I said that I am not accustomed to using coded messages. The fundamental issue—

The fundamental issue that will confront the Government at Maastricht is that the draft treaties propose an enormous, and, to me, unacceptable, transfer of responsibility from this House, which is clearly accountable to the British people, to the European Community and its institutions, which are not. In this House we are rightly jealous of our powers and responsibilities. As I said a moment ago, we are very much aware that our authority comes from the ballot box and that what we are talking about are the rights of the British people to govern themselves under their own laws, made by their own Parliament.

It has rightly been said that it is the character of a people which determines the institutions which govern them, and not the institutions which give people their character. Yes, it is about being British and it is about what we feel for our country, our Parliament, our traditions and our liberties. Because of our history, that feeling is perhaps stronger here than anywhere else in Europe, and it must determine the way in which our Government approach such fundamental matters.

My right hon. Friend the Prime Minister has said a good deal about the Single European Act, which has many lessons for us. It is not the case, as is sometimes alleged, that the Single European Act introduced qualified majority voting in the Community—it was already in the treaty of Rome. As my right hon. Friend said, the Act extended it in certain limited areas for the express and sole purpose of completing the common or single market by 1992. That was all. In the words of article 8A, these measures were adopted

"with the aim of progressively establishing the internal market over a period expiring on 31st December 1992."

Moreover, although it was in our interests to have majority voting on some measures, it was not on others and unanimity was explicitly preserved for other important areas. As article 100A makes clear, qualified majority voting does not apply

"to fiscal provisions, to those relating to the free movement of persons nor to those relating to the rights and interests of employed persons."

We would have expected some of the Commission's directives to have been taken under that unanimity clause, which requires us all to consent.

The Commission, however, has subsequently tried to circumvent the unanimity requirements by bringing forward proposals under other articles of the treaty where qualified majority voting is the rule. It has received some support from the European Court, which made an interpretation that would not have been made by our courts.

I raise that because we should draw a clear lesson from what has happened under the Single European Act. Many of us gave assurances about the unanimity rules, fully believing that they would be honoured and that the spirit of them would be honoured. Any powers conceded to the Commission by agreement are likely to be widened in practice and extended into areas that we do not envisage. We must look at the draft proposals in that light.

The other important step in the Single European Act, as my right hon. Friend the Prime Minister said, was the agreement to strengthen and improve co-operation on foreign policy. That agreement was never made part of the treaty of Rome—and quite rightly not. There are two ways to go—the treaty of Rome, with the European Court's interpretation of it, which is quite different from ours, or an intergovernmental agreement which is binding upon us but which does not have to enter into our law and is not part of the treaty of Rome.

That agreement on political co-operation is an excellent agreement. It was wholly drafted by us in the Foreign Office—*[Laughter.]*—to whom I gladly pay tribute in connection with that agreement and hope that they will be pleased—but it was tabled after I had shown it to the Germans and the French to get their approval. It was a bit offside but, nevertheless, some would take it as a compliment.

Countries with a history and a tradition such as Britain's cannot allow their hands to be tied on defence and on foreign policy by making them or their implementation subject to majority voting. I was very grateful to the Prime Minister for what he said, because something in a speech made by my right hon. Friend the Foreign Secretary—I think, in The Hague—suggested that there might be majority voting for implementation. *[Hon. Members: "Oh."]* I know that he will take it in very good part when I say that I read it, analysed it and thought that he was going a bit wobbly. However, I am delighted to hear from my right hon. Friend the Prime Minister that it is all to be agreed and that there will be no majority voting, that we shall continue under the intergovernmental agreements and not have things attached to the treaty of Rome.

Looking to the longer perspective, the history of our dealings with the European Community seems to consist of our conceding powers, of reassurances being given about their limits, of those limits being breached, and of the European Community then coming back with a new set of demands for more power for the Commission. That is the conveyor belt to federalism. That conveyor belt will not be stopped just by removing the word "federal" from the treaty.

I do not believe that any of my colleagues want federalism, but, judging from the right hon. Gentleman's speech, the Opposition are already committed to it. Faced with this, I believe that the majority of the British people do not want to hand over substantially more powers to the European Community. I believe that our objective must be to uphold the sovereignty of Parliament which has served us so well. That is more than can be said for the use that the Commission has made of some of its powers to promote what one newspaper has rightly described as "Euro-lunacies". I shall not waste the time of the House by listing them.

> The worst thing is the realization that some of those who you most trusted were most prominent in your betrayal.
>
> *Speaking after the coup against Mikhail Gorbachev, 31 August 1991*

It was never the intention, I believe, of the founders of the European Community that the Commission should try to exercise its control over every aspect of a nation's life in that way. Again, I was very grateful to my Foreign Secretary—*[Laughter.]* It is perfectly all right—my right hon. Friend is used to both praise and blame from me. Agreed? Excellent. Good.

Mr Hurd: My right hon. Friend had a number of Foreign Secretaries in her time. I accept the tribute on behalf of them all.

Mrs Thatcher: I am not quite sure whether he should.

However, that is why the Government are right to resist strongly—as my right hon. Friend said—attempts by some countries to bring education, health, social affairs, immigration and security into the treaty of Rome. We dealt with immigration under the Single European Act by a declaration which said that nothing in the Act should prevent us from making our own arrangements at borders to stop immigration, terrorism and crime. That is already agreed, and I hope that it will not be removed from the end of the Single European Act.

The right hon. Gentleman referred to the social charter. I have never for one moment regretted being isolated in opposing the social charter. If I had not opposed it, it would have been assumed that we had agreed to many of the directives—there are about 40 under that charter—and there would have been implied commitment to them. There is not. It was absolutely right to oppose it. Moreover, it would have placed unnecessary burdens and restrictions on our industry, it would, of course, have caused more unemployment and it would have been an unwarranted intrusion into our national affairs.

Most dangerous of all when it comes to the transfer of powers is the draft treaty on economic and monetary union. My right hon. Friend has already said that he will reject most of the political proposals. Economic and monetary union and being in charge of one's own economic policy go to the heart of our democracy and our powers. If one gives that up, one will have given up the capacity to make the main policies for which we are here and which affect the life of our nation.

Moreover, of course one is judged in an election on one's performance on the economy. Of course one is judged abroad on how successful we are and on how successful we were in transforming our economy from a socialist economy to an enterprise economy.

That will be the battleground for an election. It would be pretty ironic if, when arguing about the performance on this issue on one side or the other, candidates had, in the next breath, to say, "It may be that we shall pass all these powers over to the Community and other institutions." That is an enormous battery of powers, as one has seen from the economic and monetary union.

Money Bills and the general economic policy are the exclusive responsibility of this elected House. We are not, in my view, entitled ever to give away those responsibilities or to give away the people's rights, which is what a single currency would mean. Nor do I believe that a single currency would be in this country's interests. It would require a vast transfer of resources to the poorer countries of the Community to enable them to meet the obligations of membership of a single currency—and that at a time when we in Britain are already giving more money in most years to the European Community than to the third world. *[Interruption.]* Look at the autumn statement. Many people outside——

Many people would have thought that we should give more money to the third world than to the Community. In the coming years, we shall be giving about £2.5 billion to the Community and £2.1 billion to the third world. That is before—*[Interruption.]* No wonder they do not make very good speeches—they never listen. That is before any account is taken of increased requests for structural funds because of a single currency. I think that we should take that very much into account.

Most importantly, a single currency would take away any democratic accountability for our economic policies to the people of this country. I know that some people say, "Don't worry, a single currency will never come about, because the convergence conditions will never be achieved." The convergence conditions are totally unrealistic. Indeed, I doubt if they are achievable for many countries in the Community.

Certainly, it will be difficult—*[Laughter.]* It is dangerous to assume that, because the conditions are difficult at the moment, they will stay the same. It is quite possible that the Community will change them, while still keeping the goal of a single currency. Too often in the past, we have seen what we thought was a watertight agreement being subsequently eroded.

As my right hon. Friend the Member for Worthing (Mr Higgins) has noted in correspondence in *The Times*, there is the serious question of surveillance of our economic policies by the

Commission and the duty not to have an excessive deficit. From studying the section to which my right hon. Friend referred, it seems as if we shall be under surveillance anyway on a number of issues, even though we choose to use the exemption clause in the proposed treaty.

Mr Haynes: Just a year ago, the Conservative party committed a dastardly act against the right hon. Lady. I have missed her from the Dispatch Box ever since. If she was still in the seat of power, what would she be negotiating in Europe?

Mrs Thatcher: I am making a pretty good fist of just that.

My right hon. Friend the Chancellor of the Exchequer hopes to secure agreement to an opting-out or exemption clause, and one appears in the treaty. My concern, which is shared by many hon. Members of all parties, is how effective it would be in practice, bearing in mind the fact that, even if we exercise that power, we are still required to sign up to the goal of a single currency and to sign up to the institutions designed to prepare the way for it.

How easy would it be in practice to resist the pressures to go further? We do not want to be told that, because we have agreed to take part in the earlier stages of economic and monetary union under the proposed treaty, we have no real choice left but to accept a single currency. It seems to me as if that is the design of the whole draft proposals.

First, one has to have convergence with very different conditions. Before one can enter the single currency, one has to have another set of proposals—including, for example, that one has stayed within the narrow range of the exchange rate mechanism for two years. The hon. Member for Glasgow, Govan (Mr Sillars) spotted the proposition. As my right hon. Friend the Prime Minister said, eight member states could go to a single currency. We are in the exchange rate mechanism.

If we wish to keep open the option of going into a single

currency, we have virtually no freedom of action in that time. One cannot have different interest rates. If one's interest rates are lower, currency will flow out. If one's interest rates are higher, a good deal of money might flow in artificially. One would be linked inevitably to that single currency. The rate would be 2.5 per cent. and we should be unable to operate separately.

That is the design of the treaty. It always happens little by little. We should be told that we have come so far—from 6 per cent. to 2.5 per cent., and then from 2.5 per cent. to 2 per cent. or closer—that we have no option but to join. We must totally reject that, if need be——

As the hon. Member for Govan said, in such circumstances it would probably mean coming out of the exchange rate mechanism to keep our freedom of action. That is the danger of signing up to this treaty, and I hope that my right hon. Friends will consider that carefully. My right hon. Friends the Prime Minister and the Chancellor genuinely wish to keep open the right to go for exemption, and do not wish to be put by the treaty into a kind of funnel in which one has to go automatically to a single currency.

In some ways, it would be better for those who want a single currency to be achieved to go to it by a separate agreement outside the treaty of Rome. If it is achieved through the treaty of Rome, we get all the difficulties of interpretation by the European Court. If people want a single currency, why should they not achieve it outside the treaty of Rome? We have had intergovernmental conferences outside the treaty. That would be the way to do it, and it would not get us into the difficulties that I have described, of signing up to the concept of a single currency, signing up to its institutions and being driven into what I regard as a trap.

I recall the debate on economic and monetary union on 2 November 1989, in which almost universal opposition was expressed in the House to the whole Delors concept of monetary union and a single currency. It was as recently as November

1989. I remember attending the next European Council and saying to my colleagues, "It is no good. Our Parliament just will not accept it. It goes to the heart of our parliamentary tradition." My colleagues understood that and were prepared to make provision for it.

There has been a colossal and inexplicable change, especially among Opposition Members. The Opposition seem to be prepared to give up the parliamentary supremacy that has been the heart of our constitution.

I want to reply to the point raised by the right hon. Member for Chesterfield (Mr Benn) about a referendum. If at some point in the future there should be agreement between the parties in the House to abandon the right to issue the pound sterling—not only now, but in the future—and if the House agreed to abandon the right to issue our own currency, with all that that implies, and to adopt a single currency, the people would have no choice at an election time about that enormously important point.

If the Conservative party, the Labour party and the Liberal Democrats all said, "We are going to have a single currency, we are going to abandon the powers of the House of Commons and we are going to take away your rights," people could not make their views known through the ballot box at a general election.

Whoever got into power would not then have the right to claim that they had a mandate. They would not have had a mandate because they would have deprived the people of a choice. They would have done so not on a small thing, but on a major fundamental constitutional issue which was the right of the people. The only alternative for the people would be to vote for extremist parties—something which I should regret very much. There would be extremist candidates everywhere.

My right hon. Friends must address their minds to this matter. My right hon. Friend the Prime Minister said clearly that he believed in choice. He will provide choice. If everyone believes in the precise same arrangements on exemption from the single currency but we sign up to the concept, how could the people let their view be known? If one really wants to know the answer, one can find it in Dicey on the constitution. He came to the conclusion that, under those circumstances, the only thing to do was to hold a referendum, because that states clearly the issue and the merits and demerits. In our system, it would be no more binding than previous referendums which we have held in my time in Parliament. A referendum is advisory but it is not binding. The answer may be overwhelming. We had referendums in Scotland and Wales. Constitutional issues warrant a referendum.

When will Labour learn that you cannot build Jerusalem in Brussels.

1992

Anyone who does not consider a referendum necessary must explain how the voice of the people shall be heard. Therefore, I conclude that we should let the people speak. If not, we shall deprive them of their say on rights which we are taking away not only from them but from future generations and which, once gone, cannot be restored. A referendum may not be popular with some members of my party, but I doubt whether they have thought it through.

I am grateful for the opportunity to express my views clearly. I believe passionately in this House. I have been here for 32 years, although that is not as long as some Opposition and Conservative Members. We should retain parliamentary supremacy. We should not make a massive transfer of power to the Community, which is not accountable to our electorate. Therefore, we should not join a single currency.

I understand that my right hon. Friends wish to keep open the option, but the option is inevitably open because future Parliaments may consider it. We do not have to keep it open. I understand my right hon. Friends' wish, but I want to be sure that it is genuine. *[Interruption.]* Yes, of course. So does my right hon. Friend [John Major] the Prime Minister. I wish him well at Maastricht. Judging by the performance today, he will be our Prime Minister for a long time.

SPEECH TO CONSERVATIVE CANDIDATES

Conservative Central Office, 22 March 1992

Mr Chairman, Prime Minister, Mr [Cranley] Onslow, and colleagues. I nearly said fellow candidates, because old habits die hard. But this time it's a little bit different because I'm not standing for Finchley, and because we have John Major as our Leader and Prime Minister and we could not have chosen better.

I was lucky in three elections to have a manifesto with my approach stamped upon it. This manifesto has John Major's personality stamped on it and that is absolutely right. But amid the enormous detail, in this very full document, we must make sure that the electors do not lose sight of the really big issues that are at stake in this Election.

Nor must they lose sight of the fact that the Labour and Socialist principles upon which their manifesto is founded are totally different from those which have inspired all our policies so successfully. We must make certain they know the true division between us.

When I'm on the election hustings, as I frequently am, indeed I am most days, from dawn till dusk, the most frequent phrase I hear from people of all ages and backgrounds as they come up to me in the street, the thing that strikes them most of the past 12 years of Conservative government, is this. They say, 'Thank you for what you have done for our country'. They are thanking all of us for the principles for which we stand. They are thanking all of us for translating them into practice. They are thanking all of us for having the courage to see them through to success. And they are telling us something else—that, for the overwhelming majority of people in this country, the high standing and reputation of our country overseas matters to each and every one of our citizens.

If that is to continue, our task is not yet finished. Everything we have gained could so easily be lost unless we are returned for a fourth term under John Major's leadership. So let me just make three points. I notice that famous preacher, John Donne, always made just three points, and it's a very good rule. People can't usually digest more.

First, some commentators seem to suggest that the two main parties are now lookalike. A proposition I totally reject. The fact is, Labour are still Socialist and they deliberately set out to impose more government control over people's lives. That is where their whole belief starts.

It starts with the power of government over the lives of the people. That is the reason why they increase taxation—more power for them over our money, less power for the citizen. That is why they multiply controls and bureaucracy—more power for them, less for the wealth creators of our country. That is why they like nationalisation—more control over industry. That is why they reject privatisation and wider share ownership. That is why they want more council housing—because they want to have more control over the lives of the housing of the people and to use it for political purposes as in the Camdens and the Lambeths. That is why they oppose our plans for giving your doctors and nurses, your teachers and parents, more say, more responsibility, more power to decide near the point at which the decision has to be taken. That's why they oppose our plans for doing that in hospitals and in schools—they would rather have it decided by a bureaucratic level above.

That is the essence of their creed—government controls over the lives of the people—and it runs through all of their policies. That's why they love that Socialist Delors' Socialist Charter. When will they learn? You cannot build Jerusalem in Brussels. They haven't changed their Socialist spots. They've just changed their suits.

Mr Chairman, remember this. All the reforms we have brought about, the high reputation that we have gained for our country, they fought against tooth and nail while they were going through Parliament. Our marvellous achievements, our marvellous reputation, would never have been secured unless we Conservatives had been in power for the last 12 years. And particularly the trade union reforms: it wasn't the Labour Party who fought Scargill, it was we who fought Scargill, day after day for a year through the miners' strike.

And we got our judgement of human nature right. We knew that our trade union reforms, which gave more power to the ordinary members, would give them the things they wanted. We knew they would rather work to support their families than strike.

> Everything a politician promises at election time has to be paid for either by higher taxation or by borrowing.
>
> *28 March 1992*

And, my goodness, were we magnificently supported by the working miners who believed in us, who believed in the same principles that we believed in, and only wanted a chance to demonstrate their belief.

Mr Chairman, we must continue to put across our positive policies, the principles that underlie them and the splendid results we have achieved. That each and every person is born with God-given talents and abilities and it is his right to be able to express and develop those talents and abilities, both in his interest and that of his country as a whole.

And the government's task, the government's responsibility is not to take away those talents, or diminish them, but to provide the right framework within which they and the larger freedoms may flourish.

That is exactly what we have done. That is our duty—the right framework of law for enterprise. The duty to see that the currency is sound and remains sound, so that the savings put away at the grandson's christening, will still buy the same amount of goods when he comes of age. That is what a sound currency means.

And that we keep government expenditure within the limits of comparatively low taxation so we do not have to borrow too much, or take an ever increasing amount of tax away from the people.

Human wants are not satisfied by endless political promises. The wealth of nations (and remember Adam Smith said the wealth of nations as well as the wealth of individuals) the wealth of nations comes from the boundless energies and enterprise of individuals determined to improve their lot. That is the way the wealth and the well-being of a nation is created. That is where the resources come from to improve our great public services. And why we have been able to do so much more for them than the Socialists were ever able to do before us.

Now, my second point, and it won't be quite as long as the first point—the first point went right to the heart of everything we believe in—but I assure you the second and third points get a little bit briefer. And I'm going to follow Chris. So Press please take note, you'll find we all say the same thing.

The second vital point is that we continue strong defence policies—including the nuclear deterrent whose possession was bitterly opposed by the Kinnock Socialists. It is important to realise that this century saw the rise and the defeat of fascism, at great sacrifice in two World Wars. This century also saw the rise and crumbling of Communism without a great holocaust, without another great world war. And part of the reason that happened was because we always kept our defences strong and our alliances ever-green.

That, together with the battle of ideas which we took into the Communist camp, is what brought about the crumbling of Communism. But, as always, when large empires which have been held together by force fragment—as they always do—times are very uncertain. In politics the unexpected happens. We know that from the Falklands. We knew that the day Saddam Hussein went into Kuwait. The Prime Minister and I were both involved in defeating that tyranny.

But thanks to our strong defence policy we, together with the United States, didn't hesitate in sending the Forces to the Gulf. We were able to know immediately that we had all the right ships, all the right aircraft including the tornadoes, all the right tanks, because of sound defence decisions taken eight to ten years beforehand.

If Conservative Government hadn't increased public expenditure on defence, hadn't gone for the tornado, hadn't taken all the right decisions, it would have shackled our ability to deal with the tyrant at the time when he struck.

The lesson is clear. As our generation was able to react immediately and effectively, so we must not fail future generations by denying them the same security, the same strong defence whatever happens. And it's not only having all of the tanks and equipment that matters. It is knowing that you have a government in power which has the will to use them if need be.

And now my third point. I hear the Press talking about a hung Parliament. Mr Chairman, a hung Parliament would hang the future of our country. We have been able to take strong decisions and Prime Minister Major has been able to take strong decisions and show strong leadership because we had a good sound majority behind us. Just look at some countries that have had coalition governments. You may have read about Belgium in the papers in the last few weeks. It took them 100 days to form a new government. What would have happened if anything vital had come up during that time? Did it help their main decisions? Did it help their deficit to come down? Not a bit of it. They've got one of the worst deficits in Europe. Not surprising with a coalition government. No-one has got the guts to stand up and say no to public expenditure. So they get a big deficit. Does continuous coalition government help them to stand up against the tyrant? No. When we wanted to buy munitions they wouldn't sell them to us. So, do not go for coalitions—ever.

We want a strong decisive majority which enables us to continue the way in which we have, which enables Prime Minister Major to continue the strong leadership which he has already demonstrated to the people of this country and overseas.

There can be no doubt that a new, clear mandate to Prime Minister Major offers the best hope of solving our present problems, of continuing the economic advance which the 1980s began, and of ensuring that Britain's reputation rides high in the counsels of the world.

Prime Minister, your leadership is proven. It will be our most earnest endeavour to win that further period in office, that we believe you need and we believe our country deserves.

MAIDEN SPEECH IN THE HOUSE OF LORDS

2 July 1992

Baroness Thatcher: My Lords, it is a privilege to take my place on these distinguished and tranquil Benches after 33 testing years before the mast in another place. I thank my noble friend [Lady Chalker]for her kind references to me, I thank the noble Lord, Lord Richard, for his explicit and implied references to me, and I greatly thank the noble Lord, Lord Jenkins, for parts of his speech.

Mine is a somewhat delicate position. I calculate that I was responsible as Prime Minister for proposing the elevation to this House of 214 of its present Members. That must surely be considerably more than most of my predecessors—and my father did not know Lloyd George!

As Prime Minister I made a point of following your Lordships' debates and the reports of your Select Committees and found them invaluable for the wealth of experience and worldliness which they contained. I must confess that your Lordships' voting record occasionally gave rise to other and more violent emotions, particularly when the votes were on matters of finance. My frustration was too often and unfairly visited on the thankfully broad shoulders of my noble friends Lord Whitelaw and Lord Denham. I am sure that the view from here will look quite different.

I ask for your Lordships' forbearance for speaking so soon after my arrival in your Lordships' House rather than allowing a decent interval to elapse. But Britain's presidency of the Community comes round only once every six years and in future it may be longer than that. Notorious as I am for patience and restraint, I can hardly wait that long.

As the noble Lord, Lord Richard, said, I find that the late Lord Stockton managed 33 minutes during which he was not exactly complimentary about the then government's economic policies or its handling of the miners' strike. Therefore speeches are not always non-controversial. The noble Lord, Lord Wilson, for his part spent 20 minutes trampling politely on the Government's record on training and higher education. I therefore take heart that the non-controversial tradition may sometimes be honoured in the breach. But of course what is controversial to one may be music to the ears of another. Without differences of view there would be no debate; and if Parliament lost its powers to another body there would be little point in debate.

I notice from the speeches that have already been made that one point has forcibly emerged. Bearing in mind that all three parties are of the same view about ratifying Maastricht, the electorate has had no way during the general election of expressing its view. It had in fact no choice.

Britain has usually set itself rather modest and limited objectives during its turn at holding the presidency of the EC. True, our last presidency launched the single market; and in view of some of the comments in regard to the Single European Act which I heard in this House on Tuesday, I shall have something to say in that regard later and my noble friend has already referred to it. But generally we have concentrated on organising the Community's business efficiently and drawing precise conclusions from wordy and chaotic debates.

That was necessary, but it will certainly not be enough this time. Rarely, if ever, has the Community had a greater number of important issues demanding its attention than now. Most of them were mentioned by my noble friend the Minister of State [Lady Chalker] and I shall not repeat the list which she gave so ably, but start with what is on everyone's lips and the most pressing question—that is to say, what to do about Maastricht after the Danish referendum.

Many people who travel through Europe, as I have done in recent months, are struck by the very sharp change in attitudes towards the European Community, brought about by the Maastricht Treaty. Scepticism, justifiable scepticism, is on the increase. People feel that their governments have gone ahead too fast so that now the gap between government and people is too wide. Perhaps that is not surprising when in the modern political world European Ministers spend so much time in each other's company: they get out of touch with the people and too much in touch with themselves.

The particular concerns are different in each country, but the basic misgivings are mostly the same. People feel that too many of the powers and rights, which have been theirs for decades and in some cases for centuries, are being given away to the centre in Brussels. We had echoes of that in the speech of the noble Lord, Lord Jenkins. I find it very difficult to understand that two arguments are being run alongside and they are mutually exclusive. There is far too much centralisation going on; far too much bureaucracy going on which we do not like, but nevertheless we are going to ratify the Maastricht Treaty. To me, these things do not add up.

There is also among people a good, healthy understanding that bigger is not always better and that variety is more desirable than conformity. The Danish "No" to Maastricht is just one sign of those things. A recent opinion poll shows that seven out of 10 Germans do not want a single currency and that seven out of 10 do not want either to surrender significant powers in order to have a common foreign policy.

People understand that Maastricht is more, much more, than just a technical adjustment to the Treaty of Rome. The people of Denmark saw that when they received their copies—free copies, I would stress—of the Maastricht text. One figure illustrates better than anything else the scale of the extra intrusion into the authority of national parliaments and governments and into people's lives, which Maastricht would bring about.

The Treaty of Rome provides for the Commission to have the sole right of initiative in 11 areas of policy. In Maastricht that reaches 20, to which one has to add at least five other areas of co-operation where the Commission is fully involved—that is to say, monetary, judicial and immigration matters as well as foreign policy and defence. No wonder people feel that they have a right to be consulted about such a major change in the way in which they are governed, especially in the light of M. Delors' notorious statement to the European Parliament that 80 per cent. of the decisions taken on economic and social matters will soon be taken by the European Community rather than by national governments and parliaments.

It is being alleged that no less substantial powers were conceded to the Community in the Single European Act. I hope that your Lordships will not accept that assertion, but will look at the debates in another place in 1986 about the Single European Act. I hope that noble Lords will look in particular at the assurances given at that time by the then Foreign Secretary, now my noble friend Lord Howe, and by my noble friend the Minister of State [Lady Chalker] who opened the debate.

Qualified majority voting is of course in the Treaty of Rome itself. My noble friend, the then Foreign Secretary, made clear that in the Single European Act qualified majority voting replaced unanimity only for the measures which were major components of the construction of the Common Market. He said explicitly that their scope was not indefinite. He pointed out that,

I pay tribute to John Major's achievement in persuading the other 11 Community heads of government that they could move ahead to the social chapter but not within the Treaty and without Britain's participation. It sets a vital precedent, for an enlarged Community can only function if we build in flexibility of that kind. John Major deserves high praise for ensuring at Maastricht that we would not have either a single currency or the absurd provisions of the social chapter forced upon us: our industry, workforce and national prosperity will benefit as a result.

15 May 1992

"some subjects were of such importance to the national policies of individual member states that they should remain subject to unanimity voting—namely—tax measures, measures relating to the free movement of individuals and measures affecting the rights and interests of employed persons."

He recognised that there would be some people who would be anxious that, in extending qualified majority voting to promote the achievement of an internal market, we might diminish the essential protection of our national interest. He concluded,

"I would not accept that."

He gave his reasons for doing so.

The suggestion that there is any comparison between the powers transferred to the Community in the Single European Act and in the Maastricht Treaty is misplaced. Bearing in mind the burning and urgent problems of the moment, one also has to ask: What is the relevance of the Maastricht Treaty to these? What, for example, does it do for fragile democracy in Eastern and Central Europe? It makes it more difficult for those countries to join. Last week the European Council refused even to open negotiations with the much more advanced EFTA countries. The attitude is that we have to form our own tight little huddle before we can even contemplate admitting others.

What does Maastricht do to help lift Europe out of recession? It shackles and burdens our economies with the extra restrictions and intrusive regulations imposed by the Social Charter. We found out last week that the Commission is still trying to do that despite our having opted out of that chapter of the Maastricht Treaty, thanks to the Prime Minister. Unfortunately, the Commission has not yet had its action challenged in the European Court. The Government have indicated that they may do so and I hope that they will. We shall then know where we stand on this matter.

The reason for all this is that Maastricht does not tackle today's problems. There has been a hint of that in the other speeches. The world has changed dramatically in the past two years. The Community must adapt to that or it will lose its purpose and lose support. The result of the Danish referendum is an opportunity to think again, but there is regrettably little sign from last week's European Council that the Community as a whole is ready to do that.

It was treachery with a smile on his face. Perhaps that was the worst thing of all.

Describing her betrayal by the Cabinet, 1993

Certainly, it will take more than a self-denying ordinance on the part of the Commission or a promise to give back some of the powers which it has arrogated. Its record of evading the unanimity provisions of the Single European Act deprives it of the good faith that we should otherwise have accorded it.

I am very glad that the Foreign Secretary has said (my noble friend has repeated it today) that Denmark cannot be coerced and cannot be excluded. If that were to happen the Community would be breaking its own laws which state with absolute clarity that Maastricht has to be ratified by all 12 member states if it is to come into force. If we allow that to be overridden in Denmark's case, each and every one of us will become vulnerable to being coerced or excluded on some other issue or on some other occasion in the future.

We are an association of free peoples, free to take a democratic vote. Denmark has exercised that freedom. Is it now to be suggested that she did something wrong or somehow she must change her mind? After all, fortunately our Prime Minister exercised our right to be different and not to be governed by the Social Charter and not to be governed automatically by a single currency although we agreed the idea. We have done it. We are perhaps the oldest democracy and the freest. It is not for us to criticise others. If ever it is suggested that the people of any member state cannot say "No" without an attempt at duress, that is a very serious matter for the Community and one would need to revise one's views about whether it is a community now of free peoples.

Searching for a definition of subsidiarity is not a satisfactory way forward either, if only because it is based on the notion that it is the Community which has the power which it then parcels out to the member states. The true situation should be the reverse. It should be the member states which exercise all powers, except those which are specifically and legally granted to the Commission.

My own immediate, albeit limited, suggestion at this stage is that the Government should propose a formal and binding restatement of the Luxembourg Compromise. It is not a lot, but it is a little. Your Lordships will recall that this provides that if any member state considers that its vital national interest is at stake, then no vote will be taken. It can be postponed until agreement is reached between all parties. I believe that that would go some way to restore people's confidence in the Community—and hard as it will be to get agreement, I hope that the Government will consider it because technically the Luxembourg Compromise is still there. In practice, there is some doubt as to whether and how effectively it can be used.

I make one further plea before concluding this particular section of my speech: the plea that the Maastricht Treaty be not discussed in terms of personalities—it is too important for that—but in terms of the issues involved. The Government have a most difficult and complex task on their hands with this whole issue during the British presidency. I am sure that they will acquit themselves with distinction in dealing with it and uphold the freedoms of our respective peoples.

I shall deal with the other issues that will affect our presidency more briefly. My noble friend has already dealt with enlargement. As urgent for the presidency as the Maastricht agreement is the issue of the enlargement of the Community. And it is depressing that, despite our Government's best efforts in Lisbon, other member states have refused to embark on the necessary formal negotiations. I sometimes wonder whether other governments fully comprehend the scale and the consequences of the bloodless victory over communism in Eastern Europe and the Soviet Union. In the space of two years, it has become a different world—not the end of history, as some foretold, but the return of history. First

Yalta was swept away—and a very good thing too. Now Versailles is following it, which some of us do not find surprising.

The real urgency now is to stretch out a hand to the countries of Eastern and Central Europe. We were not able to free them from communist tyranny. When they escaped, it was by their own efforts. Now we have a pressing moral obligation to sustain democracy and free economies—just as we did in earlier times for Greece and Spain and Portugal—by bringing these East European countries into the Community as soon as possible even though it would require a very long transition period. This is not just in their interests, but also in ours.

We do not want the Community to be in the position of Dr Johnson. Your Lordships will recall his reply to Lord Chesterfield's congratulations after he had completed his dictionary in the cold and poverty of his garret. He said:

"Is not a patron my Lord one who looks with unconcern on a man struggling for life in the water, and when he has reached ground encumbers him with help."

I recognise that we have association agreements with East European countries, but that is not enough for the assurance that they need. The widening of Europe to include the post-communist countries is, I believe, of much more importance than the early admission of other countries. If the European Community does not respond more rapidly to the needs of Eastern Europe, the problem will still arrive on our doorstep because many peoples from those countries will join the Community even if their governments cannot. They will vote with their feet and arrive in even larger numbers. I hope that the Government, undaunted by last week's setback in Lisbon on enlargement, will return to the charge.

There are many other pressing issues for the presidency, but I shall touch on them only very briefly. On finance, there is still plenty of room under the present own resources ceiling to do the things which are most urgent. We heard at Question time that all the money is apparently not being well used and could be put to better use. I commend the Government for their robust refusal to contemplate additional funds for the Community. There will no doubt be attempts to re-open the issue of the British rebate. I had some great budget battles in my day. The noble Lord, Lord Jenkins of Hillhead, was there and witnessed some of them and understood the point that I was trying to make. I always found that the most effective weapon was, "No"—or sometimes, "No, no, no". I am glad that this continues to be the policy, even if it is more sweetly expressed.

> I think sometimes the Prime Minister should be intimidating. There's not much point being a weak, floppy thing in the chair, is there?
>
> *1993*

Britain, with the Commission, was the main driving force behind the launch of the single market, and I pay particular tribute, joining my noble friend, to the work which my noble friend Lord Cockfield did to bring about free trade within Europe—one of the original objectives of the old EEC. I hope that we shall use our presidency for a final drive towards its completion. This is especially important, as my noble friend says, for our service industries. They are one of our particular strengths, yet their opportunities have been greatly constrained by protectionism in other member states, often masquerading under the false flag of restrictions required for regulatory purposes. The remaining obstacles should be removed quickly, and no new bureaucracies created. Indeed, in a sensible world, we would never have gone ahead with a new treaty at all until the single market had been first completed and was in operation.

At long last the Community is realising that statements, declarations and even sanctions are not a strong enough response to the terrible slaughter in what was part of Yugoslavia—not in some remote country, but little more than a two-hour flight from London, and in the heart of Europe. Some of us have been warning for a time that the use of force might become necessary. I am sure that one of the first actions of our presidency will be to help to organise sustained relief supplies for Sarajevo and for other places where people have been brutally attacked and their cities devastated. If attempts are made to interfere with those supplies, I believe that we should be ready to use the air power available to NATO in the area to deal with them. After all, we gave the Kurds air power and there is no reason why we should not have given it earlier to some of those people in Yugoslavia.

It is sad that once again the lead had to come from America, in particular from James Baker, rather than from the European Community, although we applaud President Mitterrand for his visit to Sarajevo which raised the morale of those suffering people. The fact is that with a common foreign policy we would be dependent on the lowest common denominator among the Twelve—and we all saw what that meant in the Gulf war. Tyrants are not defeated by the action of the United Nations—it does the resolutions—not by the action of the Community; tyrants are defeated by the lead of nation states which have sufficient defence to go and to do the necessary task.

I agree with my noble friend about the importance of the GATT negotiations. I recall very well that at the last European Council which I attended as Prime Minister just over two years ago, despite all my efforts my fellow Heads of Government refused even to discuss the negotiations, even though the deadline for the Uruguay Round was only three months away. It has, in fact, been extended twice and the matter is still not resolved. In the meantime, we have in fact perhaps lost a very great deal of trade which would have helped us during the recession had we come to agreements earlier.

This debate about the presidency coincides with one of the great constitutional issues of our time. In such matters your Lordships' advice carries very great weight and I am sure that we shall come back to the Maastricht Treaty and I hope that we shall debate its implications in full after the Recess.

It will be obvious to your Lordships by this time that I have never knowingly made an uncontroversial speech in my life. Nevertheless, I hope to be more controversial when we get down to discussing the details. I believe that my right honourable friend the Prime Minister can have a very great influence on the whole future of the Community. I have made my view clear on the Maastricht Treaty. For the reasons that I have indicated, I do not believe that the situation will be resolved during our presidency. I think that noble Lords know how I would vote. But there are so many other things which are more immediate and which I am certain that our Prime Minister is the best person to address. I am sure that he will do that with effectiveness and distinction. I wish him well during Britain's presidency.

ARTICLE ON BOSNIA

New York Times, 6 August 1992

Stop the Excuses. Help Bosnia Now

Terrible events are happening in Bosnia; worse ones are threatened. Sarajevo is under constant bombardment. Gorazde is besieged and likely to fall. If it does, a large massacre is feared and thousands of Serbian troops will be free to move on Sarajevo, itself swollen with refugees from other areas.

The victims and losers in this conflict suffer more than the usual penalties of defeat. Some are herded into concentration camps where, even if the worst reports of atrocities are untrue they nonetheless suffer appalling privation and can be shot for insignificant offenses. Others are driven from their homes and obliged to give up their property. Children and passers-by are shot at and killed.

This is the Serbian "ethnic cleansing" policy—a term for the expulsion of the non Serb population that combines the barbarities of Hitler's and Stalin's policies toward other nations.

Everyone witnessing or hearing of these tragic events desperately wants them to stop. But this feeling is exploited by Serbia and its sympathizers to press for a U.N. sponsored cease-fire. Reasonable as this sounds, it is an attempt to "freeze" the present situation in which the Serbs hold about two-thirds of Bosnia's territory, whereas they make up only 31 percent of the total population as against 43 percent for the Muslims and 17 percent for the Croats.

Such an outcome would consolidate and ratify aggression. It was Serbia that planned and carried out aggression against Bosnia in April. The Government of Alija Izetbegovic in Sarajevo is the legal and internationally recognized government of the Bosnian republic.

> True gentlemen deal with others for what they are, not for who their fathers were.
>
> *BBC TV, 1993*

The pretense that Serbia has nothing to do with what goes on in Bosnia is just that—a pretense. From the start there has been close coordination between supposedly independent Serbian forces in Bosnia and the Serbian high command in Belgrade, which is providing financial and military means for the war—including the all important gasoline for the Serbian forces.

It is argued by some that nothing can be done by the West unless we are prepared to risk permanent involvement in a Vietnam- or Lebanon-style conflict and potentially high Western casualties. That is partly alarmism, partly an excuse for inertia. There is a vast difference between a full-scale land invasion like Desert Storm, and a range of military interventions from lifting the arms embargo on Bosnia, through supplying arms to Bosnian forces, to direct strikes on military targets and communications.

Even if the West passes by on the other side, we cannot expect that others will do so. There is increasing alarm in Turkey and the Muslim world. More massacres of Muslims in Bosnia, terrible in themselves, would also risk the conflict spreading.

Serbia has no powerful outside backers, such as the Soviet Union in the past. It has up to now been encouraged by Western inaction, nor least by explicit statements that force would not be used. A clear threat of military action would force Serbia into contemplating an end to its aggression. Serbia should be given an ultimatum to comply with certain Western demands:

- Cessation of Serbia's economic support for the war in Bosnia to be monitored by international observers placed on the Serb-Bosnian border.
- Recognition of Bosnia's independence and territorial integrity by Belgrade and renunciation of territorial claims against it.
- Guarantees of access from Serbia and Bosnia for humanitarian teams.
- Agreement to the demilitarization of Bosnia within a broader demilitarization agreement for the whole region.
- Promise of cooperation with the return of refugees to Bosnia.

If those demands (which should be accompanied by a deadline) are not met, military retallation should follow, including aerial bombardment of bridges on the Drina linking Bosnia with Serbia, of military convoys, of gun positions around Sarajevo and Gorazde, and of military stores and other installations useful in the war. It should also be made clear that while this is not a war against the Serbian people, even installations on the Serbian side of the border may be attacked if they play an important role in the war.

American leadership in this endeavor is indispensable, as the E.C.'s paralysis has shown. But America cannot be expected to act alone. NATO, which is the most practical instrument to hand, must deal with the crisis. It is not "out of area."

The West's ultimate aim should be the restoration of the Bosnian state, backed by international guarantees within a regional pact, perhaps under C.S.C.E. supervision, and guaranteeing the rights of the three main groups in Bosnia (but not allowing for its partition into three cantons).

Such a solution would prevent the irredentist wars that the partition of the country between Serbia and Croatia would inevitably provoke. Also, keeping the Muslims in a united Bosnia would discourage their radicalization, which would be inevitable if the Muslims were to be dispersed under alien rule. A desperate Muslim diaspora—not unlike the Palestinian one—could then turn to terrorism. Europe would have created an islamic time bomb.

Serbia will not listen until forced to listen. Only the prospect of resistance and defeat will lead to the rise of a more democratic and peaceful leadership. Waiting until the conflict burns itself out will be not only dishonorable but also very costly: refugees, terrorism, Baikan wars drawing in other countries and worse.

Hesitation has already proved costly. The matter is urgent. There are perhaps a few weeks left for a serious initiative before it is too late and a Serb victory is accomplished, with terrible long-term consequences.

THE KEITH JOSEPH MEMORIAL LECTURE TO THE CENTRE FOR POLICY STUDIES

SBC Warburg, City of London, 11 January 1996

Keith Joseph, in whose honour this Lecture is delivered, had the charm of a hundred paradoxes. He was a modest man; but, unlike so many modest men, he had really nothing to be modest about. He was (that overworked, but in this case appropriate word) "brilliant"; yet he never indulged in intellectual virtuosity. He was brave; yet by nature he was timid. He could seem cerebral and remote; but he had a warm heart and impish humour that made his friendship an inexpressible delight.

Keith was also unusual in that, even when quite old and frail, he seemed somehow to remain young. The secret of this youthful spirit was the opposite to that of Faust. For in Keith's case it was the fruit of innocence. Not the innocence of inexperience, let alone of insensitivity. This was the innocence of the pure of heart—of those who have wrestled with the evils of humanity, while remaining unspotted by the world.

Keith's *goodness* was shown by the little kindnesses which marked his dealings with both political friends and opponents—he had no enemies. But Keith was more than good; he was also great. And his greatness lay in his integrity. Integrity is an old fashioned word. There are even some who will tell you it is an old fashioned thing. But, for a politician, integrity is everything.

It is not just a matter of avoiding bribes and inducements. In our remarkably financially honest *British* politics, it is not even mainly about that—(whatever learned judges may say about the matter). In politics, integrity really lies in the conviction that it's only on the basis of truth that power should be won—or indeed can be *worth* winning. It lies in an unswerving belief that you have to be *right*.

It was not that Keith wore a hair shirt from preference. He was averse to any kind of suffering, especially other people's—and applying the right remedies to the British disease was bound to require suffering. But Keith's integrity was absolute.

When he became convinced—finally convinced, after the endless discussions which were a mark of his open-minded, open-hearted style—that a proposition was correct, he felt he had to defend it. He had to fight for it. When he faced those raging, spitting Trotskyist crowds at our great liberal centres of learning, I suspect he wondered sometimes whether he would have to die for it. But there he stood. He could do no other.

This Lecture is not, however, intended as a eulogy. The purpose of recalling the turbulent times of twenty years ago when Keith Joseph and I reshaped Conservatism—with the help of a handful of others, whose dedication compensated for their fewness—is that the same qualities as Keith's are required in our Party today.

Keith Joseph's name will always be closely associated with the rethinking of Conservative principles and policies in preparation for the Conservative Government of the 1980s.

You will recall that the Party was out of office—having lost the February 1974 Election—when Keith began delivering, in the summer and autumn, a series of speeches analysing what had gone wrong, and suggesting a change of direction.

In June came the Upminster speech. Keith dared to talk about what he called the "inherent contradictions [of the]...mixed economy ". This, in the eyes of the Tory establishment, whose only real *criticism* of the socialists was that they were mixing the economy in the *wrong proportions*, was bad enough.

In my day that would have required the occasional use of the handbag. Now it will be a cricket bat. But that's a good thing because it will be harder.

On John Major's negotiations on the Maastricht Treaty, 1993

But it was the Preston speech in September—delivered almost on the eve of a second general election—which most horrified Keith's critics. In it, he dared to tell the truth about inflation: and that truth was inevitably damning for the previous Conservative Government, of which he and I had been a part.

Inflation was properly to be ascribed to the excessive growth of the money supply. And since, as Keith devastatingly observed, there was a time lag of as much as a year or two between the monetary cause and the inflationary effect, the high inflation of the summer of 1974—17 per cent and rising—was the responsibility of the Conservatives.

Keith also rightly noted that the root of the Conservative Government's failure to control inflation was fear of unemployment. But—as he and I would go on to argue on other occasions—unemployment was not an alternative to inflation, but one result of it.

Ever higher doses of inflation were required in order to have even a short term effect on jobs. And in the longer term inflation undermined confidence, pushed up wage costs, promoted inefficiency and aborted new employment.

For saying such things, Keith was publicly ridiculed and privately vilified. His colleagues accused him of disloyalty, splitting the Party and so on.

Those whom Hayek had described as "the socialists of all parties" united to denounce him. For Keith in their eyes was demonstrating the worst possible political seamanship. He was "rocking the boat". But in fact it was Keith's compass that was true—and it was the *boat* that was already adrift and threatened by total shipwreck.

Most of the economic analysis which Keith Joseph offered has since been accepted. But Keith was not only, or even primarily, interested in economics. It was simply that in the 1970s the economics had gone so devastatingly wrong that this was where any new analysis had to focus. Indeed, that remained true to a large extent in the 1980s.

Reversing Britain's economic decline was such a huge and painful undertaking that, at least until the later years, the economy had to come first.

Keith himself, though, was even more interested in social than in economic issues. He had come into politics not from personal ambition but from an idealistic urge to diminish the misery of poverty. But his one foray at this time into rethinking social policy, in the form of the Edgbaston speech, went badly wrong.

In fact, though flawed in some respects, the speech with its emphasis on remoralising society and on strengthening the family, deserves re-reading.

It does not though, reveal much about his essential philosophy, which with Keith—as with most professional politicians—remained below the surface.

The kind of Conservatism which he and I—though coming from very different backgrounds—favoured would be best described as "liberal", in the old-fashioned sense. And I mean the liberalism of Mr Gladstone not of the latter day collectivists. That is to say, we placed far greater confidence in individuals, families, businesses and neighbourhoods than in the State.

But the view which became an *orthodoxy* in the early part of this century—and a *dogma* by the middle of it—was that the story of human progress in the modern world was the story of increasing state power. Progressive legislation and political movements were assumed to be the ones which *extended* the intervention of government.

It was in revolt against this trend and the policies it bred that Hayek wrote *The Road to Serfdom*, which had such a great effect upon me when I first read it—and a greater effect still, when Keith suggested that I go deeper into Hayek's other writings.

Hayek wrote:

"How sharp a break—with the whole evolution of Western civilisation the modern trend towards socialism means — becomes clear if we consider it not merely against the background of the nineteenth century, but in a longer historical perspective. We are rapidly abandoning not the views merely of Cobden and Bright, of Adam Smith and Hume, or even of Locke and Milton, but one of the salient characteristics of Western civilisation as it has grown from the foundations laid by Christianity and the Greeks and Romans. Not merely nineteenth- and eighteenth-century liberalism, but the basic individualism inherited by us from Erasmus and Montaigne, from Cicero and Tacitus, Pericles and Thucydides is progressively relinquished."

So, Ladies and Gentlemen, against that background, it is not surprising that the Left claimed all the arguments of *principle*, and that all that remained to the Right were the arguments of *accountancy*—essentially, when and how socialism could be afforded.

It was this fundamental weakness at the heart of Conservatism which ensured that even Conservative politicians regarded themselves as destined merely to manage a steady shift to some kind of Socialist state. This was what—under Keith's tuition—we came to call the "ratchet effect". But all that was not just bad politics. It was false philosophy—and counterfeit history. Let me remind you why this is so.

Creativity is necessarily a quality which pertains to *individuals*. Indeed, perhaps the one immutable law of anthropology is that we are all different. Now, of course, individuals can't fulfil their potential without a society in which to do so. And to set the record straight—*once again*—I have never minimised the importance of society, only contested the assumption that society means the State rather than other people. Conservatives do not take an extreme atomistic view of society. We need no lectures now, or at any other time, about the importance of custom, convention, tradition, belief, national institutions or what the ancient Romans would describe as "piety". Nor do we dispute that the bonds of society need ultimately to be guaranteed by the State.

It is *Marxists*, not Conservatives, who imagined—or at least pretended to imagine—that the State would wither away. No. What marks out our Conservative vision is the insight that the State—government—only *underpins* the conditions for a prosperous and fulfilling life. It does not *generate* them. Moreover, the very *existence* of this State, with its huge capacity for evil, is a potential threat to all the moral, cultural, social and economic benefits of freedom.

> I have been in Parliament for 34 years. I cannot remember a time when politicians were so out of touch with the people and so in touch with each other.
>
> *18 April 1993*

States, societies and economies, which allow the distinctive talents of individuals to flourish, themselves also flourish. Those which dwarf, crush, distort, manipulate or ignore them cannot progress. Those eras in which a high value has been placed on the individual are the ones which have known the greatest advances.

By contrast, although the great monolithic states, empires and systems can produce impressive monuments and a high level of cultural sophistication, they are not able to mobilise the initiative of their populations to ensure that each generation can expect a better life than its predecessor.

It is only Western civilisation that has discovered the secret of continual progress. This is because only Western civilisation has developed a culture in which individuals matter, a society in which private property is secure, and a political system in which a range of competing views and interests is accommodated.

The *moral* foundation of this system—which is so spontaneous as hardly to seem a system—is the Judaeo-Christian outlook. The system's *institutional* foundation is the rule of law. Expressed like this, it all sounds very abstract. But we in Britain are extraordinarily, indeed uniquely, lucky. Because, with us, these things have become second nature and a way of life.

Over the centuries, the habits of freedom became ever more established in these islands. They and the institutions which came to embody them—independent courts, the common law, above all Parliament—were in a special sense democratised: that is, they came to be regarded as the birthright not of any class or group, but of the nation as a whole. In a more doctrinal form they have found their way into the Constitution of the United States.

All this meant that when Keith and I were struggling to shift Britain back from the Socialist State, we were also acting as conservatives, with a small 'c'. We were seeking to re-establish an understanding of the fundamental truths which had made Western life, British life, and the life of the English-speaking peoples what they were. This was the foundation of our Conservative revolution. It remains the foundation for any successful Conservative programme of government.

And that is the first lesson which needs to be drawn from the rethinking of Conservatism, which Keith inspired and led. The principles which he restated, and which formed the basis of the policies the Conservative Government pursued while I was Prime Minister, are as true and as relevant now as they were two decades ago—or indeed, give or take a little economics, two centuries ago.

The cause of *limited government* — in which the State is servant not master, custodian not collaborator, umpire not player — is the one beneath whose standard Keith Joseph and I gathered all those years ago. It is time to take it out of mothballs, brush off the odd collectivist cobweb that's hung on to it, and go forth to meet the foe.

The *second* lesson is that avoiding debate about the large issues of government and politics leads to directionless failure. Being prepared to state uncomfortable truths, as Keith insisted in doing, is the precondition for success. It is extremely doubtful whether the Conservative Party lost support because of Keith's controversial Preston speech in September 1974. But I am quite sure that without it we would never have embraced the approach that yielded, first victory in 1979, and then a remarkable string of achievements in the years which followed.

Splits and disagreements over important issues never did a Party so much harm as the absence of honest, principled debate. There is, however, one apparent lesson that we would be most unwise to draw. That is the suggestion, which one hears from time to time, that the only hope for the Conservative Party is a period in Opposition. The situation today in the Party is entirely different from that in 1974, when Keith was making his great speeches. In the present Prime Minister, the Party has a leader who shares the broad analysis that Keith Joseph and I put forward.

It is no secret that between John Major and me there have been differences…on occasion. But these have always been differences about *how* to achieve objectives, rather than *what* those objectives should be. What is required now is to ensure that those objectives are clearly explained, so that a re-elected Conservative Government can go further towards fulfilling them. The attractions of Opposition are greatly exaggerated by those who have not experienced it.

But, judging from the opinion polls, Opposition is where the electorate is at present inclined to send us. For a variety of reasons, which I shall describe shortly, I believe that this would be ill-judged on their part. The Conservative Party still has much to offer. And from Mr Blair 's New—or not so new—Labour Party there is much to fear.

But we must not ignore the present discontent. Some of it is more or less inevitable. A constant struggle is required to ensure that long-serving governments don't run out of steam. I always regarded it as necessary to combine my role as Prime Minister with that of Chief Stoker so as to keep up the pressure.

It is also true that the political world is more complicated than in the '80s. The sharp divide between the forces of freedom represented by the Conservative Party and the West on the one hand, and the forces of collectivism represented by the Labour Party and the Soviet bloc on the other, is a thing of the past.

The extent of the success we achieved in the 1980s has, in this sense, caught up with us. That may be politically inconvenient;

but I for one would not change it. During most of my political life, freedom in this country was under a direct challenge from fellow-travelling Socialists and an aggressive Soviet Union. These challenges were overcome because the Conservative Party in Britain and other right-of-centre parties elsewhere—under the international leadership of Ronald Reagan—proved too much for them. The fashionable expression is that Communism and indeed Socialism "imploded". If that means that their system was always unviable, so be it—though many of the people who now say this scarcely seemed to believe it true before the "implosion" occurred.

> I personally could never have signed this Treaty.
>
> *On the Maastricht Treaty, 12 June 1993*

But, anyway, let's not forget that the system collapsed because it was squeezed by the pressure that *we* on the *Right*—I repeat on the *Right*—of politics applied. And the Left should not be allowed to get away with pretending otherwise.

But, of course, in politics there is only gratitude for benefits yet to be received. That is why, however successful they've proved to be, governments and parties have to keep on re-applying their enduring principles to new circumstances. The Conservative Party today has problems not because our analysis has been wrong or our principles faulty. Our difficulties are due to the fact that, in certain limited but important respects, our policies and performance have not lived up to our analysis and principles.

That is why the current idea, put around by some malcontents, that the Conservative Party is in trouble because it has moved to the Right, and that this is what needs to be remedied, is boloney—and Denis might be able to suggest a still more telling description.

The test is simple. Just ask yourself: is it because the Government has *not* spent, borrowed and taxed *enough* that people are discontented? Or is it that we have gone *too far* towards increasing government spending, borrowing and taxation? The answer is obvious. We are unpopular, above all, because the middle classes—and all those who aspire to join the middle classes—feel that they no longer have the incentives and opportunities they expect from a Conservative Government. I am not sure what is meant by those who say that the Party should return to something called "*One Nation* Conservatism".

As far as I can tell by their views on European federalism, such people's creed would be better described as "*No Nation* Conservatism". And certainly anyone who believes that salvation is to be found further away from the basic Conservative principles which prevailed in the 1980s—small government, a property-owning democracy, tax cuts, deregulation and national sovereignty—is profoundly mistaken. That mistake in most cases has its origins in the acceptance of the picture of the 1980s which has been painted by the critics. That decade changed the direction of Britain to such an extent that it is unlikely that even a Labour Government would altogether reverse it—try as they might.

Inflation was brought down, without the use of the prices and incomes controls which the great and the good all agreed were indispensable. Public spending as a share of GDP fell, which allowed tax rates to be cut—and government borrowing was reduced. We repaid debt. Three hundred and sixty-four economists who claimed that it was madness to think you could get economic growth by cutting government borrowing were proved wrong: I'm told they were never the same again.

Reform of the public finances was matched by reform of the trade unions, deregulation and privatisation of industries and a great extension of ownership of houses, shares and savings—quite a lot of "stakeholding" in fact! The economic growth and the improvement of living standards which resulted from these reforms were so great that for a time materialism, rather than poverty, became the main accusation against us. "Hunting the yuppie" became the favourite sport of the neo-puritan, liverish Left.

But, of course, the reality was that the success which free enterprise brought over those years was not just expressed in conspicuous consumption—though what would we give for a few more of those yuppies today! It also allowed a doubling—that's over and above inflation—of voluntary giving to good causes.

Moreover, though we made mistakes of financial management by allowing the economy to overheat and inflation to rise towards the end of that period, the general advance of prosperity was solidly based upon real economic improvements.

Above all, there was a rapid and sustained rise in industrial productivity, which has continued. And as a result of the control of public expenditure over those years—particularly the reining back of future commitments on pensions—Britain advances towards the next millennium with a large advantage over our European competitors as regards taxation and costs.

The message from all this is not that everything in the 1980s was perfect or that everything that has followed it in the 1990s has been bad. Every Prime Minister has his—and her—regrets. The important message, rather, is that in Britain we have seen from the 1980s what works—just as we saw in the 1970s what did not. And what works here, as elsewhere, is free enterprise and *not* big government. So it would make no *economic* sense at all for us to move closer to the policies of our opponents. Rather, the *economic challenge* is to cut back the burden of state spending, borrowing and taxation still further. And trying to move towards the centre ground makes no *political* sense either.

As Keith used to remind us, it is not the centre ground but the common ground—the shared instincts and traditions of the British people—on which we should pitch our tents. That ground is solid—whereas the centre ground is as slippery as the spin doctors who have colonised it.

Ladies and Gentlemen, one of Keith Joseph's most admirable characteristics—and one which secured for him respect and affection—was that he never cast doubt on the *motives* of his opponent. So, following in his footsteps, I am not going to cast doubt on the *motives* of the Leader of the Opposition.

But what about the Party he leads? The Labour Party itself may have changed many of its policies, but it hasn't changed its spots. You can tell this from the unpleasant noises it makes when anything like profits are mentioned. There is still virtually nothing that Labour spokesmen wouldn't spend more taxpayers' money on, or wish to control more tightly. They have learned to accompany these prescriptions with Conservative-sounding rhetoric, and even some Conservative-sounding policies.

But the distinctive mark of every Labour policy, from health to education, from privatised utilities to the labour market, is *more government interference*. All sorts of worthy people believe that Mr Blair in office would control his Party, and not they him. But this would be a large gamble to take. Moreover, Mr Blair is not only human; he is also (as his record shows) by instinct a man of the Left.

Confronted with the sort of choices you face in Government—decisions which often go unmentioned in the manifestos—it is the Prime Minister's gut instincts which count. The pressures to solve problems and assuage demands by more public spending, intervention and controls can become almost irresistible—*even* for an instinctive free marketeer.

Mr Blair may believe with his head that government spending is not the universal panacea: but what about his heart—and, indeed, his gut? In any case, government is not about generalities but about specifics. Only if you have the conviction—the Conservative conviction—that it is wrong to spend more taxpayers' money unless the reasons for doing so are overwhelming—and even if *then* you don't sleep easily after doing so—are you likely, as Prime Minister, to face down the pressure.

Suspicions that a Labour government would in practice become too soft a touch on public spending are compounded by all the misty talk about boosting communities and community values. Now, communities can be sustained in two ways only—either by the State, which is what community politics, community leaders, community health, community housing, community centres and so on ultimately rely on.

Or communities can be based on genuine volunteers, sometimes local businesses, sometimes individuals with a common, freely chosen goal—like those who founded the great voluntary movements of the Victorian era which are still with us.

In some cases, to be sure, the State—often in the form of local government—can play a modestly useful part in "community projects". But the risk is that community comes to mean collective; collective comes to mean State; and thus the State expands to replace individual effort with subsidised activism.

It is free, enterprising, self-reliant, responsible individuals that Britain needs. It's when we have more of *them*, our communities will take better care of themselves. But I believe there is a still more important reason why Labour should not be entrusted with government. They may protest that they are no longer Socialists: but they have lost none of their zeal for constitutional upheaval. The Labour Party's proposals on devolution threaten chaos, and possibly the dissolution of the Union of the United Kingdom itself.

You can't lead an "if only" life. There's always a future, there's always work. I shall work till my dying day.

23 October 1993

Moreover, by embracing European federalism—through the European social chapter and, above all, the European single currency—a Labour government could deal a terminal blow to the traditions of British parliamentary democracy.

Traditionally, the Socialists believed that the State must make people equal; though an honest look at the perks and privileges of the Communist *nomenklatura* might have set them right about that. The New-look Labour Party now apparently wants the State to make people highminded and socially aware; though a thought for how difficult the Churches find it to change people's behaviour ought to induce some doubts when mere politicians start to preach.

It seems to me that New Labour has a new song—one that was made famous by Dame Vera Lynn:

> *"Wishing will make it so*
> *Just keep on wishing, and cares will go …*
> *And if you wish long enough, wish strong enough*

You will come to know
Wishing will make it so."

But it won't—any more than you can make people good by legislation.

So the limitation of government is *still* the great issue of British politics—and indeed to a remarkable degree of global politics. The threat to limited government did not end with the collapse of communism and the discrediting of socialism. It remains an issue in Western—particularly European—democracies. There is a constant tendency, in which pressure groups, vested interests and the media play a part, for government to expand.

One of Thatcher's laws—for which I owe something to Lord Acton—is that all government tends to expand, and Socialist government expands absolutely. If you start with *their* view of the State—that it exists to right social wrongs rather than to create a framework for freedom—you can never find the definitive justification for saying "no". Above all, you cannot say "no" to demands for more spending on welfare.

That is why in Sweden the share of national income the government took reached some seventy per cent. It's why it's several points higher in Europe on average than here. The dominant political philosophies of those countries have been Socialist, or Social Democrat or Christian Democrat—all of them views which hold that the State, rather than individuals, is ultimately responsible for what happens in society.

This is in marked contrast to the United States which, even when the Democratic Party is in charge, has never been converted to the idea that government—let alone the Federal Government—has the right to intervene whenever it wants. It is also in marked contrast to those Asia Pacific countries—like Hong Kong, the Little Tigers and, of course, the mighty Japan—where government's share of GDP remains very low.

Spending at just over a third of GDP in the United States, and a quarter or less in the Asia Pacific, has resulted in low taxes and high growth rates. Their example, like that of Britain in the 1980s, shows what works—just as the over-spent and over-regulated Scandinavian model shows what does not.

It was with the best intent that post-War governments spent more on welfare, believing that as the standard of living rose, people would do more to look after themselves. What we had to do, as Keith often said in earlier years, was to break the "cycle of deprivation".

But the more we spent, the greater the dependency, illegitimacy and crime became. And of course the tax burden rose. Western countries have now woken up to the problem. But they are still paralysed by it.

Here, though, Peter Lilley has been advancing steadily with social security reform, making important changes to reduce future burdens. Yet, as Peter himself often reminds us, social security still accounts for over 40 per cent of central government spending and costs every working person £15 every working day.

Certainly, the proposals increasingly favoured by the Labour Party for a much higher compulsory second pension—paid for by much higher compulsory contributions—offer no way out. It is one thing to *encourage* people to make provision for themselves, as we do with housing, health and pensions. It is also acceptable in some cases to *ensure* that people make some *minimum* contribution towards benefits, as we do through the National Insurance system.

But the Labour Party's plans would involve a large *increase* in compulsory saving which — as you would expect from them— results in a large *decrease* in *personal* liberty. Alleviating the burden of the social security budget is a thankless but vital task, for which real *Tory* stamina is required. It will not be done by financial sleight of hand.

But the possibility of a *really radical* approach to spending, requiring large scale removal or transferral of government functions, must also remain on the agenda. Last November, a brilliant and provocative Centre for Policy Studies pamphlet by Patrick Minford—*Public Spending—a twenty year plan for reform*—reminded us how far we still might go, and how great the potential gains. The spending cuts he proposes would also lead to dramatic tax cuts—with a big impact on growth.

Whether Professor Minford's proposals are deemed acceptable or not, they are extremely valuable in illustrating the possibilities. So I welcome the determination of the Chancellor of the Exchequer to bring public spending below 40 per cent of GDP. And I hope that at the next election we will be equipped with plans to bring it down over a period of years by much more.

> I was just amazed by the mixture of bile and treachery which poured out. In a speech, every word of which had clearly been carefully drafted and in a speech, which he delivered, if I might say so, better than any speech I heard him deliver ... In the end it was not my record which he assassinated. He assassinated his own character.
>
> *On Geoffrey Howe's resignation speech, BBC TV, 1993*

Limited government doesn't mean weak government, only less government. This is shown by the courageous and far reaching reforms which Michael Howard has been making in the criminal justice system. The strength of the opposition he faces from the vested interests shows he is right—almost as much as do the encouraging recent crime figures.

But today the main challenge to limited government comes not from within these shores at all, but rather beyond them—from the European Union. There is, of course, also a challenge to *self*-government—and the two are closely connected. The activity of the European Court, which can only ultimately be checked by amending the European Communities Act itself, is increasingly undermining our judicial system and the sovereignty of our Parliament.

Proposals are being made for common European defence—proposals which Michael Portillo has roundly and rightly attacked. They too are a threat to national independence. But most important, of course, is the proposed single European currency which, as John Redwood has argued, "would be a major step on the way to a single European nation".

The Prime Minister will have the support of all of us who wish to see these dangerous and damaging proposals resisted, and the present trends reversed, as he argues Britain's case at the forthcoming intergovernmental council. And we look forward to a successful outcome.

But vital as the issue of *self*-government is, it is *limited* government that concerns me today. For the European Union not only wishes to take away our powers; it wishes to increase its *own*. It wants to regulate our industries and labour markets, pontificate over our tastes, in short to determine our lives. The Maastricht Treaty, which established a common European citizenship and greatly expanded the remit of the European Commission, shows the outlines of the bureaucratic superstate which is envisaged. And Maastricht is the beginning, not the end of that process. Indeed, we are increasingly seeing the emergence of a whole new international political class. Some of them are politicians who have failed in their own countries, and so have tried their luck overseas. Some are officials who understand nothing of our *British* distinction between the legitimate powers of the elected and those of the unelected.

Almost fifty years ago, the Conservative journalist, Colm Brogan, wrote an incisive *critique* of the post-war Labour Government with its arrogant bossiness and intrusive cackhandedness. He called it *Our New Masters*. The title is equally appropriate to the "new *European* masters". And it is no surprise to me—as someone who always recognised the Socialist destination of this Euro-federalist dream—that now the Labour Party welcomes it all so warmly.

What they can't achieve in an independent, free enterprise Britain, they can hope to secure in a Euro-federalist Britain, whose people's instincts are ignored and whose parliamentary institutions are over-ridden. Self-government, limited government, our laws, our Parliament, our freedom. These things were not easily won. And if we Conservatives explain that they are now in peril, they will not be lightly surrendered.

In *The Reeds of Runnymede*, celebrating the signing of Magna Carta, Rudyard Kipling puts it like this:

"At Runnymede, at Runnymede,
Oh, hear the reeds at Runnymede:
You mustn't sell, delay, deny,
A freeman's right or liberty.
It wakes the stubborn Englishry,
We saw 'em roused at Runnymede!
...And still when Mob or Monarch lays
Too rude a hand on English ways,
The whisper wakes, the shudder plays,
Across the reeds at Runnymede.
And Thames, that knows the mood of kings,
And crowds and priests and suchlike things,
Rolls deep and dreadful as he brings
Their warning down from Runnymede!"

NICHOLAS RIDLEY MEMORIAL LECTURE

Central London, 22 November 1996

If Thomas Carlyle was even partly right in suggesting that History is the biography of great men, anyone studying the history of *our* times should also study the character and career of Nicholas Ridley. Nick defied every stereotype. He was what used to be called "an original". His temperament combined in equal measure the opposing elements of the classical and the romantic. He had a clear, analytical mind, which made him the best technical problem-solver I ever worked with. As he put it after leaving office: "I was educated as a mathematician and engineer. I see a problem and I want to put it right.... This perhaps explains why I am not a good politician. "I wish we had more such "bad politicians" today!

Free-market economics was always Nick's passion. And he had a longer, better pedigree in that respect than most Thatcherites—or indeed I may add—than Thatcher herself. His first vote against a Conservative Government baling out nationalised industries was in *1961*. To be so right, so early on, is not to have *seen* the light–it is to have *lit* it. Yet the other side of Nick's complex personality was his sensitivity. As befits the grandson of Sir Edwin Lutyens, he was a gifted and prolific painter. His cool, atmospheric watercolours conveyed his sense of wonder for the beauties of nature.

He is probably the most formidable leader we have seen since Gaitskell. I see a lot of Socialism behind their front bench but not in Mr Blair – I think he genuinely has moved.

On Tony Blair, 1994

This leads to one further revealing fact about Nick's character. He could not, of course, in any terms be considered "classless". In fact, like the Labour Leader,[Tony Blair] he must have had a whole wardrobe of old school ties. But he was also quite convinced that the *bourgeois* values of enterprise, thrift and effort were what drove our country and society forward, and that government must create the climate for these things to flourish.

And of course there was Nick's integrity. The really honest, honourable man is not always popular. He makes people uneasy because he says what they half-thought—and would rather they hadn't. But whenever you meet such people you come away feeling better for it—and the country feels better too, knowing that it can produce them.

Nick enjoyed high office, but he was usually surprised to be offered it. I think he had rather given up on entering the Cabinet when I appointed him to Transport in 1984. I wish I had brought him in earlier. He would have been a superb Chancellor. But whether in or out, he had the breadth of insight of the true, Renaissance, universal man. He was as content and proficient painting the sunset, or building his wonderful water-garden, as directing his Department.

All this confirms that Nick was one of a long British line of individualists–a term which is often used disparagingly, but which should be rehabilitated, for it explains much about our country's history, traditions and achievements.

The most persuasive defence of British individualism is contained in John Stuart Mill's little manual for freedom, *On Liberty*. Mill understood how necessary it was in a mass society, with its inherent trend towards the mediocre and the monochrome, to welcome Genius, even if to the mob it seemed like eccentricity—indeed even if it was eccentricity.

Mill wrote:

> *"The initiation of all wise or noble things comes and must come from individuals; generally at first from some one individual....... In this age, the mere example of nonconformity, the mere refusal to bend the knee to custom, is itself a service."*

Nick Ridley never "bent the knee". He could never be intimidated into believing that what was fashionable was sound, or what was accepted was true, or what was mediocre was best. He lived by his principles, trusted his judgment and had the measure of his abilities. He was unconcerned by sound-bites, unimpressed by smoothness, unmoved by pleas to fiddle or fudge the facts as he knew them to be. He dressed, smoked, ate and drank as he liked, said what he thought, did what he wanted—or more precisely did what *he* thought best.

As a result, he was often pilloried for what the critics described as his "gaffes". But one man's gaffe is another man's home truth. Even pearls begin with grit. And, as in his final interview as a Minister with a certain weekly journal, his blunt language could contain an insight that now seems prophetic. In any case, there was no point in complaining about Nick's undiplomatic openness–and I for one never did. You rarely find a man of Nicholas Ridley's guts, brains and integrity who is also made to be a political mannequin.

But though all these character traits—above all his rugged and robust refusal to follow the herd—made Nick Ridley a remarkable man, they would not in themselves be sufficient to constitute greatness. It was, rather, the impact which Nick had on *events* that qualified him for that accolade. So let us take a step back for a moment, and raise our eyes to the historical horizon.

As we review the experience of this century, we can see that one vast theme encapsulates all the rest: it is that of the struggle between state domination and individual liberty. The two totalitarian systems which we in Britain had to fight—Nazism and Communism—two *socialist* tyrannies, let's remember—represented one single model. The other was represented by *our* Anglo-American liberal political culture—our parliamentary institutions, our law, our notions of human rights and our free enterprise system based on private property.

The conflict also occurred *within* as well as between our societies. *Within the command economy and the controlled society* of the Evil Empire, captive nations and courageous dissidents staged their own resistance. *Within our open society and free polity*, left wing parties sought–and sometimes obtained—mandates to make our countries more like the socialist model. But in doing this, the Left had, of course, one large advantage. For while, the rulers of the socialist dictatorships employed the full panoply of repression against their democratic opponents, we in the West had *in free debate* to demonstrate that our system was superior. So, while for the dictators, ideas represented a danger: for us, they represented hope. It is Nick Ridley's claim to greatness that no-one in our times fought this battle of ideas more heroically, persistently and effectively than he.

He began when a very young man. And he quickly grasped that socialism was more than a matter of labels and parties, but rather in essence the extension of state control at the expense of individual freedom. This insight, so obvious to us now, was not at all so to most Conservatives then.

For there was a strong paternalistic streak in the Conservative Party when Nick and I entered politics; and it was something both of us disliked. The Tory paternalists were well-intentioned, of course; but because economics was below them–and philosophy beyond them–the main impact of Tory Governments was to legitimise and consolidate socialism.

Nick never hesitated to oppose the statism of post-War Conservatives as consistently as that of the Labour Party. From the back-benches after 1972 he aimed his barbs of unwelcome—because unanswerable—criticism at those who had fallen away from the verities of Selsdon Man (and Woman). For Nick it must have seemed a thankless, hopeless, sojourn in a wilderness populated by prowling whips and sharp-toothed party managers. But had he and others not then stayed true to their beliefs, I am not sure that we could have later turned the Party round.

With Nick's help in the Opposition years that followed we set out the philosophy which would direct the party's policies for all the subsequent years of government—a philosophy which is no less relevant to Britain's circumstances now. Let me draw attention to just three of its features.

The first and perhaps the most important insight which we Conservatives have is that government can do little that is good and much that is harmful, and so the scope of government must be kept to a minimum. Contrary to myth, most government intervention at most times in most countries is not the result of wise conclusions by enlightened men pursuing noble objectives. True, the general stated objectives may indeed seem elevated enough. And just recently we have heard proclaimed such spiritually refined objectives that it seems almost bad form to question them. But the actual intervention (or perhaps coercion would be a more accurate description) is generally the result of the ambitions of politicians, the self-interest of bureaucracies and the pressure of vested interests. And these—not the theological virtues or even the deadly sins—are what democracies must keep in mind.

When Dr Johnson remarked that patriotism was the refuge of the scoundrel, he was not, of course, attacking patriotism, only noting how easily base motives and shoddy arguments could be concealed in the trappings of high-mindedness. So too, though morality and religion are fine things, we should recall–to adapt Adam Smith–that in a democracy it is "not from the benevolence" of the politician, but from the clash of his views and interests with those of his opponents that the electors are empowered to choose their country's path. As Britain should have learned, the proper reaction to any excesses of professed idealism on the Left ... is to count the spoons.

This is not, of course, an argument for weak government, it is an argument for limited government. But the vital point is that the claims made for government as a force for *general improvement* always turn out to be bogus.

Yet it is amazing what claims have been made in the past. For instance, after the War, the nationalisation of our industries was justified as a means of safeguarding employment. It did nothing of the sort and, in spite of subsidies extracted from successful firms, the dole queues remorselessly lengthened.

Or take another example. The state effectively squeezed out private healthcare, it suppressed educational choice, it introduced welfare from the cradle to the grave and it decanted whole communities into monotonous acres of municipal housing. The planners did all this to build a utopian society of free and fair shares for all. But, on the contrary, a centralised bureaucratic system forced much of the population into a new dependency. It took a Conservative Government, with policies to which Nick Ridley made a vital contribution, to enfranchise those who had been trudging the Road to Serfdom by offering them choice and opportunities for ownership.

Or take employment laws devised to bring "social justice" to the labour market. Trade unions were strengthened with special privileges. Employers' rights to hire and fire, or indeed to manage, were subject to a tangle of regulations. And, of course, the effect was quite the opposite of that intended–or at least of that proclaimed. Trade union leaders bullied firms into bankruptcy and workers into the closed shop, and insisted on self-defeating restrictive practices. New firms shut down. Large firms wouldn't expand. So again, slowly and painfully and against the outright opposition of those who now, it seems, welcome the reforms we made, we Conservatives withdrew the state from dominating the work place. In doing so, we set Britain on course for economic success, bringing more firms, more wealth and more jobs.

I can be difficult and stubborn.

19 January 1994

Time after time, the disasters could have been foreseen. But ideology and vested interests obscured clear thought. So powerful is the temptation of politicians to step in–and so manifold are the excuses offered for their doing so–that fighting big government is the hardest task on earth.

The second principle we promoted in those days of Opposition was the fundamental importance of the rule of law. The rule of law, I should add as a barrister, is something other than the rule of lawyers. And, may I say with the greatest of respect, nor is it the rule of judges. Our great judges have certainly at times proved wise and heroic guardians of our rights. But it is for Parliament to make the laws which shape our lives.

What distinguishes our understanding of law is that it should be made by the competent, sovereign authority, that it should apply to all, including government, and that it should be administered impartially by an independent judiciary. In the 1970s it was the manipulation of law to appease the unions and left wing interests that was so shocking. In the eighties it was the contrast with the Soviet and East European totalitarian systems, based on state *diktat* and *nomenklatura* privilege, which made us appreciate anew the importance of a true rule of law. Now, in the nineties, it is the encroachment of an alien system of Community law that gives most cause for anxiety. Authority is being drained away from our national democratic and judicial institutions towards a bureaucratic entity that increasingly speaks in the tones of a new imperial power. This must be halted–indeed reversed.

The third argument we advanced back in the 1970s was about

the role of private property. Of all the rights which constitute what we call "liberty", the right to own property, though one of the more prosaic, is arguably that of greatest practical importance. Owning property gives a man independence against over-weening government. Property-ownership has also a more mysterious, but no less real, psychological effect: looking after what one owns provides a training in responsible citizenship. The saints of old often renounced their property, so as to break all attachments and rise above the world. But for most of us, the ties of property lock us into duties we might otherwise shirk: to continue the metaphor, they stop us dropping out.

So encouraging people to acquire property and savings was much more than an economic programme. It was a programme to end what I termed a "one generation society", and to put in its place a capital-owning democracy.

What then happened is history—but since history sometimes under-goes a little re-writing, perhaps I'd better remind you of how it turned out.

In the 1980s we cut back the government deficit and we repaid debt. We sharply cut income tax at both the basic and the higher rates. And to do these things, we steadily reduced public spending as a share of the national income. We reformed trade union law, and removed controls and unnecessary regulations. We created a virtuous circle: by reining back government we allowed more room for the private sector, and so the private sector generated more growth, which again allowed sound finances and low taxes.

Productivity increased. New firms started up. New jobs were created. Living standards rose. And with privatised firms making contributions to the Exchequer in place of nationalised ones draining it, there was more available to improve public services. In 1979 nationalised industries were losing £50 million a week; now privatised companies contribute £60 million a week to the Exchequer in Corporation Tax.

Yes: there were mistakes. Inflation started up again in the last years. And interest rates had to rise to beat it–which they did–with all the unpleasant consequences that brought. And the community charge–I still call it that because I like the Poles very much and have never dreamt of taxing them–the community charge, in its first year led to high bills which discredited an excellent system.

But the important point is that the *over-all* strategy we pursued in the 1980s worked precisely as it was meant to. And it transformed the reality and the reputation of Britain. Moreover, it *was* a strategy. It was not a set of policies cobbled together from minute to minute, begged, borrowed or stolen from other people. It was successful because it was based on clear, firmly held principles which were themselves based on a right understanding of politics, economics and above all human nature.

This strategy has continued in the 1990s. Our Prime Minister has shown persistence, imagination and skill in taking it forward.

Facts never do–of course–"speak for themselves". We politicians have to perform this service for them. So let me again remind you:

that unemployment in Britain is lower than in any other major European country;

that real take-home pay has increased at all levels of earnings since 1979;

that there are a million more small firms than when we took office;

that sixteen of the twenty-five most profitable companies in Europe are British;

and that foreign investment in this country has never been higher.

As Prime Minister, I was never much interested in "feel good" or even feel bad factors. I believed that if the reality was sound the reaction would ultimately be favourable. So we just got on with the job. But if the British people do *not* "feel good" about the economy today, I can only warn them that they will feel distinctly "worse" if they wake up after polling day to discover they've put in a Labour Government. Some slogans run and run: so let me repeat—Don't Let Labour Ruin It!

Yet would "Labour ruin it"? Apparently not, if you believe some people. If you'll forgive the medley of metaphors, the light has dawned, the ground has shifted and whole lexicons of indigestible words—like socialism, equality and public ownership—have been eaten. I warmly welcome the fact that the Labour Party professes, after losing four elections, to have come to terms with the 1980s. If true that is a good start. And I wouldn't rule out, after four *more* lost elections, the Labour Party coming to terms with the nineties either. Indeed, I hope they gain the opportunity to do so.

It is, of course, flattering to learn that we are all Thatcherites now. In fact, the Road to Damascus has never been more congested. But it's not really very important whether New Labour is sincere in seeing the errors of Old Labour. What is important is that they don't—indeed they can't—understand *why* the policies of the 1980s worked. And because they don't understand the philosophy behind them, they could not in the hurly-burly of government put the right policies into practice. They would be blown off course. And the reefs of interventionism are no less dangerous, and the sirens of financial profligacy no less alluring, than they were in the past.

Of course, the *ways* in which this would happen are different now—but happen it surely would. And to understand—and explain—why *that* is so we have to appreciate the fact that socialism is not dead; it is not even asleep; it is visibly stirring. In fact, we may well be fast approaching one of those rare occasions in our affairs when a small deviation to right or left brings huge rewards or the gravest dangers.

Communism and socialism were always beset by fundamental, inherent weaknesses, which became more evident as time went by. Their system failed to mobilise talent and create wealth, failed to conform to the basic human impulses to provide for one's family and to express one's nationhood, and so ultimately failed to engage the loyalties of the system's subjects. From quite early on, communism could only be sustained in power by force and by the vested interests of the elite. And when faced with a resurgent capitalist West it crumbled. All that is true. But it is not the whole truth.

Socialism in the broader sense—that is, not as defined by Clause 4 of the old Labour Party Constitution or the dogma of Marx, but as a system of pervasive state control and influence over people's lives—that socialism, corresponds to an ever-present weakness in human nature.

Idleness, selfishness, fecklessness, envy, and irresponsibility are the vices upon which socialism in any form flourishes and which it in turn encourages. But socialism's devilishly clever tactic is to play up to all these human failings, while making those who practise them feel good about it.

It is still happening. Whenever, as now, Britain enjoys the benefits of a booming economy, the Left begins complaining about the social perils of individualism and greed, attributing any number of crimes and moral deficiencies to the same capitalism they ultimately expect to pay for all their social planning.

The Leader of the Labour Party [Tony Blair] decries (I quote) "rampant individualism, the atomisation and division of society, the narrow self-interest that characterised the 1980s and helped to fracture our society"—and all sorts of empty heads nod in acquiescence.

> Today I have lost one of my dearest friends, England one of her greatest men. Keith Joseph understood that it was necessary to win again the intellectual argument for freedom, and that to do this we must start from first principles... He was in many ways an unlikely revolutionary. For all his towering intellect, he was deeply humble. He spoke boldly, however hostile the audience. Yet he hated to give offence. Above all, his integrity shone out in everything he said and did. His best memorial lies in younger generations of politicians whom he inspired. But for me he is irreplaceable.
>
> *Tribute to Lord Joseph on the day he died, 10 December 1994*

But if people thought a little more about it they would become very angry indeed. For the implication is that because someone exercises his talents to improve his position, sends his children to the best school he can afford, provides for his old age from savings and leaves something worthwhile for the next generation, he is a party to "rampant individualism", and so in some unspecified way responsible for how *someone-else* mis-uses his time or abuses his neighbours. Only, it is implied, a combination of a nanny state and preaching politicians will keep the majority on the straight and narrow paths of the "decent society".

This is not just arrogant. It is absurd. Do these left wing politicians really live in the same world as the rest of us? Crime and violence are not the result of the great majority of people being free: they are the result of a small minority of wicked men and women abusing their freedom.

Do they seriously believe that it is "rampant individualism" that led to the growth of the dependency culture, of a class of people who never work, and whose children may never work, who are habituated to a life on welfare, and whose poverty is not material but behavioural? No: welfare dependence is the classic manifestation of a still-too-socialist society.

And do these New Labour politicians understand nothing of the communist system whose legacy continues to blight Eastern Europe and Russia? In that socialist system there was plenty of individualism of a sort; and "rampant" at that: for people's whole lives were taken up in attempts to cheat the system, and indeed each other. There will always be individualism as long as there are individuals: but in a free society and a free economy individualism works to the general good—in a socialist society and a controlled economy it works against it.

But we Conservatives must never forget that for large numbers of people real freedom is an intimidating prospect. The apparent security of state provision is particularly attractive for those doubtful of their own abilities. This is not just a material but a cultural and indeed a moral problem. And it is one that only conservative believers in the system of liberty *for its own sake*, are truly able to confront.

Yesterday's socialism characterised by militant trade-unionism and burdensome state-owned industries has, in our Western countries at least, almost certainly gone for good. But in the form of a continuing tendency to intervene in people's lives for ends which are quite extraneous to the state's proper functions it is very much present.

It has, for example, re-surfaced in the language and programmes of "group rights". The process has gone furthest in the United States: though I suspect that if Britain were so foolish as to elect a Labour Government we could quickly catch up.

In America, such affirmative action programmes have not only become a heavy burden on employers of all kinds: by increasing the resentment of the majority against minorities they have precisely the opposite effect to that intended.

Closely linked to this approach is the obsessive political correctness that imperils serious scholarship in so many American universities and colleges. Concepts like truth and falsehood, beauty and ugliness, civilization and barbarism have been de-constructed to give way to judgements based on ideology. The results would be funny, if the consequences were not so serious.

Whole shelf-loads of classics written by what they call "DWEMs"—dead white European males—are nowadays consigned to "the dustbin of [whatever these people now call] history".

The great Milton is now, in the words of a Stanford University English Professor, regarded as "an ass [and]...a sexist pig". Shakespeare is still on the syllabus of Duke University–but only, in the words of a professor: "to illuminate the way 17th century society mistreated women, the working class, and minorities."

All this can be called many things—collectivism, relativism, multi-culturalism—or just good old fashioned stupidity. But it also provides a new ideological basis for socialism. For the up-side down world of political correctness is one in which strategies of social control—the enduring objective of the Left—are given free rein. Ordinary, established individual rights—rights of property, or free speech, or the right to choose one's child's education—are crushed by the imposition of collective rights. And the ultimate adjudicator is always the state.

"It couldn't happen here," you may say. But if the Labour Party have their way, it could. For it is precisely this assertion of artificial group rights at the expense of individual freedom that lies at the heart of the Labour Leader's [Tony Blair] idea of "stake-holding".

Because the politics of overt confiscation and control are out of fashion, Left-wing intellectuals, whose verbal facility has always matched their practical ineptitude, have devised this new way of undermining capitalism. Shareholders–those who own a business–and managers–those the owners appoint to run it–would be subject to pressure from an array of politically correct pressure groups and trade unions which would be given a "stake" in the business. Businesses would thus be transformed from maximisers of profit into agents of socialism.

> I cannot leave the future alone. I don't want it to go wonky or wobbly.
>
> *24 June 1995*

Labour's stake-holding economy may sound comfortingly similar to the Conservative vision of a property-owning democracy. In fact, the two are diametrically opposed. For those wielding power under Labour's plans would not be individual men and women as owners and customers: they would be all those busybody representatives of Left-wing causes and special interests that now enjoy in New-Labour-speak the vague but venerable title of "the community".

Shackling British businesses in this way–and imposing a minimum wage to boot—is precisely what our thriving economy does *not* need. And those tycoons who earned their millions in Tory Britain, but are currently attracted to New Labour, may become rapidly less cheerful if they experience stake-holding in practice.

These trends towards more intervention would, of course, rapidly accelerate if Britain were to move closer to the European model of the corporate state. Again, as with socialism, there is a problem of definition: it is not of course fascist corporatism any more than Marxist socialism which is the threat. Rather, it is a creeping but persistent, and possibly irreversible, shift towards a planned economy and a controlled society.

The Social Chapter, from which our Prime Minister wisely gained us an exemption, but which the Opposition Leader would accept, is the most obvious example. We know already—not least from the saga of the 48-hour working week directive—how the European Commission and the European Court regard their mandate of achieving closer European integration by undermining national sovereignty. Accepting the Social Chapter would give them one more major opportunity to tie up our successful businesses with regulation in order to prevent them competing successfully with the over-regulated firms of Continental Europe. And have no doubt: if *they* succeed in imposing *their* higher cost industrial system here, *we* will experience *their* high unemployment.

Attention has recently focused upon the huge and quite possibly unsustainable burden of pensions which countries like France and Germany face because of past imprudence worsened by present demography—burdens which doubtless under any single currency regime they would generously seek to share with us. But we should really not be surprised as each new day seems to bring with it some new scandal or gross injustice or absurd folly for which Europe is responsible.

Instead of gazing into the crystal ball to learn about the new European politics, we only need consider Belgium—where proportional representation ensures constant coalitions of the same political class, where parliamentary democracy has been effectively suspended, where confidence in the integrity of honest government and justice has collapsed, and where separate national groups squabble endlessly within a single state that no-one respects.

These Continental European countries' ideas, traditions and history are fundamentally different from our own. The kind of liberal individualism which J.S. Mill's *On Liberty* describes, let alone the free economy of Adam Smith's *Wealth of Nations*, never took root there. The battles between the European left and right were essentially between different brands of collectivism, and they largely remain so. Moreover, in many cases there are deep-rooted tendencies toward bureaucracy, authoritarianism and corrupt abuse of power. Indeed, European politicians, dividing their time between courts, jails and debating chambers, have recently managed to give a whole new meaning to the expression "conviction politics".

But the European Union is not the only forum in which socialism in new, drab guises is evident. And here again we need to stand back a little and reflect on the significance of that titanic global clash of systems we call the Cold War.

On this subject the revisionists have been much at work. Those who once warned of the dire consequences of daring to stand up to the Soviets can now be found explaining that the Kremlin was never in any case more than a zoo for paper tigers.

The significant worry for us now, however, is that because the revisionists minimise the importance of the struggle between freedom and socialism, they fail to grasp the fact that so much of the defeated system is still in place.

The diplomats and the members of that nebulous but ubiquitous "international community" never cease to warn against *nationalism* as a threat to peace and security. But one man's nationalism is another man's patriotism. And oddly, the new internationalists rarely consider that without British patriotism or French patriotism or American patriotism there would be no national armies to enforce international justice in the first place. Far better if the commentators worried instead about what the unstable and dangerous regimes of the world have most in common, which is not nationalism but various guises of *socialism*.

Our victory in the Cold War, unlike our victory in the Second World War, was not followed by occupation of enemy territory and the purging of those who had been the ideological opponents of freedom. In fact, only the Czechs practised this process of lustration against senior Party members; and perhaps it is significant that the Czechs have since gone furthest in creating the structures of liberty.

Generally, though, yesterday's communists have crept back into power, or never even left it; and not just political power either–the old *nomenklatura* has exploited its connections to grow rich under the new pseudo-capitalism. As a result, the world is full of seedy regimes and unsettled disputes that the socialist elites have a powerful interest in continuing.

We delude ourselves if we imagine that most of the former communist countries are steadily moving in the direction of our Western system. Rather they are, particularly in the former Soviet Union, locked into conditions that resemble more closely rule by robber barons than liberal democracy. Whether in Russia or in China or in the former Yugoslavia the one thing that most of the problem states of the world have in common is that they are largely in the hands of ex- and not always "ex-" communists.

Thankfully in recent months there is some movement in the other direction, as the socialist regimes find their failures catching up with them: in the Baltics and Balkans, non-socialist governments have been or should soon be installed in Lithuania, Rumania and Bulgaria. But what a rich and terrible irony that, forty years on from the crushing of Hungary by Russian tanks, the present Prime Minister of that country is a communist who sided with the invader against his own people. And Hungary itself is still excluded from NATO because of Western feebleness in face of Russian threats. There could be no greater symbolic demonstration of how we in the West failed to carry through to its conclusion our crusade for freedom. We now need Western leaders untainted with socialism who will raise the standard for liberty—because they actually believe in it.

Mr Chairman, the beginning of the next millennium may coincide with a real historical watershed—and socialism remains the real obstacle to crossing it successfully. Britain needs, more than ever before, a government which understands, believes in and practises the politics and economics of liberty.

For three great choices face us. First, we have to choose whether we in Britain are prepared to go further in reducing public spending and taxation so as to join the most successful world economies—or accept that half or more of our national income be taken by a paternalist state.

Secondly, we have to choose whether we are going to enjoy our freedom to trade as and where our interests demand, maximising the advantages which the economic reforms of the 1980s have given us–or whether we accept a new model of socialism, imposed by the bureaucratic super-state towards which the core countries of the European Union now seem irrevocably headed.

Thirdly, we have to choose whether we are going to strive for a truly free—which means a socialist-free—international order—or surrender the future of the post-Cold War world to socialist regimes that discredit democracy by battening on the corruption and disorder which communism left behind.

Three choices—but all adding up to one choice—the age-old choice—between the rugged grandeur of liberty and the ignoble ease of dependence. And, yes, that is a moral choice.

Let it be said of us—as we with pride and gratitude can say of Nick Ridley—that we too kept faith with freedom.

SPEECH TO A FRINGE MEETING AT THE CONSERVATIVE PARTY CONFERENCE IN SUPPORT OF GENERAL PINOCHET

Blackpool, 6 October 1999

My friends, it's nine years since I spoke at a Conservative Party Conference. A lot has happened since then—and not much of it for the better... Today I break my self-denying ordinance. And for a very good reason—to express my outrage at the callous and unjust treatment of Senator Pinochet.

But first I want to extend a personal welcome to our Chilean guests, who have come half way round the world to be with us. They should understand the deep sense of shame and anger we feel at the way in which Chile—its honour, its dignity, its sovereignty and its former ruler—have been treated.

I do not know when or how this tragedy will end. But we will fight on for as long as it takes to see Senator Pinochet returned safely to his own country. Chileans can rest assured that, however contemptibly this Labour Government behaves, the British people still believe in loyalty to their friends.

Chile is our oldest friend in South America. Our ties are very close, and have been ever since Admiral Cochrane helped free Chile from oppressive Spanish rule. He must be turning in his grave, to see Britain now encouraging Spain's arrogant interference in Chilean affairs!

President Pinochet was this country's staunch, true friend in our time of need when Argentina seized the Falkland Islands. I know—I was Prime Minister at the time. On President Pinochet's express instructions, and at great risk, Chile provided enormously valuable assistance. I cannot reveal all the details. But let me mention just one incident.

During the Falklands War, the Chilean airforce was commanded by the father of Senator Evelyn Matthei, here with us tonight. He gave us early warning of Argentinian air attacks, which allowed the task-force to take defensive action. The value of this intelligence was proved by what happened when it stopped. One day, near the end of the conflict, the Chilean long-range radar had to be switched off for overdue maintenance. That same day—Tuesday 8th June, a date etched on my heart—Argentinian planes attacked and destroyed the *Sir Galahad* and *Sir Tristram* landing ships, with heavy casualties.

Altogether, some 250 members of our armed forces lost their lives during the Falklands War. Without President Pinochet, there would certainly have been many more. We all owe him—and Chile—a great debt.

But how did the authorities, under this Labour Government, choose to repay it? I will tell you. By collaborating in Senator Pinochet's judicial kidnap.

The precise extent of Ministers' and officials' involvement with the Spanish authorities is still obscure. But we know a good deal about the catalogue of abuses which occurred. We know that Senator Pinochet was treated on his arrival, as on previous occasions, as an honoured guest. We know that the Chileans were led to believe that he was safe, when the British authorities already knew that to be false. We know that he was then arrested by night on his bed of pain, after a spinal operation, in circumstances which would do credit to a police state.

We know that he was held first in a tiny room at a clinic under sedation, and then in a house where he wasn't even allowed to set foot in the garden. We know this was done under what the courts later ruled was an unlawful arrest warrant. We know that the authorities knew it was unlawful, because they hurriedly sent lawyers to Spain to draw up a new one.

We know that Senator Pinochet's guilt was publicly prejudged by a Labour Cabinet Minister. We know that for the first time in its history the House of Lords had to set aside its ruling, because a Law Lord failed to declare an interest—and that the judge in question was then publicly exonerated by Labour's Lord Chancellor.

I never thought in my lifetime to see the honour of Britain and the reputation of British justice so demeaned as in this affair. All those responsible must be shamed, and held publicly to account.

As has been confirmed at the recent hearing, Senator Pinochet is still legally prevented from answering in a British court any of the charges against him. And his accusers do not, it seems, have to present here any evidence of guilt. Under the Extradition Treaty, the case can only be heard in Spain. That Treaty envisaged, of course, that all the courts of countries which signed the Extradition Convention would behave in an honest and equitable fashion, and that those extradited would receive a fair trial. But the Spanish judicial procedure in this matter has been little short of scandalous.

The Spanish, Socialist prosecuting magistrate has simply assembled any charge whatsoever that he thinks might fit the bill—even though there is no evidence of Senator Pinochet's involvement in, or even knowledge of, the cases concerned, and even though not one concerns a Spaniard. It is well-known that counselling this prosecuting magistrate at every stage is Allende's former political adviser, working with a network of other Marxists in Spain and Chile. The chance of Senator Pinochet's receiving anything resembling what we in Britain would recognise as "justice" in a Spanish court is minimal—not least because key witnesses for his defence run the risk of immediate arrest if they set foot on Spanish soil. What is planned there is a show-trial, with a pre-ordained outcome—lingering death in a foreign land.

In Britain, we're all Thatcherites now.

At a party in the US given in honour of her 70th birthday, 24 October 1995

All this has many implications. There are implications for Chile, where the small minority of communists who once nearly wrecked the country under Allende will now be encouraged to overturn the prosperous, democratic order that Pinochet and his successors built.

There are implications for Britain, whose interests will be jeopardised, not just in the Falklands and South America, but in isolated enclaves round the world, where friends will see how we reward past deeds of friendship.

And there are implications for heads of government everywhere, as they see that at some future date they may be hauled out of hospital in a foreign country at dead of night to face some trumped up charge.

My friends, these are vital matters for our Party to ponder. We must pay heed to the implications of an international lynch-law which, under the guise of defending human rights, now threatens to subvert British justice and the rights of sovereign nations. The people of Britain, too, should reflect on what has been revealed about the priorities of this Labour Government.

For this is a government that grovels to collaborate with Spain, whose bullying of Gibraltar is a daily outrage—yet treats our Chilean allies with contempt. This is a government which reckons that ageing spies, who betrayed our country to Soviet communism, should escape prosecution—yet obsessively pursues the frail 83 year-old Pinochet, who stopped the communists taking Chile.

This is a government which grants amnesties to unrepentant terrorist murderers—yet overturns an amnesty in Chile, and imperils that country's young democracy. My friends, this is a government which discredits and dishonours Britain.

Make no mistake: revenge by the Left, not justice for the victim, is what the Pinochet case is all about. Senator Pinochet is in truth on trial, not for anything contained in Judge Garzon's indictment, but for defeating communism. What the Left can't forgive is that Pinochet undoubtedly saved Chile and helped save South America.

But don't take my word for it. Listen instead to President Aylwin, Pinochet's democratically elected successor and frequent opponent, who said: "the Allende government was planning, with the assistance of an armed militia of enormous military power, to establish a communist dictatorship." That, Ladies and Gentlemen, is what Pinochet stopped.

As he himself admits, there were abuses in the wake of the military coup. And some of these continued. The precise responsibility for what happened can only be judged in Chile. But it is an affront to commonsense, as well as a caricature of justice, to maintain that a head of government must automatically accept criminal responsibility for everything that is done while he is in power—whether he authorised it or not, whether he overlooked it or not, whether he knew about it or not. On that basis, Messrs. Blair and Straw should accept criminal responsibility for everything done in every prison or police station throughout the United Kingdom—and then be extradited to Spain to answer for it.

Why is it, I wonder, that those queuing up to accuse Senator Pinochet of every grotesque abuse imaginable don't mention the positive legacy of his rule in Chile? What about the fact that Chile was turned from chaotic collectivism into the model economy of Latin America?

What about the fact that more people were housed, that medical care was improved, that infant mortality plummeted, that life expectancy rose, that highly effective programmes against poverty were launched?

Above all, why don't they tell the world that it was Senator Pinochet who established a constitution for the return to democracy? That he held a referendum to decide whether or not he should remain in power? That he lost the vote (though gaining 44 per cent support)? And that he respected the result, and handed over to an elected successor? But, of course, we know why none of these achievements is talked about. It's because the Left don't want them to be talked about - or even (if they can help it) known about.

The Left lost the Cold War in Chile, as they lost it everywhere else. For our Home Secretary, who visited Chile as a young left-wing activist, that must have been very distressing. It can hardly have been much pleasanter for our Prime Minister, who recently described Allende as his "hero".

The Left in Chile, and in Britain, had to abandon all the rhetoric, and most of the policies, of socialism in order to get power. But what they couldn't and wouldn't abandon was the poisonous prejudices they harboured in their youth. And this, of course, was the situation when a trusting, elderly, former Chilean ruler chose to pay one too many visits to his beloved Britain last autumn.

When the communists so nearly assassinated him in 1986, President Pinochet knew that he was being fired on by his enemies. Little could he imagine that a new, legal and political assassination was to be planned for him in the Britain he trusted as a friend.

Perhaps his enemies will succeed. Perhaps he will die here, as this country's only political prisoner. Or perhaps he will breathe his last in a Spanish hospital, awaiting some interminable, contemptible semblance of justice.

But at least he will know, and the world will know, that his friends did not abandon his cause, and that those whom the Left would like to silence—but dare not—have proclaimed the truth about his treatment.

SPEECH TO A CONSERVATIVE ELECTION RALLY – THE MUMMY RETURNS

Plymouth, 22 May 2001

It's wonderful to be here this evening, campaigning for a Conservative victory, in this enterprising port of Plymouth. I was told beforehand my arrival was unscheduled, but on the way here I passed a local cinema and it turns out you were expecting me after all. The billboard read *The Mummy Returns.*

Every general election tests character as well as policies. And this one is no exception. But our party is fortunate indeed. Under William Hague 's cool and gritty leadership we have the right man with the right message to win through.

It's more than a decade since I was in the front line of politics. But one thing hasn't changed and, I trust, will never change. Ours is a Party that knows what it stands for, is proud of its beliefs, and is in tune with the deepest instincts of the British people.

We Conservatives changed Britain for the better. And we helped change the world—bringing liberty to millions who'd never known it. Moreover—let's admit it—we changed our opponents, at least on the surface, and so made them electable. But we didn't, and we couldn't, make them believers in liberty or champions of enterprise.

New Labour's main appeal, when you get down to it, is quite simply that it's not Old Labour. And that's true as far as it goes. I had some respect for the Old Labour Party, which stood for certain principles—wrong as they were.

But today's Labour Party has no discernible principles at all. It is rootless, empty and artificial. And when anything real or human surfaces despite the spin—it's the bitter, brawling, bully that we hoped we'd seen the last of twenty years ago.

Labour's election slogan—Ambitions for Britain—is, of course, half-right. They are ambitious. But not, I'm afraid, for Britain.

They are certainly ambitious to extend the power of the state.

That's why, year after year, they have piled on taxes by stealth. The British people are paying a billion pounds a week of extra tax for the privilege of keeping Messrs Blair and Brown in Downing Street. What an incentive to evict them!

Labour are also ambitious to draw more and more people into dependency, diminishing liberty, throttling choice. That's why the Chancellor took away mortgage tax relief; took away the relief for marriage; took away the relief for private health insurance. That's why he took five billion pounds a year from those who put money into private pension schemes. And that's why he plans to make more and more elderly people subject to the means-test. He just can't stand people being independent.

Above all, our New Labour masters love to strut the international stage: it's a great deal pleasanter than facing the wrath of outraged farmers, desperate hospital patients or demoralised policemen. Mr Blair says he wants to 'lead in Europe', but the price of that is that he's expected to lead Britain by the nose into the single currency. And he's prepared to do it! I would never be prepared to give up our own currency.

The greatest issue in this election, indeed the greatest issue before our country, is whether Britain is to remain a free, independent, nation state. Or whether we are to be dissolved in a federal Europe. There are no half measures, no third ways - and no second chances.

Too many powers have already passed from our Parliament to the bureaucracy in Brussels. We must get them back. Above all, we must keep the pound.

Keeping our currency is not, as Labour would have it, just a matter of economics—though the economic case grows weaker, as the Euro grows sicker, by the day. No: a country which loses the power to issue its own currency is a country which has given up the power to govern itself. Such a country is no longer free. And neither is it truly democratic—for its people can no longer determine their own future in national elections.

To surrender the pound, to surrender our power of self-government, would betray all that past generations down the ages lived and died to defend. It would also be to turn our back on America, leader of the English-speaking peoples, to whom Europe—let's remember—also owes its freedom.

That is not our way. And where better to take a stand than here in Plymouth? Plymouth—England's historic opening to the world. Plymouth—from where Francis Drake, Walter Raleigh, and Captain Cook set out to take the ways of these islands to the uttermost bounds of the earth? Plymouth—from where the Pilgrim Fathers left in that cockle-shell vessel on a voyage which would create the most powerful force for freedom that the world has known?

My Friends, New Labour in its shrivelled heart is embarrassed by our history, scornful of our achievement, oblivious of our legacy. They think that they can remove Britain's sovereignty, just as they put up Britain's taxes—by stealth. They are wrong. But they are too arrogant and too remote to know it.

So a mighty burden rests on us. We have sixteen days to shift opinions, and to shake this rotten government to the core. That is our task. Let's be about it!

ARTICLE FOR THE *NEW YORK TIMES* – 'ADVICE TO A SUPERPOWER'

11 February 2002

"Methinks I see in my mind a noble and puissant nation rousing herself like a strong man after sleep, and shaking her invincible locks." Milton's words perfectly describe America today. After the horror of September 11 the world has seen America gather its strength, summon its allies and proceed to wage war halfway across the globe against its enemy—and ours.

America will never be the same again. It has proved to itself and to others that it is in truth (not just in name) the only global superpower, indeed a power that enjoys a level of superiority over its actual or potential rivals unmatched by any other nation in modern times. Consequently, the world outside America should never be the same either. There will, of course, arise new threats from new directions. But as long as America works to maintain its technological lead, there is no reason why any challenge to American dominance should succeed. And that in turn will help ensure stability and peace.

Yet, as President Bush has reminded Americans, there is no room for complacency. America and its allies, indeed the Western world and its values, are still under deadly threat. That threat must be eliminated, and now is the time to act vigorously.

In many respects the challenge of Islamic terror is unique, hence the difficulty Western intelligence services encountered trying to predict and prevent its onslaughts. The enemy is not, of course, a religion—most Muslims deplore what has occurred. Nor is it a single state, though this form of terrorism needs the support of states to give it succour. Perhaps the best parallel is with early Communism. Islamic extremism today, like Bolshevism in the past, is an armed doctrine. It is an aggressive ideology promoted by fanatical, well-armed devotees. And, like Communism, it requires an all-embracing long-term strategy to defeat it.

The first phase of that strategy had to be a military assault on the enemy in Afghanistan, a phase that is now approaching its end. I believe that while the new interim government there deserves support, the United States is right not to allow itself to become bogged down with ambitious nation-building in that treacherous territory. Some would disagree, arguing that the lesson of the present crisis is that neglect of failed states causes terrorism. But this is trite. It implies a level of global interventionism that almost everyone recognizes is quite impractical.

The more important lesson is that the West failed to act early and strongly enough against Al Qaeda and the regime that harboured it. And because there is always a choice in where you concentrate international efforts, it is best that the United States, as the only global military superpower, deploy its energies militarily rather than on social work. Trying to promote civil society and democratic institutions in Afghanistan is best left to others—and since those "others" now include the British, I only hope that we, too, are going to be realistic about what can (and cannot) be achieved.

The second phase of the war against terrorism should be to strike at other centers of Islamic terror that have taken root in Africa, Southeast Asia and elsewhere. This will require first-rate intelligence, shrewd diplomacy and a continued extensive military commitment. Our enemies have had years to entrench themselves, and they will not be dislodged without fierce and bloody resistance.

The third phase is to deal with those hostile states that support terrorism and seek to acquire or trade in weapons of mass destruction. We have gotten into the habit of calling them "rogue" states. There is nothing wrong with that, as long as we don't fall into the trap of imagining that they will always and on every issue fit into the same slot.

For example, Iran and Syria were both sharply critical of Osama bin Laden, the Taliban and the attacks of September 11. Nevertheless, they are both enemies of Western values and interests. Both have energetically backed terrorism: the former has just been caught out dispatching arms to foment violence against Israel. Iran is also making strides toward developing long-range missiles that could be armed with nuclear warheads.

Other critics of September 11 are a menace, too. Libya, for example, still hates the West and would dearly like revenge against us. And Sudan undertakes genocide against its own citizens in the name of Islam. As for North Korea, the regime of Kim Jong Il is as mad as ever and is the world's main proliferator of long-range ballistic missiles that can deliver nuclear, chemical or biological warheads.

The most notorious rogue is, without doubt, Saddam Hussein—proof if ever we needed it that yesterday's unfinished business becomes tomorrow's headache. Saddam Hussein will never comply with the conditions we demand of him. His aim is, in fact, quite clear: to develop weapons of mass destruction so as to challenge us with impunity.

How and when, not whether, to remove him are the only important questions. Again, solving this problem will demand the best available intelligence. It will require, as in Afghanistan, the mobilization of internal resistance. It will probably also involve a massive use of force. America's allies, above all Britain, should extend strong support to President Bush in the decisions he makes on Iraq.

The events of September 11 are a terrible reminder that freedom demands eternal vigilance. And for too long we have not been vigilant. We have harboured those who hated us, tolerated those who threatened us and indulged those who weakened us. As a result, we remain, for example, all but defenceless against ballistic missiles that could be launched against our cities. A missile defence system will begin to change that. But change must go deeper still. The West as a whole needs to strengthen its resolve against rogue regimes and upgrade its defences. The good news is that America has a president who can offer the leadership necessary to do so.

EULOGY FOR PRESIDENT REAGAN,

London, 11 June 2004
(transmitted by video link to the National Cathedral, Washington D.C.)

We have lost a great president, a great American, and a great man, and I have lost a dear friend.

In his lifetime, Ronald Reagan was such a cheerful and invigorating presence that it was easy to forget what daunting historic tasks he set himself. He sought to mend America's wounded spirit, to restore the strength of the free world, and to free the slaves of communism. These were causes hard to accomplish and heavy with risk, yet they were pursued with almost a lightness of spirit, for Ronald Reagan also embodied another great cause, what Arnold Bennett once called "the great cause of cheering us all up".

His policies had a freshness and optimism that won converts from every class and every nation, and ultimately, from the very heart of the "evil empire."

Yet his humour often had a purpose beyond humour. In the terrible hours after the attempt on his life, his easy jokes gave reassurance to an anxious world. They were evidence that in the aftermath of terror and in the midst of hysteria one great heart at least remained sane and jocular. They were truly grace under pressure. And perhaps they signified grace of a deeper kind. Ronnie himself certainly believed that he had been given back his life for a purpose. As he told a priest after his recovery, "Whatever time I've got left now belongs to the big fella upstairs." And surely, it is hard to deny that Ronald Reagan's life was providential when we look at what he achieved in the eight years that followed.

I'm under doctors' orders not to make speeches but I don't take too much notice of doctors.

Speech to Oxford and Cambridge University Students, 2002

Others prophesied the decline of the West. He inspired America and its allies with renewed faith in their mission of freedom.

Others saw only limits to growth. He transformed a stagnant economy into an engine of opportunity.

Others hoped, at best, for an uneasy cohabitation with the Soviet Union. He won the Cold War, not only without firing a shot, but also by inviting enemies out of their fortress and turning them into friends.

I cannot imagine how any diplomat or any dramatist could improve on his words to Mikhail Gorbachev at the Geneva summit. "Let me tell you why it is we distrust you." Those words are candid and tough, and they cannot have been easy to hear. But they are also a clear invitation to a new beginning and a new relationship that would be rooted in trust.

We live today in the world that Ronald Reagan began to reshape with those words. It is a very different world, with different challenges and new dangers. All in all, however, it is one of greater freedom and prosperity, one more hopeful than the world he inherited on becoming president.

As Prime Minister, I worked closely with Ronald Reagan for eight of the most important years of all our lives. We talked regularly, both before and after his presidency, and I've had time and cause to reflect on what made him a great president.

Ronald Reagan knew his own mind. He had firm principles and, I believe, right ones. He expounded them clearly. He acted upon them decisively. When the world threw problems at the White House, he was not baffled or disorientated or overwhelmed.

He knew almost instinctively what to do.

When his aides were preparing option papers for his decision, they were able to cut out entire rafts of proposals that they knew the old man would never wear. When his allies came under Soviet or domestic pressure, they could look confidently to Washington for firm leadership, and when his enemies tested American resolve, they soon discovered that his resolve was firm and unyielding.

Yet his ideas, so clear, were never simplistic. He saw the many sides of truth. Yes, he warned that the Soviet Union had an insatiable drive for military power and territorial expansion, but he also sensed that it was being eaten away by systemic failures impossible to reform. Yes, he did not shrink from denouncing Moscow's evil empire, but he realized that a man of good will might nonetheless emerge from within its dark corridors.

So the president resisted Soviet expansion and pressed down on Soviet weakness at every point until the day came when communism began to collapse beneath the combined weight of those pressures and its own failures. And when a man of good will did emerge from the ruins, President Reagan stepped forward to shake his hand and to offer sincere cooperation.

Nothing was more typical of Ronald Reagan than that large-hearted magnanimity, and nothing was more American.

Therein lies perhaps the final explanation of his achievements. Ronald Reagan carried the American people with him in his great endeavours because there was perfect sympathy between them.

He and they loved America and what it stands for: freedom and opportunity for ordinary people.

As an actor in Hollywood's golden age, he helped to make the American dream live for millions all over the globe. His own life was a fulfilment of that dream. He never succumbed to the embarrassment some people feel about an honest expression of love of country. He was able to say "God bless America" with equal fervour in public and in private. And so he was able to call confidently upon his fellow countrymen to make sacrifices for America and to make sacrifices for those who look to America for hope and rescue.

With the lever of American patriotism, he lifted up the world. And so today, the world—in Prague, in Budapest, in Warsaw and Sofia, in Bucharest, in Kiev, and in Moscow itself, the world mourns the passing of the great liberator and echoes his prayer: God bless America.

Ronald Reagan's life was rich not only in public achievement, but also in private happiness. Indeed, his public achievements were rooted in his private happiness.

The great turning point of his life was his meeting and marriage with Nancy. On that, we have the plain testimony of a loving and grateful husband. "Nancy came along and saved my soul."

We share her grief today, but we also share her pride and the grief and pride of Ronnie's children. For the final years of his life, Ronnie's mind was clouded by illness. That cloud has now lifted. He is himself again, more himself than at any time on this Earth, for we may be sure that the Big Fellow upstairs never forgets those who remember him. And as the last journey of this faithful pilgrim took him beyond the sunset, and as heaven's morning broke, I like to think, in the words of Bunyan, that "all the trumpets sounded on the other side."

We here still move in twilight, but we have one beacon to guide us that Ronald Reagan never had. We have his example. Let us give thanks today for a life that achieved so much for all of God's children.

TEXT OF RADIO MESSAGE FROM LADY THATCHER'S BROADCAST ON BRITISH FORCES BROADCASTING SERVICE TO MARK THE 25TH ANNIVERSARY OF THE LIBERATION OF THE FALKLAND ISLANDS

13th June 2007

I feel privileged, and very moved, in making this broadcast. The Falkland Islanders are celebrating the anniversary of their liberation. The memories of that time are for many as fresh as yesterday. Such intense experience unites us in spirit - even though a quarter-century has passed, and though we are eight thousand miles apart.

Today, I send my very best wishes to them—you are in my thoughts and in my prayers.

Twenty-five year ago British forces secured a great victory in a noble cause. The whole nation rejoiced at the success; and we should still rejoice. Aggression was defeated and reversed. The wishes of local people were upheld as paramount. Britain's honour and interests prevailed. Sending troops into battle is the gravest decision that any Prime Minister has to take. To fight eight thousand miles away from home, in perilous conditions, against a well armed, if badly led, enemy was bound to be an awesome challenge. Moreover, at such times there is no lack of people, at home and abroad, to foretell disaster. Then, when things go well, they are just as quick to press some hopeless compromise. So we could never at any stage be sure what the outcome of the Falklands War would be. But of two *other* things I *could* be sure—first that our cause was just, and second that no finer troops could be found in the world than those of our country.

That is still the case. Britain's armed services are unmatched in their skill and professionalism. More than that, they are the model of all that we wish our country and our citizens to be. The service they offer and the sacrifice they make are an inspiration.

The Falklands War was a great national struggle. The whole country knew it and felt it. It was also mercifully short. But many of our boys—and girls as well, of course—are today stationed in war zones where the issues are more complex, where the outcome is more problematic, and where life is no less dangerous. In these circumstances, they often need a different sort of courage, though the same commitment.

So, as we recall—and give thanks for—the liberation of our Islands, let us also recall the many battle fronts where British forces are engaged today. There are in a sense no final victories, for the struggle against evil in the world is never ending. Tyranny and violence wear many masks. Yet from victory in the Falklands we can all today draw hope and strength.

Fortune *does*, in the end, favour the brave. And it is Britain's good fortune that none are braver than our armed forces. Thank you all.

APPENDIX 1

The Margaret Thatcher 'Dead Parrot' Speech

At the 1990 party conference Margaret Thatcher brought the house down with an hilarious take on the *Monty Python* 'Dead Parrot' sketch. Her then political secretary, John Whittingdale (now a Conservative MP), recounted how this came about in his entry in the book, *Margaret Thatcher: A Tribute in Words & Pictures.*

John Whittingdale:

Of all the demands on the Prime Minister's time, the one that occupied the most was speech-writing. Every speech went through at least ten drafts and major speeches many more. As Margaret Thatcher's Political Secretary, my job was to co-ordinate the preparation of speeches to Party audiences. My year was divided between fixed points: the Central Council meeting, the Scottish Conference, the Local Government Conference, the Women's Conference and most important of all the Party Conference in October.

Work would start on the Party Conference speech at least a month in advance. At a preliminary meeting, the Prime Minister would set out her ideas as to the areas that the speech should cover. This was usually done in an unbroken flow of raw Thatcher thought which our in-house speech-writing team, and those that I would commission from outside, would have to turn into draft speech form. Subject areas would be allocated between speechwriters and they would then be sent off to prepare paragraphs on each topic for inclusion. Once we had collected a number of contributions, these would be tacked together in a rough structure and the process of refinement and polishing would begin.

It was an immensely time-consuming process and at least once in the preparation of every speech, the Prime Minister would lose confidence in the whole process, tell us that it was all useless and demand that we start again from the beginning. The next few hours would be spent slightly tweaking the sections and then reinserting them while assuring her that they were completely different from the original. At the early stages, we would be meeting once a week. This would then increase to everyday and then the whole of the weekend before the Conference would be spent working on the text at Chequers.

Once we got to Blackpool, Bournemouth or Brighton, the whole time would be spent in the Prime Minister's suite surrounded by paper, with a core team which was boosted by those drafted in to make suggestions and improvements. A single critical word at the wrong time could undo weeks of work and my job was as much to keep well-meaning but destructive critics away as it was to bring in and encourage contributors. The average length of a Party Conference speech is about forty minutes. I worked on three and in each case Margaret Thatcher spent at least eighty hours working on the text: two hours for each minute of the speech. Those actually writing the speech spent much more.

The hardest and most important parts of the speech to write were the jokes. Margaret Thatcher is not naturally a joke-teller although she has a dry sense of humour. However, she recognises that without jokes, a speech is flat and dull. A good joke-writer was therefore valued above all others. On our core team we had two principle joke-writers: the late Sir Ronnie Millar and John O'Sullivan, a journalist and commentator who had been brought in to the Number Ten Policy Unit. They had very different styles and each brought a different kind of humour. However, in each case, Margaret Thatcher frequently required persuasion that what they had written was indeed funny.

In 1990, the Party Conference speech was particularly important. Margaret Thatcher was under heavy attack and had recently suffered the resignation of her Chancellor, Nigel Lawson. Her speech had to be as good as she had ever delivered. A few weeks earlier, the Liberal Democrats had unveiled their new Party symbol. It was supposed to represent a bird taking wing, but in the mind of John O'Sullivan it immediately became a dead parrot. He decided that he would write a section of the Speech devoted to mocking the Liberal Democrats and would include a section of *Monty Python*'s 'Dead Parrot' sketch. To anyone familiar with *Monty Python* it was a terrific idea and very funny. Unfortunately, the Prime Minister had not even heard of *Monty Python*.

When we came to read through the draft of the speech, Mrs Thatcher paused when she reached the dead parrot section and looked at John O'Sullivan as if he were completely mad. We knew that this would happen and so had prepared our strategy in advance. 'This is,' I explained, 'one of the most famous comedy sketches ever written. It will be instantly recognisable to every person in the audience.' I was slightly less certain of this latter point, knowing Conservative audiences, but all of us present insisted to the Prime Minister that it would be the highlight of her speech.

The joke survived that read-through but I knew that she was not convinced. On each subsequent occasion, whenever we reached the parrot section, she stopped and said: 'Are you sure that this is funny?' After about the third or fourth occasion, she tried a new tack. 'I need to see the sketch,' she said. 'If I am to deliver it then I need to get the inflexion absolutely right.' As it happened, I had at home a video of the *Python* film *And Now for Something Completely Different*, which contains the dead parrot sketch. I therefore brought it into the office the next day.

One of the more surreal moments during my time at Number Ten followed. Sitting in my office watching the dead parrot sketch were Margaret Thatcher, John O'Sullivan, Robin Harris who was also helping with the speech, Peter Morrison her PPS and myself. At any time, it is a very funny sketch. But the absurdity of the situation made it all the more amusing and I and the three others found it so hilarious that we had tears rolling down our cheeks. Margaret Thatcher, on the other hand, was all the more mystified. It was not her type of humour and she found it difficult to see why we were laughing so much. However, given that we all were, she accepted that it must be funny and so, true professional that she was, she attempted to master the emphasis and inflexion of John

Cleese's delivery. She did so brilliantly and was soon able to deliver faultlessly the famous lines: 'This parrot is no more. It has ceased to be. It has expired and gone to meet its maker.'

In the days leading up to the Conference, the Prime Minister required constant reassurance that people would find the lines funny. She was clearly still full of doubt. However, I was able to get to enough people in advance whose opinion she was likely to ask that she was eventually persuaded. Every time we ran through the speech, I found myself laughing at the passage which simply added to the Prime Minister's puzzlement.

Finally, we got to the day of the speech. The text was finished, it had been typed up on to the autocue and we had completed the final rehearsal at which she practiced her delivery and the inflexions of the speech. However, as we waited for her to go on to the stage to deliver the speech, she was still worrying about the passage and looking for reasons that it might not work. Just as she was about to go on, another doubt arose in her mind. She looked at me and said anxiously: 'John, Monty Python – are you sure that he is one of us?'

To try to explain to her that *Monty Python* did not really exist would have been to risk disaster. I therefore did not even try and instead said to her: 'Absolutely, Prime Minister. He is a very good supporter.' Thus reassured, she went on to the platform to give the speech. She did so perfectly and received the biggest laugh of all when she delivered with perfect comic timing the words of the dead parrot sketch.

APPENDIX 2

Reconstruction of the Cabinet Meeting on 22 November 1990

Author's note: Some time ago, back in 2006, I had intended to write a book about the month leading up to Margaret Thatcher's fall from power. Part of the incentive to do so was that there seemed to be so many conflicting accounts of what actually happened. I knew I would be able to get access to all the leading players and was looking forward to the challenge. In order to provide a putative publisher with a sample chapter I set about researching what happened at the meeting of the Cabinet on 22 November at which Margaret Thatcher announced her resignation. In the end I never wrote the book as a new job intervened, which meant I did not have the time. So as an indulgence, I have included the chapter here. It's deliberately written as a dramatic, rather than a dry, historical account, but the dialogue and events are entirely accurate.
Iain Dale
October 2010

At 6.30am two men arrived at the gates of Downing Street asking to be let in to see the Prime Minister. The policeman on the gate phoned through to Charles Powell, who was already at his desk. The two turned out to be Tory backbenchers Michael Brown and Edward Leigh. Powell gave them coffee and explained the PM was dressing and asked them to wait. They waited and waited – in vain. They were still there when the Cabinet convened at 9am. They were only put out of their misery when the PM's Political Secretary John Whittingdale told them what they had already guessed. She was resigning. Tears streamed down Brown's face as he left Number Ten through a back door, thus avoiding waiting TV cameras in Downing Street.

At 7am Cecil Parkinson was barely awake. The shrilling of the telephone put paid to that. It was one of his junior Ministers and a key member of the No Turning Back Group, Chris Chope. "She's going," he said. "You've got to do something." Parkinson had last seen the PM at 6pm the previous evening, before her confidence had been shattered by the meetings with her Cabinet members. So confident was he that she was heading for victory, and that the Cabinet was supporting her, he had gone out to dinner with his wife and some friends. A few hours earlier, the *Sun*'s Trevor Kavanagh had got wind of what was about to happen and had rung the Parkinson house to check if he knew anything. Parkinson had already gone to bed and his wife Ann, a close personal friend of the PM, said she didn't want to waken him. Had she done so, there is little doubt that Parkinson would have hot-footed it to Downing Street.

After Chope's phone call Parkinson immediately phoned Number Ten, only to be told that the PM was under the hair dryer and that he should phone back in thirty minutes. In desperation he then phoned his friend of twenty years standing, Norman Tebbit. Tebbit had been with her until late the previous night working on her speech for the Censure debate. He told Parkinson the game was up and that her mind would not be changed. Parkinson decided it was pointless to phone Number Ten again.

By 7.30am Andrew Turnbull had been at his desk for an hour already. He sat there unable to concentrate. He spoke to the Prime Minister several times a day, but he knew their next conversation would probably be a fairly momentous one. The call came. It was the news he had expected, as the Prime Minister asked him to put in place the formal arrangements for her resignation announcement. The next call he made was to the Palace to arrange for the formalities of an audience with the Queen.

Woodrow Wyatt called to make a last ditch attempt to make the PM change her mind but for once, she wouldn't take his call. In fact, she didn't take calls from anyone until after the Vote of Censure debate was over, later in the afternoon.

Peter Morrison phoned Douglas Hurd and John Major to advise them of the Prime Minister's decision. John Wakeham and Kenneth Baker were also tipped off by Morrison.

Shortly after 8am Denis Thatcher phoned his daughter. "There have been all sorts of consultations and your mother..." Carol interrupted him. "I know, Dad." Nothing further was said.

At 8.30 every Thursday morning it was usual for the Prime Minister to hold a short briefing in preparation for Prime Minister's Question Time. As usual, Bernard Ingham, Charles Powell and John Whittingdale were with her. It was a subdued meeting and no one was really concentrating.

The regular Thursday Cabinet meetings were a matter of routine for most of those who attended them. This one was different. Cabinet meetings normally start at 10.30am but this one had been brought forward so as not to clash with a memorial service for Lady Home, which was to be held later in the morning at St Margaret's Church, opposite the Houses of Parliament. Normally, the Cabinet would gather for coffee fifteen minutes before the meeting and gossip about the latest political machinations, before the Prime Minister would rush into the room, apparently always in a hurry. That was the signal for the rest of them to take their seats around the famous oval table.

But on this morning the atmosphere was strained to say the least. The few remaining Thatcher loyalists eyed up the rest of their Cabinet colleagues and could barely bring themselves to speak. In her memoirs, Margaret Thatcher recalls: "They stood with their backs against the wall looking in every direction except mine." According to Cecil Parkinson Kenneth Clarke was the only one who was showing the remotest sign of life, telling "anybody who cared to listen that if the PM did not resign before noon that day, he would do so himself".

Thatcher's arrival was normally the signal for everyone to file into the room and take their places, but it seemed there was a delay. John MacGregor had been held up in traffic. The awkward silence continued for an unbearable ten minutes. At 9.10 the Cabinet filed in. The PM was in her usual chair, half way along the table in front of the fireplace. They took their places in silence – even the sound of the chairs being pulled back seemed to grate. For the first time in living memory, the woman who had dominated her Cabinet for eleven years seemed powerless. The aura had gone. Still, there was silence. Cecil Parkinson noticed her reddened, swollen eyes. A carton of tissues sat next to her on the table. While the Cabinet were taking their seats she picked a tissue from the box and dabbed her eyes. The dreadful silence continued. Slowly, Margaret Thatcher opened her handbag and pulled out a creased piece of paper. The Cabinet knew what was coming, but the performance had to be played out nonetheless. She read in a slow, halting, and emotional manner:

> *Having consulted widely among my colleagues, I have concluded that the unity of the Party and the prospects of victory in a general election would be better served if I stood down to enable cabinet colleagues to enter the ballot for the leadership. I should like to thank all those in the Cabinet and outside who have given me such dedicated support.*

She faltered several times and broke down sobbing. She wasn't the only one. David Waddington, Tony Newton, John Gummer, Michael Howard and John Wakeham were all in tears. Cecil Parkinson later wondered why Mr Wakeham should be so upset, when it was he, in Parkinson's opinion, who had largely brought about the events they were witnessing.

Half way through the statement she was so upset that Cecil Parkinson, already on a light fuse, shouted to the Lord Chancellor, who was sitting to her left, "For Christ's sake you read it, James." Lord Mackay briefly put his arm round her shoulder and said gently, "Let me read it, Prime Minister." This brief interjection broke the unbearable tension and allowed the Prime Minister a few moments to gather herself. She stiffened both in resolve and body language and said, "No! I can read it myself."

Norman Lamont recalls her "referring to the events of the last few days and to the advice she had had 'from so many of you' that she could not win and should not fight on. The way she put it implied that she did not agree and thought us spineless." It was after these words that the worst breakdown occurred.

James MacKay, the Lord Chancellor, then read out a short tribute to the Prime Minister. She listened, eyes glistening and red and broke down again. She regained composure and told the Cabinet they must unite behind a candidate to beat Michael Heseltine. "We must protect what we believe in," she flashed.

Kenneth Baker then spoke in his capacity as Chairman of the Party. "You have and will always continue to have the love and loyalty of the party. You have a very special place in the heart of the party. You have led us to victory three times and you would have done so again. Those who have served you recognise that they have been in touch with greatness." He, also, was close to tears.

Douglas Hurd referred to this "whole wretched business" and said he wanted to put on record the superb way in which the Prime Minister had conducted business at the Paris conference, particularly with regard to the pressures of the leadership election on her.

The Prime Minister then called a halt, saying she could deal with routine matters but not sympathy. She was still in a highly emotional state and felt she might lose her composure entirely if such tributes went on for much longer.

She ended proceedings by telling the Cabinet that any new leader would have her total and devoted support. It was assumed this did not include Michael Heseltine. "Well, now that's out of the way, let's get on with the rest of the business," she said.

The meeting then broke for ten minutes and coffee was served while courtesy calls were made to the other party leaders and the Speaker. The atmosphere was considerably lighter than that preceding the meeting. A formal statement was issued by the Downing Street Press Office at 9.25.

The Cabinet then resumed and quickly skimmed through the rest of the normal agenda by 10.15. The final decision taken was to send an armoured brigade to the Gulf. Douglas Hurd's mind was elsewhere though. He knew that events would move fast.

Kenneth Baker passed a note to Hurd asking if he had come to an agreement with John Major about the candidacy. Hurd sent a note back saying they were issuing a joint statement declaring that they had worked closely together in the past but the best way of uniting the party was to let both their names go forward in the next ballot. He then passed the draft statement to Baker who regarded it as a "perfectly masterful composition". Hurd then tried to catch Tom King's eye to ask if he would act as his proposer on the second ballot. King didn't get the hint.

By the close of the meeting the Prime Minister was close to tears again, according to Kenneth Baker. She invited Ministers to stay behind for yet more coffee. By now she was fully composed and was keen to know her colleagues' views on what might happen in the second ballot.

No one was keen to be the first to leave, although Douglas Hurd didn't hang around long. Cecil Parkinson's most vivid memory from the conversation was when somebody—allegedly Kenneth Clarke—said "we are going to pin regicide on Heseltine". For a moment the PM looked puzzled and issued a devastating reply: "Oh no, it wasn't Heseltine, it was the Cabinet." Parkinson said this was said without the slightest hint of rancour. "It was, to her, a simple statement of fact," he said. Douglas Hurd, however, had other things on his mind and left immediately. Norman Lamont caught Michael Howard's eye. They were both anxious to go. While Heseltine was out there campaigning, important time was being lost. After what seemed an age, Margaret Thatcher sensed what others were thinking and told everyone to leave and "stop Heseltine".

As the Cabinet trooped out of Downing Street, Kenneth Baker, ever with an eye for the TV cameras, made a short statement outside the door of Number Ten, saying: "This is a typically brave and selfless decision by the Prime Minister. Once again Margaret Thatcher has put her country and the Party's interests before personal considerations. This will allow the Party to elect a new leader to unite the Party and build upon her immense successes.

If I could just add a personal note, I am very saddened that our greatest peace-time Prime Minister has left Government. She is an outstanding leader, not only of our country but also of the world. I do not believe we will see her like again."

John Wakeham followed suit. Asked about her mood, he said "Well, her mood is, like always, she does her duty, she's—of course she's sad." It was rather an understatement.

While Denis attended the memorial service for Lady Home, the Prime Minister—for she still held that office—was driven to Buckingham Palace informing the Queen in person of her decision to resign. It was not a long audience. The Prime Minister was well aware she had the speech of her life to make in the House of Commons in just a few hours' time. It was to be an occasion she, and the country, would have cause to remember for many years to come.

APPENDIX 3: CAREER CHRONOLOGY

13 October 1925 – Born in Grantham

23 February 1950 – Fights Dartford constituency at General Election

25 October 1951 – Fights Dartford constituency at the General Election

8 October 1959 – Wins Finchley constituency at General Election

5 February 1960 – Makes maiden speech in the House of Commons

February – October 1960 – Parliamentary passage of MT's Public Bodies (Admission of the Press to Meetings) Bill

9 October 1961 – Appointed Parliamentary Secretary at the Ministry for Pensions and National Insurance in Harold Macmillan's Government

28 October 1964 – Appointed Opposition Spokesman on Pensions

5 October 1965 – Appointed Shadow Spokesman for Housing and Land

19 April 1966 – Appointed as Shadow Treasury Spokesman under Iain Macleod

12 October 1966 – Makes first speech from the platform at the Conservative Party Conference

10 October 1967 – Appointed to the Shadow Cabinet as Shadow Spokesman on Fuel and Power

10 October 1968 – Gives annual Conservative Political Centre lecture on "What's wrong with politics".

14 November 1968 – Appointed Shadow Transport Spokesman

21 November 1969 – Appointed Shadow Education Spokesman

19 June 1970 – Appointed Secretary of State for Education in Edward Heath's Cabinet

May 1974 – Forms Centre for Policy Studies think tank with Sir Keith Joseph

4 February 1975 – Defeats Edward Heath in first round of Conservative Party leadership election

11 February 1975 – Elected leader of the Conservative Party

28 March 1979 – Labour Government is defeated on a motion of no confidence

3 May 1979 – Leads Conservative Party to general election victory with a majority of 43.

12 June 1979 – Budget cuts standard rate of income tax from 33p to 30p but VAT is nearly doubled to 15 percent

5 May 1980 – Orders SAS to storm Iranian embassy after terrorist siege

5 January 1981 – First reshuffle involved the sacking of Norman St John Stevas

1 March 1981 – Refuses to bow to IRA hunger striker's demands for political status

14 September 1981 – Second Cabinet reshuffle sees sacking of Ian Gilmour and Christopher Soames and promotion of Nigel Lawson, Cecil Parkinson and Norman Tebbit. Jim Prior moved to Northern Ireland from Employment.

2 April 1982 – Argentina invades the Falklands

2 May 1982 – Gives Task Force permission to sink Argentinean battle cruiser General Belgrano

14 June 1982 – British forces capture Port Stanley ending the Falklands War

9 June 1983 – Leads Conservative Party to a second General Election victory with a record majority of 144

11 June 1983 – Reshuffles Cabinet. Nigel Lawson becomes Chancellor, Leon Brittan becomes Home Secretary and Sir Geoffrey Howe goes to the Foreign Office

25 October 1983 – Condemns US invasion of Grenada

22 April 1984 – Breaks off diplomatic relations with Libya over shooting of WPC Yvonne Fletcher outside the Libyan Embassy

12 October 1984 – IRA bomb explodes in Brighton Hotel yards from Margaret Thatcher's room

15 December 1984 – First Meeting with Mikhail Gorbachev at Chequers

19 December 1984 – Signs agreement with China transferring Hong Kong to China in 1997

20 February 1985 – Addresses both Houses of the US Congress

3 March 1985 – National Union of Mineworkers calls off year long coal strike

5 September 1985 – Cabinet reshuffle sees Douglas Hurd, John MacGregor, Kenneth Clarke and Kenneth Baker join the Cabinet.

15 November 1985 – Signs Anglo- Irish Agreement

9 January 1986 – Defence Secretary Michael Heseltine resigns from the Cabinet over the Westland Affair

17 February 1986 – Signs the Single European Act

15 April 1986 – Allows US bombers to fly from Britain to bomb Libyan targets

11 June 1987 – Leads Conservative Party to a third General Election Victory with a majority of 101

15 March 1988 – Budget cuts basic rate of tax by 25p and the top rate to 40p

20 September 1988 – Makes controversial speech in Bruges

26 June 1989 – Nigel Lawson and Sir Geoffrey Howe secretly threaten to resign if MT does not agree to their policy on joining the Exchange Rate Mechanism

24 July 1989 – Cabinet reshuffle demotes Sir Geoffrey Howe. John Major becomes Foreign Secretary

26 October 1989 – Nigel Lawson resigns as Chancellor. John Major takes over

5 December 1989 – Wins Conservative Party leadership contest by 314 to Sir Anthony Meyer's 33 votes with 27 abstentions

14 July 1990 – Key Cabinet ally Nicholas Ridley resigns following anti-German comments

30 July 1990 – Another ally, former PPS Ian Gow, is killed by an IRA car bomb

2 August 1990 – Iraq invades Kuwait. MT is with George Bush at Aspen

3 October 1990 – Bows to pressure from Chancellor John Major to enter the ERM

27 October 1990 – Special EC summit in Rome prompts "No, No, No" to a single currency

1 November 1990 – Sir Geoffrey Howe resigns from the Cabinet

22 November 1990 – Resignation as Conservative Party Leader

28 November 1990 – Last Day as Prime Minster

June 1991 – Announces she will stand down as an MP at the next General Election

9 April 1992 – Stands down as Member of Parliament for Finchley

30 June 1992 – Takes her seat in the House of Lords as Baroness Thatcher of Kesteven

2 July 1992 – Makes her maiden speech in the House of Lords

October 1993 – First volume of memoirs, *The Downing Street Years*, is published

22 April 1995 – Appointed to the Order of the Garter, the UK's highest order of chivalry

October 1995 – Second volume of memoirs, *The Path to Power*, is published

June 1997 – Endorses William Hague for the Conservative Party leadership race

October 1999 – Gives her first speech to a Conservative Party Conference in 9 years

June 2001 – Supports Iain Duncan Smith for Conservative Party leader

March 2002 – Published her third book, *Statecraft: Strategies for a changing world*

26 June 2003 – Is widowed when her husband, Denis Thatcher, passes away

11 June 2004 – Delivers a eulogy via videotape at Ronald Reagan's funeral

13 October 2005 – Celebrates her 80th birthday, among the Royal Family and the Prime Minister

February 2007 – Becomes the first Prime Minister of the UK to be honoured with a statue in the Houses of Parliament while still living.

APPENDIX 4: SELECTED READING

Abse, Leo, *Margaret, Daughter of Beatrice* (Jonathan Cape, 1989)

Arnold, Bruce, *Margaret Thatcher: A Study in Power* (Hamish Hamilton, 1984)

Berlinski, Claire, *There is No Alternative: Why Margaret Thatcher Matters* (Basic Books, 2008)

Campbell, John, *Margaret Thatcher Volume One – The Grocer's Daughter* (Vintage, 2007)

Campbell, John, *Margaret Thatcher Volume Two – The Iron Lady* (Vintage, 2007)

Cosgrave, Patrick, *Margaret Thatcher: A Tory and Her Party* (Hutchinson, 1978)

Cosgrave, Patrick, *Thatcher: The First Term* (Bodley Head, 1985)

Dale, Iain, *Memories of Maggie: A Portrait of Margaret Thatcher* (Politico's Publishing, 2000)

Dale, Iain, *Margaret Thatcher: A Tribute in Pictures and Words* (Weidenfeld and Nicolson, 2005)

Freedman, Sir Lawrence, *The Official History of the Falklands Campaign* (Routledge, 2007)

Gardiner MP, George, *Margaret Thatcher* (William Kimber, 1975)

Geelhoed, Bruce, *Margaret Thatcher In Victory and Downfall* (Praeger (US), 1992)

Harris, Kenneth, *Thatcher* (Weidenfeld and Nicolson, 1988)

Jenkins, Simon, *Thatcher and Sons: A Revolution in Three Acts* (Penguin, 2007)

Junor, Penny, *Margaret Thatcher: Wife, Mother, Politician* (Sidgwick and Jackson, 1983)

Lewis, Russell, *Margaret Thatcher: A Personal and Political Biography – Updated* (Routledge, 1983)

Mayer, Allan, *Madam Prime Minster* (Newsweek Books (US), 1979)

Money, Ernle, *Margaret Thatcher: First Lady of the House* (Leslie Frewin, 1975)

Murray, Patricia, *Margaret Thatcher: A Profile* (W.H. Allen, 1978)

Ogden, Chris, *Maggie: An Intimate Portrait of a Woman in Power* (Simon and Schuster (US), 1990)

Ranelagh, John, *Thatcher's People* (HarperCollins, 1991)

Sharp, Paul, *Thatcher's Diplomacy: The Revival of British Foreign Policy* (Palgrave Macmillan, 1999)

Smith, Geoffrey, *Reagan and Thatcher* (Bodley Head, 1990)

Thatcher, Carol, *Diary of an Election* (Sidgwick and Jackson, 1983)

Thatcher, Carol, *Below the Parapet: Biography of Denis Thatcher* (HarperCollins, 1996)

Thatcher, Carol, *A Swim-on Part in the Goldfish Bowl* (Headline Review, 2008)

Thatcher, Margaret, *Speeches to Conservative Party Conference 1975-88* (CPC, 1989)

Thatcher, Margaret, *The Downing Street Years* (HarperCollins, 1993)

Thatcher, Margaret, *The Path to Power* (HarperCollins, 1995)

Thatcher, Margaret, *Statecraft: Strategies for a Changing World* (HarperCollins, 2002)

Thompson, Andrew, *Margaret Thatcher: The Woman Within* (W. H. Allen, 1989)

Wapshott, Nicholas and Brock, George, *Thatcher* (Macdonald, 1983)

Wapshott, Nicholas, *Ronald Reagan and Margaret Thatcher: A Political Marriage* (Sentinel, 2007)

Watkins, Alan, *A Conservative Coup* (Duckworth, 1991)

Young, Hugo, *The Thatcher Phenomenon* (BBC Books, 1985)

Young, Hugo, *One of Us* (Macmillan, 1989)